The Varieties of Political Experience in Eighteenth-Century America

EARLY AMERICAN STUDIES

Daniel K. Richter and Kathleen M. Brown
Series Editors

Exploring neglected aspects of our colonial, revolutionary, and early national history and culture, Early American Studies reinterprets familiar themes and events in fresh ways. Interdisciplinary in character, and with a special emphasis on the period from about 1600 to 1850, the series is published in partnership with the McNeil Center for Early American Studies.

A complete list of books in the series is available from the publisher.

The Varieties of Political Experience in Eighteenth-Century America

RICHARD R. BEEMAN

PENN

University of Pennsylvania Press

Philadelphia

10   9   8   7   6   5   4   3   2   1

Published by
University of Pennsylvania Press
Philadelphia, Pennsylvania 19104-4011

Library of Congress Cataloging-in-Publication Data

Beeman, Richard R.
    The varieties of political experience in eighteenth-century America / Richard R.
Beeman.
        p. cm. — (Early American studies)
    Includes bibliographical references (p.) and index.
    ISBN 0-8122-3770-6 (cloth : alk. paper)
    1. United States—Politics and government—To 1775. 2. Political culture—United
States—History—18th century. 3. Regionalism—United States—History—18th century.
4. Democracy—United States—History—18th century. I. Title. II. Series.
E188.B44 2004
320.973'09'033—dc22   2003068874

To Mary

Contents

The election was unanimous and will I hope always be such, as making parties and divisions among the inhabitants can never be for their interest.
—Sir William Johnson to H. Glen, December 28, 1772, reporting on results of Tryon County election to the New York General Assembly.

* * *

SHERIFF: Gentlemen Freeholders, come into court, and give your votes, or the poll will be closed.

FREEHOLDERS: We've all voted.

SHERIFF: The Poll's Closed, Mr. Wou'dbe and Mr. Worthy are elected.

FREEHOLDERS: Huzza—huzza! Wou'dbe and Worthy for ever boys, bring 'em on, bring 'em on. Wou'dbe and Worthy for ever!

WORTHY: "I'm much obliged to you for the signal proof you have given me to-day of your regard. You may depend upon it, that I shall endeavor faithfully to discharge the trust you have reposed in me.

WOU'DBE: I have not only, gentlemen, to return you my hearty thanks for the favours you have conferred upon me, but I beg leave also to thank you for shewing such regard to the merit of my friend. You have in that, shewn your judgment, and a spirit of independence becoming Virginians.
—Robert Munford, *The Candidates* (1770)

* * *

Every Election should be considered as voting in a new Assembly.
The Consideration that such or such a Gentleman has represented us several years is vague in itself. Let us reflect what Services has he done? . . . What measures has he proposed for the Good of his Country, or what opposed, which were moved to their Detriment? Has his Behaviour been worthy the solemn Trust reposed in him?"
—*Pennsylvania Gazette,* September 22, 1773

* * *

The Committee notes with disapprobation the behavior of one John Hobson, which was very illegal and tumultuous; in offering to lay wagers the Poll was closed when it was not; in proclaiming at the Courthouse that the Poll was going to be closed, and desiring the Freeholders to come in and vote, and then, violently, and by striking and kicking them, preventing them from so doing, by which Means many Freeholders did not vote at the said election.
—Report of the Committee on Privileges and Elections, Virginia House of Burgesses, March 8, 1758

Introduction

Some fifteen years ago Edmund S. Morgan began his study of the origins of democracy in England and America with a quote from that remarkable Scottish sage, David Hume. "Nothing is more surprising . . . ," marveled Hume in 1758, "than to see the easiness with which the many are governed by the few. . . . When we enquire by what means this wonder is brought about, we shall find, that as Force is always on the side of the governed, the governors have nothing to support them but opinion. 'Tis therefore on opinion only that government is founded; and this maxim extends to the most despotic and military governments, as well as the most free and most popular."[1]

I have been powerfully impressed by the wisdom in Hume's observation ever since encountering it in Professor Morgan's excellent study, and if his book was intended as a history of the evolution of ideas about democracy during the seventeenth and eighteenth centuries, this one is intended as a history of the political behavior that led to that democratic result.

As my study of eighteenth-century American political behavior has progressed, it has become increasingly clear to me that the journey to a democratic America was neither inevitable nor did it unfold along a single, straight path. As the election commentaries in the epigraph suggest, there existed across eighteenth-century America an extraordinary diversity of belief and practice in respect to the relationship between political leaders and ordinary citizens. It is hardly surprising, given the variety of attitudes and expectations implicit in those commentaries, that historians of eighteenth-century America have used widely diverse descriptions of their own in their reconstruction of the political world of the eighteenth century—descriptions that run the gamut from authoritarian oligarchy to egalitarian democracy. And, indeed, even when confronted with a *single* description—Robert Munford's evocations of election-day behavior in *The Candidates* being perhaps the most widely cited example—historians have often constructed radically different interpretations of its meaning.

While some of our confusion about the character of eighteenth-century American political life may be the result of our failure as students of history to make sense of the evidence before us, it also may be that the eighteenth-century world that we are seeking to comprehend was an inherently confusing and contradictory one. In spite of some of the sources of unity among the residents of the colonies—a common language, a shared legal and constitutional tradition, and, perhaps most important, their common identity as subjects of the king of England—the American colonies were in fact extraordinarily disconnected from one another, displaying among themselves and within themselves significant varieties of political behavior. Throughout the hundreds of localities within America there existed an array of different—and often contradictory—expectations about what the political process was all about—about the very *definition* of politics itself.

While some still clung to an idealized conception of politics as "the art and science of government," with "natural aristocrats" acting as stewards for the public good, many others were moving toward more modern conceptions in which the representation of "interests" would come to be the means by which political leaders would serve the "general welfare." And closely tied to how one conceived of politics were different conceptions about the role of ordinary people in the political process—on the responsibilities and responsiveness of local officeholders and on the relationship between voters and candidates, between elected representatives and local constituents, and between legislatures as whole entities and the populations they served. Indeed, the fact of that diversity may be the *only* generalization that we can make about eighteenth-century American political culture. So varied were the expectations within America on all of these questions on the eve of the Revolution that it becomes impossible to talk about a single *American* political culture; rather, the essential fact of political life in the American colonies in the eighteenth century is that there existed numerous, diverse political cultures, diffuse and fragmented, often speaking altogether different political languages.

There was on the eve of the American Revolution no one universally accepted mode of "correct" political behavior. Certainly one of the challenges facing the American colonists as they confronted British officials on such crucial issues as the location of sovereignty, the meaning of "consent," and the nature of representation was to forge some agreement among themselves about the meaning of those concepts. And even more certainly, as Americans began to discuss the feasibility of *union* once the Revolution was under way, those discussions could hardly go forward with much hope of success unless Americans began to work out some common understanding of the essential character of their multitudinous local polities.

However fragmented the American polity may have been, most colonies were moving, slowly and unevenly, in the same direction. In addition to portraying some of the varieties of the prerevolutionary American political experience, this book also seeks to trace at least the beginnings of one of the staple stories of American political history: the growth of "democracy." Although most people living in America before the Revolution certainly would not have described political developments in their world with the term democracy, at least a few discerning observers would have acknowledged that important changes were under way which made it increasingly difficult for political leaders to ignore popular pressures. But popular pressure does not inevitably lead to democracy, and though our twenty-twenty hindsight helps us see the ways in which the Revolution against British rule and its aftermath helped shape a democratic future for America, we should not lose sight of the variety, contingency, and lack of clear political direction that characterized most political behavior before the Revolution. *We* may know that eighteenth-century Americans were on a path that would lead them toward a democratic republic, but they did not.

While much of my own research over the course of my career has focused on eighteenth-century American politics, this book is primarily an effort at synthesizing the work of others. My effort at synthesis comes at a time when the existing paradigm for the study of colonial American politics—what some have termed the republican synthesis—is under sustained attack from cultural historians who view much of that earlier work as both excessively reliant on elitist sources and too detached from the day-to-day practice of politics to be a serviceable explanation of the forces shaping political behavior for the great mass of Americans.

My thinking about eighteenth-century American politics has been shaped significantly by the work of those historians who have reconstructed the intellectual origins of classical republican and radical Whig political thought in early modern England and traced the evolution of that thought into more popular and, eventually, liberal, democratic forms in America in the late eighteenth and nineteenth centuries. Bernard Bailyn and J. G. A. Pocock in particular have been the historians who gave initial shape to the republican paradigm, but the list of historians who have refined and elaborated the paradigm, often disagreeing with one another but in the end interested in similar questions, is a long one—Pauline Maier, Gordon Wood, Michael Kammen, Joseph Ellis, Jack P. Greene, Jack Rakove, Lance Banning, Joyce Appleby, Richard Bushman, John Murrin, and many, many more.[2]

While we may be reaching a point of diminishing returns with respect to sketching out the character of the eighteenth-century *intellectual* tradition, nevertheless much of the most interesting recent work on late-eighteenth and early-nineteenth-century American politics—including that from historians such as Saul Cornell, Edward Countryman, Sean Wilentz, and David Waldstreicher, who explicitly dissent from particular aspects of the eighteenth-century republican synthesis—is shaped powerfully by that interpretive paradigm, for the *language* of eighteenth-century politics persisted even while social, economic, and political behavior were departing dramatically from that ideal.[3]

Recent criticism of the body of scholarship on republican ideology as elitist and overly abstracted notwithstanding, I remain impressed by the vitality of that scholarship and believe that it continues to serve as a useful point of departure for any study of eighteenth-century American politics. Having spent much of my professional career reading the primary literature of eighteenth-century American politics, I am convinced that the persistence and ubiquity of the language of republicanism—with its emphasis on virtue, disinterestedness, and the public good and their antitheses, self-interest and corruption—is simply too powerful to ignore. But that language, whatever its power and persistence, is only a starting point, and the analysis of eighteenth-century American politics that follows is intended to test, not endorse, the power and efficacy of republican rhetoric in shaping the reality of eighteenth-century American political behavior.

The words "politics" and "political behavior" carry with them multiple meanings. The conventional definition of politics as the "art and science of government" is probably too restrictive to be serviceable even for the traditional societies of eighteenth-century England and America, for such a definition would confine us to the formal, institutional realm in which public policies are formulated and implemented. At the other extreme, some would include in their definition of politics any contest or negotiation over power, whether in the public or private realm and whether between men of roughly equal social standing or in relationships that move across lines of gender, race, and class. The conception of politics that guides this study is that which seeks to comprehend those *public* activities involving collective conflict or contestation and the efforts at resolving those contests.[4] In particular, I am concerned with the question that so fascinated David Hume—the means by which "the many are governed by the few"—and therefore I will focus primarily on the relationship between citizens and political leaders in the realm of electoral politics, as well as that relationship as those political leaders went about the business of carrying out the responsibilities of governance.

I have, wherever the historical record permits, attempted to tell this story as much from the point of view of ordinary residents of the colonies as from those political leaders who were supposed to serve them. One strategy for uncovering the behavior of the many as well as the few is to leave the halls of government and to observe those other public venues in which the business of politics was contested and negotiated—in taverns and at militia musters, county fairs, and other such civic gatherings. We have much scantier evidence about these comings together in prerevolutionary America than we do for the era of the early Republic, but I have attempted to use what evidence is available to help answer David Hume's question.[5]

I have sought in my organization and placement of the chapters in this book not only to illustrate what I think are the most important typologies of political culture existing in eighteenth-century America, but also to give a sense of the direction in which all of the prerevolutionary American polities, whatever their differences, were moving. The opening chapter on "The Traditional Order of Politics in England and America" seeks to identify those English intellectual and institutional traditions on which political life in America was, at least in theory, supposed to be founded. In chapters 2 and 3 we will get a glimpse of the way in which those traditions were both embraced and transformed in Virginia and Massachusetts, the two oldest British colonies in North America. However different the social and intellectual foundations of those two colonies may have been from each other, by the eighteenth century the political leaders of both the Old Dominion and the Bay Colony shared in common an unusually tenacious commitment to maintaining and nurturing their version of traditional English notions about the construction of a proper social and political order. Although they fell far short of emulating idealized classical republican notions of virtue, deference, and the disinterested pursuit of the public good, the societies over which they ruled did, more than any others in colonial America (or, indeed, perhaps England itself), approach that ideal.

Hudson River valley manor lords and low-country South Carolina planters and merchants were no less committed to replicating English social and political norms than their counterparts in Virginia and Massachusetts, but, as I attempt to demonstrate in chapters 4 and 5, their efforts, occurring as they did within societies that were at once both highly stratified and institutionally unsettled, led to a structure and style of politics that was more oligarchical than anywhere else in America. In the next two chapters I seek to characterize the structure and culture of politics in the backcountry societies of the South and northern New England. The social and political structures of those societies were, particularly by the mid-eighteenth century, moving in two, sometimes opposing, directions: they were not only in the process of assimilating the values and structures of their parent cultures, but they were also, by the very differences that they exhibited from the parent cultures, reshaping the cultures of the colonies of which they were a part. And of course it was in those societies as well that the tragic conflict of interests and cultures between Europeans and Native Americans would be played out, often with important consequences for the political relationships between earlier and more recently settled regions. Chapter 6, which deals with the southern backcountry, is itself a comparative analysis, for in spite of important similarities in the physical landscape of the western region of Virginia and that of North and South Carolina, the political cultures that evolved in those two regions displayed important points of difference.[6] As we will see in chapter 7, the powerful forces of climate and geography would operate to shape distinctly American attitudes toward self-reliance and personal independence in that part of Massachusetts that would eventually become the state of Maine. At the same time, however, an equally powerful political culture emanating from Boston and eastern Massachusetts would operate to mitigate potential sources of division between the periphery and the center of the Bay Colony.

Chapter 8 seeks to comprehend the complicated interplay of cultural values and political interests at work in the colony of Pennsylvania. Founded upon a set of religious and political beliefs that pointed toward a modern, liberal democratic American future, Penn's colony in the eighteenth century was, perhaps more than any other, one where popular and oligarchic political forces operated simultaneously. In Pennsylvania, as in the Carolinas, the conflicts of interest and attitude between eastern and frontier residents would prove to be sources of instability. Indeed, as the issues of white-Indian relations and of political representation provoked ever greater conflict between east and west in Pennsylvania during the 1750s and 1760s, its political culture would become, on the eve of the Revolution, among the most unstable anywhere in America.

If the backcountry and frontier regions of the American colonies represented one aspect of the nation's democratic and egalitarian future, then the longest settled and most populous commercial centers of the Northeast represented the other. It would be in those urban centers that America would begin its journey toward independence and nationhood. That journey was filled with conflict among men and women of differing social and economic standings, ethnicities, and religious beliefs, but out of that conflict would emerge the world's first pluralist democracies. In chapter 9 we will get at least a glimpse of the way in which the residents of Boston, New York City, and Philadelphia mobilized themselves in response to the changes in British imperial policy during the 1760s. Although that chapter is emphatically *not* intended as a full-scale account of the events leading to the Revolution in those cities, I hope that it will at least suggest the ways in which the mixture of urban and imperial politics proved to be potentially combustible. Finally, chapter 10, "The Unfinished Revolution in American Political Culture," seeks in tentative fashion to explore some of the connections between the political cultures of prerevolutionary America and those emerging in the immediate aftermath of the Revolution.

There are a few things that the reader should not expect from this analysis of prerevolutionary American politics. I have not attempted to give a comprehensive account of the substantive policy issues that provoked conflict between royal officials and provincial leaders or of those issues that caused division among provincial leaders and their constituents. There were indeed a myriad of political issues that arose within individual colonies—those concerning taxation, currency, land distribution, defense, and British trade policy among them—and the story of the discussion and resolution of those issues within and among the colonies is an important one. But that is not the story that this book seeks to tell, and thus I will touch on those issues only when they become important as a context for understanding the main themes of the book. I also do not provide an analysis of the political cultures of every one of the thirteen North American mainland colonies. I have tried to make intelligent decisions about focusing on those colonies that I think are most helpful in illustrating some of the most important typologies of political behavior existing in eighteenth-century America, but certainly the political cultures of some of the individual colonies not discussed in this book—New Hampshire, Rhode Island, Connecticut, New Jersey, Delaware, Maryland, and Georgia—may display some distinctive features that are not found in the colonies that I have discussed.[7]

Perhaps the single most important decision that I have made was to depart in significant instances from an organizational structure that revolved around each colony as a political unit. I have concluded that the political cultures of the various regions of the American backcountry and frontier and of the northeastern cities were sufficiently distinct from the individual colonies of which they were a part to warrant separate treatment, but I am also well aware that my strategy occasionally runs the risk of obscuring important connections—both cultural and political—among settled, urban, and frontier areas within the colonies of which they were a part. I hope that my strategy sheds more light on the varieties of political experience in eighteenth-century America than it obscures. It not only highlights important differences within individual colonies but also helps us to understand better the direction in which American politics were moving as the American Revolution approached. Although the chapter organization of the book is regional rather than chronological, those colonies and regions covered in the latter part of the book display more visibly some of the features that would eventually come to characterize politics everywhere in America. None of the American colonies had embraced democracy before the Revolution, and, indeed, most of the independent American states would stop far short of incorporating democratic ideals into their new constitutions in the aftermath of the Revolution. But even though the story that this book seeks to tell is an incomplete one, I do hope that it will give the reader some better sense of the process—unwitting, confused, and conflicted as it may have been—by which Americans came to create for themselves a political identity founded upon democratic principles.

Chapter 1
The Traditional Order of Politics in England and America

There was of course no "traditional order" of politics in early America or, for that matter, in seventeenth- and eighteenth-century England. Indeed, perhaps the only certain political tradition in England was one of profound uncertainty, a political culture in which conspiracies and plots against kings and ministers were commonplace and in which violence was a standard means by which individuals of any rank in society achieved their political ends.[1]

Seventeenth-century England in particular was in nearly constant, and sometimes violent, change. The tradition of the "divine right" of monarchical rule had taken a severe beating during the reign of the Stuart monarchs, with the toll including one king, Charles I, executed, and another, James II, driven into exile. The fall of James II and the accession of William III in 1688, in addition to marking the final rejection of claims by monarchs to divine right, also created a void in which Englishmen would lack the structures by which to provide leadership and coherence for their nation. While members of Parliament had been successful yet again in toppling a king, they had not yet developed the leadership structures capable of ensuring either their own ascendancy or an orderly government for the people whom they were supposed to be serving. And while the aristocracy had undergone its "crisis" and the gentry "risen" in the sixteenth and early seventeenth centuries, by the late seventeenth century the aristocracy was yet again resurgent and engaged in alternating patterns of partnership and contest with the gentry for control of the political life of the nation. Indeed, as J. H. Plumb has noted, "by 1700 England seemed to have escaped the danger of arbitrary government only to succumb to political anarchy."[2]

Just a half century later, however, the political landscape in England would look noticeably different. Indeed, the ascendancy of Parliament under the Hanoverian kings would be so striking that by the mid-eighteenth century that development would seem, at least for some, to have been inevitable. But for those whose lives extended back as far as Queen Anne or beyond, the traditions of parliamentary ascendancy or of political stability seemed anything but secure. At least some of the stability of English politics in the eighteenth century was the product of an oligarchical concentration of power in Parliament in the hands of a relatively small circle of Whig gentry men and aristocrats, and, in the eyes of both Tory and radical Whig critics, amounted merely to the exchanging of one kind of arbitrary government for another.[3]

The British North American mainland colonies, all of them except Georgia founded in the midst of the political tumult of the seventeenth century, had even fewer stable traditions on which to draw. Not only did the political structures of those colonies reflect the different and rapidly changing conditions of the eras in which they were founded, but the social visions of the colonies' various founders also ran the full range, from utopian to mercenary. And even had the political institutions of the colonies mirrored precisely those of England, the credentials of those who initially sought to lay claim to political authority in America were far shakier than those of their counterparts in England. To be sure, in the eighteenth century the American colonies would experience their own version of "parliamentary ascendancy," with the attendant creation of a more experienced and prosperous provincial political elite, but the members of the American provincial ruling class would nonetheless lack many of the essential ingredients—most notably the power of an extensive patronage—enjoyed by their English counterparts. And, finally, the people over whom they ruled were, increasingly, both more diverse in ethnic and religious heritage and, because of the plentitude and diversity of economic options open to them, decidedly more independent and obstreperous in their attitude toward authority than their English counterparts.

The Object of Government

Virtually all Englishmen—be they Whigs or Tories, residents of Yorkshire or Cornwall, Georgia or New Hampshire—would have agreed that the object of government was to promote the public good. That concern for the public good stretched back to Aristotle's *Politics*, and was echoed by virtually every writer from Polybius to Machiavelli to James Harrington, Lord Shaftesbury, William Blackstone, and Lord Bolingbroke, and to John Adams and Tom Paine. Although Englishmen and Americans alike were confused and conflicted about what form of government they desired—monarchical, republican, or democratic—all of those competing concepts rested on the rationale that they were devoted, first and foremost, to the public good.[4]

For James Harrington, whose thoughts about politics were shaped by the parliamentary struggle against the Stuart kings, governments were instituted to serve the "common right or interest."[5] William Blackstone, writing a century later, after the ascendancy of Parliament over the monarchy was well advanced, identified the "happiness of the community" as the object toward which governments were obligated to strive. John Adams, writing on the other side of the Atlantic, echoed Harrington and Blackstone, insisting that "there must be a positive Passion for the public good, the public Interest, Honour, Power and Glory, established in the Minds of the People, or there can be no Republican Government, *nor any real liberty.*" And from the other end of the American political spectrum, Tom Paine would find himself in rare agreement with Adams when he averred that "What is called a *republic* is not any *particular form* of government. It is wholly characteristical of the . . . object for which government ought to be instituted . . . *res-publica,* the public affairs, or the public good."[6]

This concern for the public, or universal, good was intimately tied to a view of society as a corporate whole, a polity in which all citizens, regardless of conditions of birth, occupation, wealth, or social status, were bound together in common purpose. Alas, human history offered plentiful evidence that mankind was not always capable of sacrificing private passion and interest to the public good without some guidance and persuasion (or, indeed, coercion), and it was for this reason that governments were instituted. The great challenge facing all governments—from Aristotle's Greece to Adams's and Paine's America—was how to create an institutional structure in which the citizens enjoyed an acceptable measure of personal liberty while at the same time maintaining an acceptable level of collective order throughout the society so that the public good could be served.

The notion of liberty, while it elicited general approval from all, would prove to be a contested and confused one in the early modern world. In the America of Andrew Jackson, the term liberty would come to have nearly unambiguously positive connotations and would come to be associated with the individual's liberty against government interference—the right of individuals to operate more or less free from government restraint. But in the classical world of Aristotle and the early modern world of Machiavelli, Harrington, and Adams (but, notably, *not* Thomas Paine), this expansive notion of individual liberty was never so positively embraced, for private liberty just as often was thought to result in the triumph of private interest over the public good, of passion and licentiousness over reason and order. It was this tendency of individuals to use their liberty to excess that created the necessity of institutions of government capable of imposing order on the society at large.[7]

Even the most radical political theorists on both sides of the Atlantic in the eighteenth century, though quick to point out the evil inherent in most governments, admitted that those governments were necessary. As Paine put it in *Common Sense,* "Society is produced by our wants, and government by our wickedness; the former promotes our happiness *positively,* by uniting our affections, the latter *negatively* by restraining our vices. . . . Society in every state is a blessing, but government, even in its best state, is a necessary evil. . . . Government, like dress, is the badge of lost innocence."[8] However much one might lament the need for governments, they were necessary if one wished to harness the destructive impulses of unrestrained liberty.

Most societies throughout recorded human history had solved the problem of finding an adequate balance between societal order and personal liberty by imposing a heavy-handed dose of order, usually through the coercive use of governmental power, a power monopolized most often by a small group of men whose claim to that power was based on hereditary privilege or wealth. The notion that the people themselves and not a small group of hereditary rulers should be responsible for deciding where the balance point between order and liberty should rest was not well advanced even by the mid eighteenth century. The repudiation of theories of divine right of kingship and the ascendancy of Parliament, though tied in some ultimate, logical sense to ideas of popular sovereignty, did not lead Englishmen or Americans directly or quickly to the idea that the people themselves, rather than a small, select cohort of the privileged few, should exercise primary power in public affairs. However much English members of Parliament may have used the rhetoric of popular rights in their struggle to increase their prerogative at the expense of the king, their goal was *parliamentary* sovereignty, not *popular* sovereignty. And Americans, no less the Englishmen, remained devoted to the idea of monarchy until just a few months before their Declaration of Independence.[9]

Republicanism, Monarchy, and the Genius of the English Constitution

By the beginning of the eighteenth century, Englishmen and Americans would have readily agreed on what sort of government they did *not* wish to have. Their survey of the history of politics from the time of the Greeks to their own day, and in particular their reaction to the excesses of the Stuart monarchs, gave them an instinctive fear of and revulsion against arbitrary government and, in particular, a fear of the corrosive and corrupting effects of excessive monarchical power. "Love of power," the eighteenth-century Englishman Henry St. John, Lord Bolingbroke, wrote, "is natural, it is insatiable; almost constantly whetted, and never cloyed by possession." On the other side of the balance sheet, virtually everyone in Anglo-American society would have agreed that some measure of political liberty was essential to any harmonious polity. Liberty, however, was a fragile and vulnerable commodity in the face of the aggressive and propulsive way in which monarchs and their lackeys had exercised political power. Liberty was, Bolingbroke observed, "a tender plant, which will not flourish unless the genius of the soil be proper for it; nor will any soil continue to be so long, which is not cultivated with excessive care."[10]

The question of the appropriate balance point between the exercise of power by governments and their officials and the free expression of personal liberty by the subjects of those governments was one that had prompted debate, disagreement, and bloodshed in virtually every corner of the globe at every point in human history. In the period from the mid-seventeenth to the mid-eighteenth century, a collection of political thinkers and activists on both sides of the Atlantic articulated a set of notions about government and society aimed at locating more certainly where that balance point actually lay. Tracing its origins to classical Greece and republican Rome, the ideology of *republicanism* would, in its idealized form, prove to have enormously broad appeal across a wide range of class and cultural conditions. Of course part of the appeal lay in the fact that no one really agreed on what the constituent parts of republicanism were; like the notion of liberty, it was a protean concept infinitely elastic and susceptible to multiple and contradictory meanings. America's John Adams, though he had spent most of his career defending his own version of "republican liberty," confessed late in his life that he had "never understood" the concept and that it might, depending on the circumstances, "signify any thing, every thing, or nothing." "The customary meanings of the words republic and commonwealth," Adams wrote, "have been infinite. They have been applied to every government under heaven; that of Turkey and that of Spain, as well as that of Athens and of Rome, of Geneva and San Marino."[11]

As historian Gordon Wood has noted, eighteenth-century republicanism "did not so much replace monarchy as transform it."[12] Indeed most eighteenth-century Englishmen and Americans tended to think of monarchy and republicanism not as mutually exclusive, but rather as nearly indistinguishable from each other. While at the far extremes of radical Whig and Tory ideology the two conceptions of government and society may have been seen to be mutually antagonistic, in the minds of most people notions of monarchy and republics could be quite comfortably accommodated. Two of the greatest political thinkers of the mid-eighteenth century— David Hume and the Baron de Montesquieu—located much of the genius of the English system of government in the way in which monarchical and republican principles both supported and offset each other. Both believed as well that the dynamic element in that combination was the republican one. For Hume, the monarchical form "owed all its perfection to the republican." Montesquieu, though he believed that virtually all eighteenth-century European governments were mixtures of both monarchical and republican forms, praised England's "beautiful system," which "may be justly called a republic disguised under the form of monarchy," precisely because the republican aspects of its character were so well-advanced.[13] However much Englishmen on both sides of the Atlantic may have prized the republican character of their monarchy, though, their faith in the monarchy as an essential component of their constitutional system was virtually unshakeable. Pennsylvania's Benjamin Rush was in the forefront of America's struggle for republican liberty and independence in 1776, but when he visited England in 1768 and "gazed for some time at the [king's] throne," he reported that he felt as if he were "on sacred ground."[14]

Most eighteenth-century Englishmen and Americans shared Montesquieu's conclusion that the English government—and, equally important, the English *people*—had come closer than any other society in recorded history to finding the proper balance point between the needs for public order and for liberty. Part of their explanation for the favored situation of Anglo-Americans was no doubt an ethnocentric one, rooted in the belief that the English were a people of superior private and public virtue. An equally important part of their explanation was constitutional and institutional: they believed that the structure of the English Constitution, with its division of power among the monarch, the nobility, and the commons, provided them with a system of mixed government that was solidly rooted in the reality of the English social structure and that therefore provided a dependable base on which to maintain a proper balance between public order and private liberty. The ideal of the English Constitution evoked a chorus of admiration in England and America. Edmund Burke would describe it as a system "in a just correspondence and symmetry with the order of the world," one which exemplified "the method of nature in the conduct of the state." In Boston, Samuel Adams would echo Burke nearly exactly, terming the English Constitution a thing of "excellency . . . which appears eminently to have its foundation in nature."[15]

Like the concepts of "liberty" and "republicanism," the notion of an "English Constitution" was, as Englishmen on both sides of the Atlantic would discover during the struggle leading to the American Revolution, a protean concept. Americans, operating with a seventeenth-century conception of the Constitution as a bulwark against arbitrary power, would find themselves confronting Britons who possessed an eighteenth-century conception of their constitution as the guarantor of parliamentary supremacy. Even before the Revolution, Englishmen and Americans would constantly differ both between and among themselves on how best to preserve the balance of governmental power and human liberty that their system of mixed government was supposed to achieve.[16]

Ideals and Realities of Provincial Government in America

While most Americans, perhaps even more than most Englishmen, would have had a difficult time articulating precisely where the balance of power in a system of mixed government should rest, they did at least share with their fellow Englishmen the belief that some form of mixed government was desirable and, moreover, that the political structures of their own colonies (or at least most of them) more or less mirrored that of the mother country. As Dr. William Douglass of Boston phrased it, the colonial governments, "in conformity to our legislature in Great Britain . . . consist of three separate negatives; thus, by the governor, representing the King, the colonies are monarchical; by the Council, they are aristocratical; by a house of representatives or delegates from the people, they are democratical: these three are distinct and independent of one another, and the colonies enjoy the conveniences of each of these forms of government without their inconveniences, the several negatives being checks upon one another. The concurrence of these three forms of government seems to be the highest perfection that human civil government can attain to in times of peace."[17]

As Bernard Bailyn and others have noted, the Americans' determination to equate their own colonial charters to the English Constitution was more an exercise in wishful thinking than in sober political analysis. In reality, both the outward forms and actual operation of the colonial governments differed from the English system in a number of important respects. In the royal colonies in particular (which by 1750 included all but Rhode Island, Connecticut, Pennsylvania, and Maryland) the theoretical balance among monarchy, aristocracy, and the people at large was heavily tilted toward the monarchy. The king alone appointed the royal governors, who in turn appointed the members of the upper houses of assembly. Those individuals, however, were not independent members of a titled nobility, but merely ordinary citizens dependent upon the governor's patronage for their positions. The governor's formal powers over the lower house of assembly were far greater than those exercised by the Hanoverian kings. The governor not only had the authority to veto all provincial legislation but also could prorogue and dissolve the assembly.[18] Moreover, royal governors arrived in the colonies carrying detailed sets of instructions spelling out the categories of colonial legislation that they should veto automatically, together with other categories of legislation that should be subject to a "suspending clause," preventing the execution of such legislation until explicitly approved by the monarch's Privy Council in England. Finally, the power of the Crown over the colonial judiciary, which had been explicitly limited in England by the Act of Settlement of 1701, was far more extensive in the colonies, giving to the king's agents, the royal governors, the power not only to make all judicial appointments, but to remove judges at their will as well.[19]

Whatever theoretical advantages the monarch may have possessed in the colonial versions of mixed government, those advantages were consciously and consistently undermined in the day-to-day operations of those provincial governments. If there was one institutional development shared in common by the governments of England and America during the eighteenth century, it was the rise to prominence and dominance of the lower houses of assembly. The extension and consolidation of political power in those houses in America occurred first in America's two corporate colonies—Rhode Island and Connecticut—where the balance between ex-

ecutive and legislative power had from the early seventeenth century onward consistently tilted in favor of the lower house of the legislature. Emulating the ascendancy of the House of Commons in England, the lower
houses of assembly in both the proprietary and royal colonies had asserted
their claims over a wide range of legislative functions—the initiation of legislation, control over their own internal legislative proceedings, primary responsibility for matters relating to taxation and finance, and, ultimately,
even the salaries of members of the executive branch.[20]

Historians have given varying accounts of how the colonial assemblies accomplished their ascendancy. Jack P. Greene is most struck by the "rather
prosaic manner in which the lower houses went about the task of extending and consolidating their authority, with the infrequency of dramatic
conflict." For Greene, the rise of the assembly occurred gradually and quietly, in the course of routine business, mirroring similar developments that
were occurring in the House of Commons in England. Bernard Bailyn, by
contrast, has seen in the disjunction between the theoretical powers of
royal governors and the actual exercise of power by colonial assemblies a
source of constant, chronic political instability. "Swollen claims, and
shrunken powers," he argues, "are always sources of trouble, and the
malaise that resulted from this combination can be traced through the history of eighteenth-century politics."[21] Bailyn and Greene do, however,
agree on the end result—a political system in which, by the middle of the
eighteenth century, America's political leaders had seized from royal governors primary responsibility for governing their colonies. The increasing
political independence achieved by America's ruling class was, however,
neither so well advanced nor even so well recognized as to constitute either
a common "tradition" or even a common goal in prerevolutionary American political life. Rather, those very same provincial American leaders who
were working so aggressively to aggrandize the power of the "popular"
branch of their legislatures and to undermine the powers of the monarch's
agents continued to extol the virtues of the monarchy, of mixed government, and of a "balanced" constitutional system.

The Character of the Good Ruler in England

As the first settlers of Massachusetts made their way from England to their
colony, the governor of the new enterprise, John Winthrop, instructed his
fellow colonists on the character of the social and political hierarchy they
could expect there. In his infinite wisdom God had, Winthrop informed
them, ordained that "in all times some must be rich some poore, some high
and eminent in power and dignitie, others meane and in subieccion." One
hundred and forty-six years later another Massachusetts colonist, John
Adams, would utter a secularized version of the same message when he defended the concept of a "natural aristocracy" and emphasized the impor-

tance of "a Decency, and Respect, and Veneration . . . for Persons in Authority." In Virginia, too, there existed from the very beginning an instinctive assumption that there was an integral relationship between social authority and political power, and that an orderly and well-governed society would be one whose leaders possessed the appropriate traits of wealth, education, gentility, and liberality. True, that formula for society faltered badly in the earliest years of Virginia's settlement. The treasurer of the Virginia Company, George Sandys (himself the son of the archbishop of York and brother of three members of Parliament) lamented the "miserablie poore" quality of Virginia's political leadership, a condition made all the more serious by the decidedly unvirtuous character of the people over whom they ruled, "a more damned crew hell never vomited."[22] But, by the beginning of the eighteenth century, through the paradoxical combination of plentiful and relatively inexpensive land and the ability of white Englishmen to exploit that land through the coercion of unfree African labor, Virginia had produced a class of men of sufficient attainment to lay claim to an "English" definition of political leadership that assumed an identity between social authority and political power.

In fact, the English traditions of government and of representation from which Americans would base their views on the character of a good ruler were in flux during the seventeenth and eighteenth centuries. Those Americans who wished to emulate the traditions of their English counterparts were forced to shoot at a moving target, never certain where they were aiming or what exactly it was they were shooting.

Certainly one of the most venerable of the English traditions of government was the notion of the divine right of kingship—the notion that the king was God's lieutenant on earth, doing the deity's divinely appointed work. In this scheme there was little need for the monarch to seek the consent of his subjects, for he obviously had an inside track into all that was good and just and virtuous. Belief in the notion of divine right required a substantial measure of credulousness even in an age more inclined to accept hierarchical schemes of governance than our own, and the combination of the distinctly ungodlike character of James I and Charles I, and the increasing unruliness of the English Parliament brought the doctrine under increasingly critical scrutiny even by the time of the founding of the first American colonies in the early seventeenth century. By the time of the English civil war and the execution of Charles I, the doctrine of divine right was, along with the king himself, on its way to extinction.[23]

The most logical alternative to the divine right theory was put forward by the Levellers, a group of political activists whose ideas came to prominence during the English civil war. Contrary to the implications of the name attached to their movement, the Levellers did not wish to do away with all distinctions in society, but only to abolish all hereditary political institutions, including the monarchy and the House of Lords. Moreover, they wanted to make the House of Commons genuinely representative by expanding the suffrage and devising ways in which members of Parliament could be held accountable to their constituents and to the rule of law. All of these notions would eventually find their way into the institutional practices of the independent American nation, but the influence of the Levellers in England declined sharply after 1650 with the assumption of political power by Cromwell's New Model Army. Because the Levellers were primarily political activists rather than political theorists and writers, their ideas were never articulated in a way that was easily accessible to subsequent generations. As a consequence the ideas of the Levellers, though potentially congenial to the social and political climate of the American colonies, never had much of an audience or impact there.[24]

Most of the politically powerful in England—whether lords or commoners—were less interested in forging a direct connection between the governors and the people whom they governed than they were in weakening monarchical power and strengthening the powers of the other branches of Parliament. In that sense the Glorious Revolution of 1688, though carried out in the name of the people, was in fact a revolution whose principal effect was to aggrandize the power of a largely unreformed Parliament. While the "popular" quality of the relationship between representatives and constituents increased markedly during the years between 1689 and 1715, as the various factions in Parliament scrambled for position and preferment, after 1715 the ruling Whig Party in Parliament, basing its power on patronage and the assertion of prerogative, was a more obvious symbol of oligarchy than of the triumph of principles of popular sovereignty.

At least a few in England, however, sought an alternative to the corruption that they believed to be inherent in the interest-based politics of parliamentary Whigs. The ideology of the radical Whigs was, like that of the Levellers, a minority strain of opinion in England, but, unlike that of the Levellers, it was an ideology that gained wide circulation in America. Within the classical republican tradition, virtue and liberty went hand in hand. A society's liberties could be protected only when its citizens, particularly its leading citizens, possessed virtue sufficient to put the good of the community over private gain. As Gordon Wood has reminded us, "the virtue that republicanism encouraged was public virtue." Though private virtues such as those encouraged by men such as the American Benjamin Franklin—frugality, honesty, industry—were important, they were less so than public virtue, which required that citizens sacrifice their private interests for the good of the commonweal. The word frequently used to describe this ideal, public-spirited behavior was "disinterestedness," a quality that would enable the true leaders of society to engage in public service for the public good and not private gain.[25]

Alas, much of the history of England, in common with the history of the rest of the world, had revealed the depressing tendency of most individuals entrusted with public service to allow private interest to override their attention to the public good. Indeed, it was precisely because of the precariousness of human virtue and disinterestedness that republics themselves were so precarious, so liable to corruption. It was this tendency toward corruption that motivated James Harrington in 1656 to take pen in hand to create his utopian model for *The Commonwealth of Oceana*, an attempt to lay down the requisites for good and responsible government for England. Harrington was himself not a champion of the "ancient Constitution" or of the system of mixed government, believing that the notion of a "balanced constitution" had been irretrievably corrupted, and that aspect of his political thought had little impact either in England or America until 1776, when Thomas Paine resurrected it in his all-out assault on the English Constitution in *Common Sense.* Harrington's insistence, however, that the ownership of land was the one true source of independence had substantial resonance both in England and America. The yeomen, possessing freeholds, would thus have the economic means that would enable them to cultivate in a modest way the private virtues of industry and independence; and, more importantly, the landed gentry, acquiring their wealth without exertion, would have the leisure time to cultivate the habits of civility, learning, and disinterestedness that would enable them to assume their rightful place as public servants.[26] There were within this vision of classical republicanism two notions of virtue—one for the many and the other for the few—that were in tension with each other. The first exalted the independent yeoman as a bulwark against oppression. Within that concept, the ultimate duty of a free citizen was to be prepared to enlist in a citizens' army to thwart the efforts of a tyrant to impose tyranny, but beyond that ultimate, desperate act of citizenship, were countless smaller and less dramatic acts by which the many could work to ensure that the public good was being served.

Whether enrolled as a militiaman in defense of hearth and home or as a voter assigned the task of choosing one's representative to Parliament, the true republican citizen needed the independence of action and expression that only ownership of property could give, and in that sense the classical republican tradition of liberty, at least in the English context, was a restrictive one. English classical republicans of the late seventeenth and eighteenth centuries, unlike the Levellers, believed that the ownership of property was an essential requisite for citizenship and only a society with a sufficiently broad base of property ownership—perhaps a society that looked more like America than England—could realistically claim to have a sufficient foundation of virtuous citizens upon which to build a republican form of government.

Over the course of the late seventeenth and much of the eighteenth centuries purveyors of what J. G. A. Pocock has called the "country party" tradition would invoke the image of a propertied and independent citizenry as the antidote to what they considered to be the principal threat to their society—the inclination of the monarch, and of the increasing numbers of courtiers and placemen dependent upon the monarch's patronage, to increase their power at the expense of the liberty of others. In so doing, the country party publicists would grant to commoners—or at least to those commoners who owned land—an important, albeit negative, role in English politics, that of guardians against monarchical attempts to unbalance the English Constitution.[27]

But few in eighteenth-century England—certainly not the coalition of court party Whigs who controlled the business of the Parliament nor the propertied gentry who made up one of the components of the country party and not even the urban radicals who joined forces with propertied gentry in the country party—would have suggested that the need to control monarchical power should carry one so far as to advocate the rejection of the idea of monarchy or to embrace the other extreme of unbalanced government: democracy. Nearly everyone agreed that democracy, in its pure and classical sense of equal participation by all in the affairs of the *polis*, was not only undesirable but also illogical. The New England Puritan minister John Cotton had identified the source of the illogic in the early seventeenth century: "If the people be the governors," he asked, "who shall be governed?"[28] Even in the more diluted meaning of the term—as a system of representative government through which a majority of all citizens would have a say in determining public policy—the concept was more often associated with mob rule than with effective constitutional government.[29]

Just as there was a populist side to classical republican ideology that vested in ordinary citizens important responsibilities to resist the encroachments of arbitrary monarchical power, so too was there an elitist side that stressed the importance of virtuous rule by a landed gentry committed to disinterested public service. The problem with a democratic political system, no less serious in relatively undifferentiated societies like those of America than in the more hierarchically organized ones of England, was that it minimized the chances that truly responsible leaders—those with the wisdom and public virtue so necessary to the service of the public good—would find themselves holding the reins of power.

The emphasis on property as the essential requisite for the independence that was required of a virtuous citizen led logically to the belief that superior wealth was conducive to nurturing a superior class of citizens—a "natural" as opposed to "hereditary" aristocracy. For Harrington, virtuous political leaders possessed superior skills of invention, articulation, foresight, and analysis, but those traits could be found only in those who possessed the education and leisure time necessary for their cultivation. That leisure time could be enjoyed only by landed gentlemen unsoiled by the grubby and corrupting pursuits of the marketplace. As Harrington, himself a propertied gentleman, described his mythical natural aristocracy of *Oceana*, "Ours of Oceana have nothing else but their education and their leisure for the public [good], furnished by their ease and competent riches."[30]

In the classical republican scheme of governance, the claims of the few to the support and obedience of the many were not simply asserted by the few but, rather, were to be affirmed by the many. For Harrington in particular, the deference of the many to the few was something given in a wholly voluntary fashion; in that sense the patriarchs in a deferential relationship owed "their authority less to their own superiority than to the acknowledgment—it would be proper to call it election—of their inferiors."[31] Moreover, the act of paying deference was not a passive one. The yeoman who deferred to his superiors did not lack a political will but, rather, was entrusted with the job of identifying and evaluating his superiors. Thus the acceptance of the notion of a deferential society was, in the classical sense, in no way incompatible with the idea of vigorously contested popular elections.[32]

Deference was, it should be noted, a highly idealized prescription for the way English politics should be conducted and not a reliable indicator of the way in which they actually were conducted.[33] The politicians who were most vocal in articulating classical republican ideas were for the most part either parliamentary back-benchers or country gentlemen and urban radicals out of power altogether, and the intensity of their protests against the corruption inherent in eighteenth-century English politics was an index of how far removed English political reality was from the ideals of a deferential and wholly republican political community. The reality of English politics was, depending upon to whom you listened, either one of outright corruption and oligarchy or, at best, a complicated brokering process that was shaped, and occasionally perverted, by the influence and interests of wealthy and powerful men. This wielding of influence and power was most often rationalized by English court party spokesmen in terms of a defense of prerogative: a system of titles, ranks, and privileges that was every bit as much an inherent part of English constitutionalism as the more voluntaristic and popular strains of country political thought. As J. H. Plumb has concluded in his assessment of the career of Sir Robert Walpole, the leader of the early-eighteenth-century English Parliament: "What Sir Robert Walpole and the Whigs did was to make certain that political and social authority should devolve by inheritance; the methods have been purified, and tortuous by-ways evolved for talent, but birth still remains a broad highway to power. And power by inheritance must mean a world run by patronage."[34]

Figure 1. Sir Robert Walpole. Depending on one's political perspective, Walpole was considered either the archetype of an effective parliamentary politician or a symbol of the corrupting effects of the use of political power in pursuit of selfish interest. Clandon, The Onslow Collection (The National Trust)/NTPL/John Hammond.

Voting and Representation in Eighteenth-Century England

If historians of eighteenth-century England have not agreed fully on the distribution of power and the character of political decision making in Parliament, they have disagreed even more significantly on the relationship of members of Parliament to their constituents. While some British historians have found in the concept of deference an elegant way of explaining the acceptance by the English people of the parliamentary oligarchy of the eighteenth century, there is nevertheless an abundance of evidence suggesting that the actual character of the relationships between members of Parliament and their constituents frequently lacked the voluntary and reciprocal qualities envisioned in the idealized classical republican model.

However much English court and country politicians may have differed over the practical aspects of parliamentary politics, they were, following Locke, united in their belief that the primary purpose of government was the protection of property.[35] Toward that end, they shared the belief that the right to vote should be limited to property-owning adult males. While some radical Whig politicians agitated for a more equal distribution of property in society, even they clung to the connection between property and the franchise. Although the qualifications for voting in eighteenth-century England were not uniformly imposed across the nation's counties and boroughs, voting was restricted—at least in comparison to the situation prevailing in most parts of America. In England's counties, which supplied roughly 60 percent of the nation's voters, the franchise was extended to freeholders owning land valued for tax purposes at 40 shillings per annum, though those owning lifetime leaseholds of that value were in some cases accepted as voters as well. In the boroughs, which supplied the other 40 percent of England's voters, voting restrictions varied, with the most restrictive qualifications prevailing in the bargage boroughs (those towns in which the extent of the franchise was controlled by a small group of residents), where the franchise was attached to specific pieces of property, and in the corporation boroughs, where only a few members of a self-perpetuating oligarchy were allowed to vote. It has been estimated that in 1715 these restrictions had the effect of limiting the franchise to about 23 percent of the adult male population. By the late eighteenth century the combined effects of an expanding population and increasing concentrations of political power actually caused the percentage of the voting population to shrink to about 17 percent of the free adult male population.[36]

Whether technically enfranchised or not, the vast majority of Englishmen played no role in selecting their representatives. The freeholders of Leeds, Birmingham, and Manchester, even though they may have met the property qualification for voting, were not able to vote for representatives to Parliament because their towns did not send representatives to Parliament. Of those counties and boroughs that were represented in Parliament, perhaps as many as a third were controlled by either private or government patronage. Among the remaining counties and boroughs that at least theoretically used elections to determine the outcome, a significant number selected a representative without electoral contest; for example, more than one-quarter of the elections in England's 203 boroughs were not contested or were contested only once during the period between 1700 and 1713.[37]

The relative weight of an Englishman's vote in determining the outcome of a parliamentary election also varied significantly. Linda Colley estimates that the 159,000 freeholders who voted for England's eighty county M.P.'s in 1715 were outweighed by the votes of the mere 3,500 freeholders in England's smallest boroughs, who sent 148 members to Parliament. Thus, the 1,000 freeholders in the rapidly growing port town of Liverpool, who elected 2 members to Parliament in 1700, were outweighed by the 100 voters in East and West Looe, in Cornwall, who returned 4 members to Parliament. Indeed, throughout all of Cornwall a small group of some 1,400 voters controlled the election of a total of 142 M.P.'s. In many parts of England this situation worsened after 1716, with politics becoming further removed from the people and with fewer elections being held. When elections were held, those with wealth and social connections enjoyed greater advantage in securing seats in Parliament.[38]

Historians of eighteenth-century English politics have attempted to gauge the effects of both the Whig and Tory and court and country divisions of the eighteenth century on popular involvement in politics, and the results of their efforts yield ambiguous, even contradictory, conclusions. On the one hand, country party Whigs and Tories, out of a desire to reduce the power of parliamentary politicians who enjoyed the advantage that court patronage gave to them, were increasingly inclined to advocate the elimination of rotten and pocket boroughs, a return to more frequent elections, and, in some cases, to seek support from the people "out-of-doors." It is also clear, however, that some of this increased activity made it more expensive for candidates to secure their seats in Parliament. By the mid-eighteenth century some English politicians were openly complaining about the increased expense involved in obtaining the votes necessary to gain election, and in one 1754 Oxfordshire election—the model for a William Hogarth print caricaturing the corruption of English electioneering—the two Tory candidates, Lord Wenman and Sir James Dashwood, were reckoned to have spent £20,000 to secure their election. Yet in spite of sporadic instances of increased electioneering in some constituencies, the overall trend of political contest in the constituencies over the course of the eighteenth century was toward oligarchy, not democracy. Country party politicians, their rhetorical posturing to the contrary notwithstand-

Figure 2. "The Election." One of the many sketches by William Hogarth
illustrating the corrupt and corrupting aspects of English electoral politics.
Courtesy of the Trustees of Sir John Soane's Museum.

ing, were plainly more interested in increasing their influence in the Commons, not in placing more political power in the hands of the people at large.[39]

But just as those tendencies toward oligarchy were increasing in most parts of England, there were nevertheless countervailing trends emerging in at least a few parts of the realm. H. T. Dickinson, Nicholas Rogers, and Kathleen Wilson have demonstrated that in some urban areas of England the conduct of "politics out-of-doors" was becoming progressively more open and more contested. In at least some towns, office seekers had to expend more time, energy, and money in the course of their parliamentary election campaigns and, once elected, had to pay some attention to the varying interests—sometimes expressed in the form of petitions—of their constituents. Even more notable were those extra-institutional forms of popular involvement in politics—in the taverns and coffeehouses, in street parades and rituals, and in extralegal protests and riots. Popular insurgencies in English politics were most visible in England's cities, particularly in

London, but Kathleen Wilson has demonstrated that vigorously contested elections, petition campaigns, overtly politicized street parades, and, occasionally, riots and rowdy street demonstrations were also in evidence in provincial towns like Norwich and Newcastle-on-Tyne, with populations of 20,000–40,000.[40]

The Character of the Good Ruler in Provincial America

There has been an impressive volume of historical analysis dedicated to explaining how a classical republican ideology that was on the fringes of political life in eighteenth-century England became a mainstream ideology in eighteenth-century America. The American colonial societies lacked both a visibly present monarch and a hereditary class of nobles. The relatively wide distribution of property in America also provided at least the potential for the broad base of independent and virtuous citizenship envisioned by the classical republicans. Moreover, as we have seen, the provincial leaders of the American colonies quite consciously drew on classical republican ideology as well as on the more mainstream precepts of English constitutionalism in their defense of colonial prerogative against both parliamentary and monarchical claims. At the same time, the more egalitarian, open-ended, and geographically mobile character of the American social order tended to muddle traditional assumptions about the relationship between political leadership and the social hierarchy. Just as the ranks of the propertied citizenry in America were more extensive than in England, so too was the gap between ordinary citizens and the "natural aristocracy" of America much smaller, rendering the distinction between the many and the few much fuzzier and the process of identifying leaders and followers more uncertain.[41]

This disjunction between the traditional expectations and the reality of American political life—whether manifested in the gap between the theoretical claims and actual exercise of royal prerogative or in the difference between the ideal and the real character of the "virtuous" political leader— would prove to be a source of both dynamism and instability in the politics of the various American colonies. The intellectual tradition of politics that those colonies had inherited from England was itself a confused and contradictory one—a dying, but occasionally resuscitated, tradition of divine right; a radical, but stillborn, tradition of popular politics as articulated by the Levellers; a conservative Whig ideology which used doctrines of popular sovereignty to justify Parliament's supremacy over the king, but which tended to leave members of Parliament free from meaningful oversight by their constituents; and, finally, the classical republican tradition, a tradition that itself was used, largely ineffectively, by a disparate collection of conservative agrarian gentry men and urban radicals whose views on the proper direction for English society were often at sharp variance with one another. When one adds to this the more fluid and unsettled social environment of America, one can understand some of the confusion many Americans must have felt as they tried to understand how the game of politics was played. As we will see, there would emerge in America a multitude of options for the conduct of politics—different rule books in different colonies, even in different regions within colonies. In that sense the provincial outposts of British Empire in America were not only moving apart from the metropolitan center that had guided their creation but were often frequently moving apart from one another as well.

The Imperatives of a Provincial World

No matter how severe the conflicts within Parliament or between Parliament and the king or between lower houses of assembly and royal governors in America, there was one fact of life in early-eighteenth-century England and America that conditioned the political life of all those societies: the social world of all save a handful of court politicians and cosmopolites was an extraordinarily narrowly bounded one. For most Englishmen—whether living in Essex County, England, or Essex County, Massachusetts—most of the sum and substance of their government's impact was seen and felt not through the agency of the monarchy or the Lords or the Commons, but through the administration of government and justice at the local level. That tradition of localism, though shared by residents of England and America, also provided an opportunity for the development of myriad diverse and even antagonistic political cultures.

As English historian Alan Everitt has noted, the three most striking characteristics of English society in the early modern period were its diversity, its insularity, and its continuity. That diversity was reflected not only in the different ethnic backgrounds of the British highland Celtic population and the lowland Saxons, but in the great differences in patterns of economic development and social organization separating a sheepherding family in Yorkshire from a farming family in Cottenham (where open-field farming persisted well into the seventeenth century) or a farm family in East Anglia (where enclosure of fields was an ancient custom) or a mining family in Warwickshire.[42] The insularity was born of a society that remained in the late seventeenth century overwhelmingly rural. While one in every ten English citizens lived in the metropolitan center of London, the rest lived on a vastly smaller scale, with the majority of the citizenry living in villages containing between 250 and 450 residents. Those villages communicated with one another in a relationship of what Peter Laslett has called "reticulation," an intricate network in which the economies of the smaller villages were closely tied to those of the larger market towns (whose population averaged around 1,000) by lines of trade and commerce.[43] These economic networks notwithstanding, the social and institutional structures of those villages retained a striking insularity. The administration of the business of the Anglican parish, the activities of local constables to maintain the peace, even the implementation of legislation emanating from the metropolitan center of Parliament and London—as in the case of the poor laws—were for the most part encapsulated within the much smaller world of the village. Finally, the continuity of the system was founded on the fact that the rhythms of preindustrial life—the effects of the enclosure movement notwithstanding—remained roughly constant from England's feudal past up through the whole of the eighteenth century. Patterns of family formation, of the organization of work, and of social relations among the different ranks in the society were conditioned by the number of hours of daylight and the dictates of the change in the seasons, the chance occurrence of flood and drought, and by the richness or meagerness of the soil—all matters impervious to legislation from Parliament or decrees from a monarch in the metropolitan center.

The collective effect of these patterns assured that the structure of political life—both in terms of political relations within local agricultural communities and the relationships of those communities to the metropolitan center—would change very little between the medieval era and the eighteenth century. The Stuart kings of the seventeenth century, particularly Charles I, had attempted to bring England's localities under greater centralized control, but, as in so many of their attempts at increasing monarchical power, their efforts were thwarted by both the forces of tradition and the jealousy with which local oligarchies guarded their power.

The Englishmen who journeyed across the Atlantic carried with them those same parochial attachments, creating in the process communities that gave new meaning to the word "provincial." Perhaps no group protected its local identity more fiercely than the original Puritan settlers of New England. At least a part of the motivation behind their decision to relocate to New England came from the threat by Charles I to impose the ecclesiastical authority of the Church of England on local Puritan communities. Moreover, Puritan Congregational Church doctrine—with its insistence on the autonomy of each local community in selecting ministers and establishing the criteria for church membership and governance—carried with it powerful localistic implications. While the covenanted Puritan communities would eventually lose some of their compactness and cohesiveness as successive generations of New Englanders were faced with the choice between declining opportunity in their original communities and the prospect of more plentiful and less expensive land to the west, New England's communities remained strikingly insular well into the eighteenth century. Like their English counterparts, they established intricate networks of trade with other communities within their region, but they demonstrated an impressive tenacity at preserving local control over their lives and in ignoring dictates from both the metropolitan center of London and the provincial centers of Boston or Hartford.[44]

The history of America was not the history of New England writ large, and the social structures created in the southern and middle colonies were not only different from those of New England but, as Jack Greene has recently argued, probably more significant in terms of the subsequent development of the American nation. The homogeneity that characterized New England society was considerably disturbed by the immigration of Africans and Scots-Irish to the southern colonies. The middle colonies were diverse in their ethnic makeup even from the outset, a diversity that was only accentuated as increasing concentrations of German and Scots-Irish settlers made New York City and Philadelphia their points of disembarkation.[45]

Public officials in the provincial centers of government in every colony would discover that the best-laid and most socially progressive plans of a chief executive could never succeed without the acquiescence of those in the hinterland. William Penn's vision of neat, orderly grid plans for every Pennsylvania town vanished as Pennsylvanians found it more convenient to spread themselves out across the countryside. From this unplanned precursor to suburban sprawl, the towns—more often loosely organized settlements—were often strikingly different in ethnic and religious makeup from one another, with English Quakers, Scots-Irish Presbyterians, German Lutherans, Amish, and Mennonites preferring to organize their polities in ways most congenial to their particular religious and ethnic cultures. Even in Virginia, the one place in which historians have seen the extension to the hinterland of a dominant English "gentry culture" to be the most pervasive, the spirit of localism often blunted the effects of legislation emanating from both London and the provincial center of Williamsburg. In the 1660s Governor William Berkeley devised an economically rational plan to diversify Virginia's one-crop agricultural economy, but when confronted with the reality of an independent and highly dispersed citizenry, his efforts to implement the plan met with ignominious failure.[46] A century later the Virginia Tidewater gentry could take some measure of satisfaction in the ways in which they had been successful in transmitting many of their values and styles of life to portions of the hinterland, but the reality of political life in mid-eighteenth-century Virginia, as we will see, suggested that the number of local variations in the definition of genteel politics was endless. By the time one reached the outposts of British political authority on the Carolina and Georgia frontier, one encountered a political system that went beyond localism and approached social disintegration. While the reports of itinerant Anglican minister Charles Woodmason on the state of civilization in the Carolina backcountry betray an hysteria and animus that make him not wholly trustworthy as an informant, his characterization of the "low, lazy, sluttish, heathenish, hellish life" prevailing there suggests a society not only disconnected from metropolitan and provincial centers but also without much of a local community life.[47]

Diversity and Convergence in Anglo-American Politics

As we stand back and try to take stock of the expectations that Englishmen on both sides of the Atlantic had about their governments and about those men who served in their governments, it is clear that they were undergoing a long, slow, and confusing transformation of political life and thought, a transformation from the medieval to the modern. The English and Americans shared at least a few items of political faith and of political experience. They believed that governments were necessary to preserve order and liberty in society, but they also believed that too great a concentration of power within a government might endanger the very order and liberty that governments were instituted to secure. They venerated the monarch both as a vital component of their government and as the symbol of their common nationality, yet they had evidence before them that their monarchs had sometimes abused the trust that the people had placed in them. Within that conflicted view of government and of the men serving in government, most eighteenth-century Englishmen and Americans probably did maintain qualified optimism about their own governments. Their admiration for "mixed government" as well as their admiration—overinflated as it may have been—for the superior virtue of the English people, provided the primary sources for that optimism. Nor were the English the only ones who admired their government. The Baron de Montesquieu, commenting on Harrington's critique of the English Constitution, defended it as the best in the world. According to Montesquieu, Harrington's effort at constructing his mythical Commonwealth of Oceana was misguided because "for want of knowing the nature of real liberty, he busied himself in pursuit of an imaginary one; and that he built a Chalcedon, though he had a Byzantium before his eyes."[48]

Most Englishmen and Americans in the eighteenth century, some with much greater enthusiasm than others, probably accepted the utility—even the desirability—of hierarchy, of a natural ordering of men and women in society and of a direct connection, at least for men, between social authority and political power. Yet that same general acceptance of a hierarchical political order, when set against the historical certainty of the corrupting effects of concentrations of political power, set up a paradox in which the need to maintain the hierarchy and the need to preserve human liberty were always in tension.

One person's tension is another person's balance, and it is fair to say that both were inherent parts of the Anglo-American political systems. Those who embraced the classical republican aspiration for England's future were probably the most concerned about both certifying the virtue of those at the top of the political hierarchy and in creating the necessary balance in government that would render even the less virtuous incapable of imposing tyranny. While there was nothing in the conditions of America that should have made the colonists there any more optimistic about being able to identify a group of leaders who were visibly more virtuous than their counterparts back in England, there probably was in the social landscape of America a condition that made the prospect of both dispersing power and of closely overseeing those who held power more realistic. The existence of a large population of independent freeholders in America created at least the potential for the sort of independent electorate that Harrington had envisioned for his mythical commonwealth. As we will see, on most occasions in the eighteenth century the potential American electorate remained somnolent. Some of that sleepiness was the consequence of their provincialism and insularity, their unconcern about public affairs beyond their own family or farm or immediate locality. Some was also the consequence of simple habit; though possessing personal independence and armed with the franchise, few had any strong notion about what to do with it. Occasionally, however, and in a few places, when they awakened from their slumber, they did discover some of the latent power that they possessed—power ultimately capable of shaking mighty empires.

The chapters that follow will in their individual parts highlight the extraordinary diversity and lack of agreement within America on what politics were all about. Running through those chapters, however, and made more explicit in the final chapter, are those sources of convergence that would, by the time of the Revolution, shape a conception of politics different from that anywhere else in the early modern world.

Chapter 2

Eighteenth-Century Virginia
In Pursuit of the Deferential Ideal

The Great Seal for the independent commonwealth of Virginia, adopted on July 5, 1776, portrays powerfully the commitment of one group of America's revolutionary leaders to create a commonwealth—virtuous and uncorrupted—true to the ideals of classical republicanism. Described in detail by Edmund Randolph, the independent state's first attorney general, in his *History of Virginia*, each side of the seal featured a central human figure, each female. On one side was Virtus, "the genius of the Commonwealth"—dressed like an Amazon—resting on a spear with one hand and holding a sword in the other; she was treading on tyranny—represented by a man prostrate, with a crown fallen from his head and a broken chain (symbolizing the shackles of British tyranny) in his left hand and a scourge in his right. Over the head of Virtus was the word *Virginia,* and at the bottom, *Sic semper tyrannis.* The symbolism could not have been any clearer: without virtue, tyranny would reign supreme. But Virginia's political leaders believed that their society, unlike Rome's, was a virtuous one, and to symbolize that belief they placed on the other side of their seal a group of three women. In the center stood Libertas, the Roman embodiment of individual liberties, flanked by Ceres, goddess of agriculture, holding a cornucopia in one hand and an ear of wheat in the other and, on the other side, Aeternitas, goddess of permanence, holding a globe and phoenix and intended to depict the immortal quality of Virginia's experiment in liberty. At the bottom of that side of the seal were the words *Deus nobis hoc otia fecit,* God endowed us with these retreats."[1] Forged together, the two sides of the seal represented the extraordinarily self-conscious belief of Virginia's revolutionary elite in an agrarian world in which virtue and liberty were intimately connected.

The political leaders of prerevolutionary Virginia, perhaps more than their counterparts in any other colony in America, seemed to cultivate those attributes that were later portrayed on the Virginia seal. The roster of republican statesmen to emerge from Virginia during the last half of the eighteenth century is truly a remarkable one. Four of the new nation's first five presidents—George Washington, Thomas Jefferson, James Madison, and James Monroe—were products of the political culture of mid-

Figure 3. The Virginia Revolutionary Seal, 1776 (front and back). Painted by Virginia Clark Taylor, 1949. Courtesy of the Library of Virginia.

eighteenth-century Virginia, and, indeed, when one looks beyond Virginia's presidential dynasty, the evidence of superior political leadership is as impressive for its depth as it is for the luminousness of its leading lights: John Robinson, Peyton Randolph, George Wythe, Robert Carter Nicholas, Edmund Randolph, Richard Bland, George Mason, John Marshall, Patrick Henry, Edmund Pendleton, a long line of Lees from Arthur to Richard Henry—the list could be extended much further. As historian Charles Sydnor observed long ago, the system within which all of those men were elevated to positions of political power was anything but democratic, yet it was, for all of its inclinations toward oligarchy, on the whole remarkably responsive and responsible.[2] Given the role that Virginia's eighteenth-

century leaders played in the politics of the young American republic, it is not surprising that so much of what has been written about eighteenth-century American political culture has had such a distinctly Virginian accent.

In 1770 a thirty-three-year-old lawyer and plantation owner from Virginia's Mecklenberg County sat down and, most uncharacteristically for a middling planter in what was still the backcountry of Virginia, wrote a play. Though not published until 1798 and not performed until the mid-twentieth century, Robert Munford's *The Candidates* has had a powerful influence on nearly every historical treatment of Virginia written in the last half century.[3] A slapstick farce, *The Candidates* portrays nearly the entire range of character types likely to be found in Virginia political life. The venerable Worthy seems to have been created as the embodiment of the classical conception of deference. Worthy's traits—attainment of wealth that elevated him to an economic position independent of the need of favors from others, a social position that instilled in him a sense of noblesse oblige, and, most important, a disinterestedness in his political conduct—were so singular in his political community that his election, whenever he chose to run, was a foregone conclusion. It is Worthy's decision not to stand for re-election to the House of Burgesses that allows a host of obviously less-qualified claimants to enter the contest. Wou'dbe is a gentry man who shares Worthy's genteel and statesmanlike view of the role of a political representative, but who does not quite match his colleague's exalted social standing. In past years Wou'dbe had represented his county alongside Worthy, but the determination of Worthy to retire has the effect not only of opening up the contest for his own seat but also of encouraging new aspirants for the seat occupied by the more vulnerable Wou'dbe.

In the course of the election an array of candidates, hopelessly inferior in status and authority to the gentry ideal embodied by Worthy, parade before the voters for support. Sir John Toddy, a lesser gentry man of drunken and dissipated habits, promises the freeholders that, if elected, he will lower the price of rum. Smallhopes, a bullying figure noted more for his concern for horse racing than public service, strips off his shirt and prepares to fight Wou'dbe to prove he is the better man. Finally, Strutabout, the parvenu, violates the genteel code by his open electioneering and his irresponsible promises to follow the wishes of even the most uninformed of his constituents. In the end, however, the traditional, virtuous system of deferential voting triumphs; thanks to Worthy's timely decision to offer himself for public service once again, the slate of Worthy and Wou'dbe is elected by acclamation. As one freeholder commented to another, "Aye, aye, they've just come, and sit upon the bench, and yet all the votes are for them." In the final scene Wou'dbe and Worthy thank the voters for "shewing your judgment, and a spirit of independence becoming Virginians," and in turn are told by the voters, "we have done as we ought, we have elected the ablest, according to the writ."[4]

Munford's play has been influential not only because it is a rollicking good source for colorful quotations about eighteenth-century political life but also because it seems to conform to the self-image that so many of Virginia's leaders worked to create for themselves—men who were neither democrats nor hereditary aristocrats, but, rather, who were forged through some process different from any with which we are familiar today, a process by which men of genuine merit, motivated by a sense of noblesse oblige, affirmed their ability and willingness to serve the broader public good. Indeed, Wou'dbe and Worthy seem to have been crafted by Munford to embody all of those traits that James Harrington, in *Oceana*, deemed essential to good and just government. The deference paid to Wou'dbe and Worthy was not blind submission to superior social and economic power, but, rather, active acknowledgment of their superior virtue, moral character, and social authority. The freeholders who swept Wou'dbe and Worthy into office, far from lacking a political will, were taking seriously the injunction given them by the Virginia electoral laws, assessing the claims to social and political authority of the contestants and then "electing the ablest."

We need to inquire, of course, whether Munford's farcical treatment, obscure and neglected as it was in his own time, was in any way connected with the reality of political life in eighteenth-century Virginia.[5] Or does it represent a misplaced nostalgia for a genuinely meritocratic political system that never really existed? There can be no doubt that eighteenth-century Virginia produced a long line of impressive political leaders, but did those leaders come to power in the context of an ethic that would have been congenial to both James Harrington and Robert Munford? If we clear our eyes from the effects of nostalgia and wishful thinking, and analyze critically the conduct as well as the self-conception of Virginia's political ruling class, the picture that emerges is one that falls substantially short of the deferential ideal.

But at least a few of Virginia's political leaders were able to project credible imitations of two variants of the classical republican statesman. John Robinson, longtime Speaker of the House of Burgesses, and George Washington, planter, soldier, and lawmaker, by the self-conscious cultivation of their public personae and by the esteem in which they were held by their fellow settlers, came closer than any others in their society to symbolizing the spirit of *Virtus et Libertas*.

John Robinson's base of power was King and Queen County, located in that fertile and well-situated part of Virginia lying between the Tidewater and Northern Neck. He was able to combine an impressive accumulation of wealth and economic power—thirteen thousand acres of land and four hundred slaves spread across several plantations—with an inclination toward public service in a way that guaranteed to him thirty-eight consecutive years of service in Virginia's House of Burgesses, with twenty-seven of those years devoted to service as Speaker of the House. Unlike Worthy, Robinson did not have to be persuaded to serve; he obviously loved the political life, but like his fictional counterpart's, his election was always a foregone conclusion. In his long legislative career there is only one small hint that he ever encountered significant opposition in the balloting for burgess for his county. When he was elected by the freeholders in his first attempt to take a seat in the lower house of assembly in 1727, his election was contested by Gaven Corbin, a member of a family even wealthier and more prominent in the region than Robinson's. The Committee on Privileges and Elections, after examining Corbin's complaint, rejected it emphatically, taking the extraordinary step of labeling it "groundless, frivolous, malicious, and scandalous." From that moment on, the standing of John Robinson, Gentleman, went unchallenged within his home county. It was only neces-

Figure 4. Speaker of the House of Burgesses John Robinson. Many of Robinson's contemporaries viewed him as the paragon of the virtuous leader, while others may have seen closer resemblances to Robinson's English contemporary, Sir Robert Walpole. Courtesy Valentine Richmond History Center.

sary that he, like Worthy, "sit upon the bench" while his superior virtue and ability were once again validated by his neighbors.[6]

What was the secret of Robinson's success? There were, as we will see, some men in colonies such as New York and South Carolina whose wealth and economic power alone may have guaranteed them unfettered access to political power. But in Virginia the mere ownership of property on the scale of Robinson's did not automatically guarantee an individual the brand of political power that Robinson was to enjoy. There were at least a dozen men in the colony who owned at least as much land and as many slaves, and, moreover, most of Robinson's constituents were not tenants dependent upon him for their livelihoods—as was the case in some parts of New York's Hudson valley—but, rather, independent freeholders.[7] Robinson was descended from a family with impressive connections both in England and in Virginia—his great-uncle had been bishop of London, and his father had briefly served as president of the Virginia Governor's Council—but again, his claim to influence through his kinfolk could easily have been equaled by a dozen others within the colony. The Robinson family name and the wealth accompanying it also purchased for John a respectable education—first at the hands of a tutor and then at the College of William and Mary—no small accomplishment in a colony that steadfastly refused to provide public education at even the most rudimentary level for its citizens. Still though, it is notable that Robinson did not venture to England to the Inns of Court or Oxford or Cambridge as did so many of Virginia's or South Carolina's most prominent citizens.[8]

Although instructed by his superiors in London to keep a close check on the prerogatives of the Virginia House of Burgesses and on its principal leader, Virginia's royal governor Francis Faquier was nevertheless an unabashed admirer of Robinson, describing him as a "Man of Worth, Probity and Honor; the most beloved both in his public and private Character of any man in the Colony."[9] Robinson's younger Virginia colleague Edmund Randolph, himself descended from one of Virginia's most illustrious families, elaborated further. Robinson, Randolph declared, was not only a person of "sound political knowledge," but more important, a man of "great integrity, assiduity, and ability in business." When he presided over the burgesses,

The decorum of the house outshone that of the British House of Commons, even with Onslow at their head. When he propounded a question, his comprehension and perspicuity brought in equally to the most humble and the most polished understanding. To committees he nominated the members best qualified. He stated to the house the contents of every bill and showed himself to be a perfect master of the subject.[10]

Furthermore, Robinson's mastery of the parliamentary mechanics of the House of Burgesses seemed to Randolph to be melded with that one quality that was the sine qua non of any true natural aristocrat, an "independence "of judgment that enabled him to rise above petty interests and political pressures to argue for the public good—the essence, in sum, of Virtus.

To Virginia burgess Landon Carter, who often found himself at odds with Robinson on legislative matters, Robinson's dominance over the assembly could be infuriating. When Robinson proposed a series of amendments to a tobacco bill, some of which Carter believed to be unwise, they were all "agreed to Naut Signisque Loquuntur ["They speak in accord with signs of rank"]. If any dared Oppose, some severe Expression unbecoming his dignity was immediately thundered out." Robinson displayed his legislative omnipotence once again a few days later, in the course of debate on a bill to divide one of Virginia's counties, which the Speaker opposed. Carter, who was once again on the opposite side of the question from Robinson, fumed, "For there he sits and what he can't do himself he prompts others to do by his nods, nay to hollow out aloud, as the division must run to whichsoever side he sits, is enough to throw the side he is off, and I'll suffer death if these days he loses a motion."[11]

It was not legislative competence alone, however, that commended Robinson to his Virginia political colleagues, for his obvious talents as a legislator were joined with extraordinary personal warmth and ease, "a benevolence which created friend and a sincerity which never lost one." The eulogy given at his death praised him for "the many amiable virtues which adorned his private station," but most important, noted that he was "cherished by rich and poor alike" for his "liberality and humanity," those cardinal virtues in the classical republican pantheon.[12]

Most of us would of course wish to have lived lives as virtuous and public-spirited as those described in the eulogies delivered at our funerals. As we will see at the conclusion of this chapter, it was only after Robinson's death that the public at large was offered a glimpse of at least some of his deeds that fell significantly short of the disinterested classical republic ideal. And the revelation would, at least for some, bring into sharp relief the inconsistencies between the rhetoric and the reality of Virginia's political ruling class.

If there were any other eighteenth-century Virginian whom we might expect to have equaled John Robinson's reputation as a paragon of virtue and disinterested public service, that person surely would be George Washington. And certainly, at some point in his career—perhaps by the mid-1760s, after he had distinguished himself by service in the Seven Years' War, but more assuredly after the successful conclusion of the Revolution—Washington was able to ascend to a status where he served as the prototype of the virtuous republican statesman throughout all of America. What is perhaps more revealing than the situation in which the mature and militarily distinguished general found himself by the time of the Revolution was that which the aspiring colonel faced earlier in his career. Though he could boast of a respectable family lineage, it was certainly not a preeminent one, and, indeed, there were many in his home county of Fairfax who could claim more distinguished family connections. Moreover, as he calculated his rise to political prominence in his home county, Washington discovered that the pathway to political power was at least temporarily blocked by his more distinguished neighbors John West and George William Fairfax.

Fortunately for Washington, Virginia's electoral laws allowed a man to run for office in any county in which he held property, and since he also possessed landholdings in Frederick County, immediately to the west of Fairfax, some of the friends of the twenty-three-year-old colonel decided in 1755 to enter his name as a candidate for the burgesses in that county against the two incumbents, Hugh West and Thomas Swearingen. Washington was not as well known in Frederick County as he was in Fairfax, and he played no part himself in the campaign; unfortunately for him, none of his initial backers expended any effort in his behalf either, and as a consequence, he ran a distant third in the race for the two vacant seats—with West and Swearingen receiving 271 and 270 votes and Washington attracting only a scant 40.[13] While we lack any explicit commentary about the outcome from Washington himself, it is notable that the proud young colonel took the pains to copy from the poll book the names of all forty of those who had cast their votes for him.

Three years later, his reputation as a military leader on the rise, Washington made another bid for a seat in the burgesses from Frederick, and this time he was not content to play a passive role in the campaign. He declared his candidacy several months before the balloting was to take place and marshalled the support of several important men of influence in his behalf. When Washington discovered that his military duties were to take him to Fort Cumberland—some forty miles away—on the election day itself, he made elaborate arrangements to make certain that his interests were well represented nevertheless. The first step in this joining of interests was to ask his friend Colonel James Wood, the founder and leading citizen of Winchester, the Frederick County seat, to appear at the election on his behalf and personally thank the voters for their suffrages. He also made certain not only that he had the support of other men of influence in the election but also that those influential men displayed their support for him in a timely fashion.

At the election itself there were four candidates contesting the county's two seats in the assembly. Hugh West and Thomas Swearingen—the two incumbent burgesses who had defeated Washington in 1755—were running for reelection. Colonel Thomas Bryan Martin, connected by kinship to the powerful Fairfax family, was joining Washington in challenging the incumbents. Assembled around a table at the Frederick County Courthouse were the sheriff, his clerks, and the candidates (in Washington's case, the candidate's representative). Voting in Virginia was conducted viva voce, so the as-

Figure 5. Major General George Washington. The earliest portrait of Washington, painted by Charles Willson Peale in 1772 after Washington had attained national and international attention as a military leader in the Seven Years War, but before he had achieved unrivaled political power and authority. Washington-Curtis-Lee Collection, Washington and Lee University, Lexington, Virginia.

sembled freeholders (and candidates) were able to watch the course of the election as it unfolded. The first voter to approach the table was the most eminent man in the region, Lord Fairfax, proprietor of the Northern Neck, county lieutenant and senior justice of the peace of the Frederick County Court. Fairfax cast his votes for Martin and Washington. The second voter to appear before the sheriff, also casting his vote for Washington, was William Meldrum, rector of the Anglican Church in Frederick Parish and one of the most influential ministers of the region. Washington's designated representative, Colonel Wood, voted next, supporting Washington and Hugh West. Another colonel in the local militia and a leading merchant in the region, John Carlyle, then voted, supporting Washington and Martin.

As the balloting proceeded, it was apparent to all assembled at the courthouse that virtually all of the men of influence in the county had swung their support to Washington. All of those voters who were identified on the poll sheets as "gentleman" voted for Washington, as did the county's three ministers—one a Presbyterian, another a Baptist, and Meldrum, the Anglican. The strategy of marshaling a prominent display of support early in the election was, at least in this case, highly successful, as Washington raced to an early lead that only grew as the day wore on. When the poll was closed, the vote stood Washington 310, Martin 240, West 199, and Swearingen 45.[14]

While Washington's victory had certainly been aided by the highly visible support given him by the local worthies of Frederick County, he had also taken pains to enhance his standing with the voters before the balloting took place. He had spent £39. 6s. out of his own pocket on 28 gallons of rum, 50 gallons and 1 hogshead of rum punch, 34 gallons of wine, 46 gallons of "strong beer," and 2 gallons of cider royal—more than 160 gallons and 1 hogshead of liquor to be served to the 391 voters of the district.[15] Washington was emphatic in his belief that his hospitality on election day was not an attempt to buy votes with food and drink. He wrote to an associate that "I hope no exception were taken to any that voted against me, but that all were alike treated and all had enough; it is what I much desired; my only fear is that you spent with too sparing a hand."[16] The young Washington knew that hospitality and liberality were two of the defining characteristics of a genuine gentry man, and this display of his generosity, in combination with his ability to mobilize other men of interest and influence in his behalf, marked the beginning of a remarkably successful political career. It is noteworthy, however, that neither the display of generosity nor the marshaling of men of influence was something that occurred purely spontaneously. There was, by necessity, an element of shrewdness, of calculation, in Washington's initial ascent to political power.

Washington was, if anything, even more aggressive about marshaling the necessary interests in his behalf in his campaign for reelection in 1761, an election in which he had joined interests with his friend and neighbor,

George Mercer. Though assured that "the leaders of all the patrician families remain firm in their resolution of continuing for you," he was warned that one of his opponents, Colonel Adam Stephen, had "attracted the attention of the plebeians whose unstable minds are agitated by every breath of novelty, whims, and nonsense." Confronted by this challenge, Washington not only persisted in his practice of treating the voters but also appealed directly to Captain Van Swearingen, the sheriff responsible for conducting the poll on election day. "I hope," Washington wrote, "my interest in your neighborhood still stands good, and as I have every great reason to believe you can be no friend to a person of Colonel Stephen's principles, I hope, and indeed make no doubt, that you will contribute your aid toward shutting him out of the public trust he is seeking." Washington then pressed the sheriff even further, noting "should Mercer's friends and mine be hurried in at the first of the poll it might be an advantage—but as sheriff I know you cannot appear in this nor would I by any means have you do anything that can give so designing a man as Col. Stephen the least handle."[17] However much Washington may have disliked Colonel Stephen's courting of the "plebeians," he had no qualms about encouraging his principal supporters, as well as the sheriff, to promote his candidacy among that same class of residents.

In subsequent years, as his reputation as a man of personal courage and sound political judgment grew, Washington would not need to go to such lengths to reinforce his claims to the public trust, but at this early stage it was not sufficient merely to announce his willingness to serve. The young Colonel Washington, like so many of his fellow Virginia gentry men, could not rely simply on his own personal reputation and ability to dispense patronage to the citizens of the county; rather, it was necessary for him to join interests with other prominent local worthies and to secure their aid in rallying the voters to his side in order to gain election. While this joining of interests was not wholly inconsistent with a conception of deference that encompassed the notion of "persuasion in a tangible shape," it was, in the extent to which Washington was forced to exert himself to command the suffrages of his neighbors, certainly a step away from classical notions of deference. Indeed, what we find in Washington's case, as with so many other of America's aspirants to office, is that the popular impulses in American politics, though certainly not articulated or structured into a shape that we can call "democratic," were nevertheless working to change the way politics in local communities was conducted.

It was almost certainly no accident that men like Robinson and Washington, who were able to rise to positions of political power and then to appear to effortlessly enhance and exercise their personal authority in the political realm, were also owners of large numbers of slaves. Many years earlier William Byrd II had, while enunciating the patriarchal ideal to which

he aspired, also made explicit the connection between patriarchal authority and chattel slavery.

Besides the advantage of a pure Air, we abound in all kinds of Provisions without
expence (I mean we who have Plantations). I have a large Family of my own, and
my Doors are open to Every Body, yet I have no Bills to pay, and a half-a-crown will
rest undisturbed in my Pocket for many Moons together. Like one of the Patriarchs,
I have my Flocks and my Herds, my Bond-men and Bond-women, and every Soart
of Trade amongst my own Servants, so that I live in a kind of Independence on
everyone but Providence. However this Soart of Life is without expence, yet it is attended with a great deal of trouble. I must take care to keep all my people to their
Duty, to set all the Springs in motion and make every one draw his equal Share to
carry the Machine forward. But then 'tis an amusement in this silent Country and
a continual exercise of our Patience and Economy.[18]

Robinson and Washington lived in a world in which their relationships
with their slaves shaped their attitude toward power and authority. Try as
they might, these self-confident, manly men could not ignore altogether
the coercive elements of their command over their "Bond-men and Bond-
women" nor, perhaps, could they escape occasional doubts about whether
their mastery over their labor force would go on unchallenged infinitely.
And if they occasionally experienced those doubts about the automatic deference of their slaves to their will and their judgment, then they might be
able to depend even less on acts of deference from their more independent and obstreperous free white constituents.[19]

If George Washington had to exert himself to earn the suffrage of his
neighbors in Frederick County, then Landon Carter of neighboring Richmond County should have been able to count on a smoother, more effortless path to social authority and political power. He was born in 1710 into
what was almost certainly Virginia's wealthiest and most prominent family,
and every aspect of his upbringing instilled in him the assumption that he
should expect the unquestioned deference of those around him. Landon's
father, Robert "King" Carter, had at the time of his death in 1732 amassed
an estate of 330,000 acres. King Carter's estate at Corotoman was one of the
few in Virginia that could bear comparison with its counterparts in England, and his political career, which included service at every level of government—in the vestry, in the county court, as speaker of the House of
Burgesses, as treasurer of the colony, and member of the Governor's Council—was equaled in its luminosity by perhaps only that of John Robinson.[20]

Landon's upbringing was a textbook example of the nurturance of a
member of the Virginia aristocracy. Sent at age nine to private school in
England where he received the sort of classical education expected of English gentlemen, he returned to Virginia at age sixteen, and briefly attended
the College of William and Mary; he then moved into his father's business
of plantation management. By the time of his father's death in 1732 Lan-

don would have a substantial plantation patrimony to manage. The fourth of King Carter's sons, Landon would inherit eight of his father's plantations which, added to 15,000 acres of land in the western portion of Virginia's Northern Neck, would offer him an impressive start. Over the course of his life Landon was married three times—to members of the Wormeley, Byrd, and Beale families—and with each marriage both his property and his access to people of influence increased. By the early 1740s, when he had completed his own plantation house—Sabine Hall, overlooking the Rappahannock River—Landon Carter's holdings in the Northern Neck alone totaled over thirty-five thousand acres. Most of that vast domain was under active cultivation, tended by a labor force amounting to more than four hundred slaves.[21]

For Landon, as for his Carter forebears, the economic power that came with great wealth was only a means to an end. It was in public life that one earned the respect of one's neighbors, which was the hallmark of social and political authority, and Landon set himself on that path early in his adulthood. He began his service on the Richmond County Court in 1734, a tenure that would persist continuously until his death forty-four years later. In the years that followed, he would gain election to the parish vestry of the Anglican Church and would earn appointment from Governor William Gooch as commander of his county's militia. By all accounts Landon Carter approached these opportunities for public service at the local level with a conscientiousness and diligence that should have marked him as a man of superior virtue, a gentry man guided by an ethic of noblesse oblige that should have set him apart from nearly all others in his locality. Indeed, his political creed was, as an expression of aspiration at least, the very embodiment of those values embodied in the Virginia seal of 1776. Fully cognizant of the imperfect and avaricious nature of mankind, Carter believed it to be the particular responsibility of men of his character, virtue, and upbringing to attend to the "Good of the Community." He repeatedly spoke of the "true sense of duty" that motivated him to take on the burdens of public service, and he regarded his labors in the field of politics and government as an important part of the obligation that men of his privileged rank and station in life owed to society in return for those favors that God had bestowed on them.

Carter sincerely believed that his service both on the Richmond County Court and in the House of Burgesses was motivated by nothing more than the purely altruistic desire to bring "order," "dispatch," and "decency" to the "Publick business," and even when he was ill, he would drag himself out of his sickbed in order to serve "so good a cause as forwarding the Administration of Justice." Believing as he did in the concept of the virtuous republican statesman, Carter claimed to be committed to a system of government in which the citizens at large, and not a narrowly composed aristocracy, identified those men best able to serve the public good.[22] By all rights Landon Carter believed his service within his county *should* have caused him to be identified as one of those virtuous few, earning him speedy elevation to political office and influence beyond the boundaries of his home county.

Landon Carter's Northern Neck constituents, however, much to his chagrin, were not always so conscientious in recognizing their patron's superior virtue. He would present himself to the voters as a candidate for a seat in the House of Burgesses in 1735, 1742, and 1748, and on each occasion he was rejected by his constituents. Carter finished a poor fourth in the contest for the burgesses in his first attempt in 1735; since it came only a year after he had embarked on service on the county court, he could perhaps rationalize that defeat fairly easily—he was, after all, only twenty-five at the time and the successful candidates, John Woodbridge and William Fantleroy, though not of his exalted social position, were nevertheless men of property and experienced politicians in the bargain. But the defeat in 1742, once again at the hands of Fantleroy, clearly rankled. Carter was convinced that Fantleroy's conduct at the 1742 election proved conclusively that he did not deserve the responsibility of a burgess. In a petition to the Committee of Privileges and Elections of the House of Burgesses, Carter protested that Fantleroy had been guilty of engaging in unfair election practices, thus preventing the voters from carrying out their duty to "elect the ablest." Specifically, Carter charged that "one William Jordan, an open Abettor of the Interest of Mr. Fantleroy, did, according to his Appointment, meet many of Mr. Fantleroy's Friends, who were Freeholders, at the Public Bridge over the Rappahannock Creek . . . and brought with him about 2 Gallons of Rum, and treated the Company to Drams." Carter's complaint went on to charge that Fantleroy, "the Sitting member, appeared to be intoxicated with strong Liquors, and none who voted for Mr. Carter appeared to be so, except one Thomas Lewis." Subsequent testimony also indicated that Jordan, Fantleroy's principal supporter, had boasted that he "would give a Hogshead, or a Hundred Gallons of Rum, rather than Mr. Carter, the Petitioner, should go Burgess."[23]

The Committee of Privileges and Elections, which contained several Carter family friends and relations, sided with Landon Carter, ruling that while Fantleroy himself had not done anything improper, the improprieties committed by his supporter William Jordan were sufficiently injurious as to void Fantelroy's election. Unfortunately for Carter, a majority of members of the whole House, many of whom had no doubt committed improprieties at least as serious, reversed the decision of the committee and ordered Fantleroy to be seated as a duly-elected burgess, a result that must have deeply wounded a hypersensitive young planter who naturally assumed that high political office would be as much his natural inheritance as his land and his slaves.[24]

In fact, mere ownership did not guarantee automatic respect or obedience, even among those slaves whose labor he theoretically commanded. If William Byrd II found keeping "all my People to their Duty" an "amusement," Landon Carter found it a constant source of exasperation. His diary seethes with frustration over acts both of lack of respect and outright disobedience on the part of his slaves. He ranted at the perfidy of "my man Bart," who had run away because "I [Carter] had ordered him a whipping for saying he then brought in two loads of wood when he was coming with his first load only. . . . He is the most incorrigeable villain . . . alive, and has deserved hanging." Such disrespect and disobedience could only be explained, Carter claimed, by the fact that "slaves are devils," and any "kindness to a Negroe" was "the surest way to spoil him."[25] With these displays of the imperfections in his world plainly before him, it was difficult to avoid the conclusion that the gentry ideal of deference and patriarchy were, at least for him, maddeningly out of reach.

Landon Carter, in addition to being oversensitive both to his natural entitlements and to the ways in which others refused to recognize them, was also persistent, and he was finally successful in gaining election to the burgesses in 1752. Once a member of that body, he distinguished himself as a member uncommonly committed to the diligent pursuit of the public good. He almost immediately was appointed a member of some of the most important standing committees in the House, and after 1756 he served as chair of the important Committee on Courts of Justice. Moreover, he used his skills as a writer to become a highly effective defender of the prerogatives of the House of Burgesses, publishing pamphlets and essays defending the House on such important issues as the Pistole Fee, paper currency, and the Two Penny Act. Even as his influence in the House expanded, however, he continued to fret about the way in which his fellow legislators failed both to recognize his own superior wisdom and virtue and to behave with the dignity and decorum befitting burgesses. In particular, he believed that too many of his fellow burgesses were "favourers of Popularity" who were too often swayed by the "sentiments of [their] constituents" rather than by "Reason and Conscience." The consequence, he thought, was mischievous legislation which, though it might serve the interests of "one part of the Community," too frequently sacrificed the good of the whole.[26]

In particular, Carter chafed under the dominance of John Robinson during the entire period in which the two served together in the House; he was appalled at the "political" character of Robinson's leadership and, believing that Robinson was at the head of the "favourers of popularity," was convinced that he—by dint of birth and upbringing—was the more virtuous and public-spirited of the two. How could it be that one as self-interested as Robinson could prevail so consistently and so easily over one so obviously public-spirited as Landon Carter? Carter similarly recorded in his diary all those instances in which his fellow burgesses lapsed from what he believed to be the "Rules of Parliamentary decency." When he invoked standards of parliamentary dignity and decorum, his model was always the House of Commons, and it is clear that he was speaking not only of technical matters of parliamentary procedure, but also of the gentility and civility that he believed to be the mark of a gentleman-statesman. Carter noted with disapproval in April 1772, in the midst of the growing revolutionary crisis, that the burgesses sat up "regaling or gaming till 12 every night, and rise very late, mostly unprepared and in the morning very unfit for business, by which means designing men carry on scandelous and injurious laws ... which unless they had been thrown out would ruin the Country."[27] And of course he was most aggrieved when he was not accorded the respect due a gentleman-statesman. During his first term as a burgess he sponsored a bill "for lessening the Number of Doggs in some Counties"; various "wise heades" in the House made jokes about the failure of the bill to distinguish between "doggs and Bitches," and at least one "Buffoon" rose to oppose the bill in verse, hoping to "send it to the Lethean Shoar where he hoped never to hear of it more." Carter regarded his bill with deadly seriousness, expressing puzzlement that his fellow burgesses should find levity in such a serious matter. After all his labors the bill finally passed the House, only to be vetoed in the Governor's Council; Carter noted ruefully, "no reasons given for it and indeed I must believe they had none unless it was to save Doggs which some are fond of."[28]

On the whole Carter was able to win the respect, if not the universal friendship, of most of his fellow burgesses. But whatever admiration he was able to inspire among his gentry colleagues in the House, the task of securing the confidence of his constituents at home was much more demanding. After sixteen years of service in the House, he was turned out in the election of 1768, the reason for this rejection being, in his own words, that he did not "familiarize" himself "among the people." More than a year before his defeat Carter had been the object of two mean-spirited poems published in the *Virginia Gazette*, in which he was compared, unfavorably, to a variety of bugs, hairy beasts, and barnyard animals.[29] By the time those poems had appeared, Carter was already contemplating retirement, in part because of the press of his private business but also no doubt because of his distaste for the whole electioneering process. On the eve of the 1768 election he received another, friendlier piece of verse from an anonymous correspondent, perhaps his neighbor John Tayloe. The poet-critic found much to admire in Carter:

> When Carter cooly does his thoughts rehearse,
> How smoothly glides the harmonious verse
> Our fancies stop nor knows by which it is caught
> The even numbers or the happy thought
> His stern behavior gives no more offence
> We praise his diction and admire his sense.

But the correspondent went on to note that Carter had not given enough

> Thought how he might be rever'd
> would he strive rather to be loved than feared.
> Such is the nature of the human Soul.
> Fear may command a part, but love the whole.

In a final bit of advice Carter was counseled, "Let him relax and we are all his own."

Carter took the counseling in stride but did not relent. In a reply, also in verse, he asked, "What stern behavior ever gave offence to men admiring, if they judged with sense." He was similarly unyielding on the matter of courting love, rather than fear:

> To Court the Love of those who will offend,
> Must Justice pine or Right give up its Whole,
> To purchase Love, so painful to the Soul.

Carter's unwilliness to "court the love" of the people would cost him. Thomas Glasscock, a man significantly less qualified by traditional standards of social status and experience, would unseat him in the 1768 election.[30]

In 1776, looking back on that humiliation, Carter was still smarting over the way in which the "Adultress Popularity" often took precedence over civic virtue. Landon's son Robert Wormeley Carter met the same fate in the elections for Virginia's revolutionary convention in 1776. The victorious candidate, "a worthless, though impudent fellow, and . . . a most silly though good-natured fool," had won the election in spite of the fact that Robert Wormeley Carter had "kissed the arses of the people and very servilely accommodated himself to others"; yet, after all that effort, he was nevertheless "shamefully turned out." Carter concluded sadly that "popularity" was "an adulteress of the first order, for at any time let her be most sacredly wedded to one man she will even be grogged by her gallant over his shoulder."[31]

Voting and Officeholding in Eighteenth-Century Virginia

An analysis by historians Robert and B. Katherine Brown of patterns of voting during three of the elections in which Landon Carter was involved gives us at least a hint of some of the ways in which differing levels of wealth influenced the "adulteress popularity." In those three elections—in 1735, 1755, and 1761—voter turnout totaled 334 (approximately 65 percent of Richmond County's free adult males), 215 (37 percent), and 250 (40 percent), respectively. In the election of 1735 more than half of the voters—most of them probably tenants—did not meet the technical property qualification of ownership of at least one hundred acres; and in the less well-attended elections of 1755 and 1761, more than a third voted in spite of falling below the required property qualification. In none of those elections did anyone see fit to question the propriety of such extensive participation by citizens not legally qualified to cast a ballot. Fully 90 percent of the voters in all three of those elections owned fewer than five hundred acres, a fact that, when coupled with the extensive participation by tenants and small-property owners, gave to the voter profile in those elections a distinctly middling character.

One of the frequently voiced concerns about the participation in elections of propertyless or "dependent" voters was that their suffrage might be unfairly manipulated by the wealthy and powerful; indeed, it was primarily for that reason that the burgesses had passed laws prohibiting the giving of election-day treats, for it was thought that members of the lower orders would be especially susceptible to suasion by food and drink. Although Landon Carter had contested his 1742 election on the grounds that liquor had played an unacceptably influential role in determining the outcome, it is notable that he failed to get any significant support from either middle-class voters or the wealthiest, facts that explain his abysmal showing in that election. By the election of 1755—the peak of his electoral popularity in Richmond County—more than three-quarters of the propertyless voters cast ballots for Carter, but this was also true of the pattern of voting of middle-class and wealthy residents. By 1761 Carter's popularity in his home county was already in decline. Though he managed to gain election, he received only 133 votes, far less than the other successful candidate, John Woodbridge, who received 205, and only 10 more than the third-place finisher, Colonel John Smith. In that election, as in the others, the distribution of the vote across all classes was relatively even, although it was the support from the wealthiest 10 percent of the voters (Carter receiving 15 votes, John Woodbridge 14, and the third-place finisher Smith only 4) that gave Carter his margin of victory. By 1768 his popularity had ebbed still further, with the result being his defeat at the hands of Glasscock.[32] Landon's son Robert Wormeley Carter would regain his father's seat in 1770, only to be turned out again in 1776 in the election for delegates to the convention that would declare independence and draft a new constitution for Virginia.

This evidence relating to the political careers of a John Robinson or a George Washington or a Landon Carter—all men of impressive wealth and social standing—suggests that the combinations of personal authority, influence, and interests affecting the outcome of Virginia elections were highly variable, and that the pathway to power in Virginia—at least for Landon Carter—was not always a smooth one. Interestingly, though, the instances in which candidates like Washington or Carter faced rejection by their constituents were relatively few in number. Indeed, there were not many instances in which Virginia's eighteenth-century residents had the opportunity to participate at all in the selection of their political leaders. All of their local officials—justices of the peace, church vestrymen, sheriffs, coroners—were appointed, not elected.

Technically the royal governor was responsible for making these appointments, but in actual practice the sitting members of the court and vestry controlled virtually all of the appointment process in each of the counties in which they ruled; the sitting members of those bodies would forward recommendations for new members to the royal governor, who would in nearly all cases follow their wishes.

The result was the creation of an elaborate network of "county oligarchies" throughout the colony, oligarchies in which not only were the members of a particular county court or vestry connected to one another by virtue of family, economic status, or personal influence, but also in which court and vestry members throughout the colony were frequently connected by those same ties. Charles Sydnor, who coined the phrase "county oligarchies," provides us with many examples of the interconnectedness of Virginia's political leaders. Thomas Jefferson's grandfather of the same name had served as justice of the peace, sheriff, and militia captain in Henrico County, and his son Peter had served as justice, sheriff, surveyor, county lieutenant, burgess, and vestryman, providing for his son Thomas a well-grooved path to public service. George Washington's father, grandfather, and great-grandfather had all served as court justices, in addition to holding several other local offices. In the case of the Randolph and Lee families, in any given year in the second half of the eighteenth century one could find scores of kinsmen scattered throughout the colony— from the Chesapeake Bay to the Blue Ridge Mountains—serving as justices, vestrymen, and militia commanders, and in most years there were a half dozen or more Lees and Randolphs serving in the burgesses, often as members of the assembly's most important committees.[33]

Virginia's county court justices were charged with the responsibility of doing "equal Right to all Manner of People, Great and Small, High and Low, Rich and Poor, according to Equity and good Conscience, and the Laws and Usages of . . . Virginia, without Favour, Affection, or Partiality." Moreover, they were to be:

Men of Substance and Ability of Body and Estate; of the best Reputation, good Governance, and Courage for the Truth; Men fearing God, not seeking the Place for Honour or Conveniency, but endeavouring to preserve the Peace and good Government of their country, wherein they ought to be resident; Lovers of Justice, judging the People equally and impartially at all Seasons, using Diligence in hearing and determining Causes, and not neglecting the Public Service for private Employment, or Ease; of known Loyalty to the King, not respecting Persons, but the Cause; and they ought to be Men of competent Knowledge in the Laws of their Country, to enable them to execute their Office and Authority to the Advancement of Justice, the Benefit of the People, and without Reproach to themselves.[34]

For the most part Virginia's county court justices managed to live up to that idealized description of their character and duties. While they were not uniformly men of extraordinary wealth, they were, by and large, men of "substance and Ability of Body and Estate." In the Northern Neck bastion of gentry rule, Lancaster County, for example, the average landholding of justices of the peace in the period 1756–75 was 989 acres, four times the average in the county at large.[35] Furthermore, most of the justices appear to have taken seriously the injunctions to competence, diligence, and impartiality. Virginia's county courts functioned as a proving ground for those wealthy and prominent men who might aspire to higher levels of public service within their locale. Due to the size of the courts—they usually consisted of between ten and fifteen justices—the opportunities for service at the county level were obviously much greater than for service at higher levels in the colony's capital in Williamsburg. The range of a justice's duties was considerable, combining legislative, executive, judicial and electoral functions, and running from the routine recording of legal papers to the trying of civil and criminal cases to overseeing the collection of taxes to responsibility for the maintenance and construction of roads and bridges. Perhaps even more critical to their political future, service in those capacities put justices at the center of community life in their respective counties, for it was on court day even more than on the Sabbath that the citizens—male and female, young and old—of a widely scattered society would come together. For most Virginia residents, most of the time, local government, along with the plethora of activities that went on at its seat—elections, horse races, mercantile fairs, slave sales, and informal convivial gatherings at the adjacent tavern—*was* the government.[36]

Perhaps it was because service as a justice was considered a test of one's fitness for wider public service, or perhaps it was because the services that justices performed at the local level were watched and judged more closely by a collectivity of freeholders who were both more numerous and more independent than would have been the case in a typical English county. Whatever the case, Virginia's system of local government, at least in the well-settled counties of the Tidewater, Northern Neck, and Piedmont, was generally more responsive to the citizens it served than the equivalent governmental structures back in England. The strong tradition of local government that prevailed in Virginia's counties did not, however, create within those counties an insularity that isolated citizens or leaders from one locality from their counterparts in another. In part because of the familial interconnections that tied leaders of one county to another, and in part because of the close connection between county court service and service at higher levels in the provincial capital, Virginia's county court system was part of a dense institutional network that provided effective local service while at the same time connecting localities, where appropriate, to other agencies and institutions of government.[37]

It was most often those who proved willing and able to engage in effective service at the county level who were encouraged to stand for election to Virginia's lower house of assembly, the House of Burgesses. The formal qualification necessary both to vote and to hold public office in Virginia was ownership of one hundred acres of land or twenty-five acres and a house in town. While historians have disagreed over the percentage of Virginia's free adult males who were able to meet these technical qualifications for the franchise, it seems likely that a high percentage—probably around 70 percent—were able to do so.[38]

Most of the men who gained election to the House of Burgesses were in fact able to do so without the necessity of energetic campaigning at election time. Sixty-five percent of the elections for the burgesses during the period 1725–1775 were essentially noncompetitive in the sense either that incumbents were reelected without any indication of competition or that no poll of the voters was necessary because there was only one candidate running for each seat.[39] For the ninety-five elections between 1735 and 1774 for which returns have been preserved, voter turnout ranged from a low of 14 percent in an Essex County assembly election in 1770 to a high of 65 percent in Richmond County in 1735. The average turnout during the whole period in those elections was 43 percent, with turnout generally rising in the 1730s and 1740s and then declining thereafter. In general there was no one region within the colony in which turnout was either dramatically higher or lower, although there were clusters of counties—Brunswick, Lunenberg, Amelia, and Halifax in the Southside, and Accomack and Northampton on the Eastern Shore—where competition for public office was more intense than elsewhere.[40] The returns from these ninety-five elections almost certainly overstate the overall level of voter turnout within the colony, as turnout in the noncompetitive elections for which returns were not recorded was undoubtedly lower than in competitive elections; indeed, it is likely that voter turnout was nearly nonexistent in some of those elections.

While the turnover of legislators in the Virginia lower house of assembly during the eighteenth century was surprisingly high—ranging from around 60 percent in the 1730s and 1740s to about 30 percent during the decade before the Revolution—much of that turnover was not directly tied to successful challenges to incumbents, for such successful challenges occurred in only 6 percent of the elections held in the colony between 1728 and 1775.[41] Rather, it most likely represented voluntary decisions on the part of sitting burgesses to return to private life. Public service, especially responsible public service, took time away from farm and family. Sessions of the burgesses during the latter half of the eighteenth century would typically last between six and eight weeks, and few men desired or could afford to be away from their plantations for such an extended period year in and year out. For that reason it was not at all uncommon for the leading citizens of a county to take turns in the burgesses, moving in and out of the legislature as it suited their personal needs.

As was the case in most parts of colonial America, the county was the geographical and political unit by which representation in the lower house of assembly was apportioned. Virginia's government officials were far more conscientious than those in many colonies—particularly those to the south in North and South Carolina or to the north in Pennsylvania—in seeing to it that new counties were created in the western regions of the colony when the density of settlement warranted it. Between 1728 and 1763 twenty-four new counties were created in Virginia, with the House of Burgesses undergoing an expansion from 60 to 108 members. By 1770 the number of representatives had increased to 118 and the ratio of representatives to free adult males in the colony was 1:439, about average for the upper South (Maryland and Delaware were 1:478 and 1:374 respectively). The ratio of representatives to constituents in the New England colonies tended to be slightly lower than that in the Southern colonies and, most strikingly, the ratios in the middle colonies were much higher, standing at well over 1:1000.[42] In Virginia, as in all of the South, one needed only to own property, and not actually to live, in a county in order to serve as a burgess. The incidence of nonresident service in the burgesses was relatively small, and where it did occur, it usually did so, as in the case of George Washington's election, when an individual owned land in an adjoining county.

Taken collectively, these components of the electoral structure of Virginia suggest a society in which the franchise was relatively open, at least to free adult males, the opportunities to exercise that franchise relatively few, and the cases in which freeholders actually took advantage of their right to vote fewer still. None of these indicators, however, helps us to penetrate very tellingly into the relationship between ordinary citizens and the men whom they chose as their political leaders. As we have seen from the cases of Robinson, Washington, and Landon Carter, it appears likely that, in determining who got elected to office, questions of personal prestige and influence were more important than direct appeals to the voters based on issues. It is also clear that the deferential relationship between voter and candidate—in whatever shadings of voluntary or subtly coercive expressions of respect, interest, and influence it might have been defined—did not cease to exist after election day. The other important part of the deferential relationship—the payoff as opposed to the promise of that relationship—was that in which the few, by their conscientious service in pursuit of the public good, justified the confidence that the many had reposed in them. Again, in comparison to their counterparts in many colonies, Virginia's elected leaders did a pretty good job of delivering on their promise of responsive and responsible leadership.

As was the case in nearly all of America's colonies, it was difficult for Virginia's citizens to keep track of what their elected representatives were

Table 1. Representation in Mainland Colonial American Assemblies

	1700		1730		1770	
	Number of Representatives	Ratio of Reps to Adult White Males	Number of Representatives	Ratio of Reps to Adult White Males	Number of Representatives	Ratio of Reps to Adult White Males
Connecticut	42	1:108	79	1:187	138	1:258
Delaware	18	1:25	18	1:96	18	1:374
Georgia					25	1:102
Maryland	46	1:114	50	1:295	58	1:478
Massachusetts	80	1:137	91	1:244	125	1:368
New Hampshire	13	1:74	17	1:124	34	1:363
New Jersey	23	1:114	24	1:287	24	1:910
New York	20	1:168	26	1:320	27	1:1065
North Carolina	22	1:94	31	1:154	81	1:315
Pennsylvania	26	1:134	30	1:336	36	1:1301
Rhode Island	26	1:43	30	1:102	65	1:167
South Carolina	30	1:21	38	1:52	51	1:192
Virginia	44	1:191	54	1:289	118	1:439

Adopted from Jack P. Greene, "Legislative Turnover in British America, 1696 to 1775: A Quantitative Analysis," *WMQ*, 3d ser, 38 (1981).

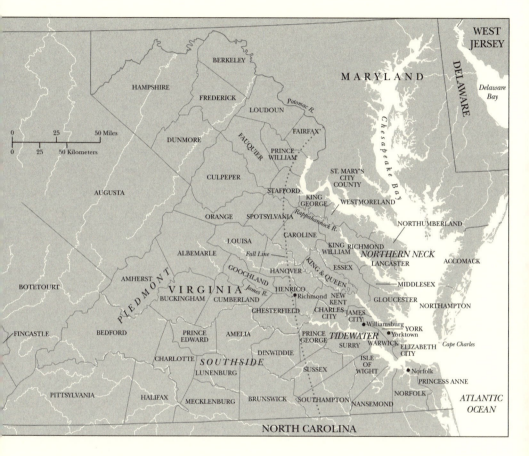

Map 1. Virginia counties circa 1775.

doing. The proceedings of the legislature were virtually never reported in the few newspapers that existed in the colony, and, even had they been, it would have been difficult to learn much about a representative's behavior from those reports, as the Virginia House of Burgesses did not record the names of those voting "aye" and "nay" on any issue during the entire colonial period. Moreover, it would have been difficult for a casual visitor to the assembly to get a glimpse of the proceedings, as there was no provision for a visitors' gallery.

If it was difficult for Virginia's residents to keep an eye on what their representatives were doing once they had arrived in Williamsburg to serve in the burgesses, they were able to communicate quite effectively with those representatives within their own localities. Although Virginians rarely issued formal instructions to their representatives telling them how to vote on a specific issue, they did make frequent use of the device of the legislative petition. John Trenchard and Thomas Gordon, authors of one of the most important series of radical Whig writings in eighteenth-century England, *Cato's Letters*, affirmed the "undoubted right" of the people "to represent their public Grievances, and to petition for Redress to those whose Duty it is to right them," and Virginians were among the most active of any of the colonists in petitioning their legislators about a wide variety of public and private concerns.[43] As in most colonies, the volume of petitions from individuals and localities to the Virginia legislature steadily increased over the course of the eighteenth century. In Virginia the increase was from an average of 28.5 annually in the period from 1715 to 1720 to about 60 per year in the period from 1750 to 1755, to 88 per year in the period from 1760 to 1765.[44] The petitions that came before the burgesses fell into four general categories—petitions protesting the conduct of elections; petitions on purely private matters from individuals asking for relief or redress, usually in accordance with well-defined legal traditions; petitions from groups within a particular locality, asking for some public improvement or relief; and, finally, petitions from numerous individuals across the whole colony asking for legislative action on some matter of public policy of a more general concern. Of the 68 petitions presented to the burgesses between 1728 and 1775 contesting the conduct of elections, the greatest number involved questions about the qualifications of voters in the elections.[45] By far the greatest volume of petitions were on private matters from individuals and ranged from requests for the granting of a divorce (which was still under the control of the provincial assembly or, more specifically, the assembly's Committee on Religion) to requests from widows and veterans for pensions, requests for tax relief, or payment for services rendered to the colony. Although free white males were the originators of most individual petitions, women, free blacks and, rarely, slaves also had petitions heard by the burgesses.[46]

The local petitions most frequently related to requests for improvements, such as the provision of a ferry across a river or improvements in a road or in the navigation of a particular river. These were often petitions engineered by the burgesses themselves, who understood well the way in which the voice of the people could be used to legitimate the worth of projects that they were sponsoring. Another important class of local petitions had to do with the division of counties and parishes; a constant occurrence in a colony in which population growth and western expansion created continual pressure for an increase in government services. These petitions often provoked counterpetitions, with one group of petitioners advocating division of a county or parish on the grounds of convenience for local citizens and another group opposing on the grounds of increased expense. In at least a few of the petitions advocating division of parishes, women—denied the right to vote or to hold office—were among the petitioners. Although formally excluded from the public sphere in most matters, their intrusion into that sphere on matters pertaining to religion was more easily countenanced. While the constant agitation for division of counties and parishes was a frequent source of conflict within the colony, the mechanism by which those conflicts were mediated—petition campaigns in which nearly all social classes in a locality were enlisted and then consideration and decision by the House of Burgesses—was one that most often served the public interest of the colony as a whole.[47]

Petitions on general matters of public policy affecting the entire colony were the fewest in number, a hardly surprising outcome given the persistent localism that Virginians shared with nearly every other American colony. Occasionally, though, mobilizations of citizens that cut across geographic boundaries would occur. Beginning in 1750, petitions from members of dissenting religious groups, complaining of infringements on their religious freedom—from the banning of the performance of marriage ceremonies by dissenting preachers to more direct attempts at breaking up religious meetings and intimidating the congregants—were read before the burgesses with increasing frequency. Furthermore, in the immediate aftermath of the Revolution, that stream of petitions would become a flood as members of dissenting religious groups launched the largest petitioning campaign in the history of any American colony. In that campaign the citizens' voices would be heard by the thousands, culminating in the disestablishment of the Protestant Episcopal Church.[48]

Although Virginians were nearly always ready to mobilize themselves, in concert with their elected representatives, to promote and protect their interests on purely local concerns such as the building of a bridge or the moving of a county seat, this locally oriented political activism most often did not carry over to the electoral process—as evidenced by the fact that some 65 percent of elections in the colony went uncontested. It is of course difficult, in the absence of explicit testimony, to determine what combination of apathy and contentment caused such a high proportion of Virginia's elections to be uncontested or, even when the sheriff bothered to take a poll, why so few voters failed to participate.

Whatever the mixture of respect, contentment, and apathy that went into the selection of the members of Virginia's ruling class, there is ample evidence in the record of governance of eighteenth-century Virginia to justify at least some of the claims to virtuous and public-spirited behavior by the colony's leaders. The Virginia burgesses worked hard at their jobs, spending six to eight weeks a year in Williamsburg tending to the public business and acting on a greater number and a wider variety of matters than any legislature in America. Whereas the legislatures of New York, Pennsylvania, and South Carolina passed only minimal amounts of legislation (in New York about eighteen laws per year, in Pennsylvania almost always fewer than ten, and in South Carolina around a dozen), the Virginia House of Burgesses' legislative output averaged thirty per year, ranging in the 1750s from a low of thirteen to a high of sixty-eight.[49]

In addition to their legislative activism the burgesses provided a wide range of "constituent service" through their activities on the standing committees of the House, ranging from the granting of divorces to providing pensions and poor relief. Whereas much of the legislation coming from even moderately active legislatures like that in New York was regulatory in nature, much of that coming from the burgesses was aimed at economic development. Over the course of the eighteenth century, for example, the House of Burgesses, most often responding to demands from individual localities, established a set of comprehensive policies for the cultivation, inspection, and marketing of tobacco. That the burgesses themselves, who most often had the largest investment in the tobacco economy, were the primary beneficiaries of this legislation in no way diminished the value of those policies to most other free white residents, whose economic interests, though on a smaller scale, were equally bound up in the tobacco economy. Later in the century the burgesses would undertake to do the same thing for other commodities—flour, naval stores, hemp, and salted meats. Although much of this legislation was regulatory in nature, telling settlers what they could not do, a substantial amount of it was aimed, through a combination of incentives and regulation, at promoting economic development.[50]

In acting aggressively and responsibly in attending to the public's interest, the burgesses were at same time steadily enhancing their own power and prerogatives at the expense of the royal governor and the few other royal officials in the colony. As Jack P. Greene has convincingly demonstrated, the ascendancy of lower houses of assembly in the eighteenth-century South and of the men who dominated those assemblies was the result of a combination of historical developments on both sides of the Atlantic.[51] On the English side a dynamic by which the Parliament itself—and in particular the House of Commons—was steadily increasing its power and prestige at the expense of the Crown, coupled with an implicit imperial policy of salutary neglect which gave freer rein to parallel efforts at legislative independence in the colonies, would create opportunities for colonial legislatures to expand their prerogatives. On the other side of the Atlantic the prevailing ethic among Virginians was one that encouraged the colony's planter-gentry to assume that their power and prestige were equal to their counterparts in the House of Commons. And by midcentury a few of Virginia's royal governors were inclined to encourage them in their thinking. William Gooch, in his farewell address to the General Assembly in 1749, complimented them on "the Spirit and Prudence with which you have transacted the . . . weighty Concerns of the Government," and "publicly acknowledge[d] the real Pleasure I have so frequently had, in reflecting upon the Conduct of our Assemblies."[52] What a far cry from a century earlier when Governor William Berkeley had, with some justification, denounced those who aspired to power in the province as "a rabble crue, only rascallity and meanest of people, there hardly being even two among them we have heard of who have estates or are persons of reputation."[53]

The consequence of these developments was a cordiality of relations and a fluidity of movement up the political ladder, from the justices in the county courts, ostensibly appointed by the governor, to the burgesses, supposedly at his beck and call, to the members of the Governor's Council, who by design were supposed to be wholly loyal to the governor, to the governor himself. In fact, though, even the leading members of the Governor's Council—men like Robert "King" Carter and William Byrd II—as a result of practices of plural office holding and of their deeply rooted interest in the soil of provincial Virginia, were in the end spokesmen for provincial, not royal power. These cordial relations would of course be dramatically disrupted beginning in 1763, with the attempts by the English to reorganize their empire, but for the first two-thirds of the eighteenth century the harmony of relations among all of the constituent parts of the body politic was notable. This pattern of genteel mutual respect may have reached a high point just a few years before the Stamp Act crisis of 1765, with the arrival of Royal Governor Francis Faquier. Although he would eventually face the first sustained resistance from provincial agitators during the protests over the Stamp Act, his initial impression of his subjects was highly favorable. He called Speaker of the House John Robinson the "darling of his country, as he well deserves to be for his great integrity, assiduity and ability in business," and he would develop similarly warm feelings for the young Thomas Jefferson, who as a student at William and Mary was invited into a regular dinner circle at the Governor's Palace that included George Wythe and a professor of philosophy at the college, William Small.[54]

Sources of Dissonance

There were, to be sure, rumblings of discontent that could be discerned if one were listening carefully. As the Revolution neared, Virginia was increasingly not simply an "English" society wedded to the values of traditional England. The most profound signifier and cause of this transformation could be discerned in the religious life of the colony. The beginnings of the "evangelical revolt" in Virginia first became apparent in the early 1740s in Hanover County, in the eastern Piedmont, when a group of ordinary citizens, inspired by the sermons of George Whitefield (who had preached in Williamsburg in 1739), began meeting together. In 1743 William Robinson, a New Side Presbyterian, came to preach, and the Hanover residents, many of them Scots-Irish, began to identify themselves as Presbyterians. The most profound currents of evangelical religious sentiment, however, emerged in Virginia beginning in the mid-1750s with the insurgence of the radical separate Baptists.

The visible and forceful emergence of evangelical religion in Virginia has most often been described as an "internal revolt" and a "rejection of the style of life for which the gentry set the pattern and a search for more powerful popular models of proper conduct."[55] In fact, the primary forces behind the growth of first the Baptist and later the Presbyterian and Methodist churches were not internal, but external. Not only was the evangelical faith carried to Virginia by ministers who had earlier been active in New England and the middle colonies, but, overwhelmingly, those Virginians attracted to the austere, but intense Christianity of the Evangelicals were newcomers, many of them from Scotland and Ireland, settling not in those parts of the colony where the Anglican-gentry culture was well established, but, rather, in the backcountry where the convergence of economic power, social authority, and political authority among the Anglican gentry was much less visibly evident.[56]

It cannot be underestimated, though, how the intense religiosity and the social gospel preached by the Evangelicals was, at least initially, troubling to all parts of the established order in Virginia. The more egalitarian structure of evangelical church organization; the "unlearned" quality of the ministry, who claimed their authority by inspiration from God and not on formal training; the lack of distance between minister and congregation; the highly emotional, rather than rational, quality of church services; and the theological message itself—with its exaltation of piety and explicit rebuke of worldly behavior—all seemed at odds with the tenets of a classical republican ideology. That ideology, however much it distrusted concentrations of power, nevertheless reposed its greatest trust in virtuous, wealthy, propertied men who were very much of the world, not above it. Even those Anglican gentry men who conceived of themselves as the most virtuous and the most capable of recognizing the public good found their vision of that public good limited by a conception in which their identity as British subjects and members of the Church of England were synonymous. Those gentry were almost certainly sincere in their belief that the Evangelicals represented a dangerous threat to the fabric of their social order, and the very strength of the Baptists' faith—their advocacy of another, alternative world of faith—must have been distinctly troubling to a group whose values and traditions had been so long dominant. Many Anglicans were not at all pleased that the growth in the numbers and influence of the Evangelicals threatened to "quite destroy pleasure in the Country," and at least some were able to mobilize local legal authorities against that threat. In 1771 one evangelical preacher, Brother Waller, was interrupted in his exhortations by the Anglican parson of the parish, the sheriff, and a few others. As Waller proceeded to lead his congregation in prayer, he

was violently jerked off the stage; they caught him by the back part of his neck, beat his head against the ground, sometimes up, sometimes down, they carried him through a gate that stood some considerable distance, where a gentleman [the sheriff] gave him . . . twenty lashes with his horsewhip.[57]

The separate Baptists were not the only religious dissenters in Virginia. There had always been modest numbers of Quakers in the colony, the numbers of Presbyterians in the Piedmont and Upper Valley were steadily increasing during the eighteenth century, and German Lutherans were present in substantial numbers in the Upper Valley counties of Frederick, Augusta, and Rockingham and in smaller numbers in a few Piedmont counties. Yet there is little in the record that suggests that any of these groups provoked the sustained hostility generated by the separate Baptists. Their manner of worship—and often their religious message—were, far more than those of Quakers, Presbyterians, and Lutherans, simply too deviant from the dominant culture to be easily tolerated.[58]

As the Revolution approached, the Baptists would find themselves in a state of uneasy coexistence with the Anglican gentry who dominated the political life of the colony. The Anglican gentry ruling class resisted calls from more ardent Anglicans to legislate an end to the evangelical insurgence by banning outdoor or nighttime religious gatherings or by refusing to acknowledge the legality of wedding vows given before Baptist ministers. For their part, the Baptists persevered in their religious practices, even though that perseverance caused them to be branded as deviant by the dominant gentry culture. But those Baptists chose, at least for the present, not to mount a political insurgency aimed at guaranteeing them the right to carry out their religious practices as they saw fit.

When Virginia declared its independence, evangelical activists came to realize that their participation in the common cause of the Revolution might give them important political leverage in their struggle for a more secure grant of religious liberty. As we will see in chapter 6, the Evangelicals in Virginia would mount a concerted popular mobilization, centering around a massive petitioning campaign unprecedented in the previous history of American politics, aimed at persuading the dominant Episcopalian majority in the legislature to put an end to the privileged status of the established Episcopal Church. And the members of that legislature, some more reluctantly than others, would endorse Thomas Jefferson's Bill for Religious Freedom, perhaps not because they were any more comfortable with the prospects of religious zealots in their midst, but because they had the wisdom to see that the separation of church and state was the only alternative that could buy social peace while leaving their economic and political hegemony intact.

Virginia's prerevolutionary ruling elite also displayed a limited conception of the public interest in the area of education. It was an article of faith that qualities of "learnedness" were among the essential components of virtuous leadership; it was similarly an article of faith that such learning was wasted on all but the most able—specifically, those men with the aptitude and the leisure time that enabled them to cultivate their minds to the fullest. The logic of that faith required that society provide excellent educational opportunities at the top level of society but rather little else. That is, of course, the way education in England evolved, with networks of private tutors, a few excellent "public schools," and, finally, the universities of Oxford and Cambridge. For those with a professional bent the Inns of Court or an apprenticeship in a merchant house also prepared young men who were ready to make their way in the world.

In general the system of education that came into being in eighteenth-century Virginia mimicked the English ideal, but only in the most superficial sense. The tutors and private schools available to young men and women in Virginia were hopelessly inferior to their English models, and the College of William and Mary, which even when Thomas Jefferson attended in 1760 had a faculty consisting of only four professors—two in philosophy and two in divinity—was a far cry from Oxford or Cambridge.[59] Moreover, unlike their counterparts to the north, Virginia's planter gentry could see little need to expend public funds to disseminate some modest measure of learning to the ordinary citizens of the colony. While the prerevolutionary Virginia legislature did nothing to prevent local agencies of government from establishing and financing public educational institutions in their communities, it also did nothing to promote such initiatives. Local governments, although they were charged by law with the responsibility of seeing to it that parents did not neglect the education of their children, were lax both in enforcing that injunction and in establishing charity schools for orphans or other children who were not in a position to receive an education from their parents. To be sure, no one seemed much to care—the record of petitions to the legislature on the subject is bare—but so long as one's ability to take a place among the virtuous and learned leaders of the Old Dominion depended upon access to education, then the pathway to such a position was blocked for all but the wealthy.

Most obviously, classical republican definitions of either liberty or the public good in both England and Virginia worked not only to promote those conditions for some part of the population but also to severely limit them for others. As Linda Kerber and others have reminded us, traditional republican ideas, while they gave to women important authority and standing within a largely private and domesticated sphere, systematically excluded them from participation in the polis.[60] In fact, before 1699 the various suffrage laws of Virginia were altogether silent about women, leaving open at least the possibility that female property-holders (most commonly unmarried women with inheritances, or widows) might be eligible to vote. There is, however, no evidence in the seventeenth century that suggests either that women voted or that any of them expressed discontent over being denied the vote. A 1699 revision of the suffrage law specifically declared its "true intent and meaning . . . that no woman sole or covert . . . shall be enabled to give a vote or have a voice in the election of burgesses."[61] The fact that women were not voting in Virginia elections does not, however, mean that they were invisible in that most public of spheres nor that their influence was not on occasion felt. The election-day treat—that familiar, if illegal aspect of the day—often found women at the center of the action, both as recipients and providers of the food and drink so often enjoyed by voters and nonvoters alike. Insofar as the tavern was itself an important site for politicking, a woman like Jane Vobe, who ran one of Williamsburg's busiest taverns for more than thirty years, was in an important position to affect outcomes.[62] More generally, though, the presence of women at election-day treats was used to defend their legality, with those responsible for the treats arguing that they were staged not for the purpose of buying votes, but rather as a general display of hospitality toward the community at large.

While it is difficult to discern the weight of influence exercised by wives upon their husbands as they contemplated how they might vote in an election, it should perhaps not surprise us to discover pieces of evidence that suggest that such influence was sometimes present. In 1769 the *Virginia Gazette* reported the case of Suds the barber, whose wife advised him to withold his vote from either of the two candidates for the burgesses until he had a better idea of how his interests would be best served. Each candidate patronized the barber, giving him generous tips, thus leaving the matter of his vote still in doubt. One of the candidates, however, returned for a second shave, tipping him once again, at which time Suds declared his allegiance, voting "as his wife and interest dictated."[63] Similarly, Robert Munford's *The Candidates* accords women a prominent place in the election-day drama (or farce). Two of the characters in the play, Lucy and Sarah, are credited with being especially knowledgeable about the candidates and with being able to influence the votes of their husbands. The struggling Wou'dbe's candidacy is given a substantial boost by the women of the county, who are impressed by his service to his neighborhood. On the other hand, women also come in for their share of ridicule, most having to do with suggestions of sexual improprieties with one or another of the candidates. Naturally, Munford's play is a broad-brush farce, and as John Kolp and Terri Snyder have argued, the silly or self-interested behavior of both men and women is given equal treatment. If anything, the women in the play seem more capable of giving careful consideration to a candidate's merits than the men.[64]

There is some evidence that suggests that on at least some occasions women did use their control over property to extend their political influence. The most obvious example of this occurred after the Revolution, in 1787, when Anne Holden of Accomack County gave identical twenty-five-acre gifts of land to Joseph Boggs and Elijah Milburn, stipulating that the property was intended to enable them to "vote at the Annual Elections for the most Wise and Discreet men who have proved themselves real friends of the American Independence [sic]." Although few women were as obvious in their intentions as Anne Holden, in some parts of Virginia as many as one-fifth of the electorate owed their ability to meet the property qualification for voting to women who transferred portions of their property rights to them, and in at least a few contested elections during the 1750s and 1760s, it is apparent that the transfer of property was a bone of political contention.[65]

Looking beyond the formal realm of politics, we can catch at least glimpses of a social world in which the wives of planter gentry were visible, and visibly empowered, in the public sphere. The fancy-dress balls over which women of the upper gentry presided had an explicit civic and public function, particularly as the Revolution approached. The women present at these balls—well dressed, well coiffed, and accomplished in manners—were more than mere ornaments to their husbands; their accomplishments as well as their appearance made powerful statements about their rank and status in Virginia society.[66]

Still, what is perhaps most striking about prerevolutionary Virginia society, and, indeed, about nearly all of the polities of colonial America, is the extent of the distance that separated most women from the public sphere. While the protests leading up to the American Revolution, especially the boycotts of British manufactured goods and the exaltation of "domestic" products, would allow women of even middling means to step tentatively into the public sphere, the most notable fact about the public activities of women prior to the Revolution is the paucity of evidence attesting to such a step. Even in that most basic of civic activities, petitioning the county court or the assembly for special consideration or for redress of grievances, participation by women in the colonies was exceptionally rare. As Cynthia Kierner has argued, when women submitted their petitions, they entered a male-dominated environment—one in which females were rarely present in the courtroom and, when they did appear, were usually expected to sit not in the main body of the chamber, but in the visitors' galleries.[67]

Classical republican values tended not merely to justify the exclusion of dependent people from active participation in the polis but also to evoke at times a fear of such participation. Some recent historians, viewing social relations in prerevolutionary Virginia through the lenses of race, gender, and class, have emphasized the underlying state of tension in which these outwardly self-confident Virginia gentry may have lived. Often heavily indebted to Scottish factors and London merchants, frequently in acrimonious debtor-creditor conflicts with small landowners, tenants, and poor whites, embroiled in ethnic and religious conflict with Scots-Irish immigrants, threatened by Indians on the frontier, and living amidst slaves held in bondage against their will, Virginia's political and economic elite may well, from our twenty-first-century pespective, have had ample reason to feel that their hegemony was anything but secure.[68] One might think that these stresses and strains in the social order would have registered more significantly either in formal electoral processes or in the more informal realms of social and political intercourse—in the taverns, militia musters, or county fairs—but what is most striking is the degree of outward stability and tranquillity that prevailed. By the mid-eighteenth century the dependent white population of Virginia was small enough and fluid enough that it did not evoke fears of an insurgence of the landless, and, indeed, frequently those male Virginia residents who did not meet the formal property qualification for voting were nevertheless allowed to cast ballots in some elections and, more generally, were made to feel connected to the political process.

The unfree and dependent black population was quite another matter. Try as they might, it was difficult for the gentry to ignore the coercive features of the slave system, and at least a few white Virginians made note of the obvious contradiction between their ostensible love of liberty and the practice of holding slaves. Writing to Quaker leader Robert Pleasants, Patrick Henry labeled the institution "as repugnant to humanity, as it is inconsistent with the bible, and destructive to liberty." In virtually the same breath, however, he explained, "Would anyone believe, I am the master of slaves of my own purchase! I am drawn along by the general inconvenience of living here without them."[69] The existence of a system of chattel slavery was, at least up until the Revolution, an accepted fact of life in the North American mainland colonies. There were relatively few individuals, especially in the southern colonies, who were willing to go beyond Henry's rhetorical musings and still fewer who were sufficiently free of their powerfully ethnocentric British cultural heritage to be inclined to allow the African—slave or free—a meaningful place in the life of the polis. But the double-edged quality of republicanism, especially in its American context, would eventually assert itself with respect to the African as well as to women and dependent whites. Although not expansively egalitarian, it did, in its emphasis on popular consent and on the role of the people as a bulwark against corrupt concentrations of power, constitute a bridge to a more egalitarian future.[70]

Anglo-Virginians of all social classes would have to travel a long way before they were willing to face up fully to the contradictions inherent in their declamations in favor of "republican liberty" and their attachment to slavery, but some of the stresses and strains within Virginia's elite political culture were apparent at least to a few on the eve of the Revolution. The final stages of the career of John Robinson, one that seemed at least superficially to typify the personae and the integrity of Virginia's ruling class, leave us with some troubling afterthoughts about the health of a political culture that placed such enormous faith in the virtue of its leading citizens.

Robinson served not merely as the Speaker of the House of Burgesses but, simultaneously, held the important post of Treasurer of the colony. If Robinson's service as Speaker was testimony to his preeminent prestige among Virginia's political ruling class, his position as treasurer gave him real power; it was also potentially very lucrative, for it gave Robinson significant control over patronage. That he was able to combine the prestige of the speakership and the power of the treasurer in his sole person suggests something of the inappropriateness of using the terminology of the court-country division in England to describe the politics of Virginia, for if there was one office that signified the pinnacle of provincial leadership, it was the speakership, and if there was one office next to that of the royal governorship itself that represented royal authority, it was that of the treasurer. In effect, Robinson had become Virginia's version of Robert Walpole, the extraordinarily powerful leader of the House of Commons who buttressed his parliamentary authority with strong support from King Georges I and II.

Robinson, like Walpole, was not averse to using his power to help his friends and allies. Part of that power was brought to bear on May 24, 1765, when a bill to establish a public loan office was introduced on the floor of the assembly. The bill called for the creation of a fund of £240,000 to be borrowed in Great Britain at 5 percent interest and to be paid back by yearly taxes on tobacco exports and by a poll tax. The ostensible purpose of the fund was to redeem some of the paper money the colony had issued during the Seven Years' War as well as to provide for a fund for future capital projects. In fact, though, it appears that there was one other, unstated, purpose of the proposed loan office fund. During the previous years the combined effect of several bad tobacco crops and the expenses of the Seven Years' War had caused a number of Robinson's close friends to go deeply into debt. Robinson, eager to help his friends out of a difficult spot, lent them money to help them extricate themselves from their debts: a magnanimous gesture indeed, the only trouble being that most of the money loaned to Robinson's friends—a veritable who's who of Virginia provincial politics, including Edmund Pendleton, Carter Braxton, Peyton Randolph, Benjamin Harrison—came straight from the public treasury.

As early as 1763 a number of burgesses, Richard Henry Lee in particular, were beginning to voice private concerns about irregularities in the treasurer's office, but the proposal for the loan office brought the issue for the first time into at least semipublic view. When the bill was debated in the House, Patrick Henry, a newly elected burgess from the Virginia Piedmont, rose to oppose it, exclaiming: "What sir! It is proposed then to reclaim a Spendthrift from his dissipation and extravagance by filling his pocket with monies?" Since visitors were not allowed in the chamber and debate was not recorded, Henry's charges would never be revealed to the public at large. In fact, Henry and the critics of Robinson's generosity were outnumbered in the assembly. But the Governor's Council, realizing that "to tax the People that are not in debt to lend to those that are highly unjust . . . ," killed the measure before it could go to the governor for his approval.[71]

Robinson died the following year, and it was only at that time that the lawyers handling his estate discovered the full magnitude of his indiscretion. The total sum owed to Robinson amounted to £250,000, more than £100,000 of which had come from the colony's treasury. One of the executors of Robinson's estate was also one of its principal debtors, Edmund Pendleton. Pendleton would, laboriously but quietly, spend the next several years taking personal responsibility for assuring that those in debt to Robinson paid back his estate so that the money could be returned to the treasury, a commitment that not only served the cause of justice to Virginia's taxpayers but that also had the effect of keeping quiet a major scandal. In fact, if the taxpayers had known the details of Robinson's behavior, they may have been surprised to discover that he and his friends, in addition to assuming that they had a special claim to public office and public prestige, had lodged a claim on the public monies as well.

One of the other consequences of the barely suppressed scandal involving Robinson and his indebted friends was that in the next session of the legislature a coalition of burgesses, in choosing Robinson's successor, would move forcefully to separate the offices of Speaker and treasurer. While Robinson's close friend and hand-picked successor, Peyton Randolph, was elevated to the speakership, Robert Carter Nicholas, an avowed critic of Robinson's handling of the public funds, mounted an aggressive and successful campaign for the treasurer's post. Neither Nicholas nor

Richard Henry Lee nor, indeed, Patrick Henry, were political radicals bent on overturning the traditional structure of Virginia politics, but they were, in their emphasis on the corrupting aspects of concentrations of power, part of a political insurgency that served notice on the traditional ruling elite in Virginia that they would need to be more inclusive and conduct their business more openly than they had in the past.

The Robinson affair clearly indicated that even in that colony whose leaders most self-consciously assumed the mantle of disinterested and virtuous public servants, the obstacles to achieving the classical republican ideal—rooted both in human nature and in the social, economic, and racial differentiation endemic within the colony itself—were formidable indeed. Virginia's prerevolutionary leaders were amazingly successful in ignoring and obviating contradictions within their order of politics, but as the American Revolution approached, at least some of these contradictions would be brought more clearly into view.

Chapter 3

The Character of the Good Ruler in Eighteenth-Century Massachusetts

If there was a man in eighteenth-century Massachusetts who was—by family lineage, careful nurturing as a youth, and conscious application as an adult—well-suited to traditional notions of political leadership, it was Thomas Hutchinson. His roots in Massachusetts could be traced all the way back to that extraordinary and indomitable early-seventeenth-century religious heretic, Anne Hutchinson, but nearly all of his forebears after Anne's exile made their names and their fortunes as merchants, not as provocateurs. The Hutchinson family name and fortune grew through the steady application of Puritan work habits—prudence, diligence, thrift, and, of course, piety—to the business of trade, and members of each successive generation were usually able to leave to their children a bit more than they had started with. As Thomas Hutchinson's biographer, Bernard Bailyn, has noted, "They were accumulators, down-to-earth, unromantic middle-men, whose solid, petty-bourgeois characteristics became steadily more concentrated in the passage of years until in Thomas, in the fifth generation, they reached an apparently absolute and perfect form."[1]

Young Thomas would enter Harvard College in 1723 at age twelve, following a long line of Hutchinson family members to attend that preserve of the virtuous elite. His class rank, determined by the long-standing, but only hazily defined method of calculating the "supposed dignity of the families" of the matriculants, was three in a class of thirty-eight.[2] Although those rankings were subjective, Thomas's rank was probably a pretty good approximation, somewhat below Samuel and William Browne, who received their number one and two rankings because their father, the wealthiest merchant in Salem, had given substantial gifts to Harvard's endowment. The rankings were not unimportant to a young man's career at Harvard, for they would determine the order in which he would eat at the dining commons, in which he would recite his lessons, and in which he would march in the college's numerous processions. Indeed, those rankings had real relevance to political success later in life: in the eighteenth century if a general court representative had ranked in the top half of his Harvard class, he had an 80 percent chance of emerging as a significant leader of the House.[3]

Figure 6. Thomas Hutchinson at the age of thirty. Painted by Edward Truman, 1741. Massachusetts Historical Society, Boston, MA, USA/Bridgeman Art Library.

We know little about Thomas Hutchinson's academic performance at Harvard, aside from the fact that he graduated with a master's degree three years after entering, choosing as the topic of his thesis, "Is a College Education of Service to One who Travels?" If his youthful college career was like his later career, though, it was probably marked by diligence, attention to detail, formidable self-control, and prudence. "My temper," he wrote, "does not incline to enthusiasm," an assessment echoed by the departing Royal Governor Francis Bernard, who, upon handing over the reins of government to Hutchinson in 1769, remarked that "[You] are a much prudenter man than I ever pretended to be"; Bernard added, perhaps with an undercurrent of disapproval, you "will take care of yourself."[4]

That combination of prudence and attentive self-interest allowed Thomas Hutchinson to steadily build both his fortune and his political career. By 1776 he had increased the original capital inherited from his father fifteenfold; he owned eight houses, two wharves and assorted lots and commercial properties in Boston, and a wonderful "country" home on a hundred acres in Milton, Massachusetts, this last being one of his few real enthusiasms. He entered politics in 1737, at age twenty-six, beginning a career in the lower house that lasted until 1749, when he was appointed to the Governor's Council. His political career would provide a substantial income for him. Between 1749 and 1776 he would serve—often holding multiple offices simultaneously—as councilor, agent to the colony in London, judge of the inferior court of common pleas, judge of the probate court of Suffolk county, chief justice of the superior court of the colony, lieutenant governor, and, finally, governor. Through all of those years of public service, one encounters not a hint of affection or enthusiasm for him among his constituents, but as Governor Thomas Pownall observed in 1757, even those who differed with him on matters of policy continued to admire and respect him because of his "disinterestedness and integrity."[5]

If the Virginia of "Worthy," "Wou'dbe," and Washington has been the most often cited example of a deferential society, then Puritan New England has run a close second. While John Winthrop's original injunction "that in all times some . . . must be highe and eminent in power and dignitie; others meane and in subieccion" no longer elicited universal assent by the mid-eighteenth century, New England has nevertheless seemed remarkable for the consistency of its commitment to traditional notions of order and hierarchy. The classical republican attachment to virtue required that those entrusted with public office rise above selfish interest to serve the public good and, as Richard Bushman has noted, the notion of interest became a particularly important one—for good and for ill—to the residents of Massachusetts. In its private sense—connoting selfishness and, more powerfully, greed—interest was the human impulse that needed to be transcended or at least neutralized. As it was used in a more public, collective sense—as in the republican concern with the "people's interest"—it was supposed to be the guiding principle of those who dedicated themselves to public service. John Adams, who seemed at times to consider himself the supreme keeper of his society's public virtue, defined it thusly: "The interest of the people is one thing—it is the public interest. . . . The interest of a king, or of a party, is another thing—it is a private interest, and where private interest governs, it is a government of men, and not of laws."[6]

In order for republican government to survive, Adams maintained, "there must be a positive passion for the public good."

In the colony of Virginia provincial leaders and royal officials—representatives of court and country—worked together in remarkable harmony in pursuit of their definition of the public good. In part because of the self-confident Anglophilia of most of Virginia's provincial leaders and in part because of the ways in which the imperatives of the Virginia tobacco economy harmonized with those of England's mercantilist empire, the day-to-day conduct of politics was generally marked by cooperation between provincial leaders and royal administrators. As the Virginia jurist St. George Tucker observed, the politics of the colony were remarkably free of "party spirit," with the only divisions arising in the polity stemming from "differences of opinion," which "different men coming from different parts" of an "extensive Country might well be expected to entertain."[7] By contrast, the very character of the political culture in Massachusetts was shaped by the frequent competition for power and authority between provincial and royal agencies of government.

Massachusetts had been founded as a corporate colony, and, most likely by oversight, King Charles I had granted the initial settlers of the colony remarkable independence. As Richard Bushman has noted, "Monarchy rested so lightly on Massachusetts Bay in the seventeenth century as to seem weightless."[8] The freemen of the Massachusetts Bay Company elected the members of the general court (the colony's lower house of assembly), the deputy governor and governor—and together those individuals assumed virtually all authority for the governance of the colony. Indeed, such was the spirit of governmental independence nurtured in the Bay Colony over the course of the seventeenth century that in 1678 the Massachusetts General Court informed King Charles II that "the lawes of England are bounded within the fower seas and doe not reach America."[9]

With the revocation of the Massachusetts Bay Company charter in 1684 and the conversion of the colony into an entity subject to direct royal control in 1691, the character of government and its relationship to the colony's residents would change. As royal governors, now appointed by and responsible to the Crown, sought to assert the prerogatives of the English state and its monarchy on the citizens of Massachusetts Bay, they would have to do so in the context of a people fully accustomed to provincial autonomy. Moreover, the character of political relations in Massachusetts—the ways in which ordinary settlers of the Bay Colony would view both their government and the people who claimed to speak in their name for the government—would be shaped by the ensuing conflict between representatives of the king and those claiming to speak in the name of the people.[10]

The function of the people in Massachusetts politics, however, was largely negative, acting as a check against the aggressive tendencies of monarchical power. After 1691 provincial Massachusetts citizens began to manifest a growing conviction that those sent to govern them from afar could be motivated only by selfish interests and not by any meaningful attachment to the good of their provincial communities. In complaining to the Privy Council in London about the conduct of their royal governor, William Burnet, in 1728, the members of the general court were explicit in reiterating their belief that the self-interests of royal officials and the public interest of the province were inimical. "It is and has been very well known in this as well as other nations and ages," the assembly complained, "that Government at a great distance from the Prince or Seat of Government have great opportunities and sometimes too prevailing inclinations, to oppress the people." The remedy, according to the assembly, was to interpose the assembly, representative of the people, between the royal placemen and those whom they sought to oppress. The issue in 1728 was assembly control over the governor's annual salary, which the assembly believed vital if they were to have any control over his self-aggrandizing tendencies, but whatever the specific irritant, through much of the eighteenth century Massachusetts's provincial leaders would invoke the rights of the people in their almost obsessive concern about the "covetousness" of royal placemen.[11]

This concern about combating covetousness and self-interest could not help but spill over into internal provincial politics. In Virginia the ruling gentry wielded power with self-confidence, apparently secure in the conviction that they were the most virtuous, and therefore the least corruptible, members of their society. That attitude, though, led not only to an impressive ease of command but also, ultimately, to such excesses as Speaker John Robinson's pilfering of the public treasury. Political leaders in Massachusetts, concerned to the point of paranoia about the way in which power corrupted, could never achieve that ease of command, but neither were they as likely to allow themselves to fall into the behavior that led to the embarrassment of John Robinson and his friends.

The spokesmen for provincial interests in Massachusetts would use the language of popular rights as their principal weapon in their contests against royal authority and, in so doing, would, in Richard Bushman's phrase, turn "the struggle between governor and the lower house into an extended legal controversy rather than a raw contest for power."[12] But however much provincial leaders claimed to be acting in the name of the people, they also fully expected the people to be virtuous enough to recognize who their natural leaders should be—not a group of royal placemen but, rather, local patrons who by dint of their property, talent, and connection to their local communities were most likely to be able to distinguish between private and public interest. Those provincial leaders of Massachusetts Bay who sought to maintain the traditional connection between economic power and social and political authority, while at the same time defending provincial prerogatives from encroachments by royal authorities, were, at least in their idealized conception of their duty, required to devote special effort to demonstrate that they were deserving of deference, that the people at large were, from respect as well as from an attention to the public good, electing to honor them with their votes.

The means by which Massachusetts citizens were supposed to identify those "natural aristocrats" who were best suited to govern them were variants on those criteria for virtuous and godly behavior articulated by John Winthrop in his original statement about the Massachusetts social hierarchy in 1632—property, family, piety, and education. Each of those criteria was in reality related to wealth, and those who best satisfied the criteria were most likely to be among the most prosperous citizens in their communities. But wealth alone, particularly in Massachusetts, was not sufficient. Indeed, with very few exceptions, the Massachusetts economy did not generate the kind of enormous fortunes that enabled one, visibly wealthy group to set itself above all others. Rather, the process by which families and individuals established their claims to political authority was one of gradual accumulation, not only of property but of other, nonpecuniary claims to authority. Thus, families like those of the Hutchinsons or Stoddards were able—by careful management of their material resources, investment in a Harvard education for their sons, and further expenditures of time spent in diligent service at the local level—to accumulate the requisite claims to power and influence within their communities.

In nearly every case this process of accumulation—of the bringing together of economic power and social and political authority—occurred initially and primarily within local communities. Nearly sixty years after the Revolution, Alexis de Tocqueville, in commenting on the phenomenon of "municipal independence" in the United States, was particularly struck by the ways in which "circumstances have peculiarly favored its growth in New England," for it was there, he noted, that the local institutions of church, court, and town meeting operated with the greatest vitality.[13] Tocqueville was partially correct in identifying the New England spirit of localism with a robust assertion of the popular will. In Massachusetts, unlike Virginia and, indeed, much of the rest of America, most of the important local offices were elective.

In the Bay Colony, popularly elected local officials were entrusted with a significant amount of authority within their communities. At the center of this popularly based tradition of municipal independence was the town meeting, "the original and protean vessel of local authority."[14] Acting on a 1635 general court mandate authorizing them to legislate in any manner not repugnant to the laws of the colony and to "choose their own particular officers," New England towns and townspeople aggressively sought and seized control over most of those political and legal endeavors occurring within their towns, from the construction of public works to the punishment of wrongdoers. The principal embodiments of the power and autonomy of the towns, the "ruling fathers," were those individuals designated "select-men," certified to be "able and discreet, of good conversation."[15] Elected annually in the town meeting, the selectmen were given significant authority over the administration and interpretation of local business.

Historians have fought pitched battles over the question of whether the selectmen were agents of entrenched oligarchy or in the vanguard of modern democracy. The mountain of evidence that we now have before us suggests once again some of the confusing ways in which eighteenth-century American politics, rooted in English tradition, were stumbling toward more modern forms of governance. The very conception of ruling fathers suggests a class of men set apart by characteristics of wisdom, virtue, and social station, and for much of the seventeenth century the selectmen seem to have comprised a visible elite, notable for their wealth, position in their local church, and lengthy public service. Yet if Massachusetts's selectmen constituted an oligarchy, then they were, as Kenneth Lockridge has observed, "a peculiar oligarchy," for they were elected to their positions by a broadly based and active electorate.[16]

The property qualification for voting in Massachusetts town elections was a "ratable estate" worth at least £20, but as in nearly all other matters in the colony, individual localities were free to enforce the qualification as stringently or leniently as they might choose. In most towns the combination of widespread property ownership and lax enforcement contributed to a broadly inclusive electorate, comprised of at least 75 percent of the towns' free adult males.[17] Over the course of the eighteenth century, voters in Massachusetts were less and less likely to automatically elect the same individuals to office year after year. The average length of service for selectmen in most Massachusetts towns was on the whole shorter in the eighteenth century than in the seventeenth, and there were also more frequent instances in the eighteenth century of incumbents being defeated for reelection.[18] Equally important, over the course of the eighteenth century, power at the local level, initially concentrated in the hands of a small group of selectmen, was increasingly diffused among as many as forty different elective offices, ranging in dignity and influence from moderator of the town meeting to town constable, town treasurer, town clerk, town assessor, and town gravedigger. Moreover, there was an increasing determination on the part of the whole people, gathered together in the town meeting, to take a direct part in the most important decisions, whether in approving tax rates or building a new schoolhouse or even, in some cases, to matters of such limited scope as passing on the merits of appeals of individual tax assessments.[19]

If power was being exercised directly by the people in the town meeting, there were other, countervailing forces at work in the government and legal apparatus lying just above that of the towns—in the appointment and authority of county justices of the peace. John Adams, ever attentive to matters of rank and station, noted in his *Defense of the Constitutions of the United States*, that the office of justice of the peace had "generally descended from generation to generation, in three or four families at most."[20] Those county justices were appointed by royal governors, not elected by their neighbors, and their power and responsibilities increased steadily over the course of the eighteenth century. Initially held in suspicion when introduced into Massachusetts during the period of the Dominion of New England, royally appointed justices of the peace of the late seventeenth and early eighteenth centuries were only infrequently elected by their neighbors to serve in the Massachusetts General Court. But by the mid-eighteenth century there was a much closer correlation between judicial power at the county level and political power in the provincial lower house of assembly, with the percentage of representatives in the general court who also held posts as justice of the peace rising from 7 percent in 1703 to 45 percent in 1737 and to 71 percent in 1763.[21] If the prevailing ethic in the towns was one of harmony and consensus, as some have claimed, the matters over which the justices of the peace exercised authority were frequently fraught with conflict. Those courts were the sites of countless appeals of unpopular decisions made in the town meeting as well as the initial sites where most of the criminal cases in the colony were heard. Those county justices, besieged with complaints from citizens in the towns, would no doubt have been surprised to hear their society described as harmonious and consensual.[22]

If the town meeting was the center of popularly based authority and the county courts the agency of royally based authority, then it was in the Massachusetts General Court that the battle between "popular rights" and "royal prerogative" was most consistently waged. The extent to which the people at large in Massachusetts cared about that battle or, indeed, the extent to which local leaders in the Bay Colony were willing to leave their communities to join in the battle varied across time and space. The election records for eighteenth-century Massachusetts are unfortunately very scanty. The three towns for which we have the most information—Lynn, Salem, and Boston—are probably those in which competition for office was greatest, thus most likely exaggerating the extent of voter participation. In Lynn the average voter participation in assembly elections was 28.8 percent (in six contests), in Salem it was 25 percent (in seven contests), and in Boston, for which we have records for more than fifty contests, it was just under 25 percent. Although there were small variations in those rates of participation from year to year, they do not seem to have been connected in any obvious way with any of the principal political upheavals of the century—which included the recurrent divisions relating to currency, control over the governor's salary, and the controversy over the land bank in 1740 and 1741. In the communities inland from the coast, for which we have far fewer records, candidates usually ran unopposed. Indeed, about half of the inland settlements did not even agree to hold elections, and in several that did conduct them, the majority voted in favor of sending no representative at all on the grounds of excessive cost. In 1763 Governor Francis Bernard reported to the board of trade that of 168 towns, most of which were eligible to send two representatives, 64 sent no representatives at all, 104 sent one, and only 4 sent two. What this suggests is that however much some provincial leaders may have invoked popular rights in their contest for power with royal officials, a good many citizens remained either unaware or unconcerned that those rights might possibly be endangered.[23]

It may be that the ordinary citizens of colonial Massachusetts chose venues other than the polling place as an outlet for political expression. David Conroy has argued that the taverns of Massachusetts "were becoming focuses for the participation of ordinary colonists in local and sometimes even provincial politics." He has found at least one prominent provincial Massachusetts political leader, the often cranky and cantankerous John Adams, to testify to the leveling tendencies of tavern politicking. Adams complained that the taverns "are becoming in many places the nurseries of our legislators." His puritanical sense of propriety was offended by the "swearing" and "carousing" that one encountered in the tavern, but even more disturbing to him was the way in which the customers "plott(ed) with the landlord to get him, in the next town meeting and election, either for selectman or representative." Adams was of the opinion that public life in the tavern allowed "artful men" to gain "sway among the rabble of the town," with the consequence being that the traditional methods of choosing the best and most virtuous man for public office were being subverted.[24]

Adams's grousing to the contrary notwithstanding, there is little evidence that tavern life had much of an impact on either the character or the outcome of Massachusetts politics, at least before the onset of the Revolution. Voter apathy remained the norm in most towns, and there seem to be strikingly few cases in which tavern owners were able to use their positions as convivial hosts to advance their political fortunes. Tavern owners may have been slightly more likely than members of other occupation groups (other than lawyers!) to hold appointive or elective offices, but most of those tavern keepers who held public offices were men like Adam Cushing of Weymouth, a Harvard-educated member of one of the colony's leading families, or James Fowle of Woburn, another Harvard-educated man, whose road to success in Massachusetts politics owed more to his incisive scholarly mind that it did to his ability to serve grog and toddy.[25]

There were individual exceptions to the general prevalence of voter apathy at election time, nearly all of them due to local circumstances. In a 1740 election in Cambridge the candidacy of a wealthy merchant, John Vassal, was opposed by the deputy sheriff, Samuel Whittemore, who publicly upbraided Vassal for being "no more fit to discharge the said trust than the horse that he, the said Samuel then rode on." True to the litigious instincts of members of the Bay Colony, Vassal first sued Whittemore, claiming that he had been "damnified" by his statement, and then Whittemore countersued Vassal. Vassal was in fact able to win election fairly easily, but the controversy did manage to elevate voter turnout to 45 percent[26]. But the Vassal-Whittemore contest was decidedly extraordinary. Most elections in Massachusetts were foregone conclusions, with the victorious candidates running unopposed. As John Waters has noted, one of the difficulties in making any meaningful generalization about any aspect of electoral behavior in Massachusetts is that individual towns had such autonomy in setting the ground rules for elections—altering the legally stipulated property qualifications or deciding not to bother to send representatives at all—that no consistent pattern of either democratic or oligarchic behavior emerges.[27]

Once a candidate gained election, there existed within eighteenth-century Massachusetts a wide variety of attitudes among assemblymen toward the responsibilities of service. In contrast to Virginia, where each of the counties in the colony was conscientious in sending representatives to the House of Burgesses, almost a third of the towns in Massachussetts did not bother to send any representatives to the general court. Even among those towns who did attempt to send representatives, a startlingly high proportion of them, particularly from the western part of the colony, simply did not show up. Typically, there were no more than 100 representatives out of a possible 350 present in the assembly for even the most important votes, and most likely far fewer at other times. This fact was not lost on either the royal governors or those in the House who sought to oppose them, for it was reckoned that a solid core of 35 or 40 representatives would be sufficient to carry the day on any issue.[28]

Among those who did appear at the assembly sessions, there was a gap between those relatively few men who served often and who played an active role in the affairs of the assembly and those who put in an appearance, but did not have an appreciable effect on the proceedings. During the mid-eighteenth century a dozen or so men controlled more than 50 percent of the business transacted by the various select committees appointed in the House, and another twenty or thirty accounted for most of the rest. The variable operating most clearly in determining a representative's diligence was interest, either personal interest or that of the constituencies being represented. Overwhelmingly, the most active members, both by the standard of years of service and by the number of important committees on which they served, were members of the mercantile communities of either Boston or the eastern coastal port towns. Although those areas elected fewer than one-quarter of the members of the assembly, they supplied more than half of the leaders. At the other extreme, inland farm towns contributed more than 65 percent of the members of the general court, but only 20 percent of the leaders. These men, often not notably different in social rank and wealth from their constituents, also were the most likely to be absent from the sessions.[29]

Perhaps the most interesting group of representatives in the assembly were those from the Connecticut Valley. That assembly delegation included some of the most prominent men in the colony—men like Israel Williams, John Worthington, and Joseph Hawley—who by dint of their large landholdings and monopoly over local offices in Hampshire County earned the designation of "River Gods." The River Gods were capable of extraordinarily effective action in the assembly when either their own personal interests or those of their constituencies were threatened, but when that was not the case, they, too, were content either to sit quietly in the assembly or, more likely, simply stay at home. Once again, all things being equal, intense localism was what drove political behavior in colonial Massachusetts.[30]

As a consequence, most representatives to the Massachusetts General Court were primarily committed to representing local, and not more broadly provincial or imperial, interests.[31] What is less clear is the process by which those local interests were identified and articulated. Two of the long-standing institutional means by which constituent interests in England and America were articulated were the devices of the group petition to the legislature and of instructing representatives.[32] The Massachusetts General Court received a huge volume of petitions, averaging well over two hundred a year from 1750 forward (by contrast, the Virginia House of Burgesses received between sixty and ninety annually, and the legislatures of New York and South Carolina infrequently received more than a dozen annually). The greatest volume of those petitions pertained to purely personal matters (e.g., appeals of financial or legal judgments, divorce petitions) and a reasonable number of purely locally oriented matters (e.g., requests from a town for the building of a road or bridge); the legislature did not receive many petitions from groups on issues of colonywide concern. The reason for this lies not in any diffidence on the part of townspeople in speaking their mind on those issues, but rather on the existence of a superior alternative forum—the town meeting—in which constituent interests could more effectively be formulated. Prior to 1732 only one town out of seven in Massachusetts saw fit to make an appeal to the legislature on any of the numerous decisions made within the town meeting, and while after 1750 that ratio increased to about one out of every five, townspeople in Massachusetts were in general willing to let the decisions of their local government stand without protest of any kind.[33]

Whereas the incidence of legislative petitioning on matters of colony-wide interest was relatively infrequent in Massachusetts, the frequency with which residents in town meetings instructed their representatives was higher than in other parts of America. This was particularly true in Boston, where after 1720 the practice became something of an annual ritual, with a large committee of townsmen being formed each year to prepare the instructions, which would then be presented to the representatives. In a face-to-face meeting between constituents and representatives, the latter would be instructed to "act with courage and zeal on prosecuting those good designs which may tend to the peace and welfare of these His Majesty's good subjects and secure those rights and privileges which by the royal charter we have a just claim to."[34]

Most of the acts of instruction outside of Boston occurred not on issues dividing residents within the province, but rather on contests of power between royal governors and the assembly, with the device of the instruction being used to buttress popular claims against royal prerogative. In most of these cases it seems less likely that the instructions represented an assertion of opinion from the grass roots than they did an orchestration of public opinion from above, with the goal being the enhancement of provincial interests at the expense of royal agencies of government. For example, one of the issues that frequently provoked instructions was the effort by successive royal governors to gain control over their salaries; the representatives who opposed that move—nearly everyone serving in the general court—found it convenient to collect opinion from their constituents supporting their position.[35]

On at least one occasion, however, instructions figured prominently in a conflict between opposing interests within the province. In 1754 representatives primarily from farming towns in the interior managed to push through the assembly an excise tax on rum. The tax would have fallen with particular severity on towns in the east, for further to the west the drink of choice was locally distilled cider. Easterners were momentarily saved from the burdens of the tax by Governor Shirley, who, sympathetic to those in the east and recognizing the bill's controversial character, refused approval until representatives could consult their constituents more fully on the matter. Shirley's suspension of the bill occasioned a flurry of instructions from towns to their representatives, particularly in the east of the province, where opinion against the bill ran high. Among the records of those instructions that have survived, twenty-six towns opposed the excise, with nine supporting it. At its next session the assembly debated a motion to consider the instructions from the towns on the excise, and, after "a large debate thereon," a majority in the assembly explicitly refused to be bound by them. In so doing, they were adopting the line of argument put forward

by one of the pro-excise pamphleteers, who, when confronted by a preponderance of instructions in favor of repeal of the excise, lectured the assembly members that "the business of a representative is to consult the
good of the whole body, and to take particular care that the town he represents, does not pay a greater proportion of the charges of government
than it ought to do . . . I take [this] to be the proper business of a representative, and not to follow the humor of his constituents, when it is evidently contrary to the good of the community."[36] Self-serving as that advice
may have been, it suggests that there was not full agreement among the citizens of Massachusetts on the question of a representative's responsibilities
to his local constituents. In the case of the excise, however, most of the representatives continued to keep their own counsels. After refusing to consider the instructions, they went on not only to repass the excise but also to
order that one of the most inflammatory pamphlets against the excise be
burned by the hangman and its publisher jailed. Governor Shirley, no
doubt reluctantly, this time signed the bill into law.[37]

In fact, those who supported the excise most fervently probably came
from western towns that did not have such a strong tradition of instructing
their representatives. That those towns did not use the formal practice of
instruction does not mean that they were altogether lacking some sort of
understanding between representatives and constituents about the representatives' responsibilities once elected to the legislature. Short of formal
instruction, residents in town meetings regularly spoke their minds to their
representatives about those matters that were of most concern to them.
The great preponderance of those expressions of opinion were, again,
purely local in nature, as in the repairing of a road or a bridge.[38]

If the connection between representatives and constituents was of necessity a close one within the context of the town meeting, it was much
less close once the representative journeyed to Boston to sit in the general
court. The proceedings of that body were closed, and the House did not
publish a record of debate; indeed, before 1740 it did not even record
the division on votes, and after that date it did so only on subjects of great
controversy, such as that surrounding the land bank in 1740 and 1741 or
the liquor excise in the mid-1750s. Members of the House justified their
continued isolation from public opinion on grounds of freedom of speech,
arguing that representatives would have the best opportunity to speak their
minds, free of reprisals, if they could do so behind closed doors, with
neither governors nor constituents monitoring their speech. That there
was not significant agitation from local townspeople to open up the proceedings of the House to greater scrutiny suggests, as in the case of the
frequent failure of towns to send representatives to the legislature, a peculiar contradiction between the frequent invocation of popular rights
and the persistent apathy of citizens about most matters of provincial
politics.

It was no doubt this combination of apathy and acceptance of received traditions about the "good ruler" that allowed Thomas Hutchinson to continue to advance his career as a politician while at the same time appearing to defend royal prerogatives. Indeed, Hutchinson's career in Massachusetts politics, perhaps more than that of any other individual in the colony, brings into relief some of the confusion that existed there as late as the mid-eighteenth century about relations between royal and provincial prerogatives, the relationship between public servants and their constituents, and the very concept of representation itself.

As we have already seen, when Hutchinson began his political career, he appeared to epitomize one of those virtuous, disinterested leaders who, by dint of the collective value of his family lineage, educational attainment, economic endeavor, and devoted service to what he reckoned to be the public good, could be assured of an uncontested place in the highest political councils of his colony. But as we will see in chapter 9, the coming of the American Revolution would dramatically alter Hutchinson's relationship with his constituents in Boston and Massachusetts. It is a painful and tragic story of a man driven by a sense of duty and righteousness but wholly out of touch with the deeply held beliefs of the great mass of residents whom he claimed to serve. The story of this erosion of his claims to deference, however, began long before Ebenezer Mackintosh and the South End Mob started rioting in the streets of Boston in the summer of 1765.

Thomas Hutchinson's election as a representative to the Massachusetts General Court in 1737 was the beginning of an impressive political career. His power and influence within the colony grew rapidly during those early years; he immediately became a leader within the lower house, and by 1746, at age thirty-five, he had gained election as Speaker, the pinnacle of power within that branch of the government that most clearly represented provincial interests. Given the speed of his ascent, it is perhaps not surprising that Hutchinson developed so early in his career strong confidence in the rectitude of his own course of action on almost any political issue. One of the issues about which he felt special conviction was the threat to the fiscal integrity of the colony and to its well-being by the constant political agitation to create a land bank that would ease a chronic currency shortage in the colony by allowing public and private banks to issue currency using the lands of the banks' subscribers as security. During the late 1730s and 1740s, the great bulk of popular opinion in Massachusetts favored the creation of land banks, but Hutchinson, whose grasp of the economics of public finance probably exceeded that of anyone in the colony, was emphatically committed to more conservative, hard money policies, and he used all of his skills to help a succession of royal governors block efforts to implement the land banks.

In 1738, beginning only his second term as Boston's representative to the general court, Hutchinson received a set of instructions from the

Boston town meeting requesting that the town's representatives support the emission of more paper money. When the instructions were presented to him, he "publicly argued against them, as iniquitous, and declared that he would not observe them." At least one citizen present at the town meeting, in response to Hutchinson's empathic rejection of their instruction, called out that the meeting should "choose another representative," but the dissident citizen received no support for his call to unseat Hutchinson.[39] Up to that point at least, Bostonians were content to record their opinions, but not to demand that their elected representatives embrace those opinions. By 1749, elevated to the position of Speaker of the House and at the pinnacle of his power as a provincial leader, Hutchinson again publicly defied the wishes of his Boston constituents, siding with Governor William Shirley in proposing that a parliamentary grant of £183,000 given to the colony in payment for its expenditures during the conquest of Louisbourg be used to retire all outstanding paper money, putting the colony on a firm specie basis once again, an emphatic retreat from any attempt at easing currency shortages. Hutchinson got his way, using his considerable influence and that of the governor to get a bill to that effect through an assembly that had been inclined toward more, not fewer, issues of paper money.

Hutchinson's course of action was probably the right one, considering that from that time forward the Massachusetts economy prospered in an environment of stable specie currency. Whatever the ultimate wisdom of Hutchinson's economic policies, his constituents in Boston did not see things that way. In the elections held in May of 1749, they turned on him with a vengeance; he received only 200 votes out of a total of 684 cast. Shortly after his defeat he wrote his Harvard classmate and friend Israel Williams explaining the result. The 200 who voted for him, he was confident, "were the principal inhabitants, but you know we are governed not by weight but by numbers." Hutchinson knew that the bulk of the support for the land bank came from the "plebeian" part of the population, and he recognized, ruefully, that "one of their votes will go as far in popular elections as one of the most opulent."[40] It was, alas, a damnably difficult system in which to assure the election of virtuous and disinterested men.

Hutchinson would be rewarded by Governor Shirley in the same year of his defeat with a seat on the Governor's Council, and he would be the most influential member of that body until his elevation to lieutenant governor, working tirelessly, if usually unsuccessfully, to increase the power of the upper house at the expense of the popular branch. In his exertions we can recognize another reality of political life in eighteenth-century Massachusetts: power and influence were not commodities easily attained, even by men as accomplished as Hutchinson; rather, they were hard-earned. Although Hutchinson's merchant career continued to flourish during his years of political ascendancy, it is plain that the bulk of his interests and energies were devoted to politics. Convinced that his superior personal character and talents required that he assume a role as leader of his colony, Hutchinson was driven in his political career by a self-conscious desire to earn a place in the history of his province. Yet greatness required earnest application to the task at hand, and Hutchinson's correspondence—to provincial politicians in Massachusetts and to royal officials in London—was devoted single-mindedly to advancing the causes in which he believed. Was all of this effort "disinterested"? Hutchinson certainly believed so, for he was convinced that all of his exertions were aimed at the advancement of the public good. But it was equally true that they were aimed at the enhancement of the power and reputation of Thomas Hutchinson.

Hutchinson's efforts as an increasingly weighty member of the royal elite would enhance his power and influence, but he would pay a price. Although he retained, at least up until the fateful year of 1765, the respect of many provincial leaders within the lower house, among ordinary settlers he would become identified increasingly with royal and not provincial interests. However much Hutchinson was convinced of the righteousness of his cause, this diminution in popular support for him would play out in disastrous fashion in the politics of the coming of the Revolution.

Thomas Hutchinson's good friend and longtime correspondent Israel Williams offers another good example of the way in which New England's political leaders had to work diligently, and often self-interestedly, to maintain their privileged positions. Among the River Gods of Massachusetts's Connecticut River valley, none had greater political power than Israel Williams of Hampshire County. Born into one of the wealthiest families in the valley, he was able to consolidate social power through skillful use of an intricate web of kin relations with the two other prominent families of his region, the Stoddards and the Hawleys. After graduating from Harvard in the same class as his friend Thomas Hutchinson (his class rank was ten out of thirty-eight—certainly respectable if somewhat less exalted than Hutchinson's), he became a farmer, merchant, land speculator, and politician and involved himself in virtually every aspect of every piece of business transacted in Hampshire County. Starting with an inheritance of a house, a home lot, and 109 acres, Williams systematically acquired land in Massachusetts and New York until he owned over three thousand acres, a substantial amount by New England standards. The principal merchant and manufacturer in his region, he supplied his county not only with a large portion of its imported goods but also with most of the potash and linseed oil it exported.[41]

Williams began his political career as selectman for the town of Hatfield in 1732; the town elected him its representative to the general court the following year, and he subsequently added positions as justice of the peace, judge of the Hampshire Court of Common Pleas, colonel in the local militia, and member of the Governor's Council. As a resident of a colony in which plural office holding was commonplace, he occupied many of these positions simultaneously. So great were his power and influence that his fellow townspeople called him the "monarch of Hampshire." Unlike his friend Thomas Hutchinson, who always sought to articulate a view of politics that comprehended a public good that embodied the interests of not only the colony as a whole but the whole empire as well, Williams view of politics was decidedly local and hardly disinterested. He spent his entire life in battles, petty and grand, in which he aggressively used his influence to promote his interests. When the general court was not dealing with issues of concern to Williams or to Hampshire County, he often skipped the session; when there were such issues—a bill to give him a ten-year monopoly on the manufacture of linseed oil, for example, or one relating to the distribution of political patronage in the Connecticut Valley—he worked hard to ensure that his prerogatives were respected.[42]

In county politics Williams rewarded his friends and punished his enemies. When fellow townsman Gideon Lyman, campaigning for the general court, identified himself as one of the "honest Plowmen" in opposition to one of the "great men," Williams—who certainly considered himself of the latter class—did not let the challenge pass. He formally requested Governor Francis Bernard to remove Lyman as justice of the peace on the grounds that "he made it his business, in a low private way, to slander and abuse those of the County who were noted for supporting Government."[43] Though Williams lost that fight, he did not lose many others. From 1733 to the Revolution few candidates gained seats in the general court or on the county bench in Hampshire who had not joined interests with Israel Williams.

Williams's dominance was not based purely on the affection and respect of his fellow residents. His use of power and patronage as colonel and commander in chief of the Hampshire militia during the Seven Years' War—when escalating conflict on the frontier made high office in the militia more than merely honorific—provides a striking case in point. Williams's personnel decisions in reviving the county's weakened militia forces consistently consolidated the network of men loyal to him; his procurement practices in refurbishing disused frontier posts achieved a similar result, and many of his strategic choices for the defense of the Connecticut Valley benefited some communities while hurting others. When neighbors opposed his policies, he did not hesitate to marshal support from powerful allies in the legislature and from the governor himself. Accordingly, as the toll of war mounted, residents voiced complaints about Williams's strategic decisions and self-serving practices.[44]

By the end of the war Williams was still entrenched as "monarch" of Hampshire, but the seeds of popular dissatisfaction had been sown. As resistance to British policy surfaced during the 1760s and early 1770s, Williams's close association with Hutchinson was crucial in making Hatfield one of a handful of Massachusetts towns that usually sided with the royal governor. But after the passage of the Coercive Acts, even the combined forces of a received tradition of obedience to authority and the entrenched power of Israel Williams were not enough to withstand the popular fury. In February 1775 Williams and his son were seized by a mob, placed in a house with a blocked chimney, and smoked all night until Williams emerged the next morning, smudged and disheveled, apparently ready to condemn the Coercive Acts.

But Williams's smokehouse conversion to the patriot cause would not last. In May of 1775 he refused to sign a declaration committing himself to the defense of American liberties, and from that time on, though he was permitted to remain free, he had lost all power in his community. By late 1776 further evidence of Williams's consorting with the enemy (in particular, some damaging correspondence with Thomas Hutchinson) had accumulated, and he and his son were arrested and jailed, where they would remain for over three years.[45]

Gregory Nobles has noted that, even when Williams was under arrest and under lock and key, his fellow townspeople regarded him as a formidable and, indeed, dangerous man. In justifying their arrest of Williams to the Massachusetts Provincial Council, the Hatfield Committee of Correspondence noted that "He has been and still is a Man of Considerable Influence with the People, and consequently has persuaded a considerable number of Persons not only in this Town but we apprehend more or less in every Town to adopt his Sentiments." In fact, the townspeoples' fears of Williams's continued influence were to prove groundless. When he was finally released from prison in 1780 and given the partial freedom of staying in his hometown of Hatfield under house arrest, he emerged disgraced and despised. He died eight years later, an object of scorn in a community that he had once dominated.[46]

The Otis family, though lacking an early forebear as colorful as Anne Hutchinson, had roots in the Massachusetts Bay Colony that went easily as deep as those of the Hutchinsons. John Otis I had immigrated from the West Country to Massachusetts Bay in 1630. Settling in Hingham, he became a solid, middling farmer, serving his town in a variety of capacities. Successive generations would build on the Otis family fortune and family name.[47] His eldest son, John Otis II, moved around 1661 to Scituate, in Plymouth Colony, and proceeded to expand both his land holdings and political influence in his new home. At his death he had at least tripled his patrimony, owning substantial properties in Hingham, Scituate, and Barnstable.[48] Following in the tradition of his father and grandfather, John Otis III would enhance the family's record of accumulation both of property and prestige. Settling in Barnstable, he not only retained ownership of an impressive array of farm properties but also started the Otis family on what would be a highly successful road toward mercantile wealth. Largely due to his leadership, Barnstable was one of the few ports outside Boston that was able to compete successfully with Boston as a center of trade. The combination of trading, shipping, and whaling would make John Otis III a genuinely wealthy man. He was also the first in his family who was able to move his career as a public servant beyond the local level. He began as Barnstable's representative to the general court in 1692, the year in which the colony's new royal charter went into effect; his service in that body was well regarded, and he was soon elevated to the Governor's Council.[49] His eldest son, John IV, was perhaps the first member of the Otis family who could lay claim to power and authority as a birthright, and he inherited his father's mantle with apparent ease. He was the first member of his family to attend Harvard (ranking seventh in his graduating class in 1707) and then went on to take a second degree in medicine. He returned to Barnstable, practiced medicine, maintained his father's interests in trade, and eventually shifted his interest to law, building an extensive local practice in that field. In 1747 he was elected to the Governor's Council, where he served until his death in 1758.[50]

It is John Otis IV's younger brother, James Otis, however, who provides us with our counterpoint to the careers of Thomas Hutchinson and Israel Williams. If John Otis IV's career was one of "effortless success," as characterized by Otis family biographer John Waters, then that of his younger brother, James, can be characterized as one driven by extraordinary ambition and energy. Born in 1702, James did not attend Harvard, but instead served an apprenticeship in his father's store and increasingly took command of that business. Sometime around 1730 he, like his older brother, decided to combine a career as lawyer with that of merchant, a combination that served him in good stead given the highly litigious character of commercial life in Massachusetts. While his mercantile career continued to produce profits, it was his law career that increasingly occupied his attention. By 1744 he was representing nearly half of all litigants who appeared before the Barnstable Court, an astonishing fact given that it would have been impossible for him or any other lawyer to represent both the plaintiff and defendant in all the legal actions heard by the court. John Adams's assessment of his legal talent—"Learned he is not"—no doubt is colored by the Braintree lawyer's tendency toward envy; the fact of the matter is that Otis was in extraordinary demand as a lawyer, and his practice gradually extended to include a substantial volume of cases in the Bristol and Plymouth courts as well.[51]

He was first elected to the Massachusetts General Court in 1745, after serving apprenticeships on numerous committees within Barnstable and distinguishing himself as a moderator of the town meeting. Unlike his older brother and his father, James Otis made his political reputation in the general court and not the Governor's Council. As we have seen, one of the striking aspects of the operation of the general court was the extent to which many towns, and their elected representatives, regarded their responsibilities to the court with apathy, with fully a third of the towns in the colony not bothering to send representatives to the lower house, and among those towns that did, a large number of representatives attending only sporadically and participating in the business of the House in only a limited way. James Otis, from the very first day of his service in the House, would be numbered among those dozen or so activist members. As in the case of every colonial assembly in America, one of the keys to power and influence was active involvement in the committee work of the House, and from his first term onward, Otis would take on a range of committee assignments that grew steadily in number and importance. On the whole he allied himself with the royal governor, William Shirley, itself not unusual during the late 1740s and 1750s, as Shirley was remarkably successful in bringing remarkable stability and harmony to the governance of the colony. Given his loyal service to the colony and his increasing influence among an inner circle of legislative advisers to the governor, Otis had every reason to believe that his political career, like that of his brother and father before him, would continue to advance to higher levels in the years to come.[52] In the fall of 1756, however, James Otis experienced real political adversity for the first time. At that time Otis resigned his seat in the general court, expecting to obtain a seat on the Governor's Council. Unfortunately, at that point his ally and political sponsor, Governor Shirley, had fallen into disrepute back in London and was recalled, to be replaced by Thomas Pownall. Although Otis thought he had the backing of Pownall, he was mistaken, and by the beginning of the new year, Otis found himself out of office. In August of 1757, searching for reasons for his fall from grace, he wrote himself a memo diagnosing the source of his woes. The essence of the problem, as he saw it was that:

my Business would Be Effectually Done upon the new Governours comeing for Mr T Hutchinson and Mr Olliver would Be his advisers and that they had a Bad opinion of my Conduct and that Mr Hutchinson had said that I never Did Carry things while in the Court By any merit But only By Doing Little Low Dirty things for Governor Shirley such as Persons of worth Refused to medle with and that Shirley made use of me only as a Tool for [their] Purposes.[53]

And thus was born a rivalry with the Hutchinsons and the Olivers that would sustain him, and his son, James Otis Jr., for the next two decades. Otis would try once again for a council seat in May of 1759 but was again rebuffed, this time under circumstances that made him doubt the loyalty of even his successor in the general court, Edward Bacon. Refusing to give up, he ran for the general court in 1760, displacing Bacon, and tried from the inside to promote his elevation not only to the Governor's Council but also

Figure 7. James Otis, Jr. Ever-vigorous in defense of local and popular rights, both Otis and his father, James Otis, Sr., owed much to their political ascendancies to traditional avenues of patronage within the structure of royal government in Massachusetts. Courtesy of the Bostonian Society/Old State House.

to a position as justice on the colony's superior court. Although he accomplished neither of those goals in the 1760 session, he did, through vigorous effort on his part, achieve something of perhaps equal importance: at just the time when the harmony between representatives of royal and provincial authority was becoming strained, James Otis Sr. was elevated to the speakership of the Massachusetts General Court.[54]

It was at this stage that the careers of James Otis Sr. and his equally ambitious son, James Otis Jr., became intertwined. James Otis Jr., recipient of a Harvard education that his father lacked, would make his name and his livelihood as a lawyer in Boston. Like his father, he started his political career as an ally of the royal governor; in his case, the governor was Shirley's replacement, Thomas Pownall, and James Junior, serving his merchant clients in Boston, would work diligently to ensure that the governor was friendly to their interests. Not unimportantly, the son also worked to mend his father's fences with Pownall, with the consequence of reviving James Senior's hopes for appointment to the council and to a superior court justiceship by 1760. Unfortunately, Pownall's service as governor of Massachusetts was short-lived, and by the end of that year he had moved on to a more lucrative governorship in South Carolina. He would be replaced by Francis Bernard, a man who would soon set himself against both of the Otises.

When Chief Justice Samuel Sewall died in September 1760, James Otis Sr. had his long-awaited opportunity for a seat on the Massachusetts Superior Court and Francis Bernard had his first opportunity to make an important patronage decision. He seized that opportunity and instead of James Otis Sr., appointed Thomas Hutchinson, who already was holding positions as lieutenant governor, member of the Governor's Council, judge of probate for Suffolk County, and commander of Castle William. The senior Otis was deeply disappointed by the decision, but perhaps more important, his son was infuriated by it, considering it an affront to the family's honor. In a bitter exchange with Hutchinson, whom he believed had betrayed an earlier promise not to accept the position, James Junior "swore revenge," a gesture that would later convince Tory Peter Oliver that the "Hydra of Revolution" had first emerged out of the jealousy and disappointment of the younger James Otis over his father's rejection.[55] From that time forward, James Senior, though still an important factor in Massachusetts politics, would leave center stage to his son, who during the years immediately preceding and following the Stamp Act became the most articulate and vocal defender of provincial rights in the Massachusetts Assembly, as well as being the mentor of another emerging Boston politician, Samuel Adams. James Otis Jr.'s role in the Revolution would take a peculiar turn, however. Beginning in 1768, he was increasingly inclined to defend the interests of the royal government; more importantly, signs of mental illness, which close observers had begun to suspect earlier, were becoming more pronounced. As a consequence James Junior, alienated from most of his Boston townspeople, including his protégé Sam Adams, and increasingly morose and irascible, was driven to the sidelines in a conflict he had done so much to initiate. He would die in the year America achieved its independence, 1783, an embittered and severely troubled man.

James Otis Sr.'s career would also take some unusual twists and turns during those years, but his ending would be somewhat happier than that of his son. In 1771 he finally received his long-desired appointment to the Governor's Council, at the pleasure of his old nemesis Thomas Hutchinson, who saw Otis's appointment as an opportunity to regroup some of his support in the lull following the repeal of the Townshend duties. It would prove to be only a temporary truce. Though James Otis Sr. was hardly a radical advocate of independence, by the time of the passage of the Coercive Acts he had reluctantly concluded that the Parliament was acting in a wholly unconstitutional fashion. While he continued to sit on the Governor's Council, he nevertheless supported his colony's efforts to initiate an independent government. When the Barnstable town meeting considered how to instruct its delegates on the question of American independence in 1776, James Senior sided with those arguing in the affirmative. Ironically, his old political opponent, Edward Bacon, took the other side, and in the town meeting's initial vote, in which only a quarter of the citizens were present, Barnstable became the only town in Massachusetts to oppose immediate independence. At this point James Otis Sr. quietly but firmly began to use both his political and economic power in the town to bring potential Loyalists into line, and at his death in 1778 the town was in the patriot camp.[56]

These stories of the political careers of Thomas Hutchinson, Israel Williams, and James Otis Sr. and Jr. offer us at least a few common threads with which to tie together the fabric of mid-eighteenth-century Massachusetts politics. Most obviously, each of the four was able to begin his political career several notches above the usual entry-level position because of the patrimony—economic and political—that they enjoyed, courtesy of their forebears. Their subsequent advancement in the political system of their colony was for the most part achieved rapidly and smoothly. Up to this point the career paths of the four are similar, with each enjoying the powers and preferments that so often fell to affluent and well-connected young men in the colony. But however predictably their initial political careers may have followed traditional pathways to power, they would eventually diverge in notable ways. Although in Massachusetts there often existed a division of interest between a provincial and royal elite—the former with its base of power in the lower house of assembly and the latter deriving its power from patronage emanating from London and then flowing through the royal governors—the careers of Hutchinson, Williams, and the two Otises suggest, in varying ways, a much murkier picture of the division between the supporters of popular rights and of royal prerogative. In fact, all four men sought support and legitimation on both sides in the contest of provincial versus royal prerogative. Although Thomas Hutchinson would by the mid-1760s become a much detested symbol of the evils of excessive concentrations of royally derived political power, he was in the early years of his political career able to achieve a manageable balance between his duty to his provincial constituents and his duty to the Crown. It was only in 1749, after ascending to the pinnacle of provincial power, the speaker-ship of the House, that Hutchinson began to be identified as a defender of royal prerogative *against* provincial interests. Yet even after his departure from the House and his elevation to the Governor's Council, Hutchinson would continue, at least until 1765, to enjoy substantial support from those provincial politicians who were not as friendly to royal prerogative as he.

Israel Williams's position of wealth and power within Hampshire County, together with the general disinterest of the citizens in that region about conflicts between provincial and royal authority, enabled him to lodge un-contested claims to both provincial and royal power. Finally, the Otises, though remembered in the aftermath of the Revolution as among the most steadfast of opponents of Thomas Hutchinson and as defenders of popu-lar rights, were in fact constantly angling for patronage and preferment from royal governors; that they were less successful than Hutchinson or Williams in doing so was not, it appears, for want of trying.

Although all four men self-consciously preached the gospel of republi-can virtue, describing their behavior as being motivated by an interest in the public good, it is plain that each, in his own way, was driven by an am-bition that sometimes clouded the distinction between individual and pub-lic interest. Israel Williams was perhaps the most obvious and aggressive in his use of public office to promote his own interests, but the Otises were not far behind. Even though Thomas Hutchinson was certainly the most self-conscious about invoking the primacy of his concern for the public good—at times setting himself against the current of popular opinion in the process—his colleague Francis Bernard was obviously talking about more than a concern for physical health when he expressed his confidence that Hutchinson could be counted on to "take care of [him]self."

Jack P. Greene, in assessing the political culture of eighteenth-century New England, has noted the "astonishing deference of the relatively ex-tensive constituencies of New England to their magisterial elites," a fact he has attributed to the "depth of New Englanders' devotion to the traditional ideal of an organic social hierarchy."[57] But the careers of Thomas Hutchin-son, Israel Williams, and both of the Otises suggest something at work more complicated than deference alone. Each of these individuals was both a recipient and a dispenser of patronage, and their accumulation of power came less from the automatic and spontaneous acclamation of their constituents than it did from a steady attention to the promotion of their own interests. And though there may have been others in the colony who identified themselves self-consciously as defenders of provincial interests— Sam Adams's father, Samuel Adams Sr., comes to mind—Hutchinson, Williams, and the Otises were pleased to accept help in their careers from either source.

As we have already seen in the case of Israel Williams and as we will see in chapter 9 in the case of Thomas Hutchinson, the revolutionary mobilization would strip away whatever veneer of deference might have remained among the aroused populace of Massachusetts and bring ruin upon those two gentlemen. Even James Otis Sr. and Jr., though they ended up in the patriot camp, were nearly as much casualties as beneficiaries of the movement for independence. There were other signs, too, that the traditional social order was giving way. Harvard College abandoned its practice of ranking entering students according to the social status of their parents just a few years before independence was declared.[58] When it came time to adopt a new constitution for the independent Commonwealth of Massachusetts, citizens in Massachusetts towns rallied against the initially proposed version—drafted by an extralegal assembly of the Massachusetts legislature—on the grounds that the constituent voice was not appropriately heard. After the initial defeat of that draft a special constituent convention was called whose members were directly elected by the people solely for the purpose of drafting a new frame of government. That frame of government was then submitted to the people for ratification, only to go into effect after a two-thirds majority of all free adult male voters added their assent.

In spite of this newfound attentiveness to the constituent voice, tradition died hard in Massachusetts. The new constitution adopted by the independent citizens of the commonwealth exhibited a strong attachment to traditional republican values. The association between property and political power was made even more explicit than it had been under the old colonial charter, with an ascending scale of qualifications necessary if citizens wished to vote (the franchise was restricted to twenty-one-year-old males who owned a freehold estate of the annual value of £3 or any estate worth £60), serve in the lower house of assembly (service was restricted to those owning a freehold estate worth £100 or a ratable estate of £200), serve in the upper house (a freehold estate worth £300 or a personal estate worth £600), or as governor (a freehold estate worth £1000). Remaining true to the vision of a republican society founded upon the virtue of its citizens, Massachusetts also continued to endorse the connection between church and state, proclaiming in its constitution that "the happiness of a people and the good order and preservation of civil government essentially depend upon piety, religion and morality." Although the revolutionary

Massachusetts Constitution greatly extended toleration to members of dissenting religious groups, it reaffirmed the special privilege of the Congregational Church as the official tax-supported church of the independent commonwealth.[59] Even after the Revolution, the course of the independent Commonwealth of Massachusetts toward liberal democracy did not run straight and true.

Chapter 4

Uneasy Oligarchs
The Manor Lords of Upstate New York

As the Indian Superintendent of the Northern District of British North America and owner of a magnificent estate in the Mohawk River valley of New York, Sir William Johnson was a man to be reckoned with. Born in County Meath, Ireland, in 1715, Johnson immigrated to the Mohawk Valley in 1737 or 1738, taking charge of a large estate owned by his uncle, Admiral Peter Warren. Over the years Johnson would add substantially to his uncle's landholding, but it was his career as a military man fighting Indians in upstate New York that provided the most important ingredient in his success. In 1755 he led the British to victory over a combined force of French and Indians from the Six Nations in a bloody battle at Lake George, where there were heavy casualties on both sides. In spite of conflicting reports about Johnson's own role in the victory (his supporters depicted him as leading the charge; his enemies had him cowering in his tent at the height of battle), King George II, smarting from earlier defeats at the hands of the French and Indians, was so relieved that he made Johnson a baronet, issuing at the same time a commission making him "Colonel, Agent, and sole superintendent of the Six Nations and other Northern tribes." In 1759, promoted to major general, he distinguished himself again as the hero of the battle at Niagara, further consolidating his power within New York.

From that point on, he built a career through the careful cultivation of his political and economic interests that few anywhere in America could match. In Albany County, his home district, Johnson worked assiduously to create a network of influence and patronage that worked to his advantage. By close alliances with a succession of royal governors, lieutenant governors, and prominent members of the assembly, he made certain that the local justices of the peace, militia officers, supervisors, and even coroners were "his people," serving his interest not only at election time but at other times as well. Johnson himself served at various points in his career as a member of the Governor's Council, but formal service in either the upper or lower houses of assembly was less important than the influence he was able to wield in all of his dealings at all levels of New York society.[1]

Sir William would eventually acquire several hundred square miles of

Figure 8. Sir William Johnson. This remarkable combination of frontiersman, Imperial British military commander, and local political magnate achieved unchallenged dominance within his political domain. Collection of the New-York Historical Society.

real estate in upstate New York through aggressive use of his power and influence as an Indian agent, but the seat of his "empire" in upstate New York was Johnson Hall, sitting on eighty square miles of prime land in Albany County. Johnson Hall was a faithful effort at creating an Anglo-Irish aristocratic seat. In Georgian style, the main building was described by one Connecticut traveler as "truly grand and noble." In the rear of the main building were two stone blockhouses, a barn, and several outbuildings. The estate featured a crannog—an artificial island in a pond—more than five hundred acres of gardens and orchards, and a small compound that housed artisans and servants. Surrounding Johnson's estate and the dwellings of his immediate dependents were carefully laid-out plots of one hundred acres each on which between eight hundred and a thousand of his tenants and their families farmed his land.[2]

Contemporary descriptions of life at Johnson Hall suggest a remarkable merging of traditional, even feudal, values and the culture and manners of the frontier. Sir William was absolute lord of his manor, dispensing both favor and punishment at his will. He preferred the role of benevolent patriarch, and his reputation as a generous landlord caused his lands to be filled quickly with tenants. Johnson was frank in his enjoyment of luxury; though he was sometimes cash-poor like so many of even the wealthiest in America, he never hesitated to purchase any adornment for his manor that might catch his fancy. This pursuit of pleasure was not confined to material matters. Johnson gave full expression to his commitment to "natural liberty," and his sexual exploits—with the wives of tavern keepers, tenants, and artisans, and with scores of the young Indian women who were a constant fixture at Johnson Hall—were the stuff of legend on both sides of the Atlantic. Benjamin Lossing, in his *Pictorial Fieldbook of the American Revolution*, reported that "Sir William is said to have been the father of a hundred children, Mostly by native women," and New York's governor George Clinton noted to Johnson himself that officials in London believed that he had at least as many children as the shah of Persia.[3] In all of this conscious mimicry of old world traditions though, there was a distinctly frontier American aspect to the scene at Johnson Hall. The doors of the manor were open at nearly all times to one and all, and at almost any time, according to most observers, it appeared "that for every white visitor there were ten to a hundred Indian guests." The most popular entertainments in Johnson's domain were not fancy dress balls or refined teas, but contests to see who could catch a greased hog or to see who could, "by contortion of feature, make the wryest face." Ralph Izard, visiting Johnson Hall from the more self-consciously genteel environs of low-country South Carolina, complained, "Sir William continually plagued with Indians, generally 300 to 900. Spoil his garden; keep his house always dirty." Lord Adam Gordon, visiting from Scotland, was equally horrified by the disorder and squalor that surrounded Johnson Hall. "No consideration," he concluded, "should tempt me to lead his life." Confronted with a multitude of descriptions about the rough and tumble character of life at the estate, Sir William's most recent biographer, James Thomas Flexner, has concluded with some justification that the behavior of the master of Johnson Hall was much closer to that of a "tribal chief" than it was to an "aristocrat."[4]

In 1772 the territory in which Johnson's estate was situated was separated from Albany County and the new county of Tryon was created. Sir William, with the help of his friends Hugh Wallace, member of the New York Council; Goldsbrow Banyar, deputy secretary to the colony; and Philip Schuyler, Albany County assembly representative, arranged the location of the county seat and laid out the boundaries for the county as well. The new county seat, named Johnstown, lay less than a mile from Johnson Hall and was planned, built, and owned by Sir William. The county gaol, courthouse, and Anglican Church (Johnson was an ardent Anglican) were all his personal property, as was the principal private establishment located in Johnstown, Tice's tavern. When it came time to select the county officers, his son-in-law and nephew, Guy Johnson, became chief justice of the Courts of Common Pleas and of the Court of Quarter Sessions; his son, John Johnson, sat on each bench as an assistant judge. Sir William, in his capacity as major general and commanding officer of New York's Northern District, selected Guy and John Johnson, along with another friend, Daniel Claus, as commanding officers of the new county's three militia regiments. A few months later, in December 1772, elections for the new county's assembly representatives were held; Sir William got together with a few of his friends and agreed to "pitch on" Guy Johnson and Hendrick Frey as their preferred candidates. Johnson made it clear to all in the county that it would be inappropriate for others to consider opposing his choices, and when the election was over, he wrote, with some satisfaction, "The election was unanimous and will I hope always be such, as making parties and divisions among the inhabitants can never be for their interest."[5]

Six months later, in June 1773, Johnson turned his attention to guaranteeing a similarly satisfactory outcome in the election of the county's five new constables. As was the case in the 1772 assembly election, Johnson carefully handpicked his five preferred candidates and made certain that no one else would have the temerity to oppose his slate. Even more impressive, though, was the way in which he managed the election itself. Although there were probably more than four hundred citizens in newly created Tryon County who would have qualified to vote in that election, only fourteen turned up at the polling place (which was of course held at the Court of Quarter Sessions in Johnstown, presided over by Chief Justice Guy Johnson). The polling was conducted, by the law of the colony, either viva voce or by show of hands, and the result was a unanimous ratification of William Johnson's selection of the five candidates. The fourteen of those who voted had, surely by design, two things in common: they were far wealthier and more prominent than the typical citizen of Tryon County, and they were all part of a densely woven network of clients of Sir William Johnson who were in his debt in various ways. Moreover, their very order of voting in that constable election suggests even more careful choreographing. Joseph Chew, "Esquire," who both conducted the tallying of the votes and voted first, was not only a prominent member of the Tryon County elite in his own right, but he owed much of his political power in the county to Johnson's patronage. Similarly, Captain William Byrne voted second, a fact dictated not only by his status as a prosperous farmer and militia officer but also by his relation by marriage to a Johnson family member. And so on down the line—a polling pattern that clearly suggests, in the words of John Guzzardo, who has conducted an extensive analysis of the poll, "a profound respect for the length of a man's identification with local society and of his subordination to the Johnsons."[6] As we have seen, combinations of economic power, politics, family prestige, and personal influence were often a potent force in shaping the conduct and the outcome of elections in Virginia and Massachusetts, but few people in America combined these ingredients more visibly and forcefully than William Johnson.

Major General William Johnson's position within the social and political hierarchy of his region of New York invites particular comparison with the place and position of that other famous general-to-be, George Washington, in the Northern Neck region of Virginia. As powerful and well respected as Washington was, he did not, at least during the prerevolutionary years, command (or, indeed, seek) the overwhelming dominance of his region's society and politics enjoyed by Johnson. Moreover, Washington's reputation was always built on a dual identity—as soldier and republican citizen—and in that latter role he was intent on gaining not only the favor but also the respect of his constituents. Toward that end, his conduct as a county court justice and as a burgess was consistently guided by a self-conscious awareness of his responsibility to represent the "best interests" of his constituents, a responsibility that required that he act as one who was simultaneously "of the people" and above any narrow and particular local interest. There is little in William Johnson's public career that suggests he ever struggled with any of the tensions inherent in being a public servant and a public leader. Perhaps because the circumstances of the frontier magnified the weight given to his military position and prowess, William Johnson devoted precious little of his time seeking to cultivate a role as one "of the people."

Many of the most prominent members of the resident provincial elite in every colony faced the challenge of serving simultaneously the interests of the people with whom they lived and the interests of the Crown. In the case of a man like Washington, the tensions inherent in serving those two masters were, at least until the years immediately preceding the Revolution, relatively minor. Thomas Hutchinson lived in a society in which the lines between provincial and royal authority were more sharply drawn, and, indeed, his own penchant for receiving royal favor was more visibly and consciously nourished. But however dedicated he may have been to serving the Crown, Hutchinson was, at least by his own standards, deeply committed to serving the people of Massachusetts, with the consequence being a turmoil within him that he found difficult to conceal.[7] William Johnson, whose wealth and power were in their entirety due to royal favor, almost certainly was not even aware of the distinction between service to the Crown and service to the people of his colony. William Johnson was a servant—a munificently rewarded servant—of the Crown.

That Johnson was able to exert such decisive and nearly effortless dominance over his constituents was precisely what Carl Becker in his landmark study, *The History of Political Parties in the Province of New York*, had in mind when he described New York politics as being composed of "three distinct classes, of which the most important was that small cohort of closely related families of wealth, commonly known as the aristocracy." (The other two, according to Becker, were a relatively small class of freeholders and a much larger class of disenfranchised citizens.)[8] The basis of the aristocracy's power, according to Becker, was their control over the land, the most impressive concentration of power being in Hudson Valley counties such as Albany and Westchester, where families such as the Livingstons, Van Rensselaers, and Van Cortlandts owned manors amounting to nearly half of the total land area of their counties. In Albany County, the Livingston and Van Rensselaerswyck manors alone composed nearly a million acres on both sides of the Hudson, a fact that gave to the owners of those properties significant coercive powers over the hundreds of individuals living on their lands.[9]

If there were any region in America in which members of an aristocracy were capable of using their superior economic power and political authority to persuade—even coerce—their fellow residents into endorsing their political dominance, then the Hudson Valley region of New York before the Revolution probably best fits that description. Not only were most offices in the colony—from militia officers to justices of the peace to sheriffs—appointive, but wealthy, well-connected oligarchs at the local level—people like Sir William Johnson—had by the early eighteenth century managed to seize effective control over nearly all of those appointments from the royal governors. So firmly established was the principle that sitting members of the General Assembly from a given county had the right to appoint and recall a host of appointive local officials that residents frequently referred to those sitting members as "the present administration."[10]

As we have seen in the case of the constable election on Sir William Johnson's estate, the existence of certain categories of elective, rather than appointive, local offices—which, in addition to the constables, came to in-

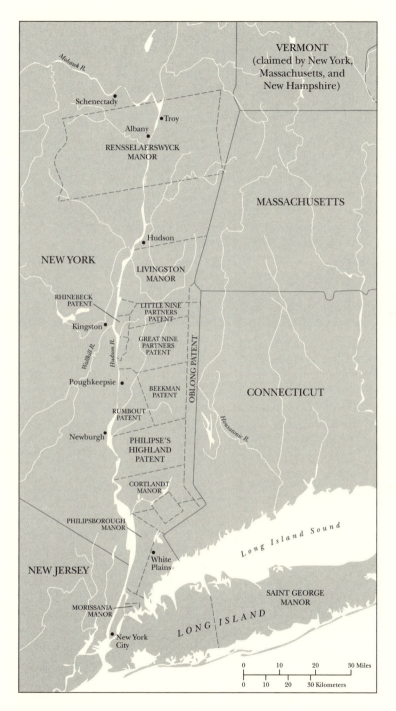

Map 2. New York, with emphasis on the Hudson Valley Manor Grants—"the concentration of land and wealth in New York's Hudson River Valley was perhaps unequalled anywhere in colonial America."

Figure 9. The Philipse Manor. Gift of La Duchesse de Talleyrand. Historic
Hudson Valley, Tarrytown, NY.

clude tax collectors, assessors, and overseers of the poor—did little to
weaken the power of local oligarchs. The real prizes in New York politics—
and the political key to controlling so much of the rest of what went on at
the local level—lay either in one of the twelve seats on the appointive Governor's Council (which simultaneously served as the governor's privy
council, the upper house of assembly, and a high court of appeal) or an
elected post as representative in the lower house of assembly.

The Governor's Council in New York, like that in nearly every colony in
America, experienced a diminution in its formal institutional power over
the course of the eighteenth century as the lower house—the most aggressive and effective advocate of provincial as opposed to royal interests—
gained in the range of its powers and prerogatives at the expense of the
royally appointed officials. However, in New York in particular, men of the
leading families, like William Johnson and Peter Warren, continued to seek
appointment as councillors because that position signified, in Warren's
words, a "little rank above the commoner sort." Moreover, though the formal political power of councillors may have been relatively slight, membership placed them at an important strategic place within the governor's
inner circle, a place in which insider information about patronage appointments, land contracts, and the licensing of land purchases from the
Indians might prove helpful to one's political interests and to one's pocketbook.[11]

There is general agreement among historians that the single most important development in the political history of eighteenth-century America was the rise of the lower houses of assembly. It was the gradual accumulation of political authority into the hands of popularly elected lower houses that both caused the steady diminution of royal authority in America and, at least theoretically, gave to those citizens who elected assemblymen a voice in politics in their colonies. There is evidence that this transfer of power from royal to popular provincial agencies of government occurred in New York as it did in most every colony, and there is evidence that much of the dynamic that propelled that transfer of power came from the aggressive behavior of provincial politicians who were eager and willing to use their status as representatives of the people as the legitimizing force in their contest for power with royal officials.

What remains at issue, of course, is whether the growth in power of provincial and local agencies of government in New York, and the consequent increase in the power of those men who served in those agencies, represented in any meaningful way an increase in the political power of the people of the colony at large. Carl Becker was only the first of many historians to note that while New York's provincial leaders may have used the rhetoric of popular rights to undermine the power of royal officials, it was the power of personality and the desire for patronage, not a genuine commitment to popular rights, that dictated political outcomes in New York.

The "political parties" that formed a part of the title of Becker's 1909 monograph were hardly modern institutions responsive to popularly based constituencies but, rather, were made up of tight alliances of "a few rich and powerful families" whose wealth was based on the combination of land, commerce, and carefully crafted political influence. In his analysis of the political infighting that occurred both between the governor and the assembly and among members of the assembly, Becker was most struck by the "medieval" quality of the political relationships created among New York's provincial leaders. The alliances that were formed among members of the colonial assembly—particularly those in the 1760s that produced a consistent division of opinion and policy between followers of the Livingston and the DeLancey families—were far from being popularly based parties, but instead were in Becker's view "prudential intermarriages" aimed at maximizing the self-interest of a small coterie of aristocratic politicians. And, he reasoned, how could it be otherwise? The franchise, by his calculations, was restricted to no more than 12 percent of the population, and even those who found themselves technically qualified for the vote were likely to find themselves subject to the severest constraints. After all, Becker argued, a "large portion of the electorate resided within the manors and on the large estates," and, with the laws requiring ballots to be cast either viva voce or by show of hands, a "common man who ventured to follow his own inclination, rather than the cue of a leader, was certainly doomed to failure, besides laying himself open to censure."[12]

Becker's book not only transformed historians' views of society and politics in colonial New York but also shaped profoundly our understanding of the nature of social and political conflict throughout all of British North America. Nearly a century after the appearance of Becker's study most historians still endorse his description of the highly stratified character of New York society, while at the same time giving us a more complicated picture of the sources of political conflict in the colony. Certainly the conduct of politics in colonial New York was unusually disputatious, with some form of conflict among competing factions nearly always on display. Although the conflict between the rich and the great mass of ordinary citizens was one obvious line of division in New York society, the sources of faction that provoked political conflict among New York's leaders were far more numerous and complex.

Above and beyond showing the normal inclination of men in power to jockey for position and preferment, New York's political leaders were frequently divided by other forces peculiar to their colony. Along with Pennsylvania, eighteenth-century New York displayed an ethnic and religious diversity unknown in other parts of America, and the sharpness of the cultural division between the Dutch in the area around Albany and Englishmen in other regions of the colony had perhaps no counterpart anywhere in America. The manor system of the Hudson Valley, in addition to creating an obvious division between a few powerful manor lords and their dependent tenants, also created divisions of interest between those political leaders representing the manors and those representing other sections of the colony. More generally, the cultural geography of the colony as a whole tended to fracture any sense of a single, organic society. There were settlements that were solidly Dutch in language and culture in the area around Albany, more ethnically and religiously mixed collections of tenants on Livingston Manor in Dutchess County, and in Westchester County a population that was more English in its ethnic makeup and more complex in its economic structure than the manor economies to the north. Further south, the "babel" of competing ethnic, religious, and economic interests in New York City; the differing interests and attitudes of the settlers in the western frontier counties of Orange and Ulster; and to the east, on Long Island, Suffolk County, composed nearly wholly of New Englanders, all contributed to a highly fractious brand of provincial politics.[13]

Political decision making in New York was rendered all the more complicated by the existence of a vast frontier to the west of the manors and counties north of New York City. Even by the mid-eighteenth century European settlement of New York from the southern border shared with New Jersey to the colonial capital in Albany did not extend more than fifty miles west of the Hudson. There is a whole other history of New York that exists side by side with that of the European settlement of the colony, that of the Algonquian and Iroquois Indian nations. Those two histories occasionally intersected—in the conduct of the fur trade and, as the importance of the fur trade diminished during the last half of the eighteenth century and as European hunger for Indian lands increased, in warfare between and among Europeans and Indians. Although issues involving the fur trade and the contest over land would at times force royal governors and provincial legislatures to turn their attention westward, for the most part, and most of the time, Indians and Europeans living on the vast New York frontier operated outside the political culture of the colony as a whole.[14]

The picture that we now have of the political culture emerging from New York's dispersed and diverse social character is one that cannot be simply characterized by words like "medieval" or "oligarchical." Most of New York's provincial leaders were more self-consciously concerned with, and sincere in their invocation of, "popular rights" in their dealings with royal officials than was William Johnson; they may indeed have been using the language of popular rights to aggrandize their own personal power, but that fact does not necessarily make their commitment to those rights any less sincere. It is also clear that the power of most of New York's provincial leaders was not quite as secure as that enjoyed by Johnson. At least some of them had to work hard—not only behind closed doors in the corridors of power of the assembly and in the county courts but also, occasionally, among the people at large—to maintain their political positions within the colony. The political parties that emerged in colonial New York were neither feudal alliances based on personal loyalty to a few wealthy and powerful patrons nor modern, popularly based machines; rather, they were a complicated phenomenon, representing the shifting powers of different ethnic, religious, economic, regional, and ideological groupings within the colony. Finally, however much members of a court faction loyal to the Crown and royal governor may have stressed the importance of prerogative and however much the members of a country faction in the assembly may have used the language of republicanism to justify their defense of rights, the dominant theme of New York politics was the aggressive pursuit and defense of interests, which frequently cut across lines of court and country or aristocracy and commoners.

The conduct of elections provides us with one view of the way in which New Yorkers regarded the relationship between the many and the few, and it is also in that area that we can glimpse some of the uncertainty and contest among New York's political leaders as they vied for power. The colony of New York, like virtually every other political entity in the British Empire, restricted the suffrage to free, propertied males. The restriction of full citizenship in the polis to males was consistent with long-standing practice throughout Europe and most of the rest of the world over the course of many centuries. While women were never fully excluded from public life either in England or the American colonies (for example, their role in the polity of the church, though never equal to that of men, was much more significant), their exclusion from formal participation in the political process was taken for granted. Indeed, it was so much taken for granted that the 1699 Virginia statute specifically banning women from voting was the only one of its kind in the colonies. As we have seen, the restriction of the suffrage to free and propertied men was closely tied to the notion—one fully congenial to good republicans—that one of the prime requisites of full citizenship was a "stake in society"—a visible attachment, by dint of property ownership, to the public good of the community. As one New York gentleman pointed out, a man with "considerable interest in the Property of this Colony" could be counted on to "consulte and promote the Means that shall preserve both." Moreover, the ownership of property, together with status as a freeman, was essential to the *independence* that was so necessary to responsible citizenship; the alternative, the manipulation by the rich and powerful of the great mass of *dependent* residents, was almost certain to lead to corruption.[15]

The technical property qualifications in New York were about the same as in other colonies; the suffrage was confined to those adult men possessing a freehold, free of encumbrances, worth at least £40. Carl Becker almost certainly overemphasized the restrictive nature of the suffrage law; its actual operation was probably not very onerous given prevailing conceptions about the relationship between property and citizenship. In addition to all of those who actually owned property outright worth at least £40, tenants with lifetime leases (a group that included nearly all of those living on the Livingston and Van Rensselaer manors) were able to vote. That the Livingstons' and Van Rensselaers' tenants were able to vote did, of course, open up just the sort of possibility that the defenders of property qualifications most feared: the possibility that the votes of dependent citizens would be controlled by those rich and powerful men who controlled their economic destiny. While the holding of a lifetime lease rendered such overt manipulation less likely, it did nevertheless create a situation—inherent in modern democratic societies today as well—in which the inclusion of economically dependent people in the polity also created a wider opportunity for one person's vote to be swayed by the superior power and influence of another. Finally, in the towns of both Albany and New York City, residents could qualify for the franchise by paying a modest fee to become freemen. While there is little agreement among historians on the precise percentage of free adult males who were able to vote under this system, estimates generally range from a low of 50 percent to a high of 80 percent, a rate of eligibility that amounted to about three times the probable rates in England at the time.[16]

As mentioned earlier, the electoral laws of the colony stipulated that voting was to be done either viva voce or by show of hands, thus making it impossible for voters to escape the eyes of their neighbors, including of course the great men of their community, as they cast their ballots. The requirement that voting be done publicly has seemed to many historians to be highly coercive, at least in its potential. Carl Becker, for example, asserted that "Every voter was watched, we may be sure, and his record was known." Certainly though, many eighteenth-century commentators from both Europe and America saw things differently. By statute New York's citizens were enjoined to select a representative who was certified to be a "fit and discreet inhabitant," and many classical republican defenders of civic virtue believed that only with open voting could ordinary citizens be trusted to designate respectable members of the community as their representatives. As Montesquieu put it, "The lower classes ought to be directed by those of higher rank, and restrained within bounds by the gravity of eminent personages." There were also, of course, more practical reasons to prefer open voting. A good many Americans agreed that open, rather than secret, balloting discouraged dishonesty at elections and kept irregularities to a minimum. It was all too easy, they argued, to "stuff the ballot box" with paper ballots, but impossible to do so if every freeholder was held accountable for his vote.[17] There obviously was another side to that argument, one that stressed the importance of each voter casting his ballot free from constraint, and opinion flutuated among members of New York's assembly, who could have changed the system had they wished. Although there were periodic attempts in the New York Assembly to move to a written ballot, that step was not taken until the passage of New York's revolutionary constitution in 1777.[18]

The structural feature of New York's political system that may have had the greatest effect in limiting the impact of ordinary citizens on the making of public policy was the extraordinarily small size of the lower house of the assembly. In 1700 it contained only twenty representatives, increasing to only twenty-seven on the eve of the Revolution. The resulting ratio of representatives to free adult males in the population—1:1065 by 1770—placed New York, along with Pennsylvania, at the very high end of the scale across America. By contrast the ratio of representatives to constituents across both New England and the South was in the range of 1:167 to 1:478, with the average being about 1:350. Moreover, unlike neighboring Pennsylvania, which elected representatives to its legislature annually, until 1743 New York held legislative elections only upon the death of the king and after that managed to hold them on the average of every five years. The most typical pattern of election in other colonies was every two years.[19]

New York's representatives were distributed reasonably evenly, if sparsely, across the colony's population. Up until 1772 each of the nine counties—Suffolk, Queens, Kings, Richmond, Westchester, Orange, Ulster, Dutchess, and Albany—sent two representatives to the assembly. New York City and

Westchester Borough each elected four. The town of Schenectady and the manors Rensselaerswyck, Livingston, and Cortlandt each elected one representative. In 1772, with the creation of Tryon and Charlotte counties, the size of the assembly increased by four. The principal source of inequity in the apportionment of representation came in the slight overrepresentation for the Hudson River valley, a consequence of the privileged status given to Rensselaerswyck, Livingston, and Cortlandt manors.[20] In fact, the inequity in simple demographic terms was not that great, as the population in the regions controlled by the manors was growing rapidly; what is less clear, however, is how a "rotten borough" system in which manor lords could control nearly completely the outcome of elections in their districts could be justified in a system of representation supposedly based on freely given consent.

One common measure either of the stability or of the competitiveness of electoral systems is the rate of turnover in the bodies to which individuals are elected. Overall rates of turnover were generally lower in New York in the eighteenth century than they were for most of the American colonies (averaging about 35 percent per election as compared to an average across America of 41 percent) and about the same as that occurring in the English House of Commons during the same period (turnover rates there ranged from about 27 percent to 35 percent).[21] There were, in fact, variations within different regions in the colony and variations within individual regions in different time periods in the eighteenth century. Turnover was the greatest in New York City, with Queens County not too far behind, but it, too, varied from decade to decade. Turnover in New York City and environs was fairly modest during much of the eighteenth century but had dramatic peaks in the assembly elections in 1726, 1737, and 1759, when it was slightly over 50 percent. By contrast the constituencies in the Hudson Valley show strikingly low rates of turnover throughout the whole of the eighteenth century. While at least one historian of eighteenth-century New York has attempted to equate the few, brief moments of high legislative turnover in downstate New York with increased concern with defense of popular rights, such a correlation is difficult to sustain.[22] The evidence neither permits nor refutes a direct correlation between elections with high voter turnout and those that resulted in high legislative turnover; it seems more likely that the rates of turnover in New York, whether very low, as in the case of the manors, or moderate, as in the case of New York City, were not the result of people being turned out of office by insurgent candidates but, instead, occurred as incumbents chose to move in or out of the legislature as their interests warranted.

The roster of representatives to the New York General Assembly from Albany, Westchester, and Dutchess counties and from Cortlandt, Rensaelerswyck, and Livingston manors during the forty-year period from 1728 to 1768 provides dramatic illustration not only of the low rates of legislative

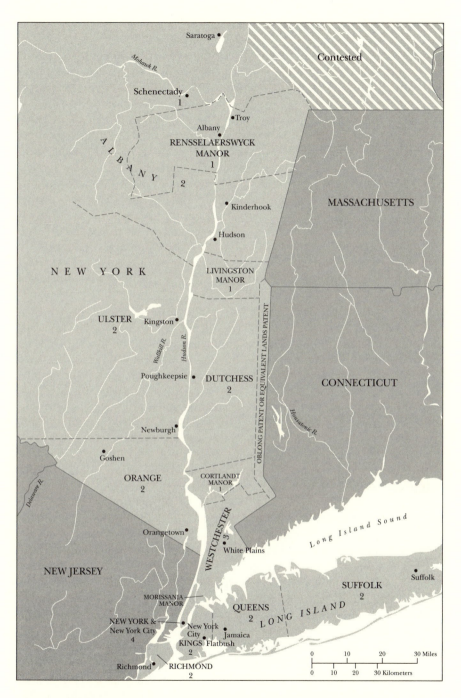

Map 3. Distribution of representatives in colonial New York, 1733–1772—Notable
for the small number of representatives in its colonial Assembly, New York's
system of representation also tended to give disproportionate power to the
Hudson Valley Manor Lords.

turnover during those years but also of the extent to which the politics of the Hudson River valley were controlled by a small, wealthy and privileged oligarchy. Albany County's two-person representation in the assembly during those years was monopolized by eight men representing five families, with two men—Philip Schuyler and Peter Winne—serving nearly forty years between them. Cortlandt Manor was represented by Philip Verplanck, Pierre Van Cortlandt's brother-in-law, for all of the forty-year period. Similarly, a Van Rensselaer served as representative from Rensselaerswyck and a member of the Livingston family served as representative from Livingston Manor in every session of the assembly during the entire period. In Dutchess County, Henry Beekman, whose landholding encompassed much of the northern half of that county, served consecutively from 1728 to 1759, when he was replaced by a Livingston. Only in Westchester did there appear to be more significant turnover from assembly session to assembly session, and even here only six families monopolized Westchester's four seats in the assembly between 1728 and 1768.[23]

In spite of the dominance of a few of New York's electoral districts by a few prominent families, the actual conduct of politics within the New York legislature was as factious, fractious, and ferocious as anywhere in colonial America. Indeed, there existed within the provincial government of New York virtually every species of conflict that one can imagine—the clash of imperial, provincial, and purely local prerogatives; conflicts of interest between commercial and landed interests and between upstate and downstate interests; and often bitter rivalries between different ethnic and religious groups—Dutch and English, Anglican, Presbyterian, and Dutch Reformed. Historians have studied exhaustively the bewilderingly complex patterns of factional political behavior in New York. Much of the political infighting of the early eighteenth century was marked by the long-standing rivalries between great men—in the mid-eighteenth century by personal contests of will between Adolphe Philipse and Lewis Morris and, subsequently, in the bitter rivalries between the Livingston and DeLancey families. One can hear, off and on during the whole of the eighteenth century, the rhetoric of a court and country division, with court politicians like Governor George Clinton (1743–53) defending the vigorous exercise of executive power in matters of finance and defense, and leading country politicians dusting off the rhetoric of classical republicanism to denounce executive attempts to usurp popular rights. It is extraordinarily difficult, however, to keep the cast of court and country party politicians straight, for country politicians seemed always ready to jump to the side of the governor when their regional or economic or ethnic interests were served by doing so, and, conversely, the governor and his friends were just as frequently willing to make those alliances with country party politicians when it suited their interests.[24]

Historian Alan Tully, in sorting through the complexity of personal, economic, regional, ethnic, and religious factionalism in New York, has concluded that there was one broad ideological divide that separated individuals into two durable factions—protoparties really—of popular and provincial whigs. Members of both factions stressed their commitment to English rights and liberties and to the rights of the lower house of the assembly in particular. Those representing the popular faction tended to express their commitment to those rights in the language of the parliamentary Whig constitutional tradition of historical rights and proved willing to work more closely with the royal governor and members of his administration on matters of mutual interest. By contrast, members of the provincial Whig faction drew more freely on the language of the English country opposition—Trenchard, Gordon, and Bolingbroke—in denunciations of ministerial corruption and executive encroachment and were, at least occasionally, willing to turn to a public arena to sound the alarm over such dangers. Tully is sufficiently impressed with the ways in which New York's political leaders aggressively organized themselves in these shifting factional alignments, always in acknowledgment and relentless pursuit of the multiple interests that were at work in their society, that he has concluded that the politics of New York, oligarchical as they may have been, were harbingers of America's liberal and democratic traditions.[25]

Edward Countryman, in surveying the many different manifestations in which party spirit presented itself—court/country, landed/commercial, English/Dutch—has shrewdly observed that the dominant contemporary nomenclature used to describe those conflicts was family names—the Livingstons, DeLanceys, Schuylers, or Johnsons. The use of family names to describe political alignments is suggestive not of a party in a modern sense but in a narrow one, suggesting the primacy of kinship and purely local loyalties over broader considerations of either interest or ideology.[26] When viewed through the lenses of an English past rather than an American future, the political alignments and infighting in the New York assembly seem perhaps less liberal or democratic than they do quintessentially English, very much a reflection of the factious, fractious, interest-oriented politics of the Whig-dominated English Parliament. The model for correct political behavior in New York provincial politics may have indeed been Robert Walpole, not the virtuous and public-spirited classical republican statesman envisioned by James Harrington. The politics of eighteenth-century Whiggism may eventually have led to the emergence of liberal democracy in England, but that would be a long, slow process, one that was hardly inevitable.

The conduct of elections for the General Assembly in New York displayed in microcosm much of the variety that characterized elections throughout the whole of America. The end result of that electoral process in New York, however, was the creation of an oligarchy that, however vehement their differences with one another or with the royal governor, confined the effective distribution of political power and patronage within the colony to a remarkably small group of men. There are two important sets of facts to keep in mind when seeking to understand electoral politics in colonial New York. First, throughout nearly the whole of the eighteenth century, popular, political campaigns in downstate New York—in New York City, in particular, but also in Queens and Westchester counties—were far more prevalent than in other areas of the colony. Indeed, the frequent occurrence of aggressive, partisan political organization at election time in New York City suggests that even though its political leaders were bound up in the same political conflicts in the legislature and with the governor as were leaders from other parts of the colony, New York City may belong in an altogether different typology from that of any other parts of the colony. (For that reason, a substantial portion of the politics of New York City will be treated in a subsequent chapter in this book.) A second noteworthy fact is that the conflicts with royal governors over the limits of royal authority, which had always played an important role in shaping the substance of New York politics, began to take on a more immediate and compelling urgency after 1764, with the character of electoral politics—in New York City, in particular, but elsewhere as well—reflecting that fact. Though Carl Becker's assertion that the Revolution in New York was "the open door through which the common freeholder and the dis-enfranchised mechanic and artisan pushed their way into the political arena" may have overstated the matter, it does appear that the coming of the Revolution did create a climate in which ordinary citizens considered their political aspirations and responsibilities.[27]

The task of determining the intensity and texture of electoral politics in New York is rendered difficult by the highly fragmentary nature of voting returns for the colony, which exist in abundance for only New York City, Queens, and Westchester, and are virtually absent for most decades for counties and manors to the north. It seems likely that one of the reasons that returns are so scattered lies in the frequency of cases in which candidates ran for office uncontested. In some of those cases, as in the elections of 1748, 1750, 1752, and 1759 in New York City, the outcome was decided without even bothering to take a poll of the voters.[28] In fact, voter turnout in New York City and adjoining counties was often quite high—often reaching 50–60 percent of the eligible voters in New York City and 40–50 percent in neighboring Queens County. In Westchester County and in the highly scattered returns for the other upstate counties, turnout fluctuated from between 15 and 38 percent, although it is likely that there were many more uncontested elections in which turnout was lower or, indeed, in which no one bothered to take a poll. In Kings and Suffolk counties on Long Island, and on the three manors that formed their own electoral districts—Livingston, Rensselaerswyck, and Cortlandt—nearly every election went un-

TABLE 2. VOTER PARTICIPATION IN NEW YORK ASSEMBLY ELECTIONS, 1698–1769

Year	New York		Queens		Westchester		Other		
	Number of Votes	Percentage	Number of Votes	Percentage	Number of Votes	Percentage		Number of Votes	Percentage
1698			389	54.5					
1699	632	80.0							
1701	224*	55–60							
1733					420	32.9			
1734	442								
1737	812	55.4	726	48.6			Albany	636	35.3
1739	633	41.8	728	48.4					
1745	177	10.7					Ulster	117	14.2
1748			800	50.1	289–500	14–30			
1750			755	45.8	476	14.0	Richmond	151	38.5
1761	1,447	56.1	678	34.6					
1768	1,924	53.6	1,100	56.2	739	18.3			
1769	1,515	40.6	871	40.0			Dutchess	1296	37.0

*Total for three wards recorded.
Source: Robert Dinkin, *Voting in Provincial America*, p. 156.

contested and voter turnout, when anyone bothered to record it, was usually negligible.[29]

In the most common forms of election in New York—those that either went uncontested or were only weakly contested—the most important work done by the candidates was accomplished before election day arrived. Many of the manor lords and grandees of the Hudson Valley had a strong stake in avoiding a formal poll at election time. Albany County representative Abraham Ten Broeck voiced a feeling common among people of his rank and station when he averred prior to a 1768 election in the district that "Everybody is averse to a poll."[30] Ten Broeck was operating on the same assumption that caused William Johnson to give thanks when an election was unanimous, for if polling led to some other result, it would "create parties and divisions among the inhabitants [that] can never be for their interest." And of course contested elections might actually require that a candidate go out and solicit votes among the citizens. William Livingston made it clear what he thought about that sort of degrading business: "To ask a man for his vote is a confession in the candidate that he is suspicious of his own merit. 'Tis a proof of his apprehension that the sense of the public is against him."[31]

Election to public office without a contest was, however, even in a society as hierarchically structured as that of the Hudson Valley, not something that occurred without effort. In most cases the real work in an election occurred before the polling began and involved securing the "interest" of the principal families in the region. If one could secure the support of a man of Sir William Johnson's power and influence in Albany County, the pathway to power would obviously be a lot smoother. Thus we find Jacob Ten Eyck and Volkert Douw supplicating to Sir William, "If it's agreeable to you, we beg your Interest in wch you'l very much oblige us." In a subsequent election another political hopeful, John Duncan, wrote to Johnson announcing his willingness to stand for election, "provided you approve and will favor me with your Interest . . . otherwise I will think no more of it."[32] Indeed, as we have seen, such was Johnson's power in his region that there was no point for a resident to even consider a run for office if Sir William would not endorse it. And of course, one way to secure the interest of a man like Sir William was to put him in your debt. Thus, when Sir William's son John was seeking a seat in Albany in 1768, he was assured by one of his friends, Richard Cartwright, that "you may depend on the Interest of Cuyler's family, of Hanson's, and many more who would be glad to know it. Whatever Interest or connection I have you may command in that or anything else."[33]

People like Sir William Johnson, although they sought to avoid having troublesome, contested elections, also wished to make certain that those who were elected would behave properly once in office. Reflecting on an upcoming assembly election in 1750, he noted how "troublesome & Inconvenient it would be to all the Farmers to have an Election at this time of year." To avoid that trouble, he went to Albany to speak to the sitting members of the legislature for Albany County, Philip Schuyler and Hanse Hansen. Upon his arrival in Albany he "sent for them, and told them if they would do their best for the good of the County, we would not sett up any body against them now, but if they would not do good for the County, we would sett up others next time. Whereupon they promised me they would do what they could." In explaining his actions to his neighbors in an open letter, he declared, "Now Gentlemen & freinds, I thank you all heartily for your good will for me, as well as if you voted every bit, and hope whenever there is another election, you will be all as one body to stand by me."[34]

Of course not all elections, even in the Hudson Valley, went uncontested. There were two, sometimes interrelated, sets of conditions that would at least occasionally lead to contested elections, which would tend to occur only when the interests of two or more prominent families were placed in opposition to one another. When those clashes did happen, they often took place in the context of struggles with the royal governor, in which one prominent man or group of men would appeal to the people in order to legitimize their opposition to the governor. It was in this manner that, occasionally, real issues and philosophies of government were introduced into political campaigns, but nearly always it would be the superior interest of the principal men that would carry the day.

Lewis Morris of Westchester County, a longtime ally of governors Hunter and Burnet, found himself out of favor, and eventually out of a job, when William Cosby arrived in 1731 to take over as governor of the colony. Morris, skilled in court politics, appealed to the board of trade back in England, hoping that he could successfully match his royal connections with those of Cosby and come out on top. As a part of his campaign against the governor, Morris decided to run for the assembly. A seat in the assembly would not only give Morris an arena in which to conduct the provincial theater of guerrilla operations against the governor but would also provide him with parliamentary immunity from prosecution as he carried out his public, personal attacks on Cosby. As an important component of his provincial New York strategy, he enlisted John Peter Zenger, the printer of the *New York Weekly Journal*, a vehemently antiroyal paper, in his cause. The most important lasting consequence of all of this political infighting would be the trial of Zenger for seditious libel and the articulation of a slightly liberalized definition of that crime, but the conduct of Morris's election campaign against William Forster, the poor soul persuaded by Governor Cosby to stand against Morris, gives us an interesting insight into the way in which personal prestige and partisanship could be merged in New York electoral politics.[35]

Like any skilled oligarch, Morris left very little to chance, and he almost certainly knew that he had the election won before the balloting had begun. But he spared no effort in demonstrating his status as the leading citizen of his county, a man whose interest was essential if one were to get anywhere politically. According to the report in the *Weekly Journal*:

First rode two Trumpeters and 3 Violines; next 4 of the principal Freeholders, one of which carried a Banner, on one Side of which was affixed in gold Capitals, KING GEORGE, and on the Other, in like golden Capitals LIBERTY & LAW; next followed the Candidate, *Lewis Morris ESQ,* late Chief Justice of this Province; then two Colours; and at Sun rising they entered upon the Green of *Eastchester* the place of election, follow'd by above 300 Horse of the principal Freeholders of the County (a greater number than had ever appear'd for one Man since the Settlement of that County.

Forster attempted to match the display. When he arrived, he was accompanied by "two Ensigns, born by two of the Freeholders, then followed the Honorable *James DeLancy,* Esq., Chief Justice of the Province of New York, and the Honorable Frederick Philipse, Esq: second Judge of the same Province . . . and they entered the Green on the East side," where they "were attended by about 170 Horse of the Freeholders and Friends." When the two groups met at the polling place on the village green, the two candidates "very civilly" saluted each other, but at that point the contest was joined. Although Morris and his supporters were certain that a majority of the citizens present were on their side, Philipse demanded a formal poll. This demand was sufficiently unusual in a district in which most elections were decided without a formal contest that the sheriff was caught unprepared. After spending the next two hours setting up a polling place, the sheriff finally got the election under way. Once the poll began, Forster's supporters badgered the sheriff into throwing out the votes of some thirty-eight Quakers, after which the sheriff was accused by Morris's supporters of a "violent attempt on the liberties of the people." Finally, at about eleven o'clock that night the poll was closed, with 231 for Morris and 151 for Forster.[36]

What is most striking about the scene is its Englishness, the pomp and display of personal fortune and authority mixed with high-spirited combat. And though Morris was now in the role of "country party" politician opposing encroachments on his liberty by Governor Cosby, just a few years before, the roles would have been reversed. Although we do not have a full account of all of the attempts of the two candidates to win voters to their side, it would not have been at all surprising, for example, if both Morris and Forster considered it necessary to provide some inducement for their supporters to follow them to the polls. Even a man as distinguished as Henry Beekman, who enjoyed virtually unchallenged political authority in Dutchess County for thirty years in the middle of the eighteenth century, found it occasionally advisable to put on lavish election-day treats for his constituents; at one such treat he stocked his tables with beef, port, and bacon, along with a hundred loaves of bread and six barrels of cider.[37] And Robert Livingston, in commenting on the distances that potential voters had to travel to appear at election day, once confided that "the Camps will not move to an Election without being payed for their time."[38]

Although it is clear that both sides in the Morris-Forster election spent substantial amounts of time orchestrating their efforts, it is worth noting that the contests between governor and assembly, and, perhaps even more particularly, the contests between one self-interested governor and another self-interested New York provincial leader were not all that compelling to the citizens of Westchester. Voter turnout in the 1733 contest, in spite of all the pomp and ceremony, was just under 33 percent.[39]

In fact, the rivalry between Cosby and Morris would generate further electoral combat in the future. In 1737 Frederick Philipse, one of the wealthiest and most powerful manor lords in Westchester County and a supporter of Governor Cosby, would find himself opposed by John Thomas, a candidate handpicked by Lewis Morris. This time the tables were turned, as Philipse was able to bring far more personal prestige and a wider assortment of distinguished interest from around the county to the polling place than his opponent. Nevertheless, Thomas campaigned vigorously, directly assaulting both the policy preferences and the person of Frederick Philipse. Philipse withstood the challenge, but the contest left bitterness and recrimination in its wake. Thomas lodged a formal protest with the New York Assembly about corrupt practices on the part of his more powerful opponent, and Philipse, for his part, publicly reprimanded Thomas for having the temerity to challenge his authority.[40]

Further to the south the Morris-Cosby rivalry spilled over into the New York City elections, in which Adolphe Philipse, another Cosby ally, and Cornelius Van Horne, a supporter of Morris's, squared off against each other in an election that attracted an unusually high number—55 percent—of the eligible voters. Cadwallader Colden, a conservative New Yorker who didn't have much use for either side in the rivalry, commented, "Mr. Philipse has carried it by 15 votes. Such a strugle I beleive was never [seen] in America and is now over with a few bloody noses. . . . The sick, the lame and the blind were all carried to vote. They were carried out of prison and out of the poor house to vote."[41] Although the ideological substance of the electoral contests in New York City remained just as murky as it did elsewhere in the colony, the members of the political elite of that city, beginning in the 1730s, were being forced to be ever more aggressive in recruiting the electorate to their side. By the 1740s the leaders of the principal opposing factions in New York City, now centered around differences between Chief Justice James DeLancey and Governor George Clinton, were using such devices as nominating caucuses and newspaper advertisements in order to assure the election of candidates favorable to their interest. As the DeLancey-Clinton rivalry gradually was transformed into a contest for power between the DeLancey and Livingston families (with a shifting cast of characters and interests at stake) during the 1750s and early 1760s, the supporters of those two factions escalated their attempts at organizing the electorate. Petition campaigns, newspaper pamphlet wars, and open town meetings became frequent occurrences in the politics of New York City. Even in that city, however, those jumps in voter interest and participation were only sporadic. At times, when rival factions were at peace, voter participation would drop dramatically, and indeed, many times even in New York City, assembly elections were decided without the necessity of a formal poll.

As rivalries between factions and families within the New York oligarchy increased, those oligarchs were often torn between the temptation to appeal to the populace in order to gain temporary advantage over their rivals and a recognition of the risks involved. Although the Morrisites would have been horrified to encounter a genuinely democratic insurgence, their campaign literature increasingly aimed at a popular audience. In the 1734 election they affirmed that "the Almighty made us equal all," and denounced the Cosby faction for its contempt for "those they call the Vulgar, the Mob, the herd of Mechanics."[42] This sort of rhetoric, though not seized and carried to its logical conclusion by the ordinary citizens who made up the New York electorate, nevertheless could not be freely issued without consequence. The Morrisite attention to the "public humor," their appeals to the artisans and mechanics for support against the actions of the governor, and their use of the press, pamphlets, and even petitions as a means of arousing public opinion would introduce important changes into the political process. The New York General Assembly, by agreeing in June 1737 to the minimally progressive step of publishing the names of those voting "aye" and "nay" on roll call votes was at least tacitly acknowledging the right of the people to monitor the activities of those who claimed to be representing them. Similarly, by the 1760s, in order to depict themselves as champions of the popular will, followers of James DeLancey, advocated opening the doors of the assembly to the general public so that ordinary citizens could observe the conduct of their political leaders.[43] Even if their advocacy was driven primarily by a desire for momentary advantage, it was nevertheless a sign that New York's politicians were being forced to pay some heed to the constituent power.

Although the conduct of politics in New York's assembly was profoundly affected by the increasingly bitter and public rivalry between the Livingston and DeLancey families that was infecting the politics of New York City, by and large the representatives to the assembly from the Hudson Valley counties and manors remained immune from the necessity of courting popular favor in the same aggressive ways that characterized politics in New York City. Even into the 1760s and 1770s elective as well as appointive offices in the Hudson Valley were generally either monopolized or at least dispensed by the great men. We should not conclude from this, however, that the political and social orders of New York rested on wholly consensual and voluntaristic understandings. The most compelling evidence attesting to the nonconsensual character of New York politics can be found not in the election records, but in the extralegal protest of Hudson Valley tenants against the economic policies of their landlords—landlords who served simultaneously as their political representatives.

The causes of tenant unrest in New York during the 1750s and 1760s have been extensively debated among historians, with a sharp line of division between those who see that unrest as a direct outgrowth of class conflict between the rich and the landless, and those who blame the conflict on the connivance of Massachusetts colonial officials in persuading western Massachusetts settlers to expand their movement westward even farther.[44] There is no question that most of the individuals resorting to extralegal protest against the New York manor lords were New Englanders moving into lands east of the Hudson; overwhelmingly, the longtime Dutch and German tenants who constituted the bulk of the residents on the manors were quiescent. Those westward-migrating settlers from Connecticut and Massachusetts had a much stronger tradition of private ownership of land and were distinctly less deferential and more cantankerous than their Dutch and German counterparts. One memoirist, Ann Grant, herself the daughter of a wealthy New York proprietor, was forcefully struck by their "litigious . . . vulgar [and insolent] manner" and claimed that "they flocked indeed so fast, to every unoccupied spot, that their malignant and envious spirit, their hatred of subordination . . . began to spread like a taint of infection."[45] It is clear as well that the New Englanders received some encouragement in their aggressive encroachment on the proprietors' lands. From 1750 onward the Massachusetts General Court started to press its conflicting boundary claims involving land lying within the Livingston and Van Rensselaerswyck manors in Albany County, and encouraged agents and land speculators to sell Massachusetts deeds to New York tenants on those manors. Moreover, royal officials such as Cadwallader Colden, motivated both by a sincere commitment to a more equitable distribution of land within the colony and by the desire to undercut the strength of their political opponents, were themselves eager to subject to scrutiny the more dubious of the great manor lords' claims to lands on the periphery of the colony. To confuse this business further, the overlapping claims of various Indian tribes, made even more ambiguous by the vagueness in so many of the deeds conveyed by Indians, created a climate of uncertainty that emboldened the aggressive New England settlers.[46]

However important those factors may have been in exacerbating tenant unrest in the eastern region of the Hudson Valley, the root cause of that unrest was the desire of westward-moving New Englanders to achieve for themselves the goal of independence, a goal most closely associated with the ownership of property. That the manor lords, through a combination of paternalism and subtle coercion, had been able to keep most of their New York tenants reasonably content for much of the history of the colony was hardly much comfort to aggressive and assertive New Englanders who, looking at the vast tracts of uninhabited and contested land on the eastern periphery of the manors, believed they had a right to use and, eventually, own portions of that land.[47]

Beginning around 1750, all of these forces began to bubble to the surface, producing isolated, but nevertheless ominous displays of popular discontent. Occurring most frequently in the eastern sections of Albany and Dutchess counties, the protests sometimes surfaced in local courts, where settlers sued landlords for legal title to the lands on which they were squatting, but sometimes also took the form of attacks on the landlords' properties—the cutting of timber or the occupation of additional property belonging to the landlords. There were at least three parties to these conflicts—the landlords on one side, aggressive New Englanders on the other, with most long-term tenants who were generally satisfied with the terms of their existing leases either siding with the landlords or, at least, trying to stay out of the fray. But the landlords were plainly worried. Robert Livingston Jr., in spite of his years of dominance over the economic and political structures of the lands encompassed by his manor, increasingly displayed his uneasiness over the restiveness of those over whom he ruled. Writing in 1752, he acknowledged that the aggressive behavior of the New Englanders "gives me trouble, [and] makes my Tenants Insolent," and a year later, as the situation was worsening, he noted, "Those folks are Still daily troubleing me & my Tennents, Some of the Latter are Indeed near as bad as the N. England people . . . I fear the Infection will very Soon be general and then no man that has an Estate in this Province or perhaps in North America, will be Safe."[48] Although some of the danger to Livingston's authority abated, in other parts of New York, particularly on the Van Rensselaer lands at Claverack, the situation continued to deteriorate. By the winter of 1755 there were frequent instances of houses and fields being burned, violent confrontations between local officials and armed gangs of squatters, with at least three fatalities as a result.[49]

Much of the agitation quieted during the period of the Seven Years' War, but by 1766 the conflicts between landlords and squatters were renewed with increased intensity. Once again the principal sites were those parts of Albany and Dutchess counties that shared a border with Massachusetts and Connecticut. The outbreaks of violence began in Dutchess County, where landlords had been taking the offensive by asserting more vigorously their claims—often in courts of law that they themselves controlled—to lands in the easternmost regions of their patents. Between the fall of 1765 and the spring of 1766 mobs ranging in size from one hundred to five hundred men roved around the eastern parts of Dutchess County threatening ten-

ants loyal to the manor lords, burning barns, and holding extralegal tri-
bunals that denounced the manor lords and their lackeys and upheld their
right to gain title to their lands. Mindful of similar protests in America's
cities over British taxation, the protesters in upstate New York liked to think
of themselves as rural "Sons of Liberty," and in some cases self-consciously
sought a connection with their urban counterparts.[50] Robert Livingston Jr.,
who feared for the security of his holdings during the unrest of the 1750s,
once again faced the threat of armed resistance against his authority. In
June of 1767 some five hundred "levellers" marched toward his manor
house threatening to "murder the Lord of the Manor and level his house"
unless he would sign leases agreeable to them. In fact, nearly all of the protesters were unarmed, and they were driven off by an armed force of some
forty supporters mobilized by Livingston's son, Walter.[51]

Similar instances of unrest surfaced in other parts of Albany and
Dutchess counties, but that unrest never coalesced into a cohesive movement of rural protest, nor did those who styled themselves rural "Sons of
Liberty" ever succeed in making common cause with their counterparts in
the city. Many of those most conspicuous in their roles in the rural unrest
were arrested, and most of those were punished with an assortment of fines
and prison sentences. One of those perceived as a principal ringleader,
William Prendergast, was indicted for high treason, convicted, and sentenced to death by a Dutchess County jury, but the judges in the case,
themselves closely tied to the manor lords but also wishing an end to the violence, asked King George III to issue a pardon. Acting on the advice of
the Earl of Shelburne, who argued that leniency toward the protests would
"have a better effect in recalling those mistaken People to their Duty than
the most rigorous punishment," George III granted the pardon, and the
agrarian protests flickered out.[52]

The rural protests of the 1750s and 1760s were complicated affairs, and
it is plain that not all—or, indeed, not even most—of the tenants on the
manors shared the sense of grievance displayed by those participating in
the extralegal action. In the 1766 action against Livingston Manor, for example, most of the long-term tenants sided with the manor lord, a fact not
lost on the insurgents. Lacking a cohesive base of support or a coherent political platform, the protests faded in intensity. But the essential grievances
underlying them—the inequity of a land system that gave to a few men
enormous wealth while denying to the great mass of the citizens that most
American of values—an independent freehold—would not disappear.

Certainly the men at whom the tenants' grievances were directed—the
manor lords themselves—found it difficult to maintain a complacent view
of their authority following the riots. In spite of the fact that only a small
number of the rioters during the disturbances of the 1750s—perhaps no
more than eight, and most of those New Englanders—were actually tenants
on his manor, Robert Livingston Jr., was nevertheless deeply shaken by the

experience. As Cynthia Kierner has observed, the land riots threatened the values and traditions that Livingston and those like him most cherished: their property rights, their family honor, and their sense of a natural and legitimate social hierarchy. The concepts of family honor and social hierarchy were essential ingredients of Livingston's conception of himself as a political leader, as a man who earned the deference of his constituents not only by his economic power but by his care and concern for those living under his power. In a series of letters to his family and in petitions to the New York and Massachusetts legislatures, Livingston defended not only his family's legal title to their lands but also their rectitude, fairness, and generosity in dealing with their tenants over the long history of their domain over the land. He called attention to his own benevolence to those tenants who had remained loyal to him during the riots of the early 1750s, and his cousin Robert Livingston of Clermont issued a public defense of the manor system, claiming that it promoted industry and commerce by encouraging tenants to produce more than they would if they owned the land outright.[53]

There was of course a good deal of self-deception as well as self-righteousness in this defense of entrenched privilege; men like the Livingstons were quite adept at evoking principles of family honor whether faced with insurgents from below or jockeying with members of other prominent families for power and preferment. Political divisions in New York, more than in any other colony in America, tended to revolve around family allegiances, and surely some of that tendency was fueled by the obsession with family honor that men like the Livingstons nurtured and trumpeted.

In spite of increasing signs of election-day tumult in New York City and sporadic agrarian unrest in the eastern Hudson Valley, the political culture of prerevolutionary New York was remarkably resistant to change. In the first instance it was an extraordinarily provincial and localized one, even by the standards of an insular, provincial world. The very structure of the relationship among local, provincial, and royal agencies of government allowed for a peculiarity of local political development—some influenced by the Dutch, some by the English, some by amalgams of the two—and gave to each locality an independence of action that greatly exceeded the norm even among other, highly parochial American colonial entities. Nearly all of those activities that brought New Yorkers into contact with their government—care of the poor, the building and maintenance of roads, the licensing of taverns, the probating of wills, and the prosecution of civil and criminal justice—were performed at the local level.[54] All of this reinforced a political culture that gave extraordinary autonomy to political oligarchs such as William Johnson or Henry Beekman or Robert Livingston Jr. to rule their own domains as they chose. Political alliances and conflicts with colonial governors would come and go, but those political skirmishes rarely threatened the security of their reign over their vast local domains.

To be sure, local oligarchs like Johnson, in protecting their own local interests at the provincial level, also frequently used their influence for the good of their constituents. One of the notable features of the legislation passed by the New York legislature in the eighteenth century was the "place-specific" character of much of it. Unlike the legislatures in Pennsylvania or Virginia, that in New York consistently concerned itself with passing legislation to benefit single counties—the killing of wolves in Albany or the safeguarding of sheep in Kings or a law for Hempstead to prevent rams from running loose and indiscriminately impregnating local sheep. This sort of intense localism was particularly apparent when the assembly acted to apportion taxation in the colony. There were constant battles in the legislature over what the appropriate tax quota for each county should be, with each seeking to push as much of the burden as possible onto other counties. Moreover, since a county's tax burden was then distributed according to a quota system to the towns and precincts within each county, this would in turn provide another opportunity for local officials to argue over who was paying too much and who too little.[55] Though the local oligarchs of the Hudson River valley fell easily into the language of republican virtue in defending their claims to power and in justifying their actions in behalf of their interests, their aggressive use of power for their own local ends raises questions about whether the classical republican aims of serving the public good were being honored in this system. The answer may hinge on a perennial issue in either democratic or oligarchic systems—the extent of the territory over which one seeks to define the public good. The bitter factionalism inherent in New York politics suggests that most residents of that colony had not reached agreement on the geographical extent of the public good. Their primary allegiances were as subjects of the Crown and as residents in a particular locality; they expended much less energy in thinking about the public good of the colony as a whole.

A second notable feature of the political culture of New York was the extent—more than any political entity in America except for perhaps South Carolina—to which its leaders committed themselves self-consciously to English norms. Perhaps initially the result of the cultural need to excise Dutch influence, New Yorkers used the English gentry as their models for proper behavior. The frequent use of titles—from Sir William Johnson's real one to the designation of Robert Livingston as "King" Robert to the frequent references to the other "lords" of the Hudson Valley manors—attests to the self-consciousness with which many of New York's oligarchs regarded matters of rank and to the attentiveness with which they sought to reinforce their superior position in society.[56] Indeed, the very existence of the manors, granted to just a few favorites of the early New York governors in an attempt to bolster their support from key individuals, was itself resonant of earlier, feudal times. The political consequences of those grants, giving to the manors special political privileges, including their own representatives to the assembly, were strikingly similar to those enjoyed by the manor lords in the English pocket boroughs.

New York was not England, however, and the New York Assembly was not Parliament, and thus the local oligarchs of New York sometimes had to try even harder to demonstrate that they had been successful in integrating the social and political authority that marked a true gentry man. In the classical republican notion of a properly deferential society, the very function of an election was to give the townspeople the opportunity to recognize and ratify the superior virtue of their social and political betters. When Robert Livingston Jr. traveled to Albany in 1759 with some eighty voters pledged to follow his lead in the elections to be held there, he was looking forward to putting on a visible display of his social and political authority. Imagine his chagrin when the candidates he was backing refused to call for a polling of the assembled citizens. They had automatically won the election without opposition, but Livingston had been cheated out of his chance to demonstrate his power and authority.[57]

Similarly, it was precisely because of the intense factionalism that so often rocked New York politics that members of the provincial General Assembly were so concerned with reinforcing the dignity of their offices. Although they did not hesitate to sling mud at one another, they were quick to take offense when someone from outside took aim at them. Thus, in 1756, when the *New York Gazette* published a letter complaining about their inattention to conditions in Dutchess and Ulster counties, the members of the Assembly passed a resolution finding both the author of the letter, the Reverend Hezekial Watkins, and the publisher of the *Gazette*, James Parker (who also happened to be the official printer for the assembly), guilty of a "high Misdemeanour and a Contempt of the Authority of this House." Their offense, according to the assemblymen, was to have disseminated opinions "calculated to irritate the People of this Colony against their Representatives"; both Parker and Watkins spent a week in jail for their offense and were released only after they humbly confessed to their transgressions and "promise[d] to be more circumspect for the Future, and humbly beg[ged] the Pardon of the Honourable House."[58]

In 1758 Samuel Townshend, a justice of the peace in Queen's County, sent a letter to the Speaker of the Assembly asking for legislative relief for certain refugees quartered on Long Island. The assembly took umbrage, passing a resolution stating that Townshend's description of the refugees' condition reflected on the "Honour, Justice, and Authority" of the House, and sentenced him to prison for committing a "high Misdemeanour and a most daring Insult." Townshend, languishing in jail, thought the better of his request and apologized for any slight he may have conveyed, after which he was discharged with a stern reprimand from the Speaker.[59] Given the treatment received by Samuel Townshend, it should perhaps not surprise us that relatively few localities in the colony used the legislative petition as a device for registering constituent concern about the conduct of public polity. Unlike the legislature of Virginia, which received nearly a hundred petitions annually, and that of Massachusetts, which regularly received more than two hundred petitions annually in the mid-eighteenth century, that of New York received only about a dozen each year, and these most often were of a routine nature relating to matters of local public improvement.[60] Whether out of fear of giving offense or out of confidence that their manor oligarchs would look after their needs in any case, the citizens of New York were moved only rarely to try to speak directly to the legislature via a petition.

Although the abortive land riots of the 1750s and 1760s made at least a few of the manor lords of New York uneasy, for the most part their political power remained unchallenged. As we have already seen, there were a number of instances in the colony—particularly in New York City and environs—in which competition among great men resulted in a temporary mobilization of the electorate and the turning out of office of one wealthy oligarch and the installation of another. Genuine electoral mobilizations against the great men were few and far between. In the wake of the land riots, however, there were at least a few signs of an emboldened electorate. Henry Beekman, who had for many years dominated the political and economic life of Dutchess County, had arranged in 1761 for his son-in-law, the soon-to-be justice of the Supreme Court, Robert R. Livingston, as well as his cousin Henry Livingston, to succeed him as representatives to the assembly from Dutchess. Beekman was successful in dictating the line of succession in the 1761 election, but in the next election, in 1768, at a time of increasing popular unrest over the manor lords, he may have been pushing his luck. Robert R. Livingston was especially vulnerable, for he was not a resident of Dutchess County, and he was a lawyer at a time when antilawyer sentiment in the region was reaching an all-time high. Robert R. Livingston's opponent in the election, Dirck Brinckerhoff, was neither a radical voice of a discontented tenantry nor a tool of the manor lords, but rather an upwardly mobile middle-class farmer who was steadily increasing his influence in both the economic and political life of the county. Henry Beekman's tenants deserted the two Livingstons in the 1768 election, voting overwhelmingly for Brinckerhoff and his running mate, Leonard Van Kleeck. As Cadwallader Colden saw it, Livingston "had so far lost the esteem of the freeholders in that County that he gave up before half the Freeholders then present had given in their votes, tho' he had everything in his favour, which power could give him."[61] A twelve-year-old boy, William Moore Jr. of Oswego, penned a poem on the occasion:

> One night in my slumbers, I saw in a dream
> Judge Livingston's party contriving a scheme
> To set up great papers and give some great bounty
> For to be assemblymen in Dutchess County

But Leonard and Derrick are both chosen men
The Livingstons won't get a vote to their ten
So pull down your papers, talk no more of bounty
You can't be assemblymen in Dutchess County[62]

"Everything in his favour, which power could give him." These words most aptly characterize the extraordinary advantages normally enjoyed by the Livingstons, Van Renssaeler's, Beekmans, and Johnsons, and for every election in which an upstart like Brinckerhoff might pull the rug out from under his wealthier and more prestigious neighbor, there were dozens in which the powers of the manor lords went unchallenged. Yet Livingston's defeat, coming when it did, as citizens across America were voicing their concerns about representation with greater force and precision, must have been unnerving to his fellow oligarchs. Even the extraordinary power of New York's landed elite would prove insufficient to enable those privileged men to maintain their exclusive grasp on politics indefinitely.

Chapter 5

Complacent Oligarchs
The Merchant Planters of South Carolina

If the political culture of New York was one characterized by often bitter factionalism among the colony's elite but one also in which members of that elite enjoyed remarkable security in their political positions and significant insulation from popular pressures, the politics of South Carolina can be characterized as both elite-dominated and, with only occasional exceptions, factionless. William Bull, Henry Laurens, and Christopher Gadsden—three of the most eminent members of the pre-revolutionary South Carolina political elite—had different beginnings, but for that part of their adulthood occurring before the outbreak of the Revolution, they enjoyed nearly unlimited access to political power within the constituencies that they served.

William Bull II was a third-generation South Carolinian who could trace his roots in the colony back to the founding. His grandfather, Stephen Bull, had arrived in 1670, the year of the establishment of South Carolina as a proprietary colony. Accompanied by nine servants, he was immediately appointed a deputy to the proprietors and enjoyed a place on the Grand Council of the colony. Stephen Bull built his fortune through trade with the Indians of the region. By the time of his death, in 1706, the family was moving out of the Indian trade and into rice production, a move made possible in part by the elder Bull's acquisition of choice tracts of land from the Indians. His son, William Bull I, extended the reputation and fortunes of the father. He served in the Commons House from 1706 until 1719, leaving that body when he was appointed a deputy proprietor and member of the council in that year. When the proprietary government was replaced by a royal government in 1721, he made the transition smoothly, serving on the new Royal Council from 1721 until 1737, in that year becoming acting governor and, in the following year, lieutenant governor, a post he held until his death in 1755. All the while he continued his family's involvement in Indian affairs, an interest that fueled further increases in the family land-holdings.[1]

Born in 1710 at Ashley Hall, his father's 1,100-acre plantation on the river of the same name, William Bull II would receive the finest education that money and his parents' social status could buy. At a time when few Carolinians ventured abroad for their education, William II and his brother, Stephen, attended Westminster School, two of just a handful of provincial Americans to attend that training ground for the sons of the British aristocracy at any time in the eighteenth century.[2] William II continued his education in the Netherlands, receiving a medical degree from the University of Leiden, probably the foremost center for medical training in the world. Returning to Charleston in 1734, he began a career as physician, planter, and political leader that exceeded even that of his illustrious father. He was first elected to the South Carolina lower house in 1736, was elevated to the speakership in 1740 at the tender age of thirty, and served nearly continuously until his appointment to the Royal Council in 1748. In 1759 he was made lieutenant governor, serving in that post until the outbreak of the Revolution. He served during much of that time—1760–61, 1764–66, 1768, 1769–71, and 1773–75—as acting governor of the colony as well. Through it all he made certain that his family's wealth and influence expanded. His estate at the time of the Revolution—which included over 20,000 acres on several different plantations, 284 slaves, several warehouses and other real estate in the town of Charlestown—was worth something in excess of £60,000, a significant fortune by any standards in the eighteenth century.[3] Frequent intermarriage between members of the Bull family and the offspring of the Draytons, Middletons, and Pinckneys created a formidable network of wealth, social, and political power.[4]

Henry Laurens was a third-generation Carolinian, too, but he was the son of a saddler. His father, John, was, however, very successful, and by the time of his death in 1747 he was able to give his son a decent patrimony. Henry Laurens also journeyed to England for a part of his education, not to Westminster or Eton, but to the merchant house of John Crokatt, where he not only learned some basic business skills but also developed important commercial contacts. He returned home to Charleston in 1747, arriving there just four days after his father's death. As eldest son he was the recipient of his father's patrimony, and, joining in partnership with two other Charleston merchants, George Austin and George Appleby, he moved swiftly and purposefully to become one of Charleston's leading merchants, building his fortune on commissions earned in the export of rice and indigo and the importation of slaves, indentured servants, and wine. Like William Bull II, he did not content himself with mercantile success alone; ever mindful not only of the pecuniary opportunities provided by landed wealth but also of the status and dignity that was accorded to owners of fine plantations, Laurens began to acquire land and plantations. Beginning in 1762, with a three-thousand-acre tract on the northern bank of the Cooper River just above Charleston, Henry Laurens would acquire several plantations and upwards of twenty thousand acres in both South Carolina and the rapidly developing colony of Georgia.[5]

Although he lacked the political patrimony enjoyed by William Bull II,

Laurens's wealth and influence within Charleston provided a reliable substitute; he was first elected to the Commons House in 1757 and was regularly reelected right up to the time of the Revolution. Unlike Bull, who moved skillfully, if precariously, between the interests of the Crown and the province for nearly the whole of his career, Laurens was generally identified as a defender of the interests of the province, though frequently with a conservatism that caused some to wonder where his sympathies really lay. As was the case for William Bull, his extensive landholdings permitted him to run for office in multiple constituencies, sometimes simultaneously. Thus, in 1762 he was elected to the House unopposed from the parish of St. Michael, while running at the same time in Charleston's other parish, St. Philip; he could easily have secured election in that parish as well, but his friends there, certain of his election in St. Michael, felt free to support other candidates of nearly equal wealth and prestige. In subsequent years he did in fact serve dual constituencies simultaneously, running unopposed as candidate for representative in both St. Michael and St. Phillip for most of the period from 1775 to 1785.[6]

Christopher Gadsden's life story provides us with some interesting variations on the same theme. Born in the same year as Laurens, he was the son of a captain in the British merchant fleet who later became port collector for Charleston. He spent most of his childhood in England, where he acquired a mastery of Greek and Latin far superior to that achieved by most young Carolinians sent to England to obtain the patina of European culture. At age sixteen he came back to Charleston and then on to Philadelphia where he served an apprenticeship in the merchant house of Thomas Lawrence. During that time, his father died, leaving him land, slaves, and cash. Following his apprenticeship, he spent two years as a purser on a British ship and then came back to Charleston where he began his career as merchant and planter. Between 1748 and the outbreak of the Revolution, Gadsden built a business based on wholesaling, retailing, factorage, money lending, and land speculation; he owned five merchant ships, his own wharf, and several warehouses on the northern edge of Charleston, as well as stores at Cheraws and Georgetown. Like Laurens and Bull, he enjoyed success within Charleston that enabled him to branch out to establish the personae of a successful planter. In 1757 he began to build a plantation on a 1,300-acre tract on the Pee Dee River, and he added other plantations to his domain in subsequent years. By the time of the Revolution he had ninety slaves working on his plantations and another twenty-four serving him in his impressive town house on Front Street, just outside Charleston.[7] Gadsden entered the lower house of assembly in the same year as Laurens, 1757, representing the same parish, St. Philip. Like Laurens he would sit nearly continuously in that body up until the Revolution, alternating, and sometimes combining, his service as a representative of St. Philip, St. Paul, and St. Michael.

Figure 10. Henry Laurens. Painted by John Singleton Copley, Courtesy the National Portrait Gallery, Smithsonian Institution. Transfer from the National Gallery of Art; gift of Andrew W. Mellon, 1942.

William Bull II was a man who enjoyed influence and power in both royal and provincial agencies of government, managing for the most part to retain the friendship and support of fellow provincials even after ascending to the lieutenant governorship. Henry Laurens made his political career in the lower house, the principal agency of provincial power, but generally worked assiduously to stay on good terms with royal officials. Christopher Gadsden, on the other hand, was from the time he entered the lower house, a steadfast defender of popular rights, often placing himself in public opposition to royal officials in the process. But however much Gadsden may have perceived himself as representing the populace, his political career, like that of Bull and Laurens, was founded on some very traditional assumptions about political leadership.

Virtually every historian who has written about eighteenth-century South Carolina has commented on the spirit of harmony that seemed to prevail within the political order of that colony. It was a harmony, many of those historians have maintained, ensured by the combination of conscientious leadership by those prominent citizens who dominated public office in the colony and of citizen disinterest in the political process, a disinterest born in part of age-old habits of deference to individuals of superior social rank. In the words of Richard Waterhouse, "throughout the period of royal government, South Carolina's elite succeeded in maintaining a responsible, responsive, and inclusive political system." Speaking of the operations of South Carolina's lower house of assembly, Eugene Sirmans concluded that "the Commons House truly represented the interests of the people of South Carolina."[8]

While everything we know about the structure of eighteenth-century South Carolina politics supports the proposition that its political culture was characterized by elite domination and citizen disinterest, we should perhaps hesitate before accepting the characterization of the political process in the colony as "responsible, responsive, and inclusive," for nearly all of the testimony on which historians have relied to support that characterization has come from those very men—the Bulls, Laurenses, and Gadsdens—who so easily dominated the politics of their colony. Although those seemingly self-confident oligarchs may have assumed the mantle of leadership with apparent ease, we must at least attempt to look more closely at their relationship with the people whom they claimed to serve. We must also inquire about the ways in which the existence of an unfree black majority—in many areas of the eastern coastal plain an *overwhelming* majority—shaped the attitudes of all white South Carolinians toward the proper mode of governance.

Those who laid claim to social and political authority in South Carolina, in common with political leaders in every colony in the South, looked self-consciously to England for their models of correct behavior. But perhaps nowhere in America was that Anglophilic tendency more pronounced than in South Carolina. As John Drayton observed at the end of the eighteenth century, "Before the American war, the citizens of Carolina were too much prejudiced in favour of British manners, customs and knowledge, to imagine that elsewhere, than in England, anything of advantage could be obtained."[9] If there were any single English attribute to which South Carolina's social and political leaders clung most tenaciously, it was the belief in hierarchy. Boston's Josiah Quincy perhaps put the matter most bluntly in 1773, describing the society as being "divided into opulent and lordly planters, poor and spiritless peasants, and vile slaves," but virtually every visitor to the colony noted much the same thing. Johann David Schoepf, while acknowledging that the "laws of South Carolina are no more favorable than those of the other states to distinctions of rank," nevertheless observed that "even if there are not class distinctions as such, it is observable that . . . certain members of society being more nearly and closely associated, . . . [are] tacitly ascribed more or less superiority." Those at the top of South Carolina society, Schoepf noted, "in many respects think and act precisely as do the nobility in other countries."[10]

The process of emulation and re-creation of English values of gentility and hierarchy began with education. As was the case to the north in Virginia, those who aspired to elite status in South Carolina looked to England as the source of a proper education for their children. In the early years of the colony's history only a few could afford to send their children to England; before 1750 only sixteen South Carolinians were educated at the Inns of Court, four at Oxford, and none at Cambridge. But after 1750 more and more young South Carolina gentlemen whose families were more affluent and whose social aspirations to replicate English gentry culture were more sharply defined would echo William Bull's dictate that it was only in England that a "learned education" was possible and would make their way across the Atlantic for their education. From 1760 until the end of the eighteenth century South Carolina would consistently send more of its young men to the Inns of Court or Oxford or Cambridge than any other colony, including Virginia.[11]

In contrast to the advantages of those few young men at the top of Carolina society who enjoyed the privilege of a proper English education was the meagerness of educational opportunities in the colony for those who could not afford to travel across the Atlantic. The devotion of South Carolina's ruling elite to English ways meant as well that they devoted much less time or money on education at home—either public or private—than any colony in America except perhaps Georgia. As we have seen, Virginia's political leaders were similarly disinclined to commit public funds to support the education of their young, but that colony did manage to generate an ethic that encouraged private efforts—most often in the form of freelance tutors, men of admittedly dubious credentials, who offered their services to middling as well as affluent planter families. Although there were a few publicly and privately supported grammar schools in Charleston and in some of the adjacent parishes, most education of young boys and girls, even at the elementary level, occurred privately at home, or not at all. Even those who may have been willing to invest in a tutor may not always have grasped the intellectual spirit of the enterprise. One planter, interviewing a prospective tutor about his ability to instill proper discipline in his charges, asked the young man if he could "drive well," suggesting perhaps that the mentality of those charged with running a slave-based plantation may not have been wholly consonant with the business of cultivating lively minds.[12]

What South Carolinians saved by not building schools and colleges, they used in building social clubs and a wide variety of other entertainments. Although nearly all of the wealth created by South Carolina's social elite in the eighteenth century was created through the cultivation and marketing of agricultural products—rice and indigo in particular—the men and women who profited from that agricultural enterprise sought not to re-create English country life but, rather, devoted nearly their full energies to re-creating the pleasures of urban society. Charleston was decidedly not London, but in following English fashion, entertainment, and manners, many Charleston residents seemed bent on proving that it could be held in the same regard. By 1770 they had set up a host of social clubs—St. Andrew's, St. George's, the Amicable Society—all modeled after London clubs; theaters, featuring contemporary English plays of course; concerts, with English composers preferred; horse race courses, all bearing names of English race courses; or if one had a taste for slightly gamier English diversions—bearbaiting, for instance—then one could go to Ashley Ferry to find amusement.[13] Among it all there was a constant round of private parties, for if Charleston could not replicate London in the scale of its public entertainments, its residents could try to equal their London counterparts in the realm of private hospitality.

This round of entertainment and party-going provoked a variety of comment from those who observed it. Johann Bolzius, visiting Charleston in 1751, was not pleased, commenting that "the splendor, lust and opulence there has gone almost to the limit." Others, less averse to earthly pleasures, were more admiring of the degree to which Carolinians had been able to transplant European culture to the American wilderness. A young German, Johann David Schoepf, traveling through Carolina after the Revolution, noted approvingly a "finer manner of life" there than elsewhere in America. "So luxury in Carolina has made the greatest advance, and their manner of life, dress, equipages, furniture, everything denotes a higher degree of taste and love of show, and less frugality than in the northern provinces."[14]

As was the case everywhere in provincial America, the anglicization of the ruling elite in South Carolina, purposeful and self-conscious as it may have been, nevertheless fell short of reproducing the English ideal in a number of striking ways. South Carolina's aristocrats were nearly uniformly parvenus—only a handful could claim significant wealth or family back in England, and much of the newness of their wealth and superficiality of their manners showed—in their imperfect command of Greek and Latin or in the newness, even rawness, of the plantations that they had hacked out of the Carolina wilderness.

Perhaps some of the impulse of South Carolina's planter and merchant elite to live for the moment stemmed from the fact that their life expectancy was short. Although less disastrous than that experienced by the planter class in the West Indies, the demographic conditions on low-country plantations in South Carolina earned for the colony the reputation as a decidedly unhealthy place, yet another reason why wealthy planters tended to be absent from their plantations as much as possible, particularly in the summer months, preferring to live in their homes in Charleston whenever they had a chance. In the words of Johann David Schoepf, "Carolina is in the spring a paradise, in the summer a hell, and in the autumn a hospital." Childhood mortality in some low country areas may have been as high as 80 percent well into the eighteenth century, a fact that helps explain why much of the colony's population growth during the first half of the eighteenth century came from immigration and not from natural increase.[15]

There were other, more compelling reasons that drove South Carolina's elite to such lengths in their imitation of English ways. First, the economic well-being of merchants and planters alike in South Carolina was tied to the mother country, whether in the form of the economic incentives that England offered for growing rice and indigo or in the important connections with English merchants upon whom they depended for their livelihood. Even more important, the South Carolinians, more than their counterparts elsewhere in the South, were driven by a pressing need to prove to themselves and to others that they did indeed constitute a legitimate ruling class, one that was owed the deference and respect due such a class in any properly ordered hierarchical society. Some of the desperation in that attempt was the result of the uncertainty of their own claims to gentry status, but perhaps an even more profound source of uncertainty lay in the people from whom they were commanding obedience and respect. In spite of reasonably easy access to land in the Carolina up-country and on the frontier, access to the two ingredients most important to economic success—low-country land and the slave labor to exploit that land—was limited. The result was the emergence of a relatively small planter and merchant class in the low country that benefited from either the cultivation or marketing of staple crops, coexisting with growing numbers of people in the up-country and frontier whose scale of operation was not only smaller but also of a materially different kind. As that differentiation increased, the challenges posed to traditional, deferential, patron-client relations based on reciprocity of interest became more formidable.

As was the case in other southern colonies, there was another form of differentiation that was even more strikingly dramatic. The people whose labor produced the profits in the rice and indigo trade were overwhelmingly African and unfree. William Byrd of Virginia, when he likened himself to "one of the patriarchs of old," and boasted of the "bond-men and bond-women" over whom he kept careful and benevolent watch, was able for perhaps a moment to delude himself into believing that his black slaves were a form of substitute English peasantry, but the low-country South Carolina planters, surrounded and outnumbered by slaves—in some regions by as much as seven or eight to one—could never sustain that fiction. To be sure, they tried, creating a social ideal of genteel Anglophilia—often based in their Charleston home away from home, comfortably removed from the sight of toiling slaves. But nearly all of those merchant-planter oligarchs, at one time or another in their lives acknowledged the tenuousness of the social system they had created.[16]

William Bull II, who was himself nearly a casualty of the Stono Rebellion of 1739, regularly referred to the slaves of his colony as "our domestic enemy"; a year following the rebellion he took the lead in securing passage of the Negro Act of 1740, a comprehensive set of regulations that restricted the movement and assembly of slaves within the colony. Johann David Schoepf, in his otherwise admiring portrayal of South Carolina society and customs, could not escape the conclusion that "the condition of the Carolina negro-slaves is in general harder and more troublous than that of their northern brethren." He was struck by the "wretched" conditions of their lives and by a labor regimen that was "capricious and often tyrannical." "There is less concern [in Carolina]," he wrote, "as to their moral betterment, education, and instruction" than in any of the other slave states.[17]

Henry Laurens, who was sufficiently uncomfortable not only with the inhumanity of the slave trade but also with the danger that the large black majority posed to his own physical security, made a conscious decision beginning in 1762 to divest himself of that part of his business involved in the slave trade. Such was the commitment of his fellow planters to the slave system that Laurens was publicly attacked by at least one of them for abandoning the trade out of a misplaced "goodness of heart," and he had to go to great lengths in his public utterances to convince people that he had gotten out of the business only because the press of other business was too heavy to enable him to pursue the slave trade profitably.[18]

The social authority and prestige that South Carolina's planters and merchants so craved carried with it corollary responsibilities in the realm of politics and public service. In nearly every other colony in America the foundation of both social and political authority was laid at the local level, in local economic relationships and in local institutions of government. In most, but not all, of those societies, economic power, social authority, and political authority were spread across many localities covering a wide expanse of geographical terrain. In South Carolina, however, economic power and social and political authority were to a remarkable extent concentrated in the seaport city of Charleston; as a result Charleston has been likened to a city-state.[19] The vast portion of the colony's economic life—from the staple crops produced for export in the hinterland to goods imported into the colony from abroad—passed through that one city. Not only did the merchants who controlled that trade live full-time in the city but the most prominent planters of low-country South Carolina also spent much of their time there, seeking out the more active social life of the city and staying on their farms in the hinterland only when the pressing business of their plantations required that they do so. Similarly, virtually all of the vital institutions of government in the colony—the governor's office, the Royal Council, the lower house of assembly, and virtually all of the functioning judicial agencies—operated out of Charleston. Those agencies of local government that were so important in other parts of America—the town meeting or the county court—never developed in an effective way in South Carolina.

Provisions for the establishment of local institutions of government were peculiarly absent from the plans of the original proprietors, and though a revised version of the Fundamental Constitutions of 1682 ordered the governor to begin to lay out counties and provide for county courts, successive proprietary governors never followed through on those plans. Upon the conversion of South Carolina to royal government in 1720, the colony's first royal governor, Francis Nicholson, announced his plans for the establishment of local institutions similar to those existing elsewhere in British North America, but those plans were successfully opposed by Charleston merchants and lawyers on the grounds that the local courts thus established would fall under the control of local planters, making it more difficult than it already had been to collect debts from the chronically cash-poor planters. The effect of their successful opposition to the establishment of county courts was not only to stifle the emergence of a large cadre of experienced local officials responsible for the administration of government and justice but also to concentrate most of the legal business in the colony in the hands of a small number of Charleston-based attorneys, who, through their control of the provincial courts located there, assumed the legal powers that had been dispersed to local officials in others part of the Anglo-American world.[20]

Over the course of the years the assembly did take some modest steps toward assuring the administration of local justice, setting up county courts in Craven, Colleton, and Granville counties, and two precinct courts in Berkeley County, outside Charleston. At the same time Governor Nicholson also persuaded the assembly to pass a law creating local districts for the construction and repair of roads and bridges and another law incorporating the town of Charleston. In fact, none of these reforms succeeded; the Charleston Incorporation Act was disallowed by the Privy Council on the grounds that it placed extra burdens of taxation on the citizens of the town; the county and precinct courts were discredited because of a controversy over the emission of paper money in the mid-1720s and were closed altogether shortly thereafter; and the local road commissions, though they survived on paper, never proved adequate to their assigned tasks.[21]

In the absence of effective county courts, the governor of South Carolina did appoint justices of the peace, but unlike their Virginia counterparts, their authority—both social and legal—was modest. Governor James Glen complained in 1749 that the office of justice of the peace had so little esteem that it was difficult to persuade anyone to accept appointment as a justice, and there were frequent complaints about the technical and legal incompetence of those who tried to perform the duties of the office. A grand jury investigating the activities of the justices in 1737 concluded that all too often they did not perform the duties expected of them and that the office had, in general, "become contemptible."[22]

The only meaningful institutions of local government in the colony were the parishes of the Church of England, administered by two churchwardens and six vestrymen, who were elected every Easter Monday by the voters of each parish. Most parish officers did little more than repair church buildings and ensure that their churchwardens carried out their legal responsibilities to oversee elections to the assembly. Moreover, since the population of the South Carolina up-country and backcountry was increasingly made up of dissenters and unchurched, the weak claim to representativeness on the part of the already weak parish governments was made all the more tenuous.

While much of the feebleness of local government seemed to pass unnoticed, the highly centralized character of the colony's judicial system did bring complaints from outlying areas. The one provision in the legal code that had doomed the county courts was that allowing plaintiffs in any civil suit to choose the site at which the case would be heard; since most plaintiffs were creditors who lived in Charleston, the effect of this act was to cripple the already frail system of county courts that was only haltingly emerging anyway. While the judicial system that resulted—consisting of a Court of General Sessions, a Court of Common Pleas, and a Chancery Court, all sitting in Charleston—may have pleased Charleston merchants and those low-country planters who spent most of their time in Charleston anyway, it was becoming increasingly clear, particularly as population increased in the western regions of the colony during the 1740s and 1750s, that the system was not serving the public interest. The assembly received a constant stream of petitions between 1750 and 1763 about the unfair centralization of judicial authority in Charleston, but the members of the Commons House, nearly all from Charleston, steadfastly ignored those complaints. However much Charleston's planter-merchant-lawyer classes may have concurred on their fitness and responsiveness as a ruling class, at least some on the Carolina frontier begged to differ. The outspoken backcountry Anglican preacher Charles Woodmason, noted the paradox imbedded in the low-country's "principled" opposition to the Stamp Act: "Lo," he wrote, "such are the Men who bounce, and make such Noise about Liberty! Liberty! Freedom! Property! Rights! Privileges! And what not; And at the same time keep half their fellow Subjects in a State of Slavery."[23]

South Carolinians called their lower house of assembly the Commons House, and that designation accurately reflected their own aspirations for that body—a provincial version of the English House of Commons in which they, the provincial equivalents of the ruling gentry of England, would possess the same constitutional rights and command the same respect as their counterparts who served in the House of Commons. As House Speaker John Lloyd put it in 1733, "This colony was settled by English subjects—by a people from England herself . . . a people who brought with them the invaluable rights of Englishmen."[24] The New York General Assembly, dominated by wealthy, powerful men who devoted themselves to the aggressive pursuit and defense of their own self-interests and those of their localities, may in fact have been a kind of rough-hewn provincial version of the English original; the South Carolina Commons House, by contrast, was only the palest of imitations.

When South Carolina became a royal colony in 1720, its government undertook a thorough revision of the qualifications by which one could vote for members of the assembly and by which one could serve in that body. The franchise in South Carolina was, at least theoretically, one of the most open in the American colonies. By the provisions of the 1721 electoral act, any adult white male owning at least fifty acres of land or paying twenty shillings per year in taxes was entitled to vote. Up until the Revolution the colonial government offered fifty-acre headrights to all adult males applying for them, and all adult males were required to pay at least twenty shillings in taxes, making these suffrage restrictions hardly onerous. In fact, the assembly tried at various times during the eighteenth century to raise those qualifications, voting in 1744 to set the qualification at three hundred acres of land or other real estate worth at least £60. The Royal Council, caught up in a dispute over the conflicting prerogatives of the lower and upper houses, delayed over a year in adding its assent to the bill, but its members fully concurred with those in the lower house that the franchise should be restricted to men of substantial property. In the end, the bill was disallowed by the Crown on a technicality but in 1759 the assembly did succeed in raising the qualification to a freehold of one hundred acres.[25]

Throughout the colonial period the property qualifications required to serve in the government were much higher than those necessary merely to exercise the right to vote; to serve in the lower house one needed to own either a minimum of five hundred acres and ten slaves or chattel valued at least £1,000.[26] Several times during the eighteenth century the assembly also tried to raise property qualifications for service in the legislative branch. Although those attempts were disallowed by the Crown, the purpose behind them was to preserve the standing of the legislature as an exclusive body of men visibly recognizable for their wealth and social prestige at a time when average levels of wealth among planters in the low country were rising.[27]

The Royal Council of South Carolina, like that of most colonies, made no pretense of representativeness. Appointed by the Privy Council upon nomination by the board of trade, it was to be made up of "men of good life and well affected to our government and of good estates and abilities and not necessitous persons or much in debt." Unlike the appointment process to the council in many colonies, in which the board of trade routinely accepted the recommendations of the leading provincial citizens of those colonies, in South Carolina the board of trade tended to fill vacancies with their own patronage needs in mind, and as a consequence council membership was often more a reflection of political influence back in England than in the colony itself. Indeed, the tendency of the board of trade, through the governor, to appoint "royal placemen" to the council was the most significant source of tension between provincial and royal elites within the colony. The forty-nine men appointed to the South Carolina council between 1720 and 1763 were a notably wealthy—if not notably diligent—group of men. The average value of the estates for which there are inventories was over £9,000, the average landholding 7,750 acres, and the average slaveholding 172 slaves. But however impressive their wealth, their powers were steadily being circumscribed by aggressive behavior on the part of the lower house of assembly. Relying on precedents set by the English House of Commons' successful struggle to wrest control of taxation from the House of Lords, between 1721 and 1740 the Commons House in South Carolina seized virtually total control over all taxation and revenue measures, leaving the council in the position of being a merely reactive body in the legislative sense and an advisory body in the executive sense.[28] There were a few advantages to be gained from service on the council—an inside track on land grants perhaps being the most obvious—but by midcentury the overall complacency of the Royal Council in the contest between royal and provincial authority was yet another reason for the harmony that seemed to prevail among South Carolina's elites.

The Commons House, though clearly more representative of provincial than royal interests, was no less than the council dominated not only by wealthy men, but even more pointedly by wealthy men with strong commitments to upholding the slave-based economy of their colony. By the 1760s fully 100 percent of those serving in the assembly owned estates valued at £2,000 or more, with the majority of them owning estates valued at £5,000 or more. Overwhelmingly, those who rose to positions of leadership within the assembly were associated with commercial and mercantile interests. Eugene Sirmans, in an analysis of leadership patterns in the Commons House, has calculated that of the twenty-two men whom he identified as leaders during the period 1733–51, eleven were merchants, six were lawyers, four were planters, and one a doctor. Between 1751 and 1763 the same pattern persisted, with fourteen merchants and six lawyers among the twenty-seven leaders in the assembly. Perhaps even more striking than the dominance of merchants and lawyers over the business of the assembly was the extent to which nearly everyone who served there, whether a planter or a city dweller, counted slave property as a substantial portion of their wealth. Over the course of the period from 1692 to 1775 the average known slaveholding among members of the Commons House was ninety-two, an average that almost certainly understates the situation by midcentury, when average slaveholdings were on the rise and many planters were already making a regular practice of giving legal title to some of their slaves to their children before they reached adulthood. By contrast, both the percentage of members of the Virginia House of Burgesses who were slave owners and the average slaveholding among the burgesses were significantly lower.[29] The other notable fact about the composition of South Carolina's delegation to the Commons House was the way in which nonslaveholding groups—most notably the artisans and mechanics of Charleston—went virtually unrepresented in the assembly; the number of artisans and mechanics in the assembly never amounted to more than one or two in any session during the period 1721–75, and in most sessions there were no members of those occupational groups serving in the assembly.[30]

It was one thing to be able to meet the minimum requirement to exercise the franchise, but quite another to make the casting of a vote a meaningful act. Both the formal structures of representation and the prevailing attitudes toward the connection between representative and constituent suggest that South Carolina had a long way to go before the notion of direct representation became a reality. Elected for terms not to exceed three years, members of the Commons House were from 1716 onward elected not from towns or countries, but according to church parish boundaries within the colony. When parishes replaced counties as the most important electoral unit, churchwardens replaced county sheriffs as the officials responsible for supervising the conduct of elections. Although there is some reason to suspect that the churchwardens were less competent in the execution of their electoral duties than were the county sheriffs in other colonies, the real difficulty was in the slowness with which additional church parishes were created in response to the rapid growth of population in the western portion of the colony. The South Carolina lower house was always a relatively small body, consisting of thirty-eight representatives drawn from eleven parishes plus Charleston in 1730 and growing to fifty-one representatives drawn from twenty-one parishes plus Charleston by 1770. If this modest expansion in the number of parishes and representatives had evinced even a modest correlation with the actual growth in population in the colony, the situation with respect to representation might not have been so bad, but, in fact, the one portion of the colony experiencing the most rapid population growth—the up-country and the hinterland beyond the Appalachians—went almost wholly unrepresented in the assembly right up to the Revolution. In the 1740s Royal Governor James Glen, acting with the encouragement of the Privy Council, attempted to push through the assembly a bill that would have guaranteed each parish with a hundred householders or more at least two representatives in the lower house, but assembly members, virtually all of whom were from the low country and, indeed, nearly all of whom spent most of their time in Charleston, rebuffed the governor's efforts. By 1767 England's Privy Council itself was making the task of redressing the inequities in representation more difficult by its policy of limiting the growth of colonial legislatures, a policy that caused them to disallow acts passed by the South Carolina assembly establishing St. Luke's and All Saints' parishes. The following year two new parishes, St. Matthew and St. David, were created, but only when the assembly agreed to take one representative from each from two of the low country parishes in order to give some minimal form of representation to the western part of the colony.[31]

Issues of representation, along with bitter dissatisfaction about the inadequate state of local government, ultimately provoked backcountry settlers into violent resistance in the Regulator Movement of 1767 to 1769. The consequences of the political alienation of the South Carolina backcountry from the provincial center of government in Charleston will be analyzed more fully in chapter 6, but the forces unleashed by that movement—felt even more devastatingly during the bitter civil war that afflicted the South Carolina backcountry during the late 1770s and early 1780s—were hardly the sort that could be described as part of a political order that was either inclusive or harmonious. Although the low-country oligarchs may have congratulated themselves for maintaining the "harmony that we are famous for," that harmony could only be achieved by ignoring the disenfranchised and the underrepresented, who did not have the luxury of spending their time in their city homes enjoying the entertainments of Charleston.

There was one trait in the elective politics of South Carolina that was shared by all of the parishes of the colony, be they over- or underrepresented in the assembly. In spite of a widely inclusive franchise, a higher proportion of South Carolina's voters failed to exercise their right to vote

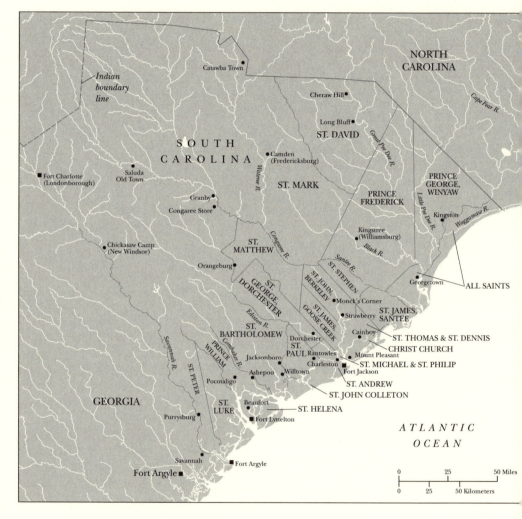

NORTH
CAROLINA

*Indian
boundary
line*

Catawba Town

Cheraw Hill

Long Bluff

ST. DAVID

S O U T H
C A R O L I N A

Camden
(Fredericksburg)

PRINCE
GEORGE,
WINYAW

Fort Charlotte
(Londonborough)

Saluda
Old Town

ST. MARK

PRINCE
FREDERICK

Granby

Congaree Store

Kingston

Chickasaw Camp
(New Windsor)

ST.
MATTHEW

Kingstree
(Williamsburg)

ALL SAINTS

Orangeburg

Georgetown

ST.
GEORGE,
DORCHESTER

ST. JOHN
BERKELEY

ST. STEPHEN

ST.
BARTHOLOMEW

ST. JAMES,
GOOSE CREEK

Monck's Corner

Strawberry

ST. JAMES,
SANTEE

ST. THOMAS & ST. DENNIS

PRINCE
WILLIAM

Dorchester

Cainhoy

CHRIST CHURCH

ST.
PAUL

Rantowles

Mount Pleasant

Jacksonboro

Charleston

ST. MICHAEL & ST. PHILIP

Ashepoo

Willtown

Fort Jackson

ST. PETER

Pocotaligo

ST. ANDREW

GEORGIA

ST.
LUKE

Beaufort

ST. JOHN COLLETON

ST. HELENA

Purrysburg

Fort Lyttelton

ATLANTIC
OCEAN

Savannah

Fort Argyle

Fort Argyle

0   25   50 Miles

0   25   50 Kilometers

Map 4. South Carolina Parishes before the Revolution.

than citizens anywhere else in colonial British America. In nearly all of the elections in the colony voter turnout remained below 10 percent of the eligible voters, and in a good many cases the only citizens to show up were the churchwardens legally charged with the responsibility of conducting the poll.[32]

Even the most controversial election of the mid-eighteenth century, that involving Christopher Gadsden's disputed election to the assembly from St. Paul Parish in 1762, attracted only ninety-four voters out of a potential voting population of more than a thousand. Actually, Gadsden regarded the fact that ninety-four voters had turned up at the election as evidence of a significant turnout and mandate, claiming that "the uncommon number of electors" who turned out that day "demand my highest acknowledgments." The controversy over the election, which hinged more on questions of the prerogatives of the governor in certifying the legality of elections than in an actual dispute about the vote totals, was obviously not a reflection of high citizen interest in the outcome. Rather, as usual, what contest there was in South Carolina politics came when insiders—in this case, the Commons House and the governor—quarreled about their respective prerogatives.[33] Many in the assembly would rally around Gadsden's claim to election in the name of popular rights, and Gadsden himself would produce several pamphlets, which in their rhetoric of rights and representation presaged many of the arguments that would be used just a few years later in the revolutionary struggle. As was the case in New York and Massachusetts and in the rhetoric of Whigs in the English House of Commons the rights being defended were in fact not popular, but parliamentary.

One student of South Carolina's history has characterized its political culture as being typified by "lack of interest," but, in a peculiar reading of the consistent apathy of the voters, concludes that the paucity of contested elections had a beneficial result, as it made "the resort to malpractice . . . unnecessary" and thus encouraged responsible service on the part of those candidates who decided to stand for public office. It is difficult, however, to find much evidence for "responsible" public service in the behavior of those wealthy merchants and planters of South Carolina who, though elected to office, either formally declined to serve or simply failed to show up at the sessions of the assembly. During the period 1730–60, more than 30 percent of those elected to seats in the Commons House refused to serve, and in some parishes it was necessary to make several attempts before finding residents willing to take on the task. For example, during the years 1736–45 in St. James, Goose Creek, one of the most centrally located of South Carolina's parishes, the voters elected a total of sixteen men in order to fill all four of the parish's seats during the three assembly terms in that decade; six of the sixteen refused to serve at all, eight served only one term, and only two served two terms. High legislative turnover, which in

some colonies may have been a sign of an active, competitive culture of
elective politics, was in South Carolina simply a function of the unwillingness of many of the colony's leading citizens to devote their time to public
service.[34]

The other notable fact about the pattern of service in the Commons
House was the extraordinary number of representatives who served
parishes in which they themselves did not live. Although by law most
colonies in America allowed individuals to serve as representatives for localities not their primary residences so long as they owned property in that
locality, only New York and South Carolina actually followed the practice of
nonresident representation on a consistent basis, and only in South
Carolina did the practice flourish. More than half of South Carolina's
parishes sent nonresident representatives to the assembly more than half
the time during the period 1721–1775; an overwhelming portion of those
nonresident representatives lived most of the time either in Charleston
or in adjacent low-country parishes. Obviously, the notion of direct,
constituency-based representation—one of the central issues at the heart of
the struggle between the American colonies and England during the 1760s
and 1770s—was only hazily defined among the citizens of South Carolina
in the prerevolutionary period.[35]

Absenteeism among those who agreed to serve in the assembly was
chronically high. Although the Commons House defined a quorum as consisting of only nineteen members—far less than half the membership—on
numerous occasions the House failed to muster the required number. In
virtually every session during the eighteenth century there were occasions
in which business could not be transacted because of the lack of a quorum,
and two assemblies, those elected in 1747 and 1749, never managed to
muster a quorum at all and, consequently, were dissolved by the governor
without ever meeting.[36] This widespread apathy on the part of both citizens
and representatives had the paradoxical effect of increasing, rather than
decreasing, the concentration of effective political power in the colony.
Though it is true that the high turnover in the assembly guaranteed that a
large number of men could claim experience as a representative, virtually
all of those men were people of property and high social standing. Moreover, their unwillingness to assume the responsibility that their election to
the assembly implied left governance to the relatively small circle of
Charleston oligarchs who were so inclined. Men like Bull, Laurens, and
Gadsden, together with a small group of lawyers such as Rawlins Lowndes,
Peter Manigault, and Charles Pinckney II, whose legal careers depended
on their political influence, served multiple terms in the assembly and
dominated the principal committee business of the Commons House. In
part the inclination of those Charleston professional people was a reflection simply of their proximity to the capital, making assembly service less
onerous for them than for men living in the hinterland. It is equally the

case, though, that the business of the assembly—decisions respecting the issuing of paper money, taxation policy, and the dispensation of legal patronage—was of more immediate interest to the professional classes than to the planters.

Ultimately, any understanding of the character of elective politics in provincial South Carolina must be joined with some understanding of the character of governance in that province. In most of the American colonies the interest the society displayed toward politics bore some relationship to the actual range of things that government could do for or to the citizens of those societies. We have already seen, for example, that the wealthy and socially powerful oligarchs of the colony of New York, though they were reasonably successful in keeping control of politics in their colony to themselves, fought constantly within the confines of the assembly to see who got what, when, and how. While presenting themselves to the voters as exemplars of classical politics—as politicians most wise and virtuous in the science and art of government—they nevertheless fought hard (and not always fairly) over the division of the spoils of politics. The fact of the matter was that there were spoils to be gotten; the New York government was a reasonably active one, doling out land grants, adjudicating among the multiple interests of an increasingly variegated economy, even regulating behavior of individuals and their farm animals in the most local of settings. The governments of Massachusetts and Virginia were even more active, playing an aggressive role in promoting economic development within their domains.

In South Carolina, however, the picture of governance that emerges is a puzzlingly paradoxical one on several levels. It is clear, for example, that members of the Commons House were every bit as intent on replicating the styles of England's political leaders as they were on replicating the social mores of the English aristocracy. Much of the parliamentary procedure of the South Carolina lower house seemed slavishly close to the English original. The New England visitor Josiah Quincy noted that at the opening of each session, a mace (according to one visitor, a "superb and elegant one which cost ninety guineas") was placed on the table before the Speaker, just as it was done in the English House of Commons. The Speaker himself was "robed in black and ha[d] a very large wig of State," which he donned when presiding over the session. And the members, again true to the English fashion, all sat in the chamber with their hats on, uncovering their heads only when they rose to deliver a speech. Similarly, the Commons House polled its members on important questions and pieces of legislation in the same manner as their English counterparts, the members "giv[ing] their votes by rising from their seats, the dissentients did not rise." On the other hand, in spite of their attachment to the outward forms and rituals of parliamentary decorum, much of their actual conduct of business presented a "very unparliamentary appearance." According to Josiah Quincy, the "members conversed, lolled, and chatted much like a friendly jovial society" rather than a deliberative body.[37]

It has often been claimed that one of the reasons why service as an elected representative in South Carolina was not much sought after and was therefore monopolized by such a small coterie of merchants and lawyers was that the job was so difficult and time consuming. The legislature was mandated by law to meet at least once every six months, with the winter session often running from January through June. During the period from 1752–1756 the Commons House was recorded as being in session an average of about ninety days a year, meeting six hours a day, six days a week.[38] This sort of legislative schedule would have been taxing under any circumstances, but given the fact that legislators were not paid for their services, it must have seemed even more so to those relative few who attended the legislature faithfully. Yet in spite of all of those days in session, the South Carolina legislature was an extraordinarily inactive body that passed relatively few laws (an average of about a dozen a year during the 1750s and 1760s) and, in the substance of its legislation, left whole areas of provincial governance, from economic development to public education, essentially untouched.

Similarly, the South Carolina legislators appeared to be in only scant touch with their constituents during their time of service. As we have seen, constituents in Massachusetts Bay and Virginia actively petitioned their legislature in the eighteenth century, but in South Carolina the legislature rarely received more than ten petitions in a given year.[39]

Perhaps one reason why the legislature undertook so little of consequence lay in its commitment to, indeed, its fetish about, unanimity. Nearly all of the business of the lower house was shaped by that commitment. The members of the Commons House did not so much elect a Speaker as anoint him; beginning in the first decade of the eighteenth century, members of the House, no matter what their private differences on the matter, elected their Speakers unanimously. The desire to avoid conflict was also reflected in the continuity—indeed, the monotony—of committee assignments, with the same few men dominating the same committees year after year. The House similarly went to great lengths to avoid divisions on votes and never publicly recorded those divisions when they did take place. It was not at all uncommon for dissenting members of the House, when they found themselves in the minority on a question, to move over to the majority precisely to ensure the illusion of unanimity in their ranks. As Peter Manigault, Speaker of the House from 1757 to 1773, once averred, he preferred to "sail with the Stream, when no Danger or Dishounour, can attend it."[40]

Rebecca Starr, comparing the cultural worlds of Virginia's planter-gentry and South Carolina's Charleston-based ruling elite, contrasts the Virginia planters' close engagement with all aspects of cultivation of their principal crop—tobacco—with the engagement of South Carolina's ruling elite—whether Charleston merchants or absentee rice and indigo planters—with more urban and cosmopolitan pursuits. Whereas the culture of tobacco inclined Virginia's political leaders to an agrarian, radical country ideology, which idealized virtue and independence and distrusted the pursuit of self-interest, the economic pursuits of South Carolina's ruling class inclined them to identify more easily with a world in which the serving of interests was not shameful.[41]

No doubt some of South Carolina's alleged political harmony resulted from the fact that the interests of South Carolina merchants and planters were on the whole similar, with their prosperity often depending on their relationship with merchants and politicians in England. Indeed, Starr argues that attentiveness to aggressive and well-coordinated lobbying back in England was more important than regular attendance in the provincial assembly, and this was the activity, she contends, at which South Carolina's political leaders excelled.[42]

Certainly members the eighteenth-century South Carolina ruling class *believed* that they enjoyed a legitimacy founded on responsible political leadership. Christopher Gadsden, looking back nostalgically on the pre-revolutionary Commons House from the vantage point of the 1780s, lauded it for "the harmony that we were famous for," a condition brought about, he believed, by "common interest" and "friendly habits."[43] Yet however much that harmony was enjoyed by the privileged few who dominated the legislature, the effort to maintain that harmony, even among men of such similar backgrounds and circumstances, may have come at the price of not addressing important, but potentially contentious, issues of public policy. That they were driven by the need for harmony suggests as well some unspoken sources of tension within their ranks. These proud, independent men, quick to challenge their neighbor to a duel at any real or imagined slight, perhaps realized how easily the polis could disintegrate into disorder and anarchy and thus declared serious disputation in the political arena out of bounds. The threat of disorder and anarchy did not come merely from within. If they had been listening, they might have heard the clamoring of those disorderly citizens in the backcountry, demanding a greater say in the government of their colony. John Rutledge for one was dismayed at their presumption, calling them a "pack of beggars" and expressing the opinion that the colony would be better off "if the Back Country was at Bottom of the Sea."[44]

And of course, the ultimate threat of disorder—a world turned upside down—was never far from view. South Carolina's political leaders went to great lengths to avert their gaze from it, but outsiders coming into their society spotted it immediately. "Slavery," Josiah Quincy wrote, may truly be said to be the peculiar curse of this land; Strange infatuation! It is generally thought and called by the people its blessing. Applicable indeed To this people and their slaves the words of our Milton: "So perfect in their Misery, Not one perceived their foul disfigurement." A few years ago, it is allowed, That the blacks exceeded the whites as seventeen to one. There are those who now tell you that the slaves are not more than three to one, some pretend not so many. But they who talk thus are afraid that the slaves should by some means discover Their superiority. . . . From the same cause have their Legislators enacted laws touching negroes, mulattoes and masters which savor more of the policy of Pandemonium that the English constitution:—laws which will stand eternal records Of the depravity and contradiction of the human character: laws which would disgrace the tribunal of Scythian, Arab, Hottentot and Barbarian are appealed to in decision Upon life limb and liberty by those who assume the name of Englishmen, freeman And Christians.[45]

That small band of gentry men who owned those slaves in such disproportionate numbers, the same men who enacted the laws of which Quincy wrote, must on some level have realized how precarious was their hold on those beings and must have clung to the solace of their internal harmony all the more desperately.

The harmony of the merchants, planters, and lawyers who ruled South Carolina would be strained, but not broken, as the Revolution neared. The events surrounding the Stamp Act and the role played in those events by the three men who were introduced at the beginning of this chapter—William Bull II, Henry Laurens, and Christopher Gadsden—give us a final glimpse into some of the ways in which the complacent world of South Carlina's oligarchs was being shaken.

William Bull II, more so than any man in the colony, had been successful in enjoying both power and respect within the circles of both the provincial and royal elites. As George Grenville and the British ministry were beginning to rethink imperial policy toward the colonies in 1763 and 1764, Lieutenant Governor Bull was elevated once again to the post of acting governor with the departure from the colony of the highly unpopular William Boone. In his initial message to the Commons House in May of 1764 he assured them that he did not intend to interfere with their own internal business and noted that, since the warm season was well upon them, he would do little to keep them in session any longer than needed. That session and a subsequent one, in January of 1765, passed with nothing but harmonious relations between the governor and the assembly. When the Commons House reconvened in July of 1765, however, the circular letter from Massachusetts calling on all American colonies to send representatives to a congress in New York to protest the Stamp Act disrupted this pattern. The royal governors of the other southern colonies, alerted to the dangers posed by the Massachusetts circular letter, refused to call the legislatures into session, but Bull not only allowed them to meet, he also refused to question either their unanimous resolution naming delegates in late July or their unanimous appropriation of £600 for their expenses in August. In his report to the board of trade on the assembly's actions in September, he conveniently omitted mention of those two particular actions, and to himself he reasoned that the Commons House, in sending delegates to New York to discuss the Stamp Act, had done nothing overtly disloyal.

Bull was faced with more difficult choices once the stamps actually arrived. Knowing from reports in others colonies that the stamps themselves might be the object of crowd violence, he ordered those that had arrived in Charleston transferred out of the line of fire to Fort Johnson, an armament on the south side of Charleston harbor. Over the weekend of October 19 there had been outbreaks of mob violence within the town aimed at those rumored to be appointed as stamp officers, but Bull minimized the extent of that violence in his public statements and emphasized that the stamps had not been distributed to stamp officers but instead were being stored at Fort Johnson. This public posture won him favor among the populace of Charleston and had the effect of dampening the potential for further violence. Indeed, at a time when Lieutenant Governor Hutchinson in Massachusetts was witnessing the destruction of his house and Lieutenant Governor Colden in New York was suffering damage both to his mercantile business (its windows smashed) and his ego (his effigy swinging from a tree), Bull was praised in an address from the Commons as one whose "conduct on the administration of government calls loudly for applause."[46]

The coming months would cause the tightrope on which this South Carolina royal governor was walking to become thinner and shakier, but he skillfully negotiated the perilous journey. The two courts under the governor's jurisdiction—that of Chancery and of Ordinary—finished their sessions just days before the Stamp Act was to go into effect, and thus Bull was spared the decision of whether to open those courts without the stamps. The chief justice of the Court of Common Pleas, with the governor's full acquiescence, closed his court on the grounds that the stamps were not yet available. Not having yet received an official copy of the Stamp Act from London, Bull was also pleased to accept the resignations of the two stamp officers, George Saxby and Caleb Lloyd.

During the next month Bull continued to play both sides. He failed to mention the Stamp Act disturbances in his opening address to the new assembly on October 29, 1765, in spite of (or perhaps because of) the likely involvement in those disturbances by at least a few members of that body. Moreover, in his report to London he minimized their seriousness, blaming them on subversive influence from New England and assuring his masters that "in all other respects the king has no subjects that express and show more loyalty to his Majesty than the people of this province." At the end of November, when the Commons House received and endorsed the resolutions of the Stamp Act congress denouncing the act, Bull again refused to set himself against the assembly, deftly justifying his failure to dissolve them on the grounds that the resolutions were intended for the king and that to intervene in the dispute before the king had an opportunity to resolve the matter would be a violation of his authority. Over the course of the next six months Bull maintained his adroit balancing act, finding a way by February of 1766 to open the port of Charleston without the stamps (still safely tucked away at Fort Johnson) and, with greater difficulty, managing to persuade the royally appointed chief justice of the Court of Common Pleas, Charles Shinner, to open his courts.

Bull was not able to satisfy everyone in the South Carolina Commons House. Christopher Gadsden, who emerged during the Stamp Act crisis as the leader of the more radical, anti-British elements in Charleston, would have preferred that the lines between the royal government and provincial authority be drawn more sharply, describing Bull as "so very obliging that he never obliged," and lamenting that "the regard for him [Bull] as a private gentleman has had too great weight in our House and occasioned great difficulties." In fact, though, if harmony was the end toward which South Carolina's leaders were working, then William Bull's behavior during the Stamp Act crisis was a testimony to the vitality of that tradition.

In the end, though, there would be other values that South Carolina's political elite would prize more than harmony, and Bull would finally fall off that high wire. As the lines between the British and the Americans were drawn ever more sharply, it was increasingly difficult for him to play the role of conciliator. When Bull left office in June of 1775, to be replaced by a new royal governor, Lord William Campbell, royal government in the colony was in collapse all around him. Although he was still well liked personally by most of his fellow South Carolina oligarchs, there was no longer any place for him within a political elite increasingly committed to the patriot cause. He spent from 1775 to 1777 in an unofficial exile at his plantation, Ashley Hall, and then, when it became clear that low-country South Carolinians were not going to come around and see the necessity of submitting to royal rule, he left for London, where he would spend much of the remainder of his life until his death in 1791. During his period of exile, there was protracted controversy within the state over the disposition of his considerable estate. Revolutionary legislation calling for the confiscation of Loyalist property put virtually all of Bull's estate at risk, but many of his friends among the provincial elite, including his political antagonist, Christopher Gadsden, worked both in the courts and behind the scenes to preserve it. Although Bull and his family would win a few legal victories that would preserve a part of his estate, the Confiscation Acts, together with the ravages of war (the British army plundered his beloved Ashley Hall in their occupation campaign of 1779), would effectively put an end to the economic power of William Bull.[47]

As Henry Laurens assessed events from his perspective as a member of the Commons House, he no doubt shared Bull's opinions both of the unwisdom of the Stamp Act and of the need to find lawful and nonconfrontational means by which to secure its repeal. Writing in early October to Joseph Brown, a justice of the peace up the coast in Georgetown, Laurens expressed his distaste for the act, but at the same time added that "I hope you as a magistrate—as a good subject—as a prudent man will do all in your power to discourage all the little apings and mockery in your town of those infamous inglorious feats of riot and dissipation which have been performed to the No'ward of us." Laurens went on to state his certainty that a "regular, decent, becoming representation of the inexpediency & inutility of that Law will have the deir'd effect & that all irregular seditious practices Will have an evil tendency, even perhaps to perpetuate that & bring upon us other Acts of parliament big with greater mischiefs." Laurens particularly feared the possibility of parliamentary retaliation, for with such retaliation, "what else would become of our Estates, particularly ours who depend upon Commerce." With that reasoning as his guiding force, he concluded that "there remains nothing for us at present to do but to shew a graceful obedience to the Law until we can procure its annihilation in a constitutional way."[48] Laurens was out of town on the weekend of October 19, when a group led by his fellow Charleston assemblyman Christopher Gadsden, calling itself the Sons of Liberty, forced the resignation of the stamp distributors and hung several suspected defenders of royal power in effigy, but he made plain his disdain for the goings-on, labeling the Sons of Liberty "Devil Burners" and claiming that they "had most shamelessly given the Lie to their pretended Patriotism, committed unbounded acts of Licentiousness & at length Burglary & Robbery."[49]

In the early morning hours of October 23 Laurens would have even greater reason to lament the licentiousness of the devil burners. Right around midnight Laurens and his wife, who was in the late stages of pregnancy, were awakened by "a most violent thumping & confus'd Noise . . . & soon distinguish'd the sounds of Liberty, Liberty & Stamp'd Paper, Open your doors & let us Search your House & Cellars." Laurens, calling to them from a window, assured them that he did not have the stamped paper, to which they replied "that they Loved & respected me, would not hurt me nor my property, but that they were sent even by some of my seemingly best friends to search for Stamp'd Paper, which they were certain was in my custody advised me to open the door to prevent worse consequences." Laurens relented and let them into his house where, in spite of "their thickest disguise of Soot, Sailors habits, slouch hats, etc.," he recognized them not as street thugs and rowdies, but as respectable (or at least previously respectable) citizens of the town. The mob made a "superficial search" of his house and, not finding anything, demanded to know where the stamps had been hidden. This demand produced not only a denial but also a small speech from Laurens, greeted alternately with applause and curses, in which he averred his detestation of the Stamp Act but maintained his commitment to pursue "a right method to obtain a repeal." The mob departed shortly thereafter, leaving Laurens to wonder, "Is it not amazing that such a number of Men many of them heated with Liquor & all armed with Cutlasses & Clubbs did not do one penny damage to my Garden not even to walk over a Bed & not 15/ damage to my Fence, Gate, or House.?"[50]

Henry Laurens would recover from his humiliation of 1775, and, unlike Bull, he would choose the winning side in the conflict with royal authority. Although he spent a part of the time between the Stamp Act crisis and the outbreak of the Revolutionary War in England overseeing his sons' education, by the time of his return from England, he would see more clearly the dangers that English policy presented to both American political liberties and his own property rights. Laurens returned to service in the legislature, in the Provincial Congress that drafted South Carolina's new state constitution, in the Continental Congress, and as a diplomat abroad, during which time he would be arrested and imprisoned for a time in the Tower of London. But when he returned once again to America, both his fortune and his political reputation were secure. Upon his death in 1792 he was widely respected by nearly all as the embodiment of the virtuous, propertied gentlemen upon whose shoulders leadership in South Carolina should rest.

Looking back on his early concern about the potentially violent course of American resistance to the Stamp Act, Laurens must have recognized that he had overreacted, for the orderly resistance that thwarted the implementation of the Stamp Act in Charleston was well orchestrated by a few members of the assembly, led by his former boyhood friend and now political rival, Christopher Gadsden. Gadsden was, more than any of his fellow merchant-planters in South Carolina, willing to disrupt the harmony of the polity if that was what was necessary to defend provincial rights and interests; he was, in the apt phrase of John Alden, "tireless, as well as tiresome, in argument," and he, more than any of his peers, followed the implications of the language of popular rights.[51] As early as January 1763, while defending himself against the royal governor's attempts to declare his election to the Commons House invalid, Gadsden had asserted that the people had "an inherent not permissive" right to select their representatives and had reasoned further that the American legislators, though they may have differed from the English Parliament in the extent of their authority, did not "differ . . . one iota" from it with respect to the basic rules of their operation. During the Stamp Act crisis, Gadsden pushed his interpretation of the English Constitution even further. As one of South Carolina's three delegates to the Stamp Act congress, he had wished that the congress had gone even further in denying Parliament's authority; the only firm, constitutional ground, in Gadsden's opinion was that based on "those natural and inherent rights that we all feel, and know, as men and as descendants of Englishmen we have a right to," and not on the legalisms of colonial charters. Upon adjournment of the congress he hurried back ahead of his fellow South Carolina delegates to direct resistance in the colony, arriving a few days before the events described with such loathing by Henry Laurens.[52] Gadsden would, at every stage in the opposition to British policy, aptly fit Pauline Maier's description of an "Old Revolutionary," lauding the superior virtue of provincial leaders like himself, denouncing British "placemen," sniffing out conspiracies of "Jacobites" within South Carolina and of corrupt, "oppressive, ministerial vengeance" from without, and, ultimately, urging South Carolina's virtuous citizens to display "manly courage" in the face of the king's attempts to enslave them.[53]

Gadsden continued his role as radical defender of popular rights through the early years of independence. He was perhaps the first in South Carolina to declare in favor of complete independence from England—doing so in February of 1776—and he was also in the vanguard of those who managed to liberalize slightly the constitution of the independent state, arguing for provisions disestablishing the Anglican Church and in favor of direct election of members of the upper house. But Gadsden was, nevertheless, a creature of his class and, ultimately, he would find the rhetoric of popular rights turned against him. In the aftermath of the Revolution one of the issues that would divide revolutionaries was their attitude toward the confiscation of Loyalist estates. Gadsden, who had declined to serve as governor of the independent state, but who had continued to serve in the legislature, was among those who supported softening provisions confiscating those estates and allowing some former Loyalists to return to South Carolina to reclaim their property. The leader of those opposing even a partial rescinding of the Confiscation Acts was Commodore Alexander Gillon, a colorful, Dutch-born merchant and shipper who had made his fortune in South Carolina before the Revolution and a reputation as a courageous naval commander during it. He was, Henry Laurens noted, a man distinguished by his "fervor for accomplishing everything by the force of his own powers."[54]

When Gillon and his followers took to the streets in protest in the early summer of 1783, their extralegal activity was initially confined to some tarring and feathering, but by midsummer that violence had resulted in four deaths. However much the violence had gotten out of hand, the great mass of the citizens of Charleston still were dead set against the return of former Loyalists, and at a large public meeting on July 21—composed principally but not exclusively of members of the laboring classes—it was unanimously resolved that the legislature be petitioned to reverse its course of reconciliation with the Tories. At this point South Carolina's merchant-planter elite became concerned not only about violence in the streets and the civil liberties of many of their former neighbors but also by the readiness of the assembled citizens to invoke and denounce the specter of "wealthy nabobs."

This radical populist insurgence was mobilized into two democratic societies—the Marine Anti-Democratic Society and the Whig Club of 600—which in turn mobilized themselves in preparation for the election of the mayor of Charleston to be held on September 13, 1784. Gillon was the standard-bearer for the radicals, and Richard Hutson was the candidate backed by the wealthy merchants, lawyers, and planters. That mayoral campaign, together with that year's assembly elections, brought forth as close to a class-oriented appeal as anyone had ever seen in South Carolina. A publication issued by the Whig Club exhorted voters to "elect no wealthy candidate who is a supplicant for your votes," and similarly cautioned the voters against supporting anyone who was among the wealthy families of this commonwealth, equally in the country as in the city . . . , yet regain their former privileges of monopolizing power, and all the honorary and lucrative offices of the State to themselves, their families and dependents; [they hope] by destroying the republican equality of citizenship . . . to introduce family influences into the government and thereby establish in their own hands an odious aristocracy of their betters."[55]

Gadsden was among those affronted by those assaults on his dignity, virtue, and judgment. He wrote several lengthy replies to his critics during the summer of 1784, and the same themes ran through all of them. In those replies he expressed what was no doubt a sincere, principled concern for establishing procedures dealing with returning Loyalists that were both humane and followed precepts of due process of law, but much of Gadsden's outrage was reserved for those who would call into question his personal character as a statesman serving the public interest. In that context he looked back fondly on those days of "natural forbearance, good humour, and harmony we were famous for," a time when "common interest, joined with the revival of old friendly habits" governed political discourse. Looking at the present political climate, he was appalled that the citizens themselves should clamor to make public policy. "Let us," he intoned, "leave national concerns to our legislature, it belongs to them, and them only. If any important matters seem to be overlooked or neglected by the House, let us address, remonstrate, respectfully for our own sakes as well as theirs." "The worthy man," he noted, "offices seek; the designing man cabals for them to give himself importance." With that image of the virtuous, republican statesman in mind—an image that strikingly resembled himself—he poured out his outrage against "detestable disturbers of the public peace and mischievous wou'd-bes." He professed an inability to understand how anyone could confuse his "disinterested" public service with "Aristocracy." The only sane path to good governance, Gadsden averred, was for the citizens to "vote with care, uninfluenced and peaceably, avoiding all innovations that have the least tendency to sap our old way of doing it." Clearly, one of those innovations was the "specious" argument that a representative should "bind himself to vote as his constituents shall direct and act, not as heretofore, but consonant to the instructions they shall give him." That innovation would, Gadsden declared, render the legislature "contemptible," reducing its members either to inaction for want of explicit instruction or to puppets on strings, its members "obsequious to the great man of the [democratic] club." It was much better, Gadsden reasoned, to "leave the members [of the legislature] untrammeled, to act by their own best judgments upon any point of importance" rather than to depend on the "parochial" views of clusters of constituents. This insistence on the importance of allowing the wisest and most virtuous men to represent the "general combined interest of all," rather than consenting to a notion of representation based on local constituencies, was of course strikingly similar to those notions of "virtual representation" put forward by George Greenville and denounced so vehemently by men like Gadsden during the Stamp Act crisis.[56]

The insurgency of Commodore Gillon and the Charleston radicals would be rebuffed at the polls, in both the city elections in the summer and the assembly elections in the fall, but Gadsden, alarmed by the attacks both on himself and on the ethic of politics by which he lived, decided not to stand for reelection. Signing off from his political career as "A Steady and Open Republican," Gadsden angrily denied the charge of "nabobship" and announced that "I by no means desire to serve in the assembly again, ardently longing to retire from all public Business."[57] With the exception of a brief return to public life to serve in the South Carolina Ratifying Convention of 1787 as a delegate favoring adoption of the Constitution and as a delegate to a state constitutional convention in 1790, Gadsden kept his promise, spending most of his remaining years tending to his commercial interests until his death in 1805.

When Josiah Quincy left his native Massachusetts and visited South Carolina in 1773, he was simultaneously impressed and revolted by many of the traits and attitudes that were nurtured in the affluent and occasionally ostentatious society of the low country. Although a self-consciously intellectual New England Calvinist, he was nevertheless more often pleased and impressed than repelled by the lavishness—from the fancy place settings to the elaborate feasts with ample liquid refreshment—with which he was entertained. Indeed, he showed a remarkably unpuritanical interest in the horse races he attended; following a day spend at the "famous Races," he was obviously impressed with the "prodigious fine collection of excellent, though high-priced horses" he had seen, and noted, with some measure of satisfaction, he "was let a little into the singular art of the Turf."[58] But in the final analysis he was deeply offended by many of the prevailing political mores of the colony. He believed that "the constitution of South Carolina is in very many respects defective," noting that in reality the "government is composed of two aristocratic parts [The Commons and the Council], and one monarchical body; the aristocratic parts mutually dislike each other." In spite of all the talk about popular rights emanating from South Carolina's lower house, Quincy "questioned whether in reality there is any third branch in the constitution of this government. Tis true they have a house of Assembly; but who do they represent? The laborer, the mechanic, the tradesman, the farmer, husbandman or yeoman? No. The representatives are almost if not wholly rich planters. The Planting interest is therefore represented, but I conceive nothing else." The members of the Commons House, all wealthy and privileged, "have in general but little solicitude about the interests or concerns of the many."[59]

The assumption of privilege on the part of South Carolina's merchant-planter oligarchs, as well as their lack of solicitude about the interests of the many, was in some measure a natural outgrowth of their attachment to traditional English assumptions about a natural social hierarchy, but the extremes to which they went in reinforcing those traditional English notions about the relationship between the many and the few can only be explained by the thoroughness of their commitment to a set of social relations founded upon the institution of chattel slavery. If Virginia's political elite was simultaneously founded upon and mildly uncomfortable with slavery, most members of South Carolina's elite displayed little of that ambivalence. South Carolina's merchant-planters relied on slavery not only for their material prosperity but also as a visible symbol of a god-given hierarchy in which they stood at the top. And, whether in the Continental Congress debating Jefferson's Declaration of Independence or in the Constitutional Convention debating the limits of federal authority over slavery, they were unabashed in their defense both of the peculiar institution and of their commitment to an unequally composed social order.

A few of them did occasionally pause to ponder the darker side of the society that they had created. Gadsden, writing shortly after the Stamp Act crisis had passed, observed that the "great part of our weakness (though at the same time 'tis part of our riches) consists in having such a number of slaves among us, and we find in our case according to the general perceptible workings of Providence where the crime most commonly though slowly, but surely, draws a similar and suitable punishment that slavery begets slavery."[60] But, in the end, even Gadsden would join forces with his fellow oligarchs in perpetuating a political system in which the few would insist on their god-given superiority over the many.

Chapter 6

The Unsettling Political Cultures of the Backcountry
The Southern Backcountry

There was no single American backcountry in the eighteenth century. Its geographic range was vast, extending northward from Massachusetts into Maine, New Hampshire, and Vermont; westward from Massachusetts, Connecticut, New York, and southeastern Pennsylvania; and southward, from Frederick County, Maryland, down through the Great Valley, Central Piedmont, and Southside of Virginia, and into those parts of North and South Carolina lying between the fall line and the Great Smokies. Just as there were important differences in backcountry societies across geographical space—differences relating to soil, climate, ethnic and religious composition, and the political institutions of which a particular geographical entity was a part—there were equally important differences generated across time. The Virginia backcountry in 1760 had a very different definition than that of 1700, and that part of Massachusetts that would become Maine displayed a different appearance in 1819 than it did in 1750.

The very concept of the backcountry, like that of the frontier, suggests a relationship with settled, seaboard societies marked by both connection and difference. All backcountry societies at every point in their development displayed—in varying degrees—points of continuity with the better-settled portions of those colonies and regions of which they were a part; at the same time those societies were—again in varying degrees—societies in motion, in the process both of becoming more like the societies that spawned them but at the same time moving toward a new, "American" definition of social and political order. In that sense backcountry societies were, as scholars from Frederick Jackson Turner to Jack P. Greene have argued, always in the process of not only assimilating the values and structures of their parent cultures but also, by the very differences that they exhibited from the parent cultures, reshaping the culture of the whole.[1] While there were important points of difference within the political cultures of the eighteenth-century American backcountries, those societies nevertheless shared a sufficiently similar path of historical development that we may be justified in speaking of a backcountry experience. All were part of a common process involving, in greater or lesser degrees, rapid and remarkable population increase, phenomenal geographic and economic mobility, the intermixture of a nearly unprecedented variety of ethnic and religious groups, and an economic base largely founded upon localized, forms of agricultural production. Those conditions produced two other common developments nearly everywhere. First they gave rise to social structures in which there was a significantly narrower range of wealth among the populace than in more settled parts of America; the social orders that resulted were emphatically not fully egalitarian, but they were ones in which the wealthiest citizens possessed substantially less coercive power than was the case in the eastern coastal regions.[2] Second the structures of political authority that came into being in these societies were, because of their newness, their distance from established centers of government, and the frailty of the economic power of many of those who sought to control them, often less efficient in their administration of government and, occasionally, less secure in their legitimacy.

The overriding ethic that conditioned behavior in all of the backcountry societies of America was one that simultaneously distinguished them from and connected them to their older, more established counterparts. That ethic was the quest for personal independence. Jack P. Greene describes independence as "freedom from the will of others. It was the opposite of dependence, which was subordination or subjection to the discretion of others. Independence implied a sovereignty of self in all private and public relations, while dependence connoted the very opposite."[3] We have already seen how the widespread adoption of that value was beginning to change the cultures of nearly every area of settlement within America, but it would be in the backcountry—whether in South Carolina, Virginia, Pennsylvania, or Maine—that the impulse toward independence would be most visibly on display, for better and for worse, in both the conduct of politics and in social relations more generally.

All of these factors—geographic and economic mobility, ethnic and religious diversity, the relative newness of political institutions, and the impulses of most citizens to pursue aggressively the goal of personal independence—served to weaken the fabric holding these backcountry societies together. The political cultures that resulted from these generally common conditions were, as Frederick Jackson Turner rightly observed, important components of a new American definition of liberty, but, as he also noted, "a democracy born of free land, strong in selfishness and individualism, intolerant of administrative experience and education, and pressing individual liberty beyond its proper bounds, has its dangers as well as its benefits."[4] If there was a single common initial consequence of this loosening of the bonds of society, it was political disorder. That disorder might serve to open up the political process and therefore to lead eventually to more democratic modes of political behavior, but just as often it led to aggressive forms of behavior in which the desire of individuals to achieve advantage, and, ultimately, dominance, led to the two extremes that lay on either side of democracy—anarchy or oligarchy.

The analysis in this chapter and the two following will focus on four examples well suited to suggest some of the broad similarities of backcountry experience as well as some of the most striking differences. This chapter will describe the expansion and dispersion of America's oldest colony—Virginia—and compare it to developments in North and South Carolina where, in spite of broadly similar patterns of social development, the political cultures that emerged were strikingly different. In chapter 7 we will move to the far northern frontier of British America, Maine, where in spite of the presence of a more homogeneous European population and a self-conscious effort by political leaders to extend the political culture of the provincial center to the frontier, the challenges to successful integration of periphery and center remained formidable. Finally, in the final section of chapter 8 we will encounter the ways in which ethnic and religious differences, an inequitable distribution of political power, and a fundamental cultural division on the question of Indian policy would bring citizens living in Pennsylvania's frontier into bitter conflict with political leaders in the provincial center.

The Formation of the Southern Backcountry

The backcountry experience of Virginia, though its origins stretched back further in time than any of the other southern colonies, was in the main connected to a continuous set of developments that affected the whole of the South—from Frederick County, Maryland, down through the Great Valley, Central Piedmont, and Southside of Virginia, and into those parts of North and South Carolina lying between the fall line and the Great Smokies.[5] Most of the settlers in that entire region were part of the same extraordinary wave of immigration, beginning in the 1720s but reaching epic proportions in the period from 1750 to 1770. In Virginia the greatest increase in the prerevolutionary period was in the Southside and great southwest, with the population rising at an annual rate of about 15 percent during the 1750s and then maintaining a steady upward momentum of about 8 to 10 percent each year until the Revolution. In North Carolina the backcountry population more than doubled during the years from 1750 to 1770, with the number of inhabitants of Anson, Orange, and Rowan counties—the center of the civil disturbances in the 1760s that would become known as the Regulation—actually tripling in just five years between 1760 and 1765. Similarly, the South Carolina backcountry, though it remained virtually unsettled through the mid-1720s, by the 1760s had a population of between 30,000 and 35,000, comprising somewhere between two-thirds and three-fourths of that colony's total white population.[6]

Life on the southern frontier was at times arduous for many of the people who had uprooted themselves from their homes on the eastern seaboard of North America or from Scotland, Ireland, or Germany, but it strains credulity to argue—as some have done—that only the myth and not the reality of economic opportunity awaited those tens of thousands of settlers who immigrated there. Those who have argued that overt class conflict was the principal cause of both the Regulator disturbances in the 1760s and 1770s and the civil disorder within the backcountry at the time of the Revolution have pointed to the fact of increasing economic differentiation within the region.[7] While it is possible to identify an emerging economic elite in the western areas of Virginia and the Carolinas, the material endowments of that elite were meager by the standards of their counterparts in Virginia's Northern Neck or the South Carolina low country. The members of the economic elite in the southern backcountry were people like the wealthiest citizen in Virginia's Lunenberg County, Henry Blagrave, who, though he had invested heavily in tobacco cultivation, amassing some two thousand acres and twelve tithable slaves by the time of the Revolution, was only a slightly more-successful-than-average planter. His estate, probated at his death in 1781, had a full inventory of slaves, horses, cattle, sheep, hogs, pails, tubs, saws, hoes, plows, harnesses, reaphooks, and jugs, as well as a hogshead of rum, a fiddle, and one wineglass, but missing altogether are those items—silver, china, crystal, a portrait or even a picture—that might suggest the life of a more refined Virginia gentleman.[8]

Far more striking than the modest attainments of those who rose to the statistical top of the economic order was the extraordinary expansiveness of the middling ranks. In the Virginia and North Carolina backcountry the number of householders owning their own land exceeded 70 percent, with the great majority of those householders owning between one hundred and four hundred acres. In South Carolina's Ninety-Six District over 90 percent of the adult male population owned land.[9] While there is ample evidence attesting to some of the rude aspects of life in the region, observers were often struck by the relative ease with which the inhabitants could support themselves. The Virginia gentry man William Byrd, on one of his trips to inspect his speculative holdings in the backcountry, commented, "Surely there is no place in the world where the inhabitants live with less labor than in North Carolina. It approaches nearer the description of lubberland than any other, by the great felicity of the climate, the easiness of raising provisions, and the slothfulness of the people." Byrd's observations betray the incomprehension of a gentry man who had never bothered to ponder the daily hardships of people living on the frontier. Nevertheless, he recognized, like so many others, that this was the "Best Poor Man's Country," a description that was applied equally to Virginia and the Carolinas as to the mid-Atlantic region.[10] Indeed, the gaps in wealth and power between the many and the few in the southern backcountry, as compared to those prevailing in those parts of upstate New York so thoroughly dominated by oligarchs such as Sir William Johnson, were remarkably slight.

Most of the members of the middling ranks who inhabited the backcountries of Virginia, and North and South Carolina were less dependent than their low-country neighbors on labor-intensive crops like tobacco, rice, and indigo and more reliant on the cultivation of foodstuffs such as wheat and corn and—of particular and overlooked importance—on the grazing of cattle, one of the easiest and cheapest ways of gaining a subsistence in a land-plentiful but labor-scarce economy. The profitability of this sort of agriculture varied from Virginia's central Piedmont to the Saluda River in western South Carolina, but the daily rhythms of this subsistence agriculture dictated a similar style of life throughout that whole region.

This picture of a uniform pattern of population increase, enhanced economic opportunity, and a fluid economic order was not one of consistent prosperity and ease; the egalitarianism of the backcountry often meant equality of hardship as well. Though the middling ranks may have enjoyed unprecedented opportunity to purchase inexpensive land, that commodity did not allow them to accumulate the surplus capital that might enable them to participate in the consumer revolution that was occurring in other parts of America. In Lunenburg County, for example, the median estate during the 1760s was valued at only £75, with the typical estate containing a few horses, some livestock, simple carpenters tools, the basic complement of farm implements, a bed (usually of straw, and without a bedstead), and a few plates and pots (but only rarely earthenware) for the kitchen. All of this was enough for an independent existence but hardly sufficient for a luxurious one. Moreover, only good fortune—or the avoidance of misfortune—separated the great mass of middling farmers from a return to dependence. Lacking surplus capital, most backcountry planters knew well that a serious illness or a fire—phenomena that touched all too many of their friends and relatives—could destroy the material basis of their independence.[11]

If the extraordinary mobility of the backcountry settlers served to enhance economic opportunity, at the same time it also worked to create chronic instability. The settlers who came to the backcountry brought with them an unprecedented variety of cultural preferences and only the vaguest loyalties to the government or traditions of a single colony. Indeed, it is clear that many of the citizens of Virginia's Southside had less identification with their colony than they did with that backcountry region, which included parts of north-central North Carolina. In Lunenburg, for example, marriage patterns were just as likely to cross colonial boundaries into North Carolina as they were to move either to the north or east, and even church congregations, at least for dissenting religions, drew members from outside the colony as well as from within.[12]

Perhaps the most dramatic sign of the impermanence of colonial or even regional attachments was the phenomenal movement of residents out of the backcountry counties. During the 1750s, when Lunenburg's total population was increasing at the rate of 16 percent annually, it was also losing its existing population at the rate of 17 percent per year, a migration pattern that assured that over 30 percent of the county's population would consist of individuals who had arrived only within the past year. This extraordinary mobility in and out of the county made the Virginia backcountry—no less than that of North and South Carolina—a moving frontier in the fullest sense of that phrase, with an uncertainty of kin and social relations that affected community stability in countless ways.[13]

The peoples who contributed to that extraordinary population increase and movement were a diverse lot. Settlement of the backcountry of Virginia occurred in two rather different streams—the east–west migration of Virginians whose primary identifications remained English and Anglican, and the north–south movement of peoples more recently arrived in America from Pennsylvania, Scotland, Ireland, or Germany, many of them members of dissenting religious groups. While the Scots-Irish were the recent immigrants who tended to be the objects of greatest scorn from others, and the separate Baptists the religious group that seemed to many the most deviant from traditional English religious forms, the challenges that ethnic and religious diversity posed came from multiple sources. In Virginia's Shenandoah Valley, which provided a migration route to settlers of all descriptions moving to the south and west, one encountered communities of German Lutherans along Stony Creek in Shenandoah County and Irish Presbyterians around Staunton in Augusta County. The settlers along Smith's and Holman's creeks in the Shenandoah were a microcosm of the ethnic and religious diversity of the middle colonies from which they had come, with Pennsylvania Quakers, Swedes, Mennonites, Germans, Welsh, Irish, and Ulster Scots living in close proximity to one another.[14]

While the presence of longtime Virginians alongside more recent immigrants would prove an important aid in assimilating that part of the backcountry to the norms of the more settled regions of the colony, it would at the same time open up the opportunity for conflict. William Byrd likened the immigration of the Scots-Irish into the Virginia Southside to barbarian invasions of the "goths and visigoths of old," and, while he was impressed with the beauty and fertility of the area in which they settled, he lamented the slothful character of its plantations, a condition he blamed on "the common case [that] in this part of the country the people live worst upon good land, and the more they are befriended by the soil and the climate, the less they will do for themselves."[15] Byrd's descriptions of the Virginia Southside and central parts of North Carolina seem a model of cultural sensitivity compared to the assessments of the Anglican minister Charles Woodmason, who set for himself the task of bringing English gentility to the South Carolina backcountry, a business that he found trying indeed. "Nor is this," he wrote:

a Country, or place where I would wish any gentleman to travel, or settle. . . . their ignorance and impudence is so very high as to be past bearing. . . . They are very Poor—owing to their extreme indolence, for they possess the finest country in America, and could raise but everything. They delight in their present low, lazy, sluttish, heathenish, hellish life, and seem not desirous of changing it. . . . Both Men and Women will do anything to come at Liquor, Cloaths, furniture, etc. rather than work for it—Hence their many vices—their gross Licentiousness, Wantonness, Lasciviousness, Rudeness, Lewdness, and Profligacy they will commit the Grossest enormities, before my face, and laugh at all Admonition.

Although he was dismayed by the habits of almost everyone he encountered, he saved particular scorn for the Scots-Irish, "the Scum of the Earth and the Refuse of Mankind."[16]

Woodmason's reactions to what he encountered in the Carolina backcountry were in part a product of an unusually tormented soul but were also shaped by a more generalized Euro-American cultural perspective unused to diversity, where ethnocentrism and provincialism were the norm rather than the exception.[17] As ethnic identity threatened to become a divisive, rather than a cohesive, force to communities, residents of the eighteenth-century backcountry would be challenged to discover new sources of identity within their communities that would allow them to affirm what they had in common rather than fight with one another about what they did not.

That ethnic diversity, in combination with the structural and spiritual frailty of the established Church of England on the southern frontier, led to an unprecedented diversity of religious life. Rhys Isaac has portrayed the character of the "evangelical revolt" in Virginia, but in depicting that movement as a response to "internal disorder"—to inherent weaknesses within the Anglican gentry culture throughout the whole colony—he has underestimated the extent to which the rise of the Evangelicals, a movement most apparent in the backcountry, was a function of a radically different kind of society. It was one in which traditional institutions of authority may indeed have been weakened by their transit across space, but in which the weaknesses of the established church were further undermined by the habits of the entirely different sorts of people—most of whom never had any connection with the religious culture of the gentry in the first place—who chose to settle there.[18]

The religious conflict that afflicted the South in the mid-eighteenth century is typically presented as a conflict between pious, austere, and generally humble Evangelicals and the wealthy, worldly, "great men" of the established church, but in fact the opposition the Evangelicals faced from leaders of the established church in the Virginia and Carolina backcountries was nowhere as aggressive or as threatening as that opposition coming from the great mass of the unchurched, who were the most prominent in scorning and disrupting their religious observances. The intensity of opposition to the Baptists may have varied from group to group within the backcountry, with the Anglicans more outspoken in their scorn for the Baptists in Virginia, and the unchurched largely responsible for harassment in parts of the Carolinas. Baptist Church records in both the Virginia and Carolina backcountry, however, testify forcefully to a religious experience that was common to evangelical adherents everywhere in the backcountry. When scores, sometimes hundreds, of converts walked into the rivers of Virginia and the Carolinas to bind themselves together through the ritual of adult baptism, they were at once setting themselves apart from those who gathered on the riverbanks to mock and scorn them and at the same time seeking to create the kind of community that was lacking in virtually any other institutional form in the spacious and often isolated backcountry. And those same individuals, by submitting themselves to the rigorous disciplinary code of the church meeting, were both affirming their intention to create some kind of order in their lives on the frontier and issuing an implicit rebuke to those many around them who chose to live their lives differently.[19]

The diversity—some saw it as disorder—of ethnic composition and religious life in the backcountry was sometimes accompanied by a remarkable looseness in the structures of family and community life as well. It was not only the hypersensitive Reverend Woodmason who was struck by that looseness. Governor James Glen, traveling through the Ninety-Six District of South Carolina in 1753, noted that though children in the region were numerous, their parents did not "bestow the least Education on them, they take so much Care in raising a Litter of Piggs. . . . The Parents in the back Woods come together without any previous Ceremony, and it is not much to be wondered at that the Offspring of such loose Embraces should be little looked after."[20] Indeed, the dominant image used by most European visitors to the backcountry was one of savagery, the feeling that European settlers, in removing themselves to the wilderness, had become, again in Woodmason's words, "as rude as the Common Savages, and hardly a degree removed from them."[21] The image recurs again and again; the Indian traders of South Carolina were reputed to be "more prone to savage barbarity than the savages themselves," and even respectable citizens in the backcountry, in the aftermath of the brutal and bloody fighting of the Cherokee Wars of 1760 to 61, "acquired such vicious habits that when the war was over they despised labor and became pests of society." In sum, the "state of nature" which many Europeans had revered in the abstract, was hardly a Lockean paradise, but often a coarse, brutal, disorderly place.[22]

Contrasting Political Cultures of the Southern Backcountry

In some important senses the economic and social conditions contributing to the loosening of the bonds of community and traditional conceptions of civility in Virginia and the Carolinas had similar effects on the political cultures of those backcountry regions. Given the independence, impermanence, cultural and religious dissidence, and general obstreperousness of the citizens in the backcountry in all of those colonies, we should not be surprised to discover how difficult it was for any southern backcountry community even to approach, let alone reach, the ideal of a deferential relationship. While many in the Virginia backcountry may at least have wished to emulate the deferential ideal of the Tidewater and Northern Neck (an ideal, as we have seen, seldom reached even in those regions), the record of contested elections in the Virginia backcountry displays a pattern of rowdiness, drunkenness, and occasional outright intimidation that suggests a very different ethic of constituent conduct. For example, the Committee on Privileges and Elections of the Virginia House of Burgesses was moved to set aside a 1758 election in Lunenburg in part because "of the behavior of one John Hobson, which was very illegal and tumultuous, in offering to lay Wagers the Poll was closed, when it was not; in proclaiming at the Courthouse that the poll was going to be closed, and desiring the Freeholders to come in and vote, and then, violently, and by striking and kicking them, preventing them from doing so, by which Means many Freeholders did not vote at said election." In neighboring Halifax County the sheriff charged that Nathaniel Terry, one of the candidates for the Burgesses,

came to me, his Coat and Waistcoat being stripped off, and his Collar open, and holding up a large Stick, threatened to cane me, and declared, if I attempted to read the Writ [of election] he would split me down, and did aim and endeavour several times to Strike me . . . with his Stick. . . . Immediately after this such a Tumult ensued, and the electors were in such a Temper, and so disorderly, and some of them drank of spiritous liquors to such excess, that I was convinced a fair Election could not have been made afterwards on that Day.[23]

When Charles Sydnor analyzed the meaning of scenes like those in his classic book, *Gentlemen Freeholders*, he depicted them as an amusing deviation from the prevailing deferential code of the Old Dominion, but those scenes, occurring as consistently as they did in the Virginia backcountry, suggest a system in which claims by political candidates to traditional notions of respect were far less secure and in which the inclination of an independent and mobile citizenry to pay deference was far more grudging at the very outset. Yet, however disorderly the conduct of politics in the Virginia backcountry may have seemed, the operation of the political system in that region was nevertheless strikingly more successful than that in

North and South Carolina, both in its ability to represent the interests of the western counties in the politics of the colony as a whole and in its ability to serve the legal and economic needs of nearly all of the settlers within their communities.

By contrast the institutional machinery and cultural ethic of both the North and South Carolina backcounty were woefully inadequate not merely for creating a system of deferential politics but, more importantly, for providing fair and just governance for the burgeoning population of those areas. Most obviously, the Carolina backcountry counties lacked adequate representation at all levels of government. In Virginia the House of Burgesses was conscientious about creating new counties when population growth in an area warranted it, thus assuring adequate provision of legal and administrative services at the local level and adequate representation for each locality in the provincial legislature. Throughout nearly the whole of the eighteenth century the ratio of representatives to constituents was uniform throughout the colony, averaging about 1:400. In the eastern regions of North Carolina, however, the ratio of representatives to constituents was about 1:150, as compared with about 1:1,500 in parts of the west. On most occasions the attitude of the provincial and royal governments in North Carolina toward the western regions was not one of aggressive oppression but of simple indifference. But that indifference often had serious consequences, particularly in the difficulties that settlers encountered in getting legal title to their lands. Settlers living in the Granville District of North Carolina had for many years suffered from inefficiency and fraud in the land office there, but with the closing of that office in 1763, at precisely the time when demand for land was peaking, the indifference of the government to settlers' needs seemed particularly outrageous.[24]

In South Carolina the situation was probably worse. Backcountry residents in that colony comprised nearly three-fourths of the colony's white population, yet were granted only three of its thirty representatives in the assembly. And while North Carolinians had at least some of the formal machinery, if not the actual substance, of local government, South Carolina's assembly steadfastly determined to concentrate political and legal power in Charleston rather than to disperse it throughout the colony. The consequences were severe for the backcountry; the provincial government of South Carolina refused to establish local courts in the backcountry until 1772, and, as we have seen, even then justice was meted out by circuit courts rather than county courts staffed by local residents.

If a large part of the problem in both the North and South Carolina backcountries was the neglect of the needs of the western counties by those politically powerful in the east, an equally important part was the breakdown in responsive and responsible relations between the few and the many in the backcountry communities themselves. The underrepresentation of the western counties of North and South Carolina in the legislature by formulas for representation devised in the east was further exacerbated by the fact that many of those western representatives, once elected, never bothered to appear in the legislature at all. Absenteeism among the representatives from North Carolina's Granville, Anson, Orange, and Rowan counties during the years 1760–70 was endemic. In South Carolina, where statutory underrepresentation of the west in the legislature was even more severe, attendance by those few western delegates who did serve in the assembly was no better. Moreover, those who did make an effort to attend the assembly sessions often did so to serve their own individual interests, not those of their constituents.[25]

The people elected to the assembly from the western regions of North and South Carolina hardly fit the gentry ideal. In North Carolina's far western Granville County the assembly representative from 1760 to 1768, Samuel Benton, had only recently been released from debtors prison prior to his election. In a region in which apathy in politics prevailed, however, Benton's energy in presenting himself as "a person calculated for what is called a poor mans Burgess" was sufficient to gain him election. Benton's ambition, it would turn out, was matched by his penchant for corruption. He was ultimately implicated in the financial scandals involving land patents in the North Carolina legislature, and at least some of his fellow citizens would lament that he and other local leaders in the Carolina backcountry had "practised upon our ignorance and new settled situation" in his rise to political power.[26]

James Carter, the most powerful political figure in Rowan County, provides an even more dramatic example. Born in Pennsylvania, by 1740 he was a "languishing prisoner" in a debtors jail in Cecil County, Maryland, a confinement occasioned when he was convicted of building a house for himself on someone else's property. Like so many others, Carter made his way further southward, first to the Shenandoah Valley in Virginia and then, sometime during the late 1740s, was one of the first Europeans to settle on the North Carolina frontier. Upon the establishment of Rowan County in 1753, Carter was made a justice of the peace, a major in the county militia, and, most important, a surveyor for the large grant of land given to John Lord Carteret, Lord Granville, in 1744.[27] The Granville grant offered to an ambitious and, as it turned out, corrupt surveyor like Carter all sorts of opportunities for personal enrichment. Serving a clientele eager, even desperate, to gain title to land, Carter was among those surveyors who overcharged for his surveys, refused to publicize his fees, and sometimes sold patents to different individuals for the same tracts. And, whether by design or sloth, he filed only "about 170 odd returns" on what should have been nearly a thousand transactions, leaving the vast majority of landowners without legal title to their lands. As one official later concluded, "there is not one single Patent that covers the Land claimed under it, owing to the

Villainy or Ignorance of former surveyors." Carter's transgressions, many of which did not become known until many years later, would not stand in the way of his election to the assembly; he would serve as Rowan County's delegate to the assembly in 1754, although his venality would finally get the best of him; in 1757 he was expelled from the assembly when it was discovered that he and several of his partners in corruption in Rowan had embezzled £500 that had been appropriated for the purpose of providing arms and ammunition for defense of the county during the French and Indian War.[28]

As we have seen, local government was virtually absent in the South Carolina backcountry owing to the refusal of the eastern-dominated assembly to create institutions of county government there. Although those local institutions did exist in North Carolina, they were so inadequate that the residents might have been better off had they been absent altogether. The local officials charged with keeping order and dispensing justice in backcountry North Carolina were as feckless, venal, and larcenous a lot as existed anywhere in America. Sheriffs embezzled tax monies and illegally seized property from those unable to pay inflated tax assessments, and justices of the peace, most of them lacking any significant political experience, used their offices improperly in pursuit of private gain. One traveler in Rowan and Anson counties in 1759 noted "a strange infatuation in the Devil possessing the Courts of Rowan and Anson," and vowed that he would "never . . . if possible" visit the area again. The local justices, another observer commented, "frequently bring down upon themselves, the contempt they deserve." Nearly all commentators were struck by the low level of learning of the justices, with one observing that the discourse in the court among the lawyers "was rather Obscene than Learned." That description was given substantive meaning in 1760 when Robert Harriss, a Granville justice and assemblyman, engaged in a drunken brawl in which he and his compatriots smeared human excrement on the face of their adversary, a local constable.[29]

A good deal of this behavior was the result of the scramblings for personal gain by a highly inexperienced and rough-cut local elite. As an Anglican missionary in Rowan County observed of the local sheriffs in the region, they were all "Persons in low circumstances" who, through the aggressive and, if necessary, corrupt use of their offices hoped to better their circumstances.[30] But at least an equal part of the problem in backcountry North Carolina was a colonywide political system that had never given serious consideration to the question of how best to govern a rapidly expanding, multiethnic society. As James P. Whittenburg has observed, "Even if the Regulation had not brought local government to a standstill in the late 1760s, the impossibility of administering—with only the meager tools provided by the assembly—an area larger than most contemporary European

nations and containing a population whose diversity was rivaled only by
that of Pennsylvania, would probably have done the trick."[31]

The combination of political inattention, government inefficiency, and
outright corruption that so often characterized political life in the North
and South Carolina backcountry brought into being a great mass of disaffected citizens who set their faces firmly against both their provincial government in the east and those local residents who claimed power over
them. When the crosscutting mixture of ethnic, economic, and religious
jealousies was added to those political grievances, the result was potent.
The intense alienation of the backcountry settlers—often ill focused and
only hazily diagnosed—had its initial manifestation in the Ninety-Six District of South Carolina in the late 1760s and had a dramatic flash point in
the Regulator uprising at Alamance Creek, North Carolina, in 1771.

The Regulator Movements

The Regulator Movement in North Carolina had its origins in the establishment of the Sandy Creek Association in Orange County in August 1766
and had its first, extralegal manifestation in an outbreak of violence in
Hillsborough, the county seat of Orange, on May 3, 1768. Over the course
of the next three years armed confrontations erupted between Regulators
and local officials and, eventually, the provincial militia in Anson, John-
ston, and Orange counties. The climax of the conflict occurred on May 16,
1771, when some 2,000–3,000 Regulators, in varying stages of prepared-
ness, met a well-armed provincial militia force of over a thousand men.
Royal Governor William Tryon, who himself commanded the militia, was
successful in subduing the Regulators, and the battle at Alamance, which
claimed thirty lives and two hundred casualties, marked the end of the
Regulator Movement in North Carolina.[32]

In South Carolina, backcountry residents similarly calling themselves
Regulators and acting in the name of law and order, engaged in a series of
vigilante actions between 1767 and 1769, directing their ire at "outlaws,"
"roguish and troublesome men," and, eventually, even "whores." In most
cases these actions took place on a small scale, as when a group of frontiersmen captured a suspected horse thief, John Harvey, stripped him
down to his undershirt, tied him to a tree with a chain, and meted out five
hundred lashes to him—all of this accompanied by the banging of a drum
and the playing of a fiddle while the blood streamed down his back. The
Regulators were free in their use of the torch, as well as the lash, setting fire
to the houses of men they suspected of thievery or corruption. The instances of violent vigilante action in the South Carolina backcountry were
sufficiently numerous and sufficiently devoid of anything remotely resem-
bling due process of law that it is hard to avoid the conclusion that many

of the backcountry defenders of law and order were far from lawful or orderly themselves. It is equally clear, however, that they had ample provocation, because the instances of lawlessness—of banditry, horse thievery, and petty crime associated with vagrancy—were sufficiently numerous to suggest something approximating a state of anarchy in the area.[33]

In a few cases larger groups engaged in more explicitly political protest, as when they presented a formal petition to the South Carolina Assembly in 1767 complaining about the prevalence of local outlaws and vagrants and the absence of local jails and other institutional checks on lawlessness in their communities. Even more pointedly, hundreds of backcountry citizens marched to three low-country South Carolina polling places during the election of 1768 to demand that they be allowed to vote in those parishes since they were denied representation in their own. In one of those parishes, St. James, Goose Creek, the Regulators actually elected three of their candidates. Unlike their counterparts in North Carolina, who put themselves in violent confrontation with provincial officials to the east, the Regulators in South Carolina sometimes operated with the acquiescence, if not enthusiastic approval, of at least a few provincial leaders in Charleston. While many in the legislature deplored their vigilante methods, they could not help but sympathize with the Regulators' demands, which at least claimed to be aimed at strengthening, not overthrowing, institutions of law and order.[34]

Whereas South Carolina Regulators engaged in vigilante action against bandits and vagrants and complained of the absence of local institutions capable of bringing people to justice, those who resorted to extralegal violence in North Carolina were deeply suspicious of both local and provincial institutions of government and of the corrupt men-on-the-make who dominated those institutions. As Roger Ekirch has noted, the Regulation in North Carolina arose "in opposition to abuses of power committed by men whose claim to authority and position in North Carolina's newly settled backcountry was extremely fragile."[35] Either of those conditions would have constituted a significant source of political instability in its own right, but when joined together, they created a nearly perfect climate for the unleashing of violence.

Historians will no doubt continue to disagree on the underlying causes of the Regulator Movements in North and South Carolina. Those movements have been variously described as being propelled by class antagonisms within the backcountry, by long-standing sectional differences between the backcountry and the wealthier and longer-settled east, and by simple jockeying for position among competing, but highly insecure, elites within the backcountry. It seems certain that all of these factors played a role in fueling the upheavals but that none played a determinative role. If there was one factor common to all of those who joined in the Regulation in both North and South Carolina it was a profound reaction—revulsion—against the disorderly conditions prevailing in their societies.

There were important differences in the composition of the Regulator Movements in North and South Carolina. There certainly is ample evidence suggesting that the leadership of the South Carolina Regulation was drawn primarily from what would have been the local political elite if the backcountry regions had possessed political institutions capable of sustaining an elite. Almost all of the South Carolina Regulators—the leaders and rank and file—were landowners, and a good many of them would go on to become the principal landowners and political leaders in their region after the Revolution. Rachel Klein, in her analysis of the composition and motivation of the South Carolina Regulators, has characterized the movement as one that linked "yeomen and aspiring planters as property holders who shared an interest in making the backcountry safe for planting." While their most immediate concern was the bandits who roamed the countryside unchecked by agencies of law and order, they also expressed a powerful—almost tribal—animus against hunters and other highly mobile individuals whose principal livelihood was not connected with the more orderly business of planting. In Klein's words, "Regulators were not . . . simply seeking to establish order. They sought to establish a particular type of order that was consistent with the needs of the planters."[36]

Certainly the most intriguing participant in the South Carolina Regulation was the itinerant Anglican minister Charles Woodmason. The same man who poured into his journal venomous descriptions of the manners and morals of the settlers of the South Carolina backcountry was also a strong supporter of the Regulators' efforts to bring some semblance of order to the region and a bitter critic of the neglect of the backcountry's problems by the low-country planter merchants who dominated the legislature. Woodmason had himself been a fairly successful merchant, planter, slaveholder, and holder of numerous local offices during the 1750s. Suffering some financial reverses in the early 1760s, he moved to Charleston where, through patronage favors from provincial and royal officials alike, he began to establish a moderately successful political career for himself, including appointments as clerk of the assembly, commissioner of pilotage for Charleston harbor, and commissioner of streets. In pursuit of patronage, Woodmason applied for the newly created post of stamp distributor in 1765, a decision that would dramatically change the course of his life. Stung by the fury of the townspeople at his intention to help enforce the hated tax, Woodmason quit his posts in the city and applied for the position of itinerant Anglican minister to the upper part of St. Mark parish, situated in the west-central portion of the South Carolina backcountry. Although it easy to ascribe Woodmason's abrupt decision to leave Charleston and his life of relative ease and privilege to disappointment and anger at his fall from grace, it is also clear that his Anglican faith ran strong and deep and that his concern for the absence of religious institutions in the backcountry was genuine. Upon receiving his appointment, Woodmason sailed for England—armed with glowing references attesting to his piety from a number of South Carolina officials, including Lieutenant Governor William Bull—and obtained his certificate of ordination.[37]

Woodmason returned from England in the summer of 1766 and took up his duties as an itinerant minister the following month. Although others had reported previously on the rude state of "English civilization" in the backcountry, Woodmason was obviously not fully prepared for what he encountered; nearly everything that he saw—from the instability of family life to the nearly total ignorance of the principles of his Anglican religion—shocked him. At the same time, though, he retained a genuine, if overly paternalistic and ethnocentric, concern for the people of the region, and he was infuriated at the hypocrisy of those low-country political leaders who carried on about "the rights of Englishmen" with respect to British authority in America while altogether denying similar rights to English subjects in the backcountry. Some of his anger was generated from sources purely personal—in particular, he felt that he had been abandoned by former friends like Henry Laurens and Christopher Gadsden at the time of the Stamp Act troubles—but some of it was founded on what he believed to be their hypocrisy. It was Woodmason, who was far superior to those around him in terms of education and command of language, who drafted the Regulator Remonstrance to the South Carolina Commons House in November 1767, and in it he turned the language of popular rights squarely on the backcountry's low-country oppressors. "We are Free Men—British Subjects—Not Born Slaves," the Remonstrance began, and "we contribute our Proportion in all Public Taxations, and discharge our Duty to the Public, equally with our Fellow Provincials, Yet We do not participate with them in the Rights and Benefits which they Enjoy, tho' equally Entituled to them." Woodmason then went on to enumerate the ways in which "the present Constitution of this Province is . . . defective, and become a Burden . . . to the Back-Inhabitants." The absence of readily accessible courts of law, inefficiency and corruption in the handling of "Land Matters," the denial of adequate representation in the legislature, and, most serious, the absence of institutions of local government and security, making it possible for "Villains . . . to range the Country uncontroul'd," were to Woodmason the very antithesis of proper English notions of law, order, and authority. This proper, law-obeying Englishman warned finally that "Oppression will make Wise Men Mad," and drive even the "many sober Persons among us" to desperate measures.[38]

Woodmason's rhetoric was shaped by his own conceptions of a "proper" English social order, prejudiced by his disdain for the hunters and other less permanently rooted folk who had helped make backcountry society deviate so dramatically from that ideal, and inflamed by his animus toward the low-country nabobs whom he felt had deserted him, but his strategy of turning the rhetoric of popular rights back on those low-country nabobs and shaming them with the obvious contradictions therein was effective. Although they would wait until the Revolution unfolded to take action (and would pay a significant price during the Revolution for their delay), the eastern oligarchs of South Carolina would eventually take steps to provide for the backcountry with the mediating institutions that would finally bring order to the region. And it overwhelmingly would be former Regulators who, newly empowered, eagerly took up the reins of government.[39]

The composition and ultimate outcome of the North Carolina Regulation was both more complex and infinitely more volatile. At least a few of the leaders of the movement were men who were—at least by the fairly low standards of the backcountry—men of property and standing. Hermon Husband, the principal leader of the insurgency, was the elder son of a prosperous planter from Maryland who immigrated to Orange County in 1755. By the late 1760s he had patented over 10,000 acres in Rowan and Orange counties. Similarly, the four other Regulators who were able to gain election to the assembly in the elections of 1769 and 1770 were all men of substantial property, represented in both land and slaves.[40] But plainly, whatever the affluence of its leaders, the North Carolina Regulator Movement was marked by a deep-seated sense of outrage over corruption and injustice that resonated particularly strongly among those at the bottom of the social order. At least some of those who cried out against corruption in the secular sphere were also in the sway of a millennial religious vision that looked to the day when society at large would be purged of corruption and vice. Hermon Husband's religion was a combination of Quakerism and New Light Presbyterianism, but the more common religious affiliation of the North Carolina Regulators was New Light Baptist, thus joining the political with the evangelical revolt.[41]

Some of the message that emerged from the Regulation was closely connected to traditional English country party ideology. One of the most frequently invoked phrases in the petitions, pamphlets, and letters of the Regulators was the good of the "Country," a condition that was constantly threatened by the corruption of "avarice" and the scramble for power. In castigating the manipulations of corrupt placemen like surveyor Samuel Benton or James Carter, they—like Charles Woodsmason—looked longingly toward the classical republican ideal of disinterested, virtuous statesmen motivated only by the "principles of virtue and honesty." Hermon Husband, in a statement that could have come out of Harrington's *Oceana*, insisted that "Where there is not virtue, there can be no liberty." His prescription for good government was to choose men who "have been unblamable in Life, independent in their Fortunes, without Expectations from others; let them be such as enjoy no Places of Benefit under the Government; such as do not depend upon Favour for their Living, nor do derive Profit or Advantage from the intricate Perplexity of the Law. In short, let them be Men whose private Interest neither doth nor can clash with the Interest or special Good of their Country."[42]

Although much of Husband's rhetoric could be used as a justification for rule by a virtuous, propertied elite, there were also strong popular themes in his message. The ideal was the virtuous yeomanry, "good industrious labouring Men, who knew the value of their property better than to let it go to enrich Pettyfogging Lawyers, extortionate and griping publicans or Tax gatherers." Lawyers came in for particular opprobrium, with some Regulator petitioners demanding that pettifoggers be prohibited from serving in the assembly. And it is clear that at least a few of the Regulators, including Husband, had a genuine concern for the poor; in his "Impartial Relation of the First Rise and Cause of the Recent Disturbances," Husband drew from chapter 5 of Nehemiah, in which the nobles were rebuked for their exploitation of the poor and in which "a Great assembly" was turned against them.[43]

Finally, the Regulators, though deprived by their isolated and largely powerless condition from participating in the protests against British imperial policy, were easily able to make the connection between British and North Carolinian corruption. The very first Regulator protest, written in August 1766, noted that "Whereas that great good may come of this great designed Evil the Stamp Law while the sons of Liberty withstood the Lords in Parliament in behalf of true Liberty let not Officers under them carry on unjust Oppression in our Province . . . as there is many Evils of that nature complained of in this County of Orange in private amongst the Inhabitants therefore let us remove them (or if there is no cause) let us remove the Jealousies out of our Minds."[44] The message was clear: the "Officers" of government in North Carolina could hardly call upon backcountry citizens to resist British oppression so long as they were responsible for similar oppression within the colony.

Whereas in many colonies elections served the function of focusing and occasionally resolving political conflict, electoral solutions were almost unheard of in the North and South Carolina backcountries. In South Carolina an electoral solution was a virtual impossibility given the denial of representation in the assembly to backcountry districts; as we have seen, a group of Regulators did descend on the low country parish of St. James, Goose Creek, in order to gain some representation for their views, but for all practical purposes South Carolina backcountry citizens were denied representation in the provincial assembly.

The scant records available for North Carolina suggest that citizen interest in elections was exceptionally low everywhere in that colony throughout the eighteenth century; in contrast to Virginia, however, there was often little in the behavior of those elected to office to suggest that voter apathy was a sign of citizen affirmation of the legitimacy of those noncompetitive elections. One significant exception was the election in Orange County in 1769 in which Hermon Husband and John Pryor, both Regulators and both turning to the avenue of elective political office for the first time, defeated the local symbol of provincial authority, Edmund Fanning, in the contest for the county's two seats in the assembly. Husband polled 642 votes, Pryor 455, and Fanning placed a distant third with only 314.[45] Voter turnout in the election was by far the highest (54 percent) in the colony's history, but this unusual mobilization of popular sentiment was not welcomed by those who controlled the provincial government. On December 20, 1770, assemblymen in the lower house expelled Husband from their ranks on the grounds that he had libeled a North Carolina superior court justice, Maurice Moore. On the same day Husband was arrested and imprisoned in the capital to prevent him from returning to the backcountry to stir up more trouble. Moreover, just a few weeks later the assembly passed a bill that made rioting a felony, and set up ground rules for the enforcement of the act, which denied those accused of rioting of due process in a number of significant respects. Husband was released six weeks after his imprisonment, but the symbolic importance of the provincial government's response to the Regulator concerns—even when those concerns were expressed by a representative duly elected by his constituents—could hardly have been lost on backcountry residents. Just as the British were denying John Wilkes his seat in Parliament and imprisoning him, provincial officials in New Bern were doing the same to Husband; both were outrages against traditional notions of English liberty, but backcountry residents, living far from London, were emphatically more upset about the imprisonment of their leader.[46]

It would be the popular reaction in the backcountry to those events that would lead to climactic confrontation between Regulators and government supporters in the Battle of Alamance on May 16, 1771. Governor William Tryon, who assumed the royal governorship of North Carolina just three months before news of the Stamp Act reached the colony, had managed, in spite of the furor caused by that news, to create reasonably harmonious relations with the North Carolina Assembly in the wake of the repeal of the Stamp Act. And, indeed, when he toured the North Carolina backcountry in late 1766, he reported his feeling of "Satisfaction [that] I found in those hilly or back settlements a race of people, sightly, active, and laborious, and loyal subjects to his Majesty."[47] But, obviously, that goodwill and harmony did not last long. The North Carolina Regulators, and Hermon Husband in particular, who almost certainly blamed the governor for his arrest, were quick to conclude that Tryon was part and parcel of the corruption they saw around them. Following two major disturbances at Hillsborough, the county seat of Orange, in May 1768 and 1770, and one in Anson County in 1769, Tryon marched a force of 1,185 provincial militia into the backcountry in May of 1771. Their firepower bolstered by artillery, the colony's militia defeated a force of 2,000 to 3,000 Regulators at Great Alamance Creek, in Alamance County. Thirty people were killed in the struggle, two hundred were injured, and seven were subsequently executed for their part in the rebellion.[48] The Battle of Alamance ended in defeat for the Regulators; indeed, it ended the Regulation.

The profound alienation that typified these outbursts of violence in the Regulator movement had its payoff during the Revolution, when the eastern rulers of North and South Carolina society asked backcountry settlers for their support in the common cause of the Revolution. The character of the "Uncivil War" in the Carolina backcountry during the Revolution has been well documented by historians. It has proven difficult to sort out the specific considerations that caused some social groups to ally with the patriots, others with the Loyalists, and, perhaps most commonly, caused still others to withhold any commitment whatever. But whatever confusion there may be about the underlying patterns of allegiance in the Carolina backcountry, there is no doubt that the Revolution in that region really was an "uncivil war," one which turned neighbor against neighbor, community against community, and significant regions of the Carolina backcountry against the patriot and provincial governments to the east. The central causes of that civil war—ethnic and religious antagonism, bitter competition for scarce economic resources, and the utter failure of outside mediating organizations to create a larger sense of the polity—added up to a nearly tribal brand of conflict, with the principal motivating forces being negative ones: the fear and hatred of one group toward another based on primordial impulses stemming from conditions of injustice. General Nathanael Greene, commander of the Continental Army forces during the most trying months of the southern campaign, was deeply impressed by the bitterness of the social conflict prevailing in the region. It was a country, Greene observed, in which "the whigs and the tories pursue one another with the most relentless fury, killing and destroying each other whenever they meet. Indeed a great part of this country is already laid waste and in the utmost danger of becoming a desert. The great bodies of militia that have been in service this year employed against the enemy and in quelling the tories have almost laid waste the country and so corrupted the principles of the people that they think of nothing but plundering one another." Even when formal warfare had ended after the battle of Yorktown, Green lamented that the South Carolina backcountry was "still torn to pieces by little parties of disaffected who elude all search and conceal themselves in the thickets and swamps from the most diligent pursuit and issue forth from these hidden recesses committing the most horrid murders and plunder and lay waste the country."[49]

That the backcountry regions of North and South Carolina were ultimately assimilated into the larger polities of first their independent states and later the independent United States is attributable more to the military victories achieved by the Continental Army elsewhere than to any inherent sense of loyalty or attachment that Carolina backcountry residents felt toward institutions of government in provincial centers in those colonies. In the immediate aftermath of the Revolution the provincial governments of North and South Carolina did belatedly attempt to make amends. Representation of western areas in the legislature was improved somewhat, and, more importantly, some of the principal demands of the Regulators—prohibitions against plural office holding and stricter controls on the activities of tax receivers—were addressed. As would be the case everywhere in the South, the most enduring source of allegiance between backcountry and the longer-settled centers of power in the Carolinas would ultimately have less to do with the conscious design of politicians than with the increasingly common commitment in both east and west to the institution of slavery—a commitment that would knit the politics, economy, and social ethic of those two societies more closely together.

But those developments occurred only gradually and at different rates of speed. The tenuousness of the Carolina backcountry commitment both to the polities of their state governments and, later, to the new national government, was everywhere in evidence—in ongoing difficulty in collecting taxes from backcountry residents, in continued absenteeism among backcountry representatives in the legislature, and, at least in the case of the North Carolina backcountry, in staunch and solid opposition to ratification of the United States Constitution. And in the years immediately preceding and following the drafting of the Constitution, the threat of separatist movements hovered in the background. The maneuvering over the state of Franklin, and, later, the activities of Aaron Burr farther to the west, all were testimony to the existence of at least an underlying threat to political integration within the new nation. Indeed, while some of Thomas Jefferson's vehemence in prosecuting Aaron Burr for his alleged acts of treason can be attributed to personal animus, we must also credit Jefferson with having a realistic sense of the tenuousness of the American nation-state, a situation that made aggressive action against those who would fragment it a necessity.

Backcountry Virginia Political Culture

The backcountry regions of Virginia never experienced the tumult that wracked the social orders of backcountry North and South Carolina. Political leaders in the Virginia backcountry, while they would never be successful in embodying a Harringtonian (or even a Washingtonian) ideal of disinterested virtue, did nevertheless work self-consciously to assimilate at least some of the traits of the political culture to the east. The political career of Lunenburg County's Matthew Marrable suggests some of the progress that many in Virginia's backcountry made toward reaching that ideal. In some respects his story parallels that of the two corrupt North Carolina assemblymen, mentioned earlier, Samuel Benton and James Carter, but the differences are instructive and relate at least as much to the political culture in which Marrable was operating as to his superior moral character. Like Benton and Carter, Marrable could boast neither an impressive family background nor a college education and, instead, would have to make use of his abundant ambition as a substitute for those advantages. Whereas Benton and Carter would use their political careers as means toward their accumulation of wealth, Marrable, like nearly all of his Virginia counterparts, would acquire at least modest wealth first and then use that wealth as a means toward the accumulation of political power. Beginning in the early 1750s, he built an estate of 3,700 acres and sixteen slaves through a combination of hard work and adroit land speculation, providing himself with an economic base for his political career. During those years, he served as a justice on the county bench and as a vestryman of his Anglican parish, two of the traditional requisites for political advancement in Virginia. Marrable understood the importance of marshaling influence and interest in order to establish claims to superior social status and political power, but, at least early in his career, he still lacked the politesse and the power to exercise those claims without experiencing substantial challenge. Marrable's first attempt at gaining election to the burgesses occurred in the same 1758 Lunenburg election in which John Hobson disrupted the proceedings by "violently, . . . striking and kicking the voters." But Hobson's behavior was not the sole cause for concern when the burgesses' Committee on Privileges and Elections investigated complaints about that election, for Marrable, who had initially emerged as the second top vote getter in the balloting and therefore one of the county's two representatives to the burgesses, had also engaged in behavior that separated a parvenu from a natural aristocrat. He treated the voters on several occasions, including feasts of seven roasted lambs and thirty gallons of rum. Although he warned recipients at his election-day treat "to take care they should not intoxicate themselves, least a Riot might ensue at the Election," it was quite obvious from the testimony about Hobson's behavior that that outcome was not averted. More seriously, the committee noted that Marrable had written a letter to David Caldwell, "a man of Great Interest in the County, strongly soliciting his Interest, in which is contained the following Words: 'This shall be my obligation to be liable and answerable to you, and all who are my Friends, in the Sum of five hundred pounds, if I do not use the Utmost of my Endeavors (in case I should be a Burgess) to divide this our county of Lunenburg in the following manner, to wit, Beginning at Byrd's Mill, running a straight line at the Head of the Nottoway.'" Caldwell, principal agent for William Byrd II's land dealings in the area, was indeed "a man of Great Interest" whose opinion of the rival candidates could affect the election, but the attempt to win his support by pledging a vote on a bill or, worse still, by promising money went far beyond any permissible definition of the deferential code. In this respect Marrable's behavior was characteristic of Strutabout in *The Candidates*, who, it was charged, told voters he would repeal their taxes, "make the rivers navigable, and bring the tide over the tops of the hills, for a vote."[50]

The House of Burgesses declared Marrable's election void and awarded the seat to the candidate who had lodged the protest, Henry Blagrave. Blagrave, as we have already seen, was, by the standards of Lunenburg, a wealthy man, but his claim to the deference of his fellow citizens was at least as shaky as Marrable's. In a subsequent election he was accused of an assortment of breaches in campaign etiquette, including instructions to the local tavern keeper that "if any person wanted Drams to let them have them" and another report that he had bribed at least one voter with a promise of a five-shilling pocketbook. Nor did Blagrave's conduct in private seem any more decorous than that in public. He was twice censured by his Baptist Church for drunken and "unchristianlike behavior" and on the second occasion remained sufficiently unrepentant that he was excommunicated from the church altogether. Lunenburg's other seat in the burgesses in that 1758 election went, virtually without a contest, to Colonel Clement Read, a man who, more than anyone else in the country, was seen as an embodiment of the successful transmission of Tidewater gentry values to the Virginia backcountry. Arriving in the region in 1733 from the Tidewater, he built the first really grand plantation house ever seen in Lunenburg and, through a combination of economic success and sober, responsible public service, managed to win not only the respect of his Lunenburg neighbors but also, through long and diligent service on some of the key committees in the House of Burgesses, a measure of recognition and respect from political leaders in the east of the colony as well. If Matthew Marrable and Henry Blagrave were floundering somewhere between the status of Wou'dbe and Strutabout, then Clement Read can be said to have achieved the status of Worthy.[51]

Both Blagrave and Marrable would move onward and upward in their political careers. Having learned a lesson about a proper joining of interests, Marrable cultivated sufficient support among the local worthies to gain a seat in the burgesses in 1760, holding it for most of the next decade. While he would never achieve the influence in the House of Burgesses of a Peyton Randolph or a Robert Carter (or, indeed, of his fellow burgess, Clement Read), he and most of those who followed him into political service from Lunenburg found themselves increasingly connected to the political institutions and behaviors of their eastern counterparts. Unlike their counterparts in North Carolina, they attended assembly sessions regularly, particularly so when business affecting the interests of their constituents was before the House. They were diligent in seeing to it that petitions from their home county were brought before the assembly, and the success of the county's citizens in getting the assembly to pay attention to their needs—whether it be in the establishment of additional tobacco inspection stations in the region or in the division of the vast, but rapidly growing county into small geographic units—was in at least some measure a consequence of their efforts.[52]

Again in contrast to the situation in North and South Carolina, where the electoral process was either nonexistent or little used, competition for public office in most of the counties in Virginia's backcountry regions was greater than it was for the colony as a whole. In particular, those Southside Virginia counties closely bordering North Carolina—counties like Brunswick, Halifax, and Lunenburg—showed exceptionally high levels of competition. In Halifax, which lies directly north of North Carolina's Orange County, the site of much of the Regulator activity, 75 percent of the elections between 1752 and 1775 were contested, with voter turnout during that entire period averaging 42 percent. Moreover, the elections were often close, with losers receiving an average of 47.4 percent of the total votes cast. And consistent with the more fluid and open-ended power structure in the county, incumbents were defeated in a third of the elections. Roughly similar patterns held true in Brunswick, Amelia, and Lunenburg, all in the same region.[53] Obviously, political conflict and contest were not absent in the Virginia backcountry, but the institutional structure of the Old Dominion provided a mechanism by which that conflict could be adjudicated.

When the Revolutionary War came to the Virginia backcountry, it would be ambitious and earnestly striving men like Marrable and Blagrave who would have the responsibility of mobilizing the populace in favor of the patriot cause. The economic hardship and personal grief occasioned by the coming of the war to the Virginia backcountry was no less than it was in the Carolinas, but the response in Virginia, both in the months preceding independence and in the dark aftermath of Cornwallis's southern invasion, was fundamentally different. Overwhelmingly, Virginia's backcountry citizens supported the patriot cause, doing so because their Whig leaders—both in their home counties and those to the east—were able to demonstrate in tangible ways that it was clearly in the interests of backcountry settlers to give their support. Unlike their Carolina counterparts, Virginia's leaders in the more settled parts of the colony had created a political structure at the provincial level that had proved responsive to the needs of the backcountry.

In the early years of the constitutional conflict with Britain, most of the western counties of Virginia, in common with most areas in America, were much less caught up in the dispute than either the commercially oriented residents of port towns or political leaders in provincial capitals.[54] Yet by 1775 Virginia's political leadership had scored remarkable success in spreading Whig institutions of protest and resistance to the backcountry. The first county committees in Virginia, originally modeled on the colonial Committees of Correspondence, began to spring up in the eastern counties in the early summer of 1774, but by mid-1775 those committees—by that time charged with the task of enforcing a boycott of all British goods through the agency of a Continental Association—had spread to virtually every county in Virginia. The committees were supposedly elected by the freeholders of their respective counties in much the same way burgesses were chosen, although in some counties it appears that the sitting members of the county court routinely assumed the position of county committeemen along with their regular duties. Whether the committees were appointed or elected, however, the fact that emerges about their composition in the Virginia backcountry is that the same moderately wealthy, earnestly striving men who had managed to control institutions of local government before the Revolution also controlled them during that struggle.

Those county committees were remarkably successful in creating and enforcing unity within the population at large, proceeding swiftly against those guilty of violating the nonimportation agreements of the Continental Association, and moving forcefully against those who were suspected of disloyalty to the patriot movement. In that sense, the coming of the Revolution in the Virginia backcountry, far from weakening the claims to political authority of a relatively fragile elite, would have the effect of enhancing the legitimacy of that elite, giving to them an expanded and more visible role in the common cause of the Revolution, a cause that would serve as a force for cohesion, rather than disruption, of Virginia's polity.[55]

There was, however, at least one area in which the assimilation of the Virginia backcountry into the larger political culture of the colony was thwarted. As we have seen, the one consistent source of cultural dissonance in the Virginia backcountry, as elsewhere, was the conflict between evangelical religious enthusiasts and their adversaries on both sides—adherents to the established Church of England and the unchurched. In the mobilization of the populace leading up to the Revolution those differences were to a remarkable extent submerged in the cause of greater immediacy—that of creating a united opposition to Great Britain. The Baptists, no less than their Anglican neighbors, wholeheartedly supported the resistance against Great Britain. Indeed, the rhetoric of American revolutionary republicanism—the call for the defense of virtue against corruption and the representation of the struggle against Britain as an opportunity for purging American society of luxury and vice—was wholly consonant with the doctrines of the insurgent evangelical movement.

The coincidence of rhetorical styles alone could not, however, have produced such unity, for Evangelicals in backcountry Carolina, though they, too, used the language of virtue and corruption, were obviously not so uniformly committed to the patriot effort. The principal difference between

Virginia and the Carolinas was that in Virginia the republican ideas of the Revolution were given expression by leaders—most notably Patrick Henry—who spoke the language of the backcountry authentically and who were capable of binding east and west, Anglican and Baptist, into a unified movement. Those leaders relied not only on rhetoric but also on a political agenda that sought to advance the interests of the backcountry, arguing for such vital concerns as the commutation of taxes in that region during the most financially trying times of the revolutionary period. In the aftermath of the Revolution, however, the Evangelicals of the Virginia backcountry would use the tactics of revolutionary mobilization to address the one grievance that had fueled their discontent before the Revolution: the privileged position of the Protestant Episcopal Church. Though it would be Thomas Jefferson who provided the lapidary philosophic phrases, and James Madison who played the role of legislative pilot in the passage of the Virginia Statute for Religious Freedom, the movement to separate church and state in Virginia was initially prompted and consistently propelled by backcountry dissenters. The session of the Virginia House of Delegates that passed Jefferson's bill in 1785 was little different in composition from the Episcopalian-dominated assemblies that had voted to restrict the rights of religious dissenters in the prerevolutionary era. However, faced with a determined political mobilization by backcountry Evangelicals in an unprecedented petitioning campaign involving many thousands of their constituents, the assemblymen of the revolutionary period—from counties in both the east and west—acknowledged that a genuine commitment to popular rights required that they give way. As a consequence the very Anglican assemblymen who had placed their names at the top of petitions supporting the church establishment were equally prominent in supporting the wishes of the dissenters in the final vote on the question.[56]

The political accommodation between Anglicans and Evangelicals achieved in 1785 would not eliminate all of the sources of antagonism that existed both within the Virginia backcountry and between the backcountry and the east of the state, but it was a sign of the vitality of a tradition of political responsiveness that had been established well before the Revolution commenced. In the eastern sections of the independent state of Virginia many citizens no doubt would have continued to link that tradition of responsiveness to long-established practices of deference and noblesse oblige, but the legitimacy of the political system in the Virginia backcountry was perhaps being founded on a concept more durable. Few of the Anglicans or Evangelicals would have been comfortable with the label of "democrat," but each side had embraced a form of egalitarian, voluntary contractualism that presaged the acceptance of an explicitly democratic ideology.

Chapter 7

The Unsettling Political Cultures of the Backcountry
The Northern Frontier

The primary direction of settlement of the backcountry in the mid-Atlantic and southern colonies was to the south and the west, with the massive migration of non-English immigrants adding new and socially unsettling ingredients to what was inherently an unsettling process. The direction of settlement of the New England backcountry was to the north, and in the case of Maine, to the north and east, and the great majority of those migrating there shared with their longer-settled New England counterparts a common English cultural and political heritage. This, along with a conscious effort on the part of the leaders of traditional New England society to transplant institutions such as the church parish, town meeting, and county court to the northern frontier, served to bind those frontier societies more closely to the provincial centers than was the case in most of the southern colonies and in Pennsylvania and New York. In spite of those cultural and political forces working toward convergence, however, the societies of the northern frontier nevertheless were fragilely constructed, and as was the case in their counterparts to the South, the road to political legitimacy and stability was a bumpy one.[1]

In 1760 there were perhaps twenty thousand people living in the fifteen incorporated towns that made up the province of Maine. The growth in Maine's population—from about two thousand in 1690—had been on the whole slow and sporadic, with small spurts of population increase interrupted by periodic wars or skirmishes with the French and the Indians that were occurring during nearly half of the years between 1690 and 1760. A contemporary map of Maine reveals a fairly clear line of settlement, stretching from the coast to about twenty miles inland and running from Berwick to the Penobscot region. The map shows a rather orderly line of towns—Kittery, York, Wells, Saco, Falmouth, North Yarmouth, Waldoboro—running up the coast and occasionally into the interior, a reflection in part of the desire of imperial and provincial governments alike to secure New England's northern frontier from hostile European interlopers. But the map fails to show a great deal about the nature of the settlement in 1760. The vast, unsettled spaces. The blanket of dark green forest that still covered most of the province, except for stretches where the white pine forest had already been harvested for masts, which were increasingly in demand in shipbuilding towns in Maine, Massachusetts, and England.[2] The map does not indicate the uncertainty of communication that existed between the provincial center of government in Boston and the towns of Maine. The colonial postal service terminated in Portsmouth, New Hampshire, and if residents of any of the towns in Maine wished to pick up their mail, they had either to travel to Portsmouth or arrange for private carriers to deliver the mail northward. And if a person made the trip—even on the one, "improved" coastal road that ran from the mouth of the Merrimack to the Penobscot region—it was likely to be an adventure. John Adams, forced to ride the roads of Maine as a circuit court judge, described a trip to Falmouth (only about halfway up the coastal road) as the most "spiritless, tasteless journey I ever took." He complained of "many sharp, steep hills, many rocks, many deep ruts, and not a footstep of man except in the road; it was vastly disagreeable."[3]

The settlement of the lands of Maine had for the most part been delegated to groups of "proprietors," but that term covers a wide variety of circumstance and behavior among Maine's economic and political elite. Most of the settled regions of Maine in the mid-eighteenth century were initially part of huge grants of land—the Pejepscot Patent, the Plymouth Patent, and the Waldoboro Patent—that in the early seventeenth century had been conveyed by the Crown to three small groups of proprietors. From the very beginning, the holders of these patents displayed a mixture of motives, ranging from the desire to extend pious settlements of Calvinists northward to the desire to enrich themselves through land speculation. Over the course of the seventeenth and mid-eighteenth centuries the claims and authority of the original proprietors were complicated by conflicting Indian claims, assertions of other Englishmen who claimed similar proprietary rights, the death of original proprietors and the complicated descent of their property to surviving relatives, and the purchase of inherited proprietary rights by others. As a consequence, there was by the mid-eighteenth century no single model for the way in which the proprietary system operated.

On the one hand, the township of New Marblehead (later to become Windham) was the product not of speculative greed, but of a 1734 petition of settlers of Marblehead, Massachusetts, asking to relocate their families to a place where land was more abundant. The resulting grant to the sixty original proprietors of New Marblehead was consistent with the desire of the Massachusetts General Court to perpetuate the original New England town ideal along the area's northern frontier. Most of the New Marblehead proprietors were men of middling wealth—two ship captains, six carpenters, four blacksmiths, a number of fishermen—and, given their seafaring

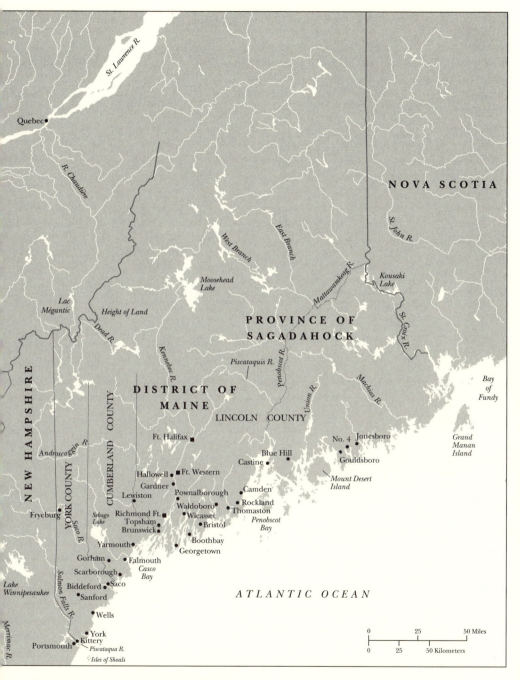

Map 5. The District of Maine, circa 1776.

and artisanal occupations, it is unlikely that they themselves migrated northward to become yeoman farmers. But their neighbors, increasingly pressed for land, did so, and the settlement became a modestly thriving agricultural community.

At the other extreme, when a consortium of Boston merchants formed the Kennebeck Purchase Company in 1749 and laid claim to three thousand square miles of land under the old Pejepscot Patent, their intent was to enjoy handsome profits as absentee lords and not to move northward to partake of the pioneer life. Even proprietors with the aggressively mercenary purposes of those involved in the Kennebeck Purchase Company, however, were able in the long run to achieve the orderly advance of settlement. As Gordon Kershaw has noted, the eighteenth-century Kennebec proprietors were every bit as adept as nineteenth-century robber barons in their expenditures of money to influence legislatures and royal governors, their employment of small armies of lawyers and lobbyists charged with gaining maximum advantage for their clients, their intervention and intrigue in the principal religious rivalries of the period, and, occasionally, in their ruthless eviction of settlers who stood in the way of their claims. Kershaw also notes, however, that, "in the long run, the Kennebeck proprietors demonstrated, if unwillingly, that aggrandizement for private gain might not necessarily run counter to the public interest."[4]

One reason for the continued success of large-scale proprietary organizations in getting provincial government sponsorship of their enterprises, aside from the fact that royal governors and legislators often directly profited from those enterprises themselves, was that private capital was often able to secure the aims of orderly settlement and the construction of public works, roads, and means of defense where public authorities lacked the resources to do so. But land policy dictated by the self-interests of land speculators also often led to division and conflict, a fact recognized by the Massachusetts General Court when it noted that the goals of orderly settlement based on widespread distribution of land were often thwarted "by reason of some Persons claiming Large Quantities of Land, which they are not capable themselves to settle, as the Law direct, nor are willing to part with to others, that offer to settle on them."[5] The result was that in at least some parts of mid-eighteenth-century Maine there was a situation in which a few individuals laid claim to large tracts of land while others who had immigrated there with the hope of securing a modest freehold had to content themselves either with squatting on the land or settling for tenancy on land owned by others.

Many of the holders of the largest land grants were absentee owners who rarely went to the trouble and expense to build grand houses on their largely speculative holdings, and the more typical pattern of land ownership and living was lots of one to ten acres in town or farms of one hundred to one hundred fifty acres in the countryside, with modest dwellings of log,

frame, or clapboard at either site. The vast landholdings of absentee proprietors to the contrary notwithstanding, the overall impression given by
the landscape of rural Maine was one of rough equality of condition.[6] The
other striking impression conveyed to outsiders certainly was one of
poverty: Reverend William Bentley, visiting from Salem, concluded that
Maine was "inhabited by poor people, whose cottages could not be exceeded in miserable appearance by any of the most miserable in Europe,"
and the aristocratic duc de La Rochefoucauld-Liancourt observed with obvious distaste that their "habitations are every where poor, low huts. . . . In
short, of all America, the province of Maine is the place that afforded me
the worst accommodation. And, considering how little reason I found to
praise the accommodations of many other places; what I have now said of
Maine must be regarded as an affirmation that the condition of human life
in that place is exceedingly wretched."[7]

More often than not the rough equality of condition that was so visible
in the Maine backcountry, like that prevailing in most other parts of the
American backcountry, was one of scarcity and hardship. One study of thirteen towns in Maine reveals that on the eve of the Revolution nearly half—
48 percent—of the taxpayers in those towns owned no land at all, with
another 47 percent possessing under five cultivated acres, and only the remaining 5 percent owning more than that. These figures almost certainly
overstate conditions of landlessness by including in the calculations young
adults still living with their parents and understate sources of wealth by ex-
cluding term lands from the calculations of "cultivated acres." Similarly,
they may overstate the extent of desperate poverty by ignoring the large
population of seafaring taxpayers who, though they may not have owned
land, nevertheless derived an independent sufficiency from the sea. They
do, however, reveal dramatically the narrow range of "affluence" enjoyed
even by people who did own property.[8] Even if residence in Maine did in
the long run offer the great majority of adult citizens the opportunity to
own land, that land often yielded only meager fruits. Whereas William Byrd
could marvel at the "felicity of the climate [and] the ease of raising provisions" in the backcountry of North Carolina and Virginia, the scarcity of
material comfort in Maine was exacerbated by the harshness of the climate
and the lesser fecundity of the soil.

One could easily imagine that the existence of a few wealthy, privileged,
and largely absentee "Great Proprietors," often guided by the desire to aggrandize their own economic interests, in conjunction with the conditions
of material scarcity and hardship that were the norm for a significant part
of the population, might create the potential for significant conflict between haves and have-nots. And for at least brief periods in the first two
decades of the nineteenth century, conditions of unrest, "decentralized
and slowly simmering," would erupt as poor white settlers, often disguised
as Indians, made explicit their unhappiness with the dominance of the

"Great Proprietors".[9] What is perhaps most surprising is not only that the unrest was not more apparent but also, the extent to which at least before the Revolution, the public behavior of the settlers of the northeastern frontier of Maine—by the mid-eighteenth century no longer predominantly English or Calvinist—continued to be shaped by traditional institutions and habits of the Puritan society that still claimed political sovereignty over them.

While those individuals designated proprietors in Maine's towns were granted privileges and opportunities for enrichment that other settlers lacked, they also shouldered significant responsibilities. By law the Massachusetts provincial government required that proprietors of towns complete a survey that provided for a compact and reasonable layout for their communities, build a meetinghouse, and hire a "learned and orthodox" minister, as well as attract a requisite number of settlers to live in the town—each in a house of a certain minimum size and standard of construction—all within a stipulated time period.[10] The requirements of peopling and financing a frontier settlement were often considerably more than what many proprietors had anticipated, and thus these statutory necessities sometimes were honored in the breach. But fulfilling those commitments was not simply a legal nicety. One of the market realities in mid-eighteenth-century Maine was that proprietors—whether resident or absent from the new towns—had to provide the necessary public services to attract settlers to their towns or those settlers would migrate elsewhere.

While the political leaders who designed the stipulations for proprietary settlements had as their goal the re-creation of the Puritan village on the frontier, few frontier settlements in Maine fully met that goal. The nucleated New England village, already itself being dissolved by the pressures of population increase and the lure of land on the outskirts of towns, was further fragmented on the Maine frontier. As Charles Clarke has noted, "in the most characteristic northern country towns, life focused on the family farm rather than on the village, which in most cases was either sharply attenuated or failed to develop at all."[11]

The reasons for this failure, if it can be called that, are not difficult to discern, being related to the interplay of geographic reality and the economic aspirations of the settlers. As in most colonies, with the possible exception of the earliest decades of the Massachusetts Bay settlement, those who immigrated to Maine did not do so by following an orderly town plan, but spread out along the valleys of rivers and streams. Some of the lands along the principal rivers of northern New England were naturally clear of trees, a fact that made starting a settlement there easier than in the otherwise wooded wilderness. More important, the principal rivers offered ready sources of transportation, and all of the rivers and streams of decent size provided sources of power for sawmills and gristmills. Similarly, though the laws of the Massachusetts Bay Colony may have stipulated that the construction of a meetinghouse be the first responsibility of the proprietors, the demands of settlers and potential settlers for other public services— such as lumber mills, gristmills, or bridges over rivers and streams—often took precedence over other matters, either political and spiritual. While for many the meetinghouse may have represented the very heart of the community, one could not expect to build a viable community without those public works that made life on the frontier viable.[12]

However dispersed and attenuated community life may have been in comparison with the closed, corporate ideal of early-seventeenth-century Puritanism, nevertheless Massachusetts, like Virginia, took pains to re-create on its northern frontier the full range of legal and political institutions that existed in the original settlements of the colony. If the Maine proprietors were in some cases slow to build meetinghouses in which the business of the town could be transacted publicly, they did nevertheless follow the mandate of the Massachusetts General Court to convene town meetings at least once a year and to choose "select-men" in those town meetings who would be responsible for administering the business of the town. Maine's town meetings met regularly, electing a large slate of town officers who performed the same range of tasks performed in Massachusetts towns. In practice, there were no property qualifications limiting a resident's right to stand for election to a town office. In the wealthier coastal towns local offices were more narrowly distributed to 4 to 5 percent of the population, whereas in the poorer, and often underpopulated, towns of the interior, as many as 15 to 20 percent of the population held local elective office at one time or another.[13] Though relatively few men selected for town offices came from the ranks of the impoverished, the typical town officeholder was very much of a middling sort. During the period between 1730 and 1785 in the coastal town of Pownalborough, service in town office was spread out among sixty-four yeomen, twenty millowners, sixteen merchants, fifteen blacksmiths, fifteen mariners, eight innkeepers, eight millwrights, seven shipbuilders, six cordwainers, four lawyers, and lesser numbers of teachers, tanners, brickmakers, and physicians. Those chosen as selectmen were generally wealthier than those chosen to lesser town offices, but even here service was spread fairly widely among the population, with average service as selectman usually being limited to three or four years, often not consecutively.[14]

As in the case of the parent colony, if the town meeting was responsible for laying down the broad lines of conduct for public behavior and making the important decisions about the expenditure of public monies on projects for the common good, the county courts were responsible for enforcing town edicts respecting the public good and the public order. As in Massachusetts, the line between administrative and judicial responsibilities among the justices in Maine was indistinct, and, as a consequence, justices at all levels were as likely to make decisions about bridges or roads or taverns as to preside over a civil or criminal trial. Perhaps even more than in Massachusetts proper, individual justices of the peace, acting in their own, very localized, districts within Maine's vast counties, were given a great deal of discretion to hear and decide on cases. More formally organized courts—common pleas, general sessions, and at the highest appellate level, the superior court—were generally composed of three or four of the most well regarded of the justices of the peace, so although judges on those courts were nearly always J.P.'s themselves, not all justices of the peace served on those higher courts.

Those serving as local justices as well as judges of the common pleas, general sessions, and superior courts of Maine constituted a distinctly smaller and wealthier group than those serving in local town offices, although by far the greater number of them can be considered wealthy only in a relative sense, within a society in which just a handful of people were truly affluent. If there was any occupational group that tended to have disproportionate influence within the court system, it was not lawyers, who numbered fewer than twenty in all of Maine during most of the period before the Revolution, but merchants from the wealthier and better connected coastal towns of the province.[15]

Overwhelmingly, the Maine court records suggest a society not only committed to adjudicating the typical suits between individuals over property but also, and more prominently, to maintaining social order and a "proper" Puritan moral code. Individual justices and the courts of common pleas and quarter sessions on which they served were intent on enforcing laws passed in Boston "against Intemperance, Immorality and Prophaness and for the Reformation of Manners," and the court records reveal that the justices were kept extraordinarily busy doing so. The justices were particularly active in combating what they perceived to be breaches of the sexual code. While it might be tempting to conclude that their close attention to this area of contact was a sign of their success in maintaining strict Puritan values in matters pertaining to relations between the sexes, it is perhaps at least as likely that their preoccupation with those matters is suggestive of the extent to which a northern frontier society posed challenges to those values. But however great the challenges, the commitment of people in the provincial center of government to extend institutions of social and political order to the backcountry as a means of maintaining traditional values is noteworthy, as is the willingness of at least a few people in those frontier communities to undertake the job of overseeing the administration of order and justice.[16]

The towns of Maine were guaranteed representation in the Massachusetts General Court under the same formula applied to towns in the Bay Colony itself, but like many of the towns of western Massachusetts, many Maine townships—in some years as many as four-fifths of them—went unrepresented in the provincial assembly, either because those elected refused to serve or because they never went to the trouble of electing representatives in the first place.[17] Some argued that the absenteeism on the part of Maine's representatives was a reflection of their feeling of helplessness in the face of the superior power of Massachusetts representatives. One resident of the interior complained:

It has been found by long experience that our members have so little weight in the legislature, that they can carry no point which is supposed to be to our advantage. . . . This had led us to think it almost a matter of indifference whether we be represented in the legislative body. . . . Though we seem to have the benefit of a representation, it in fact comes to nothing.[18]

Those who were most conspicuous in taking on the responsibilities of public service in the Massachusetts General Court, while their family lineages and attainments of wealth and prestige may not have established for them indisputable claims to natural aristocracy in the Harringtonian sense, were nevertheless readily identifiable within their communities for their wealth, family connections, and perhaps most important, their steady attention to the public business. In the immediate postrevolutionary period, about 60 percent of the 260 men elected to seats in the general court were justices of the peace, and those legislators who were also justices were more than twice as likely to actually appear in Boston to serve as those who were not justices.[19] At least a few of those who chose not to serve may have suffered from the same feelings of inferiority expressed by Samuel Nasson of Sanford, who wrote to a friend:

Others have offered to Assist to Send me again, but I cannot yet Say if I was Chosen wither I should Attend. I have lately thought I would not and it not for any reason that I have as to the Administration or that I do not like the Life but I feel the want of a proper Education. I feel my Self so Small on many occasions that I all most Shrink into Nothing. Besides I am often obliged to Borrow from Gentleman that had advantages which I have not.[20]

One student of the political leadership class in Maine has argued that life on an isolated, often dangerous, northern frontier caused most residents to focus their energies entirely on providing a subsistence for themselves and their families, frequently making for "greater dependence on the relatively few leaders of the region," but, in fact, Samuel Nasson did rouse himself to serve at least a few years as a representative to the general court.[21]

The sorts of people who managed to translate modest economic success into modest political authority at the local level in this remote land of seafaring farmers were men like Thomas Chute of New Marblehead. Chute was born in London in 1690 and immigrated to Marblehead, Massachusetts, sometime before 1725. In Marblehead he established himself as a hardworking and reliable individual, earning a living as a tailor and storekeeper, as well as running a "house of entertainment." He was also serving as deputy sheriff in Essex County, Massachusetts, at the time that he became one of the original proprietors of New Marblehead, in Maine, in 1734. Unlike most proprietors, who never lived in the towns they helped found, Chute actually moved his businesses and his family to New Marblehead shortly after its legal establishment. Indeed, Chute was not only the first of the New Marblehead proprietors to move there, he was also the first European settler of any kind, building his new home, made of logs, near the shores of the Presumpscot River, on the edge of the wilderness. Shortly after he completed his own house, Chute, his son, and a hired hand began work on a fort, fifty feet square, two stories high, with walls one foot thick, to protect the settlers from Indians in the area. When negotiations with nearby Indians broke down in the mid-1740s, all of the New Marblehead settlers, including the Chute family, ended up moving into the garrison, spending most of their time from 1745 to 1751 there. During these years, the fort served as principal domicile, church meetinghouse, and town hall for the handful of settlers who had chosen to make New Marblehead their home.

As was the case in Massachusetts, Chute proved himself an able hand in virtually every conceivable area of endeavor. He continued his tailoring business, and, sometime not too long after relocating there, began keeping a small store in his house in which he sold everything from basic foodstuffs to rum, tobacco, and wigs. He cleared land for other settlers, hauled masts to the river, and hired himself out to the proprietors building roads and bridges. Over the course of the next thirty years he built a new home—this one a frame house—and opened both a tavern and an expanded mercantile store. In both of these pursuits, whether in dispensing rum, flip, and toddy, or in selling flour and dry goods, Chute was in a good position to get to know, and get to be known by, virtually all of his fellow townspeople. He also used some of his lands to provide pasture space for the cows and other livestock of his neighbors and marketed the dairy products from neighboring farmers. All the while he continued his tailoring and hired himself out to clear some land, cut some wood, or deliver merchandise, sometimes being paid in cash, other times in barter. The sum total of all of those efforts—expended constantly over the full course of his life—was certainly not affluence, but it was a sufficiency.[22]

From the very beginning, in part because he was one of the original proprietors, but in equal measure because he was a steady hand who could be counted on, Chute's fellow townspeople entrusted pieces of the town's business to him. When they wished to present a petition to the general court, they often sent Chute to Boston to deliver it. As one of the seven original male members of the New Marblehead Church, he was made a deacon and appointed to look after the church's finances and to prepare the Sacrament. And like nearly every able-bodied male in a frontier region in a state of perpetual military mobilization, Thomas Chute gave a portion of his time to militia service. He was a sergeant and was placed in charge of New Marblehead's small contingent within the Falmouth militia company during the 1740s, and during the 1750s, was made a captain and placed in charge of his own company.[23]

Toward the end of his life, when in 1762 New Marblehead was reorganized as the incorporated town of Windham, Chute was elected by the town meeting to be the first town clerk, serving in that office for four years and then being chosen a selectman for two terms. By the time he retired as selectman, Chute was in his seventies and most of his business—economic and political—had been transferred to his son Curtis. It hardly constituted a family dynasty, but within the context of the northern frontier, Thomas Chute stood out as a man of substance and probity.[24]

If the career of Thomas Chute exemplifies the emergence of the sturdy yeoman of Maine into positions of respectability and modest political authority, then that of Enoch Freeman of Falmouth takes us closer to the center of power within one of Maine's busier and more affluent seaports. Freeman was born and raised in Eastham, on Massachusetts's Cape Cod, the son of Captain Samuel Freeman, a selectman in his town and a member of the general court. His family lineage and academic aptitude were sufficient to enable him to enter Harvard, where he graduated in the class of 1729, a fact nearly unique among those men who would constitute the ruling elite in Maine at any time during the prerevolutionary era. Being the eighth son in his family and therefore lacking any realistic prospect of inheriting his father's wealth, he initially apprenticed himself to a Boston merchant, Hugh Hall, and then subsequently entered into a contract with Hall to sell on commission some of the goods that Hall imported. The income from this enterprise, together with the network of contacts that he developed with Boston merchants, enabled him to begin his own mercantile business when he relocated to Falmouth in 1742. Falmouth, although it had been incorporated in 1658, had languished and nearly expired as a viable settlement until the late 1720s, when it finally began to establish itself as an export center for the products of both the fisheries and the forests. Freeman's timing was impeccable; an experienced, Harvard-educated merchant with good ties to Boston, he was able to establish himself rather quickly as a leading figure in the burgeoning trade in masts and other forest products. Moreover, as one of the few college-educated men in the region, he was quickly drawn into the practice of law, putting his Harvard education and his recently acquired knowledge of the law into the service of both his town and his mercantile business.

Within a few years of his arrival he was appointed a captain in the Falmouth militia, two years later a major, and by 1750 was made a colonel and placed in command of all of the militia of York County. Over the course of the next twenty years Freeman would acquire a nearly endless list of public offices, many of them simultaneously: selectman, town treasurer, notary public, justice of the peace, naval officer for the port, deputy collector of customs, register of deeds, judge of the court of common pleas, judge of probate and, beginning in 1748, representative to the general court. At the peak of his power, in 1774, he was elected by the assembly to serve as one of Maine's three representatives on the Royal Council, but like that of many others elected by the general court to serve on the council on the eve of the Revolution, his appointment was vetoed by the governor due to his patriot sympathies.[25]

Freeman's rise to political prominence within his community was not achieved without some conscious effort. Described by at least a few of his contemporaries as a man of "proud bearing and severe manners," he was not above electioneering when he thought it would help his prospects. In 1760 he sought appointment from Royal Governor Francis Bernard as temporary register of deeds, believing that being the incumbent in that post would help him gain election for a full term when the interim appointment expired. Casting about for some means of influencing the appointment, he wrote to James Otis Sr., a client for whom he sold dry goods on commission and from whom he bought lumber, and indicated that "I shall take it as a Favour if you'd Speak to Governor Hutchinson or any of my Friends about it; Governor Barnard don't know [me so] that I suppose it will not Signify much to Speak to him unless you Say Something in my Favour."[26] He was evidently successful in gaining the temporary appointment, but when he ran for election for a full term the next year, his ambition would cause him to misstep. While Freeman's influence in his hometown of Falmouth may have made him invulnerable to challenge there, the election for the post of register of deeds put him in competition with others across the whole of Cumberland County. Although Freeman initially won the election, three months later, in May 1761, the governor and general court received a petition from residents in Scarborough complaining of Freeman's overaggressive behavior in securing the votes of citizens at the Scarborough town meeting. Their complaint was that the court of common pleas at Falmouth, of which Freeman was himself a member, had set aside the votes of citizens at the Scarborough town meeting on the grounds that people at that meeting had not been sufficiently informed of the election in advance. The petitioners disputed the action intensely, "Especially as Enoch Freeman, Esq was at the meeting with a Number of his Friends from Falmouth making Interest for him before and at the very Time of the Meeting. . . . So that the whole Town was as well Acquainted with the Choice of a Register and also of the Candidates as they Eer can be of any Vote." On hearing the petition, the council and general court ordered a new election the following year, choosing, however, to retain Freeman in office until that election could be held. In the end he would withstand the challenge, as he not only gained reelection the following year but would continue to serve as register of deeds for the next twenty-nine years.[27]

Freeman's assumption of prerogative did not sit well with everyone. He was later described as a person who, by "almost overwhelming influence, which his character and position had given him, was somewhat arbitrary and overbearing; a disposition which the long possession of office is apt to nourish."[28] He was a firm opponent of New Light religion in general and of George Whitefield in particular and, as a magistrate, steadfastly defended the property rights of absentee proprietors against the encroachments of landless frontiersmen. But like so many in Boston and the principal port towns of Maine, he was not so wedded to law and order that he was able to stand by and see his interests as a merchant sacrificed at the altar of British imperial policy. As deputy collector of the customs and as a magistrate, he was bound by law to punish customs violators, but when a mob assaulted the comptroller of customs in 1769, Freeman refused to move against any of the suspected offenders. His role in the coming of the Revolution would increase—he and his son Samuel would serve on the new Falmouth Committee of Correspondence, and he would also serve in the first revolutionary Provincial Congress.

As the Revolution in Maine unfolded, and as agrarian radicals like Colonel Samuel Thompson of Brunswick sought to mobilize Maine frontiersmen in a preemptive strike against English naval ships, Freeman, like many other Whig leaders in Maine, would have to find a way to draw the line between orderly resistance to British authority and excessive mob action against all authority. For most of the period of the Revolutionary War, Falmouth would be a very disorderly place, under danger of constant attack from the British, and the security of property always in jeopardy because of the excesses of the mob. On October 18, 1775, two-thirds of the houses in the town and most of the ships in the port were leveled by a bombardment by a British naval fleet, devastation made all the more horrible by the fact that militiamen from neighboring towns, under the pretext of preventing the British from ransacking Falmouth, joined in the looting of the houses damaged in the bombardment. The Reverend Jacob Bailey reported a "multitude of villains were purloining . . . goods and carrying them into the country beyond the reach of justice." Freeman, no friend of assaults on property by backcountry mobs, was no doubt among the selectmen who determinedly carried out the orders of the general court to punish people suspected of retaining stolen property.

In fact, the disorder and destruction in Falmouth in the fall of 1775 would turn out to be a one-time explosion of randomly directed violence. Freeman and the other selectman would recover much of the stolen property, the citizens of the town would begin the task of rebuilding, and Falmouth would be successful in repulsing all other attacks—internal and external—for the duration of the war.[29] Conservative Whig leadership, in the person of Enoch Freeman, and increasingly in his son Samuel, managed to remain in command.

If Thomas Chute's career was typical of those men who rose to modest prominence in a town where great wealth and great power were beyond the means of nearly all, and if Enoch Freeman's career represents that of a man who had moved to the forefront of Maine's provincial elite, then the exceptional career of William Pepperrell Jr.—which ultimately would extend his reputation beyond Maine and Massachusetts to England itself—was one that draws attention to the ways in which the Maine frontier was simultaneously shaping and being shaped by the colony and empire of which it was a part.

There was perhaps no other family in Maine more conspicuous in its willingness to step forward and assume the responsibility and reap the rewards of public service than the Pepperrells. Few in either Maine or Massachusetts were able to achieve as much in those respects as William Pepperrell Jr., later annointed Sir William. William Junior's father had left England as an apprentice to the captain of a fishing vessel and, sometime in his late twenties, decided to start his own modest mercantile business on the Isles of Shoals in the harbor of the Piscataqua River, separating Maine and New Hampshire. Teaming up with another West Country Englishman, Pepperrell started off by buying small shares of fishing voyages until he and his partner could afford to purchase a few fishing boats of their own. He had some modest success at this when, in 1680, he left the Isles of Shoals for Kittery and for a wife, Margery Bray, daughter of John Bray, a boatbuilder there. From this point on, William Pepperrell was on a steady path of accumulation—building a substantial two-story house for himself and his wife, in "a plain place near the highway" but overlooking a cove on which the waters were sufficiently calm, even during the frequent northeasters, that it made an excellent anchorage for his expanding fleet of vessels.[30]

William Pepperrell's business, which always centered around the export of Maine's two principal products, fish and lumber, and the importation of goods from England to Boston, grew steadily during the next thirty years. He gradually increased the number of vessels in his service, as well as the venues that his exporting business served. William Pepperrell Sr.'s eldest son, Andrew, became an active partner in the business as soon as he reached adolescence, but he died in 1714, leaving only William Pepperrell Jr., then just seventeen, as the surviving heir to the firm. Although William Junior's education had been largely informal, by the time of his brother's death he had already acquired considerable experience in some of the practical aspects of running his father's firm. From that time forward he would enter into active partnership with his father. William Senior was sixty-five years old in the year of Andrew Pepperrell's death, and by 1726, when he was only thirty, William Junior was for all practical purposes fully in control of the firm, finally inheriting it outright in 1734, at his father's death.[31]

Since a good portion of the Pepperrells' merchant business was tied to the timber trade, it was only natural that once they had sufficient capital they would buy up some of the lands that produced that timber. William Junior, in particular, would oversee the expansion of that portion of the business, and by 1730 he owned several thousand acres in Saco and Scarborough. Equally important, the nature of the Pepperrells' business required a constant presence in Boston; consequently, William Junior spent much of his time there, expanding his network of business and political associations.[32]

The growing economic power of William Pepperrell Jr.—as merchant, shipbuilder, and, increasingly, owner of substantial tracts of timberland—was obviously an important factor in his political influence within his community and region, but it was not the only one. For William Pepperrell Jr., as for nearly all of the political leaders of eighteenth-century Maine, service and leadership in the militia was an important determinant of a man's standing and influence. Militia service in Maine, as nearly everywhere on the American frontier, was more than honorific. For virtually the entire span of its colonial history, Maine was caught up both in the global struggles for dominance among England, France, and Spain and locally with constant warfare with Indians. William Pepperrell Jr. was appointed captain of the York County militia when he was still in his early twenties, and he had probably assumed his father's position as a colonel and commander of all of the militia forces in the province of Maine by the time he was in his early thirties. Although Indian warfare on the northern frontier would die down for a decade or more after Captain John Lovewell led a series of brutal attacks on Indian outposts on the banks of the Kennebec in 1725, later in his career Pepperrell would have much the same sort of opportunity to enhance his standing by service in Indian wars as that enjoyed by another colonial warlord and frontier grandee, Sir William Johnson.[33]

Although William Pepperrell Sr. was nearly exclusively a businessman for whom politics was only a necessary means to an end, William Junior entered politics early, actively, and enthusiastically. As Pepperrell's biographer Byron Fairchild has noted, it "was natural and inevitable that William Pepperrell, Jr., should be chosen for political office," for throughout the entire eighteenth century, public affairs in Kittery were dominated by just a few families, of which the Pepperrells quickly became the most prominent. "Town offices were passed around among them and handed down from father to son and grandson," with more than half of the selectmen in Kittery during the period from 1693 to 1760 coming from just nine families. The same nine families furnished the representation to the Massachusetts General Court in forty-eight of the sixty-seven years of that period.[34]

In fact, reversing the normal order of things, William Pepperrell Jr. served on the Massachusetts General Court before he served as selectman, gaining election to that body by the Kittery town meeting at the age of twenty-four, in 1720. William Junior was elected a Kittery selectman in

1722, and for most of the rest of that decade served simultaneously as selectman, moderator of the Kittery town meeting, and representative to the
general court. There is no question but that he was a conscientious and effective representative of the interests of his constituents during his service
on the general court, particularly as his service related to the two matters
that were of the greatest interests to his constituents—that of frontier defense against Indians and of continuing the battle to undermine the authority of the Surveyor General of His Majesty's Woods, whose job it was to
punish encroachments on the king's woods. Indeed, he was successful not
only in holding the confidence of his Kittery constituents, but also in sufficiently ingratiating himself with the new royal governor, William Dummer,
as to gain appointment to the Governor's Council, in 1727, at the age of
thirty-one. William Pepperrell Jr. served on the council for thirty-two consecutive years, until his death in 1759, serving the last eighteen of those
years as the council's president. When his good friend Jonathan Belcher
was appointed governor of Massachusetts in 1730, he appointed Pepperrell
chief justice of the York County Court, thus confirming Pepperrell's unrivaled authority in town, county, and province.

Pepperrell's achievements in the political arena were notable by any
standard within the Massachusetts Bay Colony, but, in fact, they would extend considerably beyond his long service on the Governor's Council. One
of the paths to political power for Pepperrell had been his familiarity with
Indian affairs and, indeed, with all matters relating to the frontier. Almost
from the first month of his service on the Governor's Council until his
death, he would be a key government representative at every deliberation
with the region's Indians, in both peace and in war. It would be in this latter posture—as military leader of English forces attacking Louisbourg, the
French fort on Cape Breton, that Pepperrell would establish a reputation
for himself that would extend well beyond the Massachusetts Bay Colony.
The question of whether or not to mount an attack on Louisbourg had
been debated off and on in England and New England for several years,
but it was not until Governor William Shirley of Massachusetts, with the active support of Pepperrell, his council president, proposed an American-
led, as opposed to an English-led, assault that the proposal moved forward.
When it did, an Englishman commanded the naval forces and an American, William Pepperrell himself, commanded the ground forces. Although
others within New England lobbied for the appointment that went to Pepperrell, the factor that turned the tide, according to several observers, was
Pepperrell's popularity with the rank-and-file soldiers, many of them from
Maine, who would make up the bulk of the force carrying out the assault
on Louisbourg. In fact, Pepperrell, in spite of his long service in the militia, had never actually faced an enemy in armed combat, but military inexperience was deemed less important than his popularity, which enabled
him to raise the entire force of 4,300 men necessary for the assault within

just a few months.[35] Anti-French and anti-Catholic sentiment combined with the near-religious fervor produced by the thought of unimpeded geographic expansion, and Pepperrell's army of frontiersmen, aided by only a small English naval force, laid siege to Louisbourg and captured it on July 17, 1745. Just a little over a month later, still in residence at the captured fort at Louisbourg, Pepperrell received word that King George II had made him a baronet. One of America's few titled noblemen, Sir William Pepperrell, like Sir William Johnson of New York, earned his nobility by fighting the French and Indians.[36]

Pepperrell's imposing influence in vigorous and active structures of town and county government and in the wider circles of his colony and, eventually, the British Empire, stands in stark contrast to the situation in the North and South Carolina backcountry. Indeed, his career was far more luminous than any backcountry politician ever achieved in the more institutionally stable political culture of Virginia. A partial explanation for the difference can be found in the institutional structure of the Massachusetts Bay Colony. The northern frontier was guaranteed some measure of political influence within the politics of the colony by provisions of the 1691 colonial charter, stipulating that any incorporated town, no matter how small its population, was entitled to at least one representative in the general court and reserving for the province of Maine at least three seats on the twenty-eight-seat Governor's Council. In fact, though, Pepperrell's record of conscientious and effective service within the provincial government was unusual by the standards of Maine, and given the overall rates of absenteeism and participation among members of both the Governor's Council and the Massachusetts General Court, it should be no surprise that Maine's representatives to those bodies—lacking Harvard educations and preoccupied with the more pressing concerns of building or maintaining modest family fortunes within their localities—were, like many of the representatives from western Massachusetts towns, frequently absent from the proceedings or, at best, backbenchers who had only slight influence on the business of the general court or the council.

What is most notable about the political culture of backcountry Maine is not the cosmopolitanism of a William Pepperrell, but the intense localism—given the state of communications, isolation might be a more apt word—that prevailed in most towns in the region. These traditions of localism persisted well after the Revolution. When Silas Lee, a young lawyer in Maine, visited Castine during the debates over ratification of the federal Constitution in 1788, he noted that the people of the town were remarkably unaware that a new Constitution had been drafted in Philadelphia; they were, he commented, not only unaware of its existence, but "equally indifferent as to its establishment." The only political concerns to which the Castine residents were attentive, according to Lee, were "the sheriffs and justices of the peace."[37] Most of the rhythms and rigors of daily life

LT. GEN. SIR WM. PEPPERRELL, *Bart.*
The Victor of Louisbourg A. D. 1745.

Figure 11. Sir William Pepperrell. Like Sir William Johnson in New York,
Pepperrell's career on the Maine frontier brought him fame and power in both
the military and political realm. Photograph courtesy of the Peabody Essex
Museum.

were determined by the soil and climate, not by government policies. The principal points of contact (and conflict) with provincial and metropolitan centers of government came over territorial disputes, whether with the Crown over the extent of the royal timberlands or with the French and the Indians over land. It was on those occasions that the presence of a William Pepperrell in Boston was important, and no doubt Pepperrell's effectiveness in representing his region's interests in those crucial areas was a more important ingredient in the popular support that he enjoyed than was some mystical, surviving form of deference among Pepperrell's Maine frontiersman neighbors.[38]

The localistic impulses of Maine's towns, together with conditions of material scarcity and the insecurity of life and property on some parts of the northern frontier, could have produced the sort of conflict that occurred in the Carolina and Pennsylvania backcountry. Moreover, the combined effect of isolation and alienation could have perhaps rendered the allegiance of Maine's backcountry residents to the cause of independence tenuous. But that did not happen. According to James Leamon, the author of a comprehensive modern study of the Revolution in Maine, "Maine's residents were too isolated and too pre-occupied with surviving in a grudging environment to be much concerned over imperial issues," and, as a consequence, no one in Maine was much involved in the resistance to parliamentary authority up to 1774. With the passage of the Coercive Acts, Maine did fall into line.[39] The men responsible for securing Maine's allegiance to the revolutionary cause were men like Enoch Freeman who had previously established their authority in the towns while at the same time establishing some measure of communication with politicians and merchants in Boston. By and large those local leaders, secure in their places in their communities, presided over a conservative revolution, one that ultimately wreaked relatively little change within the social structures of the communities in which they lived.

But as we have seen in the case of Enoch Freeman and Falmouth, that ultimately conservative outcome did not always seem inevitable, for on one side the threat of British occupation and on the other the insurgencies of agrarian radicals lent a good deal of instability to the situation. Maine's vulnerability, by land and sea, as the northernmost frontier of the patriot military effort, brought even greater hardship to a citizenry already accustomed to great privation. The British took particular advantage of their naval superiority in the region, plundering Maine shipping and establishing a base of naval operations on the Penobscot River. And, from their beachhead in Nova Scotia, they sought to extend Loyalist influence south and westward into Maine. The rigors of military conflict on a vast and underdefended frontier would try the allegiance of many, but in the end Maine's towns would remain remarkably united and steadfast in their support of the patriot side. One of the effects of the war, however, was to exacerbate the conditions of poverty with which most Maine citizens had always lived. As Henry Sewall put it, "the delicious draught [of liberty] is embittered by the poisonous obtrusion of poverty and dependence," a thought echoed by Jonathan Sayard of York, who commented, "As a State we are in Miserable Circumstances. . . . People are so poor, they know not which way to turn . . . and some begin to Doubt whether independence will be so great a Blessing as it was at first thought to be."[40]

These conditions of poverty were exacerbated by the financial policies of the Boston-based state government, policies that imposed higher tax burdens and tightened credit on a population already finding it difficult to carry existing loads of taxation and debt. These of course were precisely the conditions that led to the agrarian unrest exhibited in Shays's Rebellion in western Massachusetts, and one could imagine that citizens in Maine, more isolated and suffering in at least equal measure as those in western Massachusetts, would have risen in rebellion as well. To make matters more ominous, those dislocations in an already-straitened economy coincided with a movement led by many of the most prominent leaders of Maine's coastal towns to separate Maine from the Commonwealth of Massachusetts. The leaders of the Maine separatist movement were hardly radical social revolutionaries—their primary motive was to secure greater independence and power for themselves within the context of traditional structures of government and society—but a good many in Maine recognized the possibility that the unrest of the poor and the political ambition of those local elites might be brought together in a more explosive combination.

That a violent uprising did not occur was the result of a number of factors. The most important no doubt was the essential moderation of the leaders of Maine's separatist movement; not only were they inherently nervous about an alliance with a group of agrarian radicals but also the nature of the "imperialism" imposed on them and their Maine constituents was not nearly so oppressive as to incline them to overcome that nervousness. The citizens of Maine, while in some measure geographically remote from Boston, were never politically and culturally alienated from Bostonians in the way in which the Carolina Regulators or the Paxton Boys in Pennsylvania had been during the 1760s. Moreover, there were demographic and economic forces at work in Maine in the aftermath of the Revolution that were helping to mitigate some of the hardship being experienced by its citizens. Immediately following the end of the Revolution, a veritable flood of people, many of them from eastern Massachusetts, migrated to Maine in search of greater opportunity. Between 1784 and 1795 the population of Maine increased by more than 70 percent, from 56,000 to 96,500, and by 1800 the population had increased to 150,000, nearly a 300 percent increase in just sixteen years. While in some respects that population boom increased pressure on land, the more important result, in a region where land was cheap and plentiful and capital was scarce, was to generate an internal economic revival that in the long run eased, rather than heightened, conditions of poverty. The migration of tens of thousands of lower and middling people to Maine would be accompanied by a smaller migration of extremely wealthy and politically powerful individuals—including former Revolutionary War generals such as Henry Knox and Benjamin Lincoln—who, with their money and influence would be successful in resuscitating some of the old speculative land companies such as the Kennebec Proprietors and the Pejepscot Company and create for themselves bastions of power that would make the small, town-based oligarchies in colonial Maine pale by comparison. The creation of that postrevolutionary oligarchy would itself be a new source of tension within the social order of Maine, but those social tensions would never be fully joined with political action. The separatist movement in Maine, which achieved its final success in 1820 with the passage of the Missouri Compromise and the granting of statehood to Maine, would continue to be led by men of substance, including some of the "Great Proprietors," and not by discontented agrarian radicals. In backcountry Maine, the goal of independence, in both its economic and political senses, would be achieved within traditional conceptions of law and of property.[41]

The Paradox of Popular and Oligarchic Political Behavior in Colonial Pennsylvania

By the standards of late-seventeenth-century England, William Penn's vision for his new colony in America was a remarkably progressive one, combining a commitment to ethnic and religious pluralism in the social sphere with a more generous attitude toward the role of ordinary people in the political sphere. Penn's First Frame of Government, published in May 1682, articulated his fundamental belief that "Any Government is free to the People under it (whatever be the Frame) where the Laws rule, and the People are a Party to those laws." Although it favored the governor and his council over the lower house of assembly in its apportionment of power, it was in nearly all other respects a testament to enlightened seventeenth-century Whig thought. The Frame of Government and the laws that Penn proposed along with it called for popular election of both lower and upper houses, provided for a secret ballot, rotation in office, and, most momentously, stipulated that all believers in God "shall in no ways be molested or prejudiced for their Religious Persuasion or Practice in matters of Faith and Worship."[1]

As a Quaker who first and foremost embraced the ideal of "Christian love," Penn not only wished to attract to his colony "diligent," "frugal," and "virtuous" men and women of all religions and national backgrounds, but he also pledged to the American Indian inhabitants of his new colony that he and his fellow settlers would "enjoy it with your Love and Consent, that we may always live together as Neighbours and freinds." He hoped that his colony would be marked not only by freedom and virtue but also by order and structure. One obvious product of that desire was his plan for the city of Philadelphia, with its carefully laid-out grid and its numerous parks placed at regular intervals. But Penn had similar plans for an orderly taking up of land in the countryside; he proposed the establishment of a series of contiguous townships, each to be carefully surveyed and laid out prior to settlement.[2]

William Penn returned to England from Pennsylvania only a year and ten months after he had arrived, and during the fifteen years between his departure and his return in 1699, almost nothing in his colony went precisely according to his original plan. Yet in a new Charter of Privileges, which Penn encouraged the Pennsylvania colonists to draft in 1701 as a means of protecting their freedoms from an overly zealous Parliament, Penn and the Quaker political leaders of the colony further buttressed notions of popular rights in the affairs of government. The Charter of Privileges significantly decreased the power of the council, making it essentially an advisory body, lodged all legislative power in an annually elected House of Representatives, and, empowering county sheriffs to carefully supervise elections to ensure a free and fair ballot, required the popular election of that class of local officers, as well as the county coroners, on a regular basis. Moreover, elected representatives had, at least in Penn's view, clear responsibilities to the voters who elected them. "Every representative," Penn wrote, "may be called the creature of the people, because the people make them, and to them they owe their being. Here is no transessentiating, or transubstantiating of being, from people to a representative; no more than there is an absolute transferring of a title in a letter of attorney."[3]

Penn would establish the foundation for what would become one of the freest, ethnically diverse, and religiously open societies in the early modern world, but his vision for his "holy experiment" contained within it sets of contradictions that, as the eighteenth century unfolded, would pose significant challenges to his hopes for a colony founded on notions of peace and harmony. The ship taking Penn back to England in 1684 had barely left the dock when divisions surfaced between those whom the proprietor had entrusted with executive leadership in the colony and Quaker leaders in the council and the assembly, many of them trusted friends, who increasingly disputed his policies. "I am sorry at heart for your animosities," he wrote to the colony's leaders in 1685 and pleaded with them, "For the love of God, me, and the poor country, be not so governmentish, so noisy, and open, in your dissatisfaction." A decade later, looking back on the strife he had observed from his vantage point in England, he lamented, "When I was among you, we were a People," and pleaded once again, "let me prevale thee not to strengthen that spirit and Party which runs against the ancient unity of friends."[4] This internal discord between proprietor and local Quaker leaders would be temporarily muted in 1701, when Penn, briefly resident in the colony once again, joined with Quaker leaders to create the Charter of Privileges in order to ward off parliamentary interference in the colony. With Penn's departure and, subsequently, the assumption of the proprietorship by his sons, none of whom professed their father's Quaker faith, relations between the proprietors and Quaker leaders in the assembly deteriorated once again.[5]

Similarly, while both Penn and most of the Quaker leaders who joined with him in the initial settlement of Pennsylvania shared a common commitment to creating a colony in which all Christians were welcome, they nevertheless assumed that Pennsylvania would remain predominantly a *Quaker* colony in which "weighty Quakers" would always shape public policy. But as non-Quaker immigrants from England, Wales, Scotland, Ireland, Germany, and Sweden swarmed into the colony in search of both religious freedom and prosperity, Quaker political dominance was rendered progressively less secure. Even twenty years after the colony's founding, Quakers probably did not constitute more than a third of Pennsylvania's population; by the mid-eighteenth century they constituted perhaps less than a fifth, and by 1790 they amounted to no more than 9 percent.[6] Moreover, those settlers who moved through Philadelphia into the surrounding countryside had scant regard for William Penn's initial vision of an "orderly" plan of community settlements. By 1700 the practice of "indiscriminate location" became widespread, and though most of those who situated themselves on the land in that way usually followed up by having their property surveyed and properly deeded, it vastly undermined Penn's original ideas about compact and orderly towns. Recent non-Quaker immigrants were not entirely to blame for these developments, as many of the initial Quaker grantees—those who were granted large tracts of land to be set aside as woodlands—turned around and carved up their grants and resold them to newer settlers.[7]

As European settlement spread across Philadelphia, Bucks, Chester, Berks, Lancaster, Northampton, York, and Cumberland counties, the vision of settlers of differing ethnic and religious backgrounds living together side by side, in peace, faded as well. For the most part, Germans, Scots-Irish, and English and Welsh settlers were inclined to cluster together with their own kind. By the mid-eighteenth century, the Germans, who had occupied more land in the colony than any other ethnic group, were concentrated in Berks, upper Philadelphia, Northampton, and York counties; the Scots-Irish were most numerous in parts of Lancaster County and western York County; and English and Welsh settlers were particularly concentrated on some of the best lands in Chester and Bucks counties. These trends toward residential segregation and a consequent reinforcement of ethnic identity were no doubt driven by a number of related factors: common language in the case of the Germans and some of the Welsh; the tendency of large kinship groups to immigrate to America together; the close correlation between ethnic background and religious belief, which encouraged residential proximity in the organization of church congregations; and, in the case of the Scots-Irish in particular, the need to escape the hostility of other ethnic groups.[8] The Quaker founders may have created a colony in which peoples of all ethnic backgrounds and religion might enjoy legal guarantees of freedom and toleration, but they were not able to guarantee that people of differing religions and ethnic background would live together in loving harmony.

As Pennsylvania's exploding population spread across the landscape in search of greater opportunity, another one of the casualties was William

Penn's vision of a "peaceful community." Although Penn's colony began as the one English settlement in America where notions of peace and love toward all of humankind actually seemed to triumph over the more visceral instincts of acquisitiveness and ethnocentrism, those inexorable impulses would soon come to the fore as new arrivals, most of them unencumbered by Quaker pacifistic beliefs, moved onto the periphery in search of land of their own. However inspiring Penn's original vision of a "peaceable kingdom" may have been, European-Indian relations on the eighteenth-century Pennsylvania frontier began to look depressingly similar to those in most every other frontier region of colonial America. But precisely because of the continuing commitment of the disproportionately powerful Quaker minority to principles of pacifism, the politics of European-Indian relations would develop very differently in Pennsylvania than elsewhere.

These conflicts—between Quaker and proprietary elites, between and among European settlers of divergent ethnic backgrounds and religious beliefs, and between Europeans and Indians—unfolded within a political system that historian Alan Tully has perceptively identified as simultaneously popular and oligarchic. The very antiauthoritarian character of Quakerism, together with the localized, intimate character of provincial politics, made it more difficult for aspirants to public office to lay their claims to power solely on traditional claims to deference; rather, they would increasingly need to demonstrate their affinity to the popular will. On the other hand, to a remarkable extent a small cohort of men—overwhelmingly *Quaker* men—was able to enjoy a virtual monopoly on political power within their localities by skillfully mastering the arts of patronage and the joining of interests.[9] This seemingly paradoxical coexistence of popular and oligarchic tendencies was, as we have seen, present in greater or less degree in every polity within colonial America, but it seemed to be present in a particularly striking way in Pennsylvania. Some of the explanation for this, as Tully observes, was that the combination of Pennsylvania's proprietary form of government and its radical, antiauthoritarian religious origins "produced a pride in provincialism and a way of approaching politics that . . . freed [Pennsylvanians] from the orthodoxies of British political paradigms."[10]

This chapter, and a significant portion of the next one, will seek to describe the political structures and cultures that were produced by the interaction between the ideology of the Quaker founders and the dynamic mix of demographic, economic, and ethno-cultural conditions at work in the colony. This chapter will end with an analysis of the most serious internal challenge to Pennsylvania's prerevolutionary political system—the Paxton uprising, and the next chapter will conclude with an analysis of the internal and external challenges to that system posed by the advent of the American Revolution.

The Reality of Quaker Politics and the Influence of Party

Nearly every major modern work on colonial Pennsylvania politics has focused on the highly visible contest for power within the colony between
those wedded to defending the interests and enjoying the patronage of the
proprietor and those identified with the interests and patronage of the
original Quaker settlers. Indeed, so durable and persistent were the divisions between proprietary and Quaker factions—almost from the moment
that Penn first departed from the colony in 1684 up to the very eve of the
Revolution—that many historians have referred to them as "parties," rather
than factions. Their use of the term party has been justified not only as a
way of highlighting the persistence and consistency of the divisions between Quaker and proprietary interests, but also of calling attention to the
ways in which the two sides—and the Quaker side in particular—forged
identities based on collective values as opposed to loyalties to specific individuals or interests.[11]

Much of the evidence in this chapter supports the contention that the
Quakers, in the self-conscious way in which they organized and conducted
themselves both inside and outside the assembly, did constitute at least a
"protoparty." The evidence does not sustain, however, a similar conclusion
with respect to the proprietors and those in their patronage. Too weak in
numbers and nearly aways lacking a coherent political base outside of the
patronage of the Penn family, the proprietary faction never forged an identity capable of attracting consistent popular support.

However useful the notion of Quaker and proprietary divisions may be
in understanding the jockeying for position and power among political
leaders at the level of the provincial government, it is somewhat less helpful in understanding the ways in which ordinary citizens and political leaders related to one another in the context of their local communities.
Indeed, the emphasis that historians have given to the spirited contests that
occasionally erupted between Quaker and proprietary factions may have
given us a distorted view of the more enduring sources of both the popular and oligarchic tendencies in Pennsylvania's political culture.

The technical qualifications for formal participation in Pennsylvania's
political system were similar to those prevailing in most colonies; a 1706
statute laid down the basic framework for the conduct of elections in the
colony, and that statute provided that anyone owning a 50-acre freehold in
one of the counties or personal property valued at £50 or more within
Philadelphia was entitled to vote in Pennsylvania elections.[12] Although perhaps no more than 50 to 60 percent of Pennsylvania's male residents met
that qualification, many historians have tended to agree that the percentage of male residents who might actually be allowed to vote probably
reached as high as 75 percent.[13] The job of determining who was eligible
to vote was given to a set of election inspectors, who were themselves, by a

1727 statute, elected by the "qualified voters" assembled on the day of the election. That process, which was to be supervised by the sheriff and coroner, was itself sufficiently complicated that it did, as we will see later in this chapter, occasionally provoke as much controversy as the election itself.[14]

Perhaps the most notable feature of Pennsylvania's election laws, one strongly influenced by Quaker ideology, was the provision for written ballots. In contrast to the prevailing ethic in colonies such as New York and Virginia, where the act of casting a ballot was an explicitly public one in which voters were asked for a visible display of their loyalty to one candidate or another, Pennsylvania's Quaker founders believed that the voting decisions were private, an opportunity to exercise political judgments free from outside pressure. Although supporters of a particular candidate sometimes might write out ballots and distribute them to voters in advance of the election, thereby providing an opportunity for observers to identify the choice made by the voter depending on the appearance of the ballot, it nevertheless seems likely that colonial Pennsylvania may have been the first colony or state in America to provide for something approximating a secret ballot.[15]

Although the occasional controversies that erupted during elections for representatives to the General Assembly have tended to shift the attention of historians to politics within the assembly, for most of the eighteenth century the majority of the meaningful actions of government in Pennsylvania, as elsewhere in America, occurred at the local level, and, with the exception of the city of Philadelphia, most political authority at the local level resided in the county rather than the township. Although Pennsylvania was by no means the only colony to organize its system of local government around the unit of the county, the consequences of that decision were perhaps more profound in Pennsylvania than elsewhere. Before William Penn took control of his colony, all of the lands in the territories possessed and overseen by the Duke of York were organized into ridings, townships, and parishes, and although the structures of authority in those small local units were hardly democratic, they did bring local government very close to the residents of a particular locality. In that respect the contrast with New York, which retained the Duke of York's system of highly localized units of government, is instructive. In New York's system of local government, political power was diffused across literally hundreds of different townships, with a consequent development of a sizeable class of local political leaders who tended to develop tenacious, parochial attachments to purely local issues and interests. In Pennsylvania, with political power concentrated in the centers of just a small number of county units, the number of individuals entrusted with political authority was much smaller, and the angle of vision of those local political leaders was necessarily much broader.[16]

Although the units of local government in Pennsylvania were fairly extensive, the popular foundations of local government were slightly stronger

in Pennsylvania than elsewhere. Pennsylvanians elected their county commissioners and county assessors directly; they indirectly elected their
county sheriffs and county coroners, forwarding the names of two candidates for each of those positions to the governor, who appointed one of the
two recommended by the voters. Perhaps the most important of the county
officers—the justices of the peace—were appointed by the proprietors.
Given the ongoing struggle for power between proprietary officials and
elected members of the assembly, one might think that the proprietors
would have used their power to appoint county justices as a means of
strengthening their hand at the expense of the dominant Quaker faction,
but, in fact, it appears that the proprietors used an even hand in making
those appointments, recognizing that the orderly conduct of local government required that local justices of the peace be men esteemed by their
neighbors.

The individuals who were probably most influential in determining who
was appointed justice were the sitting justices on the court or other leading
residents of the county, and they, too, tended to rise above party animosity
in making their recommendations. In 1755, for example, colony secretary
Richard Peters asked Presbyterian minister Samuel Finley for his recommendation for appointment of the justice in his locality; Finley came back
with two suggestions, one a Presbyterian and the other a Quaker. Of the
Presbyterian he said, "a man of strong judgment, strict justice, and impartiality;" he described the Quaker as "a good natured, candid, sensible
man," and concluded by saying that "my great desire [is] to have men of
wisdom, probity, and resolution employed, who [know] what [becomes]
their place and how to maintain the due dignity of it by the proper exercise of authority."[17]

Perhaps the most striking fact of political life in eighteenth-century
Pennsylvania, at least up until 1756, was the extent to which Quakers, in
spite of their dwindling importance demographically, continued to dominate public office at both the local and provincial levels. This dominance
was most dramatic in traditional Quaker strongholds, such as the city of
Philadelphia and Philadelphia, Bucks, and Chester counties, but it was also
often the case even in counties such as Lancaster or Berks, where Quakers
constituted only a tiny portion of the total population. In Chester County,
for example, Quakers probably constituted only a third of the population
by 1750, but in the elections for county commissioner between 1729 and
1754, eighteen of the twenty-one individuals elected to that position were
Quakers.[18] The Quaker monopoly on seats in the assembly was equally pronounced. During the period 1710–55, a period in which the Quaker portion of Chester County's population was declining, the county's
eight-person delegation was composed entirely of Quakers 55 percent of
the time, of seven Quakers and one non-Quaker 29 percent of the time,
and at no time did Quakers have fewer than five of the eight seats. Even in

Lancaster County, which was carved out of Chester County in 1729, Quakers tended to dominate the four-person delegation. "It is remarkable," Quaker political leader Isaac Norris observed in 1755, "that the Frontier county of Lancaster, composed of all sorts of Germans, & some Church of England Electors, have chosen all their Representatives out of ye Quakers, tho' there are scarcely one hundred of that Profession in the whole county."[19]

During the period from 1710 to 1755, Quakers held two-thirds of the seats across all of the assembly districts in the colony and, with very few exceptions, tended to occupy between 75 and 90 percent of the seats in most of those years. Moreover, for the most part, the same Quaker leaders tended to take on a disproportionate amount of public service year in and year out. Nearly all of those serving in the assembly held other local offices as well, especially as county commissioners and justices of the peace.[20] Even more striking was the relatively low turnover among those serving in the assembly; there was a steady rise in the average length of service of representatives from just a few terms during the 1690s to nearly seven terms during the 1740s. The rate of annual turnover of representatives during the whole of the eighteenth century was 29.8 percent and during the period from the mid-1730s up to the Revolution, it was consistently under 20 percent, one of the lowest rates of turnover among any of the American colonies. By way of comparison, average rates of turnover in Massachusetts during the whole of the eighteenth century stood at 45 percent, in Virginia, at 47 percent, in South Carolina at 55 percent, and in Rhode Island at 61 percent.[21]

Certainly one of the factors favoring the Quakers' continuing dominance over the business of the Pennsylvania General Assembly was the structure of representation within that assembly. As we have seen, one of William Penn's important decisions was to make the county, rather than the township, the dominant unit of political organization within his colony. Colonies like Virginia, which also used the county as the principal means of organizing local government, also made regular provision for dividing colonies into smaller units as population increased. By the practice of frequent division of counties (by 1760 Virginia had created fifty-three counties to accommodate its population of 200,000 people) Virginia was able to ensure Virginia that the services of local government would not be too physically distant from her citizens but also that newly settled areas in the colony would be extended adequate representation in the House of Burgesses. By contrast, in 1760 Pennsylvania had created only eight counties, along with the city of Philadelphia, to accommodate its population of 175,000. One of the consequences of this was that the ratio of representatives to adult male citizens in Pennsylvania was, at 1:1,301 in 1770, the highest in America. In Virginia and Massachusetts the ratios were 1:439 and 1:368.[22] When Pennsylvania did create new counties, including Lancaster,

York, Berks, Cumberland, and Northampton, its citizens were given fewer representatives in the assembly than were the original counties of Philadelphia, Chester, and Bucks. In 1760 the taxable population of the three original counties and the city of Philadelphia stood at 16,222, and each of those three counties sent eight representatives to the assembly, with the city of Philadelphia sending another two; by 1760 the combined taxable population of the five western counties, which covered an expanse of some 8,000 miles, had reached 15,443, and they were granted only ten representatives.[23] The control that Philadelphia-area Quaker politicians exercised over the business of the assembly was even greater than that possessed by the ten delegates serving Philadelphia County and the city of Philadelphia. Eighty percent of Chester County's representatives lived within a twenty-four-mile radius of Philadelphia, a fact that further consolidated Quaker cohesiveness. The consequence was a system that not only facilitated continued Quaker political dominance in a colony that was increasingly non-Quaker in its demographic composition but also one in which many of the citizens in northern and western regions of the colony found themselves living far from any agency of local government and felt themselves wholly distant from the principal agency of representative government, the colonial assembly. Proprietary Governor George Thomas, confronted by that closely knit Quaker phalanx in 1741, likened the Pennsylvania Assembly to a "conclave," rather than "a body of men who are accountable to their electors."[24]

However much the Quakers may have structured the governance of Pennsylvania to ensure their continued dominance, perhaps the most striking fact of government in Pennsylvania—particularly at the provincial level—is how little active governance actually occurred. As Alan Tully has noted, "Quaker leaders accumulated [political power] to prevent its abuse, while simultaneously expressing their ethic of self-denial by refusing to use it."[25] In practice this meant that the Quaker-dominated Pennsylvania legislature did very little legislating. Over the course of the period from 1710 to 1756 the Pennsylvania Assembly, which on average was in session for fifty days per year, enacted an average of 5.5 laws per term. There were eleven terms in which no legislation whatsoever was enacted, and there were eight terms in which between 11 and 19 laws were enacted. In New York, by contrast, the legislature enacted an average of 13.3 laws per term, during the period 1730–35 and 25.5 laws per term in the period 1740–45. In Virginia, where the burgesses possessed a much more activist view of their role as legislators, the legislature enacted more than 30 laws per year.[26]

Perhaps one reason that the number of laws enacted by the assembly was so few was that Pennsylvanians were not as active in petitioning their legislature as were citizens in other colonies. During that same 1710–56 period, the legislature received an average of 21.8 petitions per year, although, again, the volume of petitions varied widely from year to year, with some

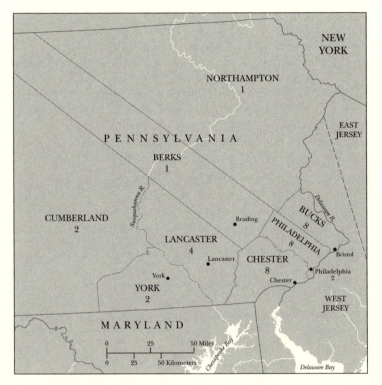

Map 6. Distribution of representation in Pennsylvania, circa 1770.

years producing just a handful and others producing as many as 50 or 60. The principal forces driving the increase in petitioning seemed to be economic difficulties, as during the period 1721–25 when the legislature received numerous petitions asking for emissions of paper money and other economic relief measures and during the period from 1754 to 1756, when issues of Indian warfare and defense aroused the citizenry.[27] New York's residents, attached to many more individual localities and demanding that their specific interests be served, nevertheless produced fewer petitions, only about 14 per year during a similar period. Virginians were far more active, directing an average of 28.5 petitions per year to the burgesses in the period 1715–20 and 60 petitions per year in the period 1750–55.[28]

Alan Tully has convincingly contrasted the impact of the different political structures and the sets of values present in New York and Pennsylvania in the character of legislation in those two colonies. Whereas the sense of self-importance of New York's myriad local political leaders demanded that they demonstrate their ability to serve the interests of their constituents through legislation, in Pennsylvania, where the structure of local government was more austere and where the needs for local officials to seek purely local solutions to their problems was significantly less, demands for legislative solutions to local problems were also fewer. Thus, while the New York legislature passed separate laws providing for the control of the wolf populations of Albany, Dutchess, and Orange counties, and special laws safeguarding sheep in Kings County and protecting property in Claverack precinct in Rensselaerswyck Manor from roaming pigs, the Pennsylvania legislature either did not deal with those problems or dealt with them in comprehensive acts aimed at addressing the problems across all of the colony's counties.[29]

While during the first three decades of Pennsylvania's existence, the legislature tended to be most concerned with laws regulating public morality—from laws suppressing profanity and public drunkenness to laws licensing public houses and regulating marriages, over time the legislature's concerns predictably turned toward the management of an expanding population and an increasingly complex economic order. Thus during the 1720s onward, the assembly concerned itself with the full range of regulatory functions, from provisions for the extermination of squirrels who ate farm crops to the lighting of streets to the regulation of immigration to the care of the poor. The assembly also became somewhat more active in protecting and promoting economic development, both in terms of regulation of particular trades and in regulating the monetary system of the colony. By far the greatest portion of the legislation enacted during the period 1710–56 though—nearly half of all laws—dealt with the routine and straightforward matters of political administration of the colony—from the establishment of courts of justice to the collection of fees and fines to the laying down of rules for the election of local officials.[30] Again, what is surprising about this legislative activity is not that it was occurring in any of these areas of public concern, but rather that it was so sparse. On the whole, the burden of government in Pennsylvania both at the local and provincial level rested remarkably lightly on the shoulders of the citizenry. Quaker pacifism made moot the elaborate set of laws and obligations involved with militia service, and the revenue needs of the government were modest and for the most part easily provided by the loan office and a modest excise. Moreover, as Alan Tully has noted, the Quaker ethic of government was guided by the belief that values such as morality, public order, and civil behavior were best nurtured not by legislation and government regulation but by an "internal commitment to 'holy conversation.'"[31] And, Tully argues, even though Quakers constituted a diminishing portion of the total population, their values about public life and public behavior continued to permeate the entire population.[32]

We are able to get at least a few glimpses of the ways in which this combination of an antiauthoritarian commitment to popular rule and Quaker oligarchy played out in the face-to-face relationships of voters and aspiring political leaders in the Pennsylvania countryside in the first half of the eighteenth century. Certainly most of Pennsylvania's political leaders, like their counterparts in other colonies, would have preferred to avoid formal electoral contests. In the case of the Quakers, who comprised such a large part of the political leadership class of the colony in the first half of the eighteenth century, that natural desire to avoid electoral competition was heightened by their Quakerly uneasiness with contest and conflict of any kind; far better that the colony's citizens reach a consensus on the identity of their leaders within their localities and select those leaders by acclamation. And it is likely, particularly in more homogeneous counties such as Chester and Bucks, where the Quakers enjoyed nearly unchallenged dominance, that uncontested elections were the rule rather than the exception.[33]

That did not mean, however, that Quaker dominance of electoral politics came without effort. Before 1756 members of leading Quaker families such as the Norrises, Pembertons, and Kirkbrides self-consciously devoted themselves not only to public service, but also to controlling the access of others to public office, and thus they played an active role behind the scenes in the selection of candidates to public office. To this end, the Quaker meetings themselves often played an important role in identifying the best candidates for local and provincial offices; indeed, there was frequently a significant congruence between those who enjoyed political power and those who commanded the greatest authority within their local Quaker meetings.[34] As the contest between the Quaker-dominated assembly and the proprietors heated up in the 1740s, this intersection between religion and politics would lead to some overheated complaints from members of the proprietary faction. William Smith, one of the most vociferous of the anti-Quaker proprietary politicians, complained that the Quakers "entered into Cabals in their yearly Meeting, which is convened just before the Election, and being composed of Deputies from all the monthly Meetings in the Province, is the finest Scheme that could possible be projected, for conducting political Intrigues, under the Mask of Religion."[35]

Not surprisingly, the result of this was an assembly composed overwhelmingly of Quakers—especially wealthy and socially prominent Quakers. Of the forty men who served Chester County in the assembly between 1729 and 1755, thirty-two ranked in the top 10 percent of taxable citizens in the county in terms of wealth, four ranked in the 80–90 percentile, three in the 70–80 percentile, and one was at 60–70 percent. Moreover, within the relatively small group of wealthy men who dominated service in the assembly, a still smaller group dominated its actual business, chairing the principal committees and serving as the prime movers behind the most important pieces of legislation.[36] Although historians have frequently highlighted the differences in both the religious affiliations and policy that divided members of the Quaker and proprietary groups, when one looks at the governance of Pennsylvania as a whole, what is most striking is the essential *similarity* of members of the Quaker and proprietary elites. Whatever their religious or political differences, they frequently belonged to the same clubs, dined together, did business together, and, more generally, operated in the same social universes.[37]

The Conduct of Elections

These oligarchic tendencies aside, certain aspects of Pennsylvania's political culture created a climate in which at least some electoral contest was inevitable. More of Pennsylvania's local offices were elective than in most other colonies, and elections were held with greater frequency. These facts, together with the generally egalitarian cast of Quaker ideology, increased the likelihood that at least some elections would be vigorously contested. As early as 1710, with the publication of *Friendly Advice to the Inhabitants of Pennsylvania* by Isaac Norris, political pamphlets began to play a role in election campaigns, and as the Quaker and proprietary rivalries flared up sporadically in the decades that followed, the volume and vituperation of the pamphlets increased as well. Indeed, a survey of the pamphlets and public announcements in the newspapers published at election time makes it clear that our modern-day practices of negative campaigning have deep and strong roots in colonial Pennsylvania.[38] The fact that elections for sheriff were held at the same time as those for the assembly further encouraged popular interest in elections, and, it is likely that many citizens considered the selection of the sheriff to be a more important decision than that of the assembly representatives.[39] By the 1750s candidates for sheriff and coroner in Philadelphia had begun routinely to solicit votes for their candidacies by taking out newspaper advertisements. Nevertheless, most aspirants for office stopped short of overtly campaigning for themselves. Most members of both the Quaker and proprietary elite would have agreed with Edward Shippen, who, when asked in 1756 by his supporters to appear on his own behalf, responded, "It is a very disagreeable task to appear to solicit for one's self." Shippen did ultimately relent, noting, "if it is necessary, I must submit," but he was uncomfortable in the role.[40]

The surges of competitive, populist impulses that took place in the first half of the eighteenth century did not occur in any regular, predictable manner, although they were most often provoked either by sporadic, and usually unsuccessful, efforts by the proprietary faction to rally popular support to their position or by purely personal rivalries within particular localities. One of the most noteworthy examples of the ways in which personal rivalry, tinged with ethno-cultural animosity, came into play at election time was the contest between John Wright and Andrew Galbraith for the assembly in Lancaster County in 1732. Wright, a Quaker bodice maker who immigrated from Lancashire to Chester County in 1714, would serve a total of twenty terms in the assembly, first as a representative for Chester County and then for Lancaster when that county was created in 1729. Although never managing to achieve great wealth in Pennsylvania, he was extraordinarily adroit in forming political alliances with the right people, and he enjoyed a steady ascendancy in political power at both the local and provincial levels, finally achieving elevation to the position of Speaker of the House in 1745. But Wright's ride to political power did hit at least one bump in the road. Andrew Galbraith, a Scots-Irishman who immigrated to Pennsylvania around 1718, began to establish his place in the Lancaster Country township of Donegal through his activities in the Donegal Presbyterian Church. Galbraith was also helpful to proprietary secretary James Logan in settling several property disputes in the region, many of them involving Scots-Irish, and the combination of proprietary support and his stature as an elder in the Donegal Presbyterian Church were probably most responsible for his initial election to the assembly in 1731. Although Galbraith served an undistinguished first term in the House, he was returned to the assembly the following year. In that year his election was challenged by John Wright, who claimed that the election inspectors had mistakenly rejected tickets with his name on them because they had contained three rather than the four candidates required by the election law. Wright insisted that if those votes had been counted he, not Galbraith, would have been elected. It seems clear as well that Galbraith had benefited from the deliberate marshaling of support of his Presbyterian neighbors in Donegal. One of the persistent pieces of the oral history of Lancaster, though not documented in the written record, has Galbraith's wife playing the key role in the election by actively campaigning among the Scots-Irish of Donegal, leading one hundred of them in the thirty-four-mile ride between their township and the county seat in Lancaster to vote for her husband.[41]

Galbraith would serve eight undistinguished terms in the legislature, but Wright would rebound to continue to be an important, and occasionally controversial, force in Pennsylvania politics. Perhaps the most notable effort by leaders of the proprietary faction to lay claim to popular political power in the provincial assembly would come during the period from 1740 to 1742, when the Quaker-dominated assembly's pacifistic defense policies caused the proprietors particular unease. When England declared war on Spain in 1739, ending a period of more than twenty-five years of relative peace among the European powers, the proprietors responded by urging the assembly to take at least some steps to put the colonies in a state of defense in order to avoid the "miseries of a City sack'd or a Province ravaged."[42] At precisely that time John Kinsey, a Philadelphia Quaker particularly committed to maintaining the colony's pacifist policies, became Speaker of the assembly, a fact that further buttressed the assembly's resistance to any meaningful effort at strengthening the colony's defenses. Frustrated by their inability to get what they wanted from the assembly, proprietary leaders Andrew Hamilton and William Allen attempted to organize slates of candidates throughout the colony that would oppose Quaker Party contenders. John Wright of Lancaster would be one of those targeted for defeat. Proprietary candidates ran spirited, but unsuccessful, campaigns in Lancaster in 1740 and 1741; then in 1742 their most vigorous effort took place. The partisan character of that election throughout the entire colony was greatly inflamed by the publication of an attack by Governor George Thomas on the assembly in which he had questioned the fitness of Quakers to govern the colony responsibly.[43] All four of the incumbent assemblymen from Lancaster at that time were Quakers, but James Hamilton, an Anglican; Samuel Smith, most likely a Presbyterian from Donegal; and Robert Buchanan, a former sheriff of the county, were urged to oppose them.

One of the other Quaker incumbents from Lancaster was a particularly colorful and combative individual named Samuel Blunston. Blunston had earlier been involved in a highly controversial action involving the capture and imprisonment of a group of Marylanders led by Thomas Cressap, who, according to Blunston and his followers, had been illegally settling on Pennsylvania lands and, worse, making unauthorized war against friendly Indians. Thus, with public opinion on the subject of Quaker attitudes toward defense and Indians more inflamed than ever before, Blunston was a particular target for those seeking to oust the Quakers from power. But he and the three other Quakers on the slate were easily able to turn aside the challenge from the proprietary candidates. According to colony secretary Richard Peters, Blunston "trumpetted ab[ou]t the Country that Robert Buchanan had 200 a[cre]s Land given him by the Proprietaries & that he

& Sam[ue]l Smith had taken Bribes to give up the Liberties of the People, that Jimmy Hamilton had given a Lot of ground in the town of Lancas[te]r to a Roman Catholick Priest to build a Romiish Chappel & that he was a great favourer of Jews & Roman Catholicks." Although the proprietary candidates tried to counter the obviously false charge, "it signify'd nothing, Sam had the Ears of the people & drove all before him by means of the Dutch & the Sheriff [Quaker James Galbraith] who p[ro]v'd false after he had given his word to act a neutral & fair part."[44]

Susanna Wright, a politically active daughter of John Wright, also teamed up with Blunston to write a public letter that was sent to "every Presbiter[ia]n Congregacion in the County & read at all publick Meetings of the Party." The letter, according to the testimony of the chagrined Richard Peters, was filled with "Lies ab[out]t your favouring a Militia with no other design than to use it for ejecting poor People out of their Possessions." Peters considered the letter as proof of the "Lengths a vindictive Spirit will carry people witho[u]t the Restraints of Honour and Concience," and acknowledged that it had had the effect of putting the people of Lancaster into a great "Ferment." "Could any one believe," Peters asked, "that Susy could act so unbecoming & unfemale a part as to be employ'd in copying such infamous Stuf?" During the election itself, according to Peters's testimony, she went up into "an upper Room in a publick House," "had a Ladder erected to the Window," and proceeded to distribute "Lies and Tickets" to those who were gathering for the election.[45]

The result of the proprietary challenge and the vigorous response by Quaker Party leaders like Wright and Blunston was a humiliating defeat for the proprietary challengers. Voter turnout in the 1742 Lancaster election reached an astonishing 56 percent of the taxable males, a figure that may have been the result of ballot-stuffing by each side, but all of the Quaker candidates enjoyed margins of victory of more than 1,000 votes, with Blunston being the leading vote-getter at 1,480, and James Hamilton, the leading proprietary vote-getter receiving only 360 votes.[46]

The proprietary challenge to Quaker dominance of the assembly met a similar fate in the Chester County elections of 1742. As in Lancaster, a politically active female, Quaker minister Jane Hoskins, would figure prominently in the campaign. In spite of her position in the Quaker community, she publicly endorsed a slate of candidates supported by Governor George Thomas and the proprietary faction. But her efforts were in vain. In Chester, even more than Lancaster, Quakers remained comfortably in control, with the principal threats to their hegemony more often coming from divisions within their ranks than from challenges from without.[47]

It was probably not an accident that women like Susanna Wright and Jane Hoskins played more visible roles in the public life of their regions than women in other colonies. Quaker theology provided at least some of the basis for greater empowerment of women; Quaker belief that the Inner

Light was available to all led to a significantly more public role for women in the business of the Quaker meeting, and this carried over to other aspects of community life. Moreover, the very Quaker conception of marriage—based on love rather than on patriarchal arrangements engineered by elders—produced a level of equality in the domestic sphere that further buttressed notions of equality in the public sphere. As Alan Tully phrases it, "In Pennsylvania, Quaker women were power brokers, not a titillating side-show, and they were power brokers, not because of familial property right in some rotten borough, but because they were part of a mixed male/female network of respected leaders."[48]

Philadelphia Elections

The proprietors' unhappiness with the Quaker-dominated assembly's refusal to cooperate on issues relating to the colony's defense had its most dramatic manifestation within the city of Philadelphia itself. The proprietors mounted their first slate of candidates in the election of 1740, but the Quakers, according to their opponents, "by their dextrous knack of lying brought down upon us about 400 Germans who hardly ever came to elections formerly." In Philadelphia County, voter turnout jumped from 11.9 percent to 37.6 percent of the eligible voters between 1739 and 1740. William Allen and his supporters tried again in 1742, this time attempting to strengthen their position both by putting Allen himself at the head of the ticket and by enlisting Conrad Weiser, the influential German Indian agent on the frontier, to send an appeal "To our Countrymen the Germans in Pennsylvania" urging them to support Allen's ticket rather than that of the Quaker Party.[49]

The polling in Philadelphia was done at the courthouse at Market and Second Streets, an area just a few blocks from the wharves, where merchant seamen, taverns, and grog shops were all densely intermixed. As the October 1 election day approached, the city was filled with rumors, the two most prominent being that the Quaker Party was bringing a veritable army of unnaturalized Germans from the countryside to vote illegally for their candidates, the other that the proprietary faction had hired a gang of merchant sailors to drive the Quakers and their supporters from the courthouse. Both of these rumors gained further credence by the fact that the 1739 election law providing for a simplified system of choosing election inspectors had expired, leaving the method of choosing those officials muddled as the 1742 election approached.

One of the means by which the Quakers had in previous years asserted their dominance in Philadelphia elections was to have Quaker Party supporters line the stairs leading from the street level to the balcony of the courthouse where election inspectors were to receive the ballots from each voter. Anyone voting for the opposition would thus have to run a gauntlet of jostling and hostile political opponents as he mounted and descended the stairs. As the election day drew near, nearly everyone in the city knew that control of the stairway of the courthouse might very well play an important role in the outcome of the election. It was therefore obviously important that the inspectors endeavor to assure impartiality in the conduct of the poll, but attempts by William Allen to persuade the Quakers to agree in advance that each party appoint four inspectors of its own choosing were futile; the Quakers insisted that the lawful way to choose election inspectors was by the traditional method, in which the voters would stand en masse behind the inspector candidates of their choosing. Representatives of the proprietary faction pointed out to the Quakers the tumult that was likely to result, particularly because of the likely presence at the election of large groups of unnaturalized Germans who planned to vote. But the Quaker representatives did not relent.

At 7 A.M. on the morning of October 1 spectators and voters alike began to assemble at the courthouse, waiting for the polling to begin at 9. As crowds gathered, word spread that bands of roving sailors had been overheard around the city saying that they planned to "knock down the broad Brims." A delegation of Quakers then went to William Allen, demanding that he do something to keep the peace. Allen, though angered by the charges, agreed to meet with a group of thirty unarmed sailors passing by who, upon questioning, reported that they were simply "going out of Town to be merry." The Quakers were not fully appeased and appealed to the mayor of Philadelphia, Clement Plumstead, but since the sailors had broken no law, he took no action, noting at the same time that the sailors had "as much Right at the Election as the Dutchmen." Following that exchange, the mayor had the sheriff read aloud a proclamation ordering everyone present at the election to behave peaceably, and, with that, the polls were opened.[50]

The first phase of the election, involving the selection of the election inspectors, was initiated by the sheriff, who asked for people to come forward to support William Allen for that post. (Allen was running both for election inspector and for an assembly seat, as was Isaac Norris, the leading Quaker candidate.) A few hardy souls stepped forward, but Allen complained that many more were obstructed from doing so by the crowd of Quakers on the stairs. Upon that complaint the sheriff sought to clear a lane for additional supporters to step forward, but that did not appreciably add to his support. Next the sheriff called for supporters of Isaac Norris to come forward, precipitating a rush of voters—English and Germans alike—to stand behind Norris at the top of the stairs. At precisely that moment, a gang of fifty to seventy sailors waded into the crowd, swinging their clubs at the Quakers in an effort to clear them from the stairs. As one witness recalled it, "The Sailors were Strangers and [I] never heard they had, or pretended to have, any Provocation, but fell on violently as soon as Isaac Norris was chosen Inspector, as if they had a Watch-word."[51] In the disorder that followed, the sheriff issued constables' staffs to citizens willing to try to repel the sailors, an act that of course increased the resulting carnage.

William Allen had taken shelter around the corner from the melee and claimed not only that he had nothing to do with the violence but also that he had neither seen nor heard it. After briefly withdrawing from the scene of battle, the sailors renewed their attack. Captain Redmond, who seemed to be serving as one of the leaders of the gang, cried out to his fellows, "Damn you, go and knock those Dutch Sons of Bitches off the Steps," and the melee was revived. This time the violence was aimed both at people and property, with the sailors breaking the windows of the courthouse as well as the heads of several of the Quakers who had the temerity to remain on the courthouse steps. Although the accounts of William Allen's behavior during this second phase of the riot are confused, at least some of the people present testified that he had in fact tried to end the violence, at one time wading into the melee and calling the sailors a "Parcel of Villains."[52]

When the riot was over and an accounting of both the mayhem and the election returns was made, fifty-four sailors had landed in jail and the Quakers had managed to win convincingly. The highest proprietary vote getter was William Allen, with only 336; all of the Quaker candidates were returned to office with totals of more than 1,400 votes each. Indeed, aside from a few broken bones among their supporters, the Quaker Party profited from the election in every conceivable way. Allen, who before the election had been given a good chance of winning, actually lost a substantial amount of his support while the riot was going on. Robert Moore later recalled that "above 300 ticketts had [Allen's] name dash'd out in his shop," because of the suspicion that he had been the man behind the rioting. The Quakers, who had increased their control of the assembly in the aftermath of the election, used the affair to further discredit the proprietary faction. Quaker Party members stage-managed a petition from their "constituents" requesting that the assembly itself—now overwhelmingly controlled by enemies of Allen and the proprietors—conduct the investigation. That investigation relied almost exclusively on testimony from members of the Quaker Party and ignored testimony from both the sailors themselves or from the many Germans who were suspected of voting in spite of not being naturalized citizens. When the investigation was over, Allen was judged to be the man behind the riot and the case was turned over to the Supreme Court—also controlled by members of the Quaker Party—for further action. At this point the governor intervened to try to protect Allen, arranging a political deal by which the charges against Allen and others would be dropped in return for the governor's willingness not only to sign a few of the assembly's bills but also to appoint John Kinsey, Speaker of the House, as the chief justice of the Supreme Court.[53]

So Allen had lost not only the election but also a large measure of public support in the future; it would be fourteen years before he was reelected to the assembly and then only as a representative of the frontier county of Cumberland. More importantly, the Quakers had consolidated their control of every branch of the government except the governorship, and even Governor Thomas's opposition to them had been dampened.

However decisive the Quaker Party's victories in Philadelphia and in the countryside in 1742, the meaning of those elections for the people at large remained ambiguous. Although the campaigning in Lancaster and Chester counties was spirited, and the election in Philadelphia tumultuous, the fact remains that the course of events in those elections was at every stage orchestrated by leaders of the Quaker and proprietary factions. To be sure there may have been other forces at work in the election. At least some of the German supporters of the Quaker Party, genuinely concerned "that a militia would subject them to a bondage to governors as severe as they were formerly under to their princes in Germany," were voting out of a sense of their self-interest.[54] It was also the case that the core of German support for the Quakers was composed of members of pacifist sects such as the Mennonites, but more generally, the Germans had reason to look to the Quakers to continue the colony's policies of religious and civil liberty. The loyalty of the sailors to William Allen and the proprietors is more puzzling. It may be that the sailors were particularly aware of the Quaker Party's weak response to the call to defend the colony, a response that had its effect not only along the western frontier but also in fortifying the Delaware River. Perhaps, too, the sailors resented the arrogance exhibited by Quaker leaders, visibly on display on that 1742 election day. On the other hand a close look at the demeanor of proprietary leaders could not have assured the sailors that the election of proprietary officials would lead to a less arrogant ruling class.

In the end neither the Germans nor the ordinary sailors would achieve an independent agency that would enable them to speak and act for themselves rather than for their political masters. After 1742 the Quakers would move to consolidate their power within the colony, occupying as many as 90 percent of the seats in the assembly for the next fifteen years. And, with the diminution of discord between the two ruling elites, neither side would see much need to mobilize ordinary citizens to help them gain advantage in their political squabbles with their adversaries. As a consequence, for the next twenty-two years voter participation in Pennsylvania elections would recede to earlier levels, averaging about 20 percent of the eligible voters, as compared to 36 percent during the elections of 1742.[55] For the most part, electoral contests in Pennsylvania, when those contests occurred at all, would remain top-down affairs.

Quaker Ideals and Frontier Realities

It is difficult to put a label on the complicated mix of Quaker egalitarianism, Quaker elitism, and occasional popular political contest within Pennsylvania. Traditional notions of deference seem to fit more awkwardly in Pennsylvania than they do in other colonies. The Quakers' antiauthoritarian theology militated against their constructing a rationale for their rule based on notions of deference, and while individual Quaker leaders may in their hearts have wished that their constituents would automatically recognize their superior virtue, there was very little about the demographic character and social structure of eighteenth-century Pennsylvania that was likely to produce that response.

The representatives of the proprietors were among the first to discover the limits of Quaker deference to constituted authority. In the first decade of the eighteenth century Speaker of the Assembly David Lloyd, in one of his many confrontations with the proprietary governor, John Evans, refused either to remove his hat or stand to speak during conferences with the governor and his council; when the governor reprimanded him for his "affrontive" behavior and demanded a "due deference" to authority, Lloyd remained slumped over in his chair and responded that the "mouth of the Countrey" deserved an "Equality" that made such deference inappropriate.[56] Similarly, Charles Norris, brother of the Speaker of the assembly, Isaac Norris, and a Quaker political insider, confided to Lancaster political activist Susanna Wright his pleasure at seeing how "our poor little G____, the other day, had like to have got a drupping on the High way by a rude Carter who would not turn out of a deep & hollow road, or more properly turn back, for he could not get up the sides with his loaded waggon."[57]

The occasional electoral skirmishes that occurred during the first half of the eighteenth century—whether prompted by the sporadic efforts of proprietary politicians to loosen the Quaker grasp over the assembly or by purely local circumstances—took place within a political system that was on the whole a relatively peaceful one, in which Quaker political dominance in the popular realm was achieved quite easily. By the mid 1750s, however, as the effects of war began to be felt more painfully by more and more Pennsylvanians, ethics of "holy conversation" and of community consensus were less obviously at work in shaping political behavior in the colony. Indeed, whatever the oligarchic features of Pennsylvania's political culture during the first half of the eighteenth century, its protodemocratic features would provide a rich environment for the playing out of those conflicts.

The Quaker commitment to pacifism had shaped the history of the Pennsylvania colony from its very inception. Whether in William Penn's insistence that citizens should rely "upon the justice of [their] cause" rather than "navies, horses, chariots, and mighty men of war" or in his commitment to winning over the "natives by just and gentle manners, to the love of civil society and Christian religion,"[58] Quaker policies toward the legal and human rights of Indian peoples and toward the role of the government in settling conflicts between Indians and Europeans were significantly different from those prevailing in any other American colony. These policies drew criticism from the very beginning from those colonists who either did not share the Quakers' benevolent and pacifistic values or resented any impediment to European expansion westward. The reluctance of the Quaker-dominated Pennsylvania Assembly to resort to military solutions to conflict on the frontier was not, it should be noted, founded in pure principle alone. The proprietors were under steady pressure from London to raise an appropriate level of financial support for British imperial war efforts, and Quakers in the assembly self-consciously used that need as a means of leverage in their struggle for power with and autonomy from the proprietors.[59] Quaker pacifism and Quaker rivalry with the proprietors were important factors in the refusal of the assembly to authorize military appropriations to defend against incursions by the French and Spanish and to make war against Indians, but an equally important impulse toward inaction came from the deeply rooted reluctance of Quaker leaders to use governmental powers for any purposes. This impulse toward "passive sovereignty" caused most members of the assembly to remain stubborn in their insistence that military expenditures were entirely the responsibility of the Penn family and to ignore the dangers posed by the renewal of military rivalries in Europe.[60]

Quaker attitudes toward Indians and toward defense were increasingly at odds with popular sentiment in a colony that was increasingly non-Quaker, but for the most part, at least until the early 1740s, the assembly managed to resist proprietary and popular pressures to vote monies for defense. By 1744, as England's long-standing rivalry with Spain and France flared up again with the beginning of the European War of the Austrian Succession, British officials in London renewed their requests that Pennsylvania contribute to the imperial war effort and make some provision for its own defense.[61] This time, after extracting some other concessions from the proprietary governor, they voted a sum of £5,000 for the "King's Use." Similarly, faced with appeals to provide assistance to a New England force that had just occupied the French fort at Louisbourg, the legislature voted £4000 for "the purchase of Bread, Beef, Pork, Flour, Wheat, and other Grain" for the occupying forces at Louisbourg, but they also made a point of reiterating their opposition to "raising of Men or providing of Arms and Ammunition."[62] In 1747, faced again with British requests that they provide for defense against French privateers in the Delaware Bay, the assembly failed to act. At that point Benjamin Franklin, by then an important figure in the Quaker Party even though he did not share the Quakers' scruples against warfare, was growing increasingly uneasy about the extent to which Quaker principles were running counter to popular opinion. Franklin took pen in hand and wrote *Plain Truth*, which offered a gentle critique of Quaker defense policies and then called for the creation of a voluntary militia that might fill the void left by the legislature's inaction.[63]

Conflicts between the Quaker-dominated legislature and the proprietors would oscillate at fluctuating levels during the next several years, but by July of 1755, as the Delaware Indians and the French began to cement their alliance and as bitter warfare between the Delawares and European settlers erupted on Pennsylvania's western frontier, the issue of frontier defense and Indian policy took center stage and would remain there for the next decade. One indication of the popular resonances on the issue was the increase in the volume of petitions coming into the assembly, which had averaged a little over twenty annually during the first half of the eighteenth century and rose to fifty in 1755 and sixty-six in 1756, nearly all of that increase accounted for by petitions on the defense question. The Pennsylvania citizens most aggrieved over the reluctance of the assembly to wage all-out war on the Indians were of course those living in the line of fire, on the frontier. As early as the fall of 1755 some westerners were threatening to "march down [to Philadelphia] and tear the whole Members of the legislative body Limb from Limb, if they did not grant immediate protection."[64] On November 24, 1755, a mob estimated at between 300 and 700 men, led by a Lancaster tavern keeper named John Hambright, marched to Philadelphia demanding increased military protection.[65]

In the face of renewed conflict between Europeans and Indians, Governor Morris urgently asked the assembly for an appropriation of £50,000 for the "King's use," but the assembly would agree to the proposal only if the proprietors conceded to allow their lands to be taxed. In order to break the deadlock the proprietors agreed to make a "contribution" to the public coffers in lieu of taxes. Following that concession, the assembly did pass both a supply bill and a militia bill, although the final products left both sides unhappy.[66]

As these conflicts were erupting in the legislature, other Quakers were trying to win back the allegiance of the Delaware Indians by peaceful means. Forming themselves into a "Friendly Association," a group of "sober" Friends, most of them residents of Philadelphia, far from the actual site of Indian hostilities, organized themselves as an extralegal alternative to government efforts to end the violence on the frontier. Over the course of several years from 1756 onward, members of the Friendly Association, often with at least the tacit support of Quaker members of the assembly, would attempt to identify "friendly" Indians and then work to protect them from aggression by their neighbors. The initiative was doomed to failure; the flames of war on the frontier were too hot to be cooled by "peaceful conversation," and, moreover, many western residents regarded the peacemaking efforts not only as ineffective but also perfidious. From their perspective a Quaker-dominated assembly was turning a deaf ear to popular clamorings for defense against hostile Indians while at the same time actually giving aid and comfort to the enemy.[67]

By April of 1756 Governor Morris and his council were preparing a declaration of war, which, among other things, included a bounty for Indian scalps—$130 for males over twelve years of age; $50 for females—and on April 12, over the objections of the assembly, they formally issued the declaration. Quaker politicians in the assembly, many of them already under pressure from their meetings to withdraw from politics in order to avoid complicity with warfare against Indians, began to do just that. On hearing of Morris's declaration, six Quakers, some of them leading members, resigned from the assembly, and at the elections the following fall, more than half of the Quaker members of the legislature refused to stand for election (although, interestingly, four of those who refused to stand were nevertheless elected by their constituents over their protestations). In fact the Quaker Party would continue to be the dominant force in the Pennsylvania legislature for the next two decades after 1756, but the political landscape in the colony would be forever changed.[68]

The unfolding of these events proved to be both an extraordinary challenge and an extraordinary opportunity for Benjamin Franklin, who had only recently moved from being clerk of the assembly to an elected member of that body. As many of the most self-consciously observant Quakers departed from politics, they created a leadership vacuum that Franklin was superbly equipped to fill. Although Quakers no longer dominated the membership of the Pennsylvania Assembly (after the Quaker defection in 1756 the percentage of Quakers in the assembly dropped to 33 percent), Quaker influence on the assembly party, or at least the influence of those Quakers who regarded their duty as public officials and opponents of proprietary prerogative as higher than that of maintaining a strict commitment to pacifistic principles, remained substantial. As Franklin himself put it, "the Quakers now think it their Duty, when chosen, to consider themselves as Representatives of the Whole People, and not of their Sect only . . . To me, it seems that if *Quakerism* (as to the matter of Defence) be excluded from the House, there is no Necessity to exclude *Quakers*, who in other respects make good and useful Members."[69] From 1756 onward, Franklin, working with Quakers such as the longtime Speaker of the House, Isaac Norris Jr., put together a coalition of antiproprietary politicians that was in its own way as formidable and effective as its Quaker-dominated predecessor. More flexible on issues of defense than its pre-1756 predecessor, the assembly party coalition was also able, through Franklin's popularity among the working-class population of Philadelphia, to bolster its claim to popular support against proprietary privilege.[70] Moreover, although hostilities between Pennsylvania backcountry settlers and Indians did not end altogether, there was, following important British victories at Fort Niagara and Quebec in 1759, at least a quieting in those conflicts.

Unfortunately, that quiet did not last long. Beginning in the summer of 1763, the Ottawa Indian leader Pontiac, provoked by the failure of the British to live up to their wartime commitments and by the murder of Teedyuscung, led a series of raids on the northwestern frontier that had backcountry Pennsylvania residents once again clamoring for aggressive action against Indians. Indian forces moved southward and eastward over the course of the summer months of 1763, capturing Fort Venango, Fort LeBoeuf, Fort Presque Isle in June and laying siege to Forts Ligonier, Bedford, and Pitt in late June and July. In late July they moved into the Juniata, Tuscarora, Cumberland, and Sherman's valleys, causing more than a thousand settlers living on the western edge of Pennsylvania's frontier to flee further eastward. According to Edward Shippen, a prominent local officeholder in Lancaster County with close ties to proprietary leaders in the colony, "every body . . . that are at Paxton, must be in great Terror, night and day, and the Poor Familys that are come thither from Juniata & other Places, in great want of the Necessarys of Life. . . . The other day at the River I mentioned to Mrs. Susey Wright, that it was thought by some people, & my self among the rest, that a good reward offered for Scalps would be the most effectual way of quelling the Indians."[71] A week later, as hostilities continued to increase, Shippen predicted, "the commissioners may think what pleases of the present calamitous Situation of the Province, but They may depend upon it, that if the poor people do not receive due Encouragement to Stand their Ground . . . the Savages will soon make inroads through the whole Province, burning & destroying everything as they go."[72] In fact the Pennsylvania Assembly did respond to the heightened threat of Indian warfare by providing for the raising of a force of some 700 men, but to many in the western part of the colony, particularly those living in the most exposed regions of Lancaster and Cumberland counties, that response seemed pathetically inadequate.

The long-simmering hostility that many backcountry Pennsylvania residents felt toward their Indian neighbors and toward the seeming indifference of Pennsylvania politicians in the east boiled over on December 14, 1763. On that day settlers in Paxton, a community lying about ninety miles to the north and west of Philadelphia in the area that is now Pennsylvania's state capital, Harrisburg, lashed out at their Indian neighbors. Suspecting that a group of supposedly friendly Indians residing on a manor in Conestoga were in fact conspiring with hostile Indians to the west, a band of some fifty armed and mounted men rode into the compound just before dawn and "fired upon, stabbed and hatcheted to Death" the three men, two women, and one small boy who they found there. They then scalped their victims and set their houses on fire. Two weeks later another band of men finished the job. Learning that the Indians whom they had not found in Conestoga a fortnight before had been placed in the Lancaster workhouse for their protection, they assaulted the workhouse, butchering all fourteen of the Indians residing there in a matter of minutes. When confronted by the band of men, the Indians "fell on their Knees, protested their Innocence, declared their Love to the English, and that, in their whole Lives, they had never done them Injury; and in this Posture they all received the Hatchet! Men, Women and little Children—were every one inhumanly murdered!—in cold Blood."[73] One observer, William Henry of Lancaster, was walking by the jail when the band of men, "well mounted on horses, and with rifles, tomahawks, and scalping knives, equipped for murder," rode into town:

And there, oh what a horrid sight presented itself to my view! Near the back door of the prison lay an old Indian and his squaw, particularly well known and esteemed by the people of the town on account of his placid and friendly conduct. His name was Will Soc; across him and squaw lay two children, of about the age of three years, whose heads were split with the tomahawk, and their scalps taken off. Toward the middle of the jail yard, along the west side of the wall, lay a stout Indian, whom I particularly noticed to have been shot in his breast; his legs were chopped with the tomahawk, his hands cut off, and finally a rifle ball discharged in his mouth, so that his head was blown to atoms, and the brains were splashed against and yet hanging to the wall, for three or four feet around. This man's hand and feet had also been chopped off with a tomahawk. In this manner lay the whole of them, men, women, and children spread about the prison yard; shot, scalped, hacked and cut to pieces.[74]

Most Pennsylvanians had developed a high tolerance for inhumane behavior toward Indians, but the barbarity of the massacres was shocking even to many of those who had previously shown little sympathy for Indian rights or Indian ways. Benjamin Franklin was one of those who took up pen to denounce the barbarities committed at Conestoga and Lancaster. Unlike most of Franklin's pamphlet writings, which were cool and controlled, and most often aimed at both the reason and self-interest of his readers, Franklin's "Narrative of the Late Massacres in Lancaster" made no attempt to hide the author's moral outrage. Taking his readers through the history of warfare—from the Greeks to the Jews to the Turks, Saracens, and Moors—he could find no instance in which the slaughter of innocent people could be justified. He noted that even before the birth of Christ, Homer, in the *Odyssey*, spoke of the "sacred rites of Hospitality," wherein innocent "Strangers, the Poor, and the Weak" were to be protected from injury. As to the Indian victims at Lancaster, Franklin lamented:

Unhappy People! to have lived in such Times, and by such Neighbors! We have seen, that they would have been safer among the ancient Heathens with whom the Rites of Hospitality were sacred. They would have been considered as Guests of the Publick, and the Religion of the Country would have operated in their Favour. But our Frontier People call themselves Christians! *They would have been safer, if they had submitted to the Turks; for ever since Mahomet's Reproof to Khaled, even the cruel Turks never kill prisoners in cold Blood.*

In describing the aftermath of the December 27 slaughter, Franklin noted that "the Bodies of the Murdered were then brought out and exposed in the Street, till a Hole could be made in the Earth, to receive and cover them." But, he averred, "the wickedness cannot be covered, the Guilt will lie on the whole Land, till Justice is done on the Murderers. THE BLOOD OF THE INNOCENT WILL CRY TO HEAVEN FOR VENGEANCE."[75]

Governor John Penn issued two proclamations denouncing the massacres in emphatic terms, each with stern injunctions that those guilty of the barbarous acts be apprehended and punished. At the same time he ordered that similar groups of peaceable Indians currently residing under the protection of the Moravians at Nain and Wechquetank and another group at Wyalusing be moved to Philadelphia for their protection. Pennsylvania's backcountry residents remained unrepentant, and indeed, with the decision to move the Indians to Philadelphia, they drew support from a number of Philadelphia and Chester County residents as well. Denouncing the "excessive Regard manifested to Indians beyond his Majesty's loyal Subjects," they expressed consternation as to how the "horrid Ravages, cruel Murders and most shocking Barbarities committed by Indians on his Majesty's Subjects are covered over and excused under Charitable Term of this being their Method of making War."[76] Nor did they confine their defense to words. On January 28 the governor received a report that "fifteen hundred Men would come down [to Philadelphia] in order to kill the said Indians, and that if Fifteen hundred were not enough, Five thousand were ready to join them." Alarmed by this news, the governor, with Benjamin Franklin as his key adviser, summoned Philadelphia citizens to the statehouse and asked them to volunteer to join an association that would confront the mob when it appeared in Philadelphia. On Monday, February 6, several hundred Philadelphians, including a substantial number of Quakers who had put aside their scruples about violence and armed themselves for the occasion, met the Paxton "Hickory Boys" at Germantown. Reports of the events of that day suggest as much a carnival as a bloody confrontation. David Rittenhouse reported that the frontier protesters "uttered hideous outcries in imitation of the war whoop, knocked down peaceable citizens, and pretended to scalp them," but, in fact, though heavily armed with rifles, tomahawks, and pistols, the Paxton Boys were under orders not to engage in violence. The following day Benjamin Franklin was dispatched to meet with the frontiersmen, ascertain the nature of their grievances, and, hopefully, persuade them to return home. Franklin, in the company of Benjamin Chew, Joseph Galloway, and Thomas Willing, was successful in achieving all of those aims. Meeting for several hours in a tavern with the leaders of the Paxton Boys, Franklin agreed to present the grievances of the frontier residents to the assembly and governor, in return for the peaceable departure of the mob.[77]

The frontier people's grievances were expressed in a two-part document,

"A DECLARATION/AND/REMONSTRANCE/OF the distressed and bleeding, Frontier Inhabitants/of The Province of Pennsylvania." The declaration was a ringing defense of the frontier settlers' past actions against the Indians, denouncing provincial officials for a policy that took "murderers" and "cherished and caressed [them] as dearest friends." The remonstrance, however, set down nine grievances, with the very first of those relating not to the issue of Indian warfare but, rather, to the denial of "the same Privileges and Immunities with his Majesty's other subjects . . . in the very important Privilege of Legislation," an injustice that stemmed from malapportionment of representation in the Pennsylvania Assembly.[78] The tone of the declaration and remonstrance was, to be sure, infected throughout with a virulent hatred of Indians that illustrates the full extent to which ethnocentrism shaped our nation's past, but running through those documents as well was a powerful sense of beleaguerment and estrangement from eastern institutions of law and government, a sense that at least some of Pennsylvania's frontier residents, though officially subject to the laws of the colony, were in fact living in a different land altogether.

Although separated by several hundred miles from those regions in North and South Carolina that produced the Regulator uprisings, the community of Paxton was similarly afflicted by a combination of ethnic conflict, economic uncertainty, an absence of stable, community-based institutions, and an unresponsive political apparatus at the provincial center. While the structure and operation of government in William Penn's colony had, on the whole, brought to southeastern Pennsylvania a remarkable measure of order, liberty, and prosperity, that same government—in its failure to extend adequate representation to the western part of the colony and in the refusal of its principal eastern leaders to comprehend the nature of conditions on the frontier—fell far short of William Penn's Whiggish ideal of a government based on the full consent of the whole people.

Lancaster County, of which the town of Paxton was a part, was itself underrepresented in the legislature; with a population of 5,635 taxable citizens, a system of proportional representation would have given the county eight, not four, representatives. But as inequitable as the underrepresentation of Lancaster County may have been, far more serious was the way in which townships like Paxton, lying on the periphery of Lancaster's 2,000-square-mile expanse, were ignored within the local governance structure of that sprawling county. The town of Paxton itself covered some 260 square miles of territory and was located thirty miles, or a day's ride, to the north and west of the county seat.[79] Almost all of the government of the region was conducted at the county seat—the administration of justice in the county courts, decisions about the building and maintenance of roads, the licensing of taverns, and the overseeing of taxation policy. If Paxton's citizens wished to vote in any of the county's elections—whether to elect the county's lone sheriff or its commissioners—they had to make that long

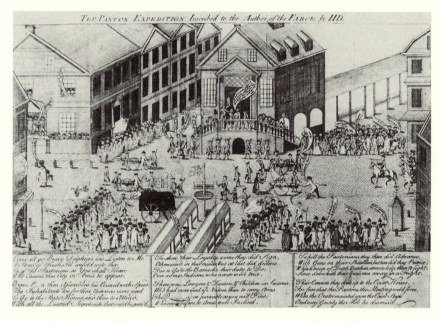

Figure 12. March of the Paxton Boys on Philadelphia. Courtesy of The Library Company of Philadelphia.

day's ride to the county seat to do so, a fact that effectively disenfranchised voters residing on the periphery of the county and enabled control of county politics by a small group of men residing near the county seat. Indeed, in the thirty-five years between the establishment of Lancaster County in 1729 and the Paxton uprising, the town of Paxton had never managed to have one of its residents in the assembly and, overwhelmingly, Lancaster's legislative delegation all during that period had the closest ties with the traditional Quaker ruling elite in Chester County.[80]

There was little in the structure of Pennsylvania politics or in the myriad local cultures within the colony that served to encourage the emergence of alternative forms of government at the township level. In Paxton township itself, the operation of "community" institutions—both political and otherwise—was negligible. The reasons for the frailty of Paxton's community are not hard to discern. Although William Penn had hoped for an orderly process of settlement radiating out from his "Greene Country Towne" in Philadelphia, the reality of settlement—in Philadelphia and elsewhere—was far messier, with the greed of public officials and private citizens alike and the cultural predispositions of the settlers themselves all getting in the way of Penn's vision. His determination to reserve 10 percent of every hundred thousand acres for himself was continued in the eighteenth century

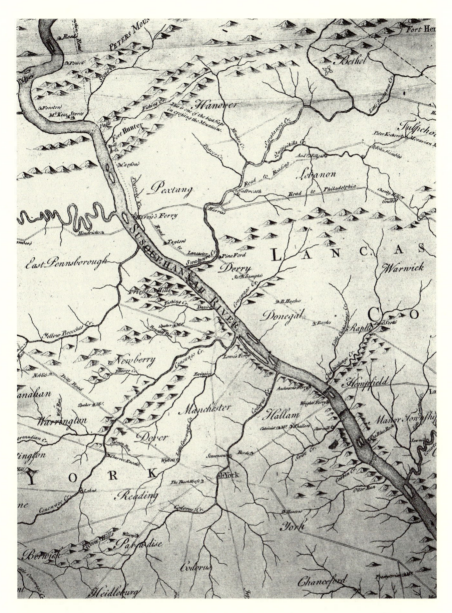

Figure 13. The Lancaster County frontier, including Paxton township, 1759.
Courtesy of the Edward E. Ayer Collection, the Newberry Library, Chicago.

by his heirs, who were aggressive about seeing to it that their 10 percent was from the best land that could be purchased from the Indians. The personal interests of the few members of the proprietary family, however, increasingly came smack up against the aspirations of the thousands of Palatine and Scots-Irish settlers who flocked to western Pennsylvania during the years between 1720 and the outbreak of the Paxton riots. During the years between 1718 and 1733, at a time when the pace of immigration into the backcountry was changing from a trickle to a flood, the Pennsylvania land office was closed due to legal uncertainty over the claims of Penn's heirs to land in the province. The consequence was that the tendencies of backcountry settlers to squat on the land—taking up parcels without legal title—were encouraged even further.[81] James Logan, writing to Hannah Penn in January, 1726 was nearly beside himself over the uncertainty of land ownership on the frontier. "I doubt not," he wrote, "but there are at this time Near a hundred thousand Acres possess'd by persons who resolutely sitt down and improve, without any manner of Right or Pretense to it." He blamed a good portion of the difficulty on "An unruly sort of Palatines," who "have, by encouragement from the Govt, entered upon . . . about 20 thousand acres in one Tract." Even more alarming though was the extent of squatting by the Scots-Irish. "They have," Logan wrote, "generally taken up the western lands; and as they rarely approach me to propose to purchase, I look upon them as bold and indigent strangers, giving as their excuse, when challenged fore titles, that we had solicited for colonists, and they had come accordingly."[82]

The uncertainty of land titles in the region only exacerbated the natural inclinations of all backcountry settlers—whatever their ethnic origins—to be suspicious of residents unlike themselves. Though William Penn's laudable policies with respect to religious toleration may have restrained official harassment of ethnic minorities, they were certainly insufficient to guarantee peace, harmony, and mutual trust among Quakers, Mennonites, Scots-Irish Presbyterians, and Germans, who often came in contact and contest for land and cultural hegemony. Governor James Hamilton, writing in 1752, made no effort to hide his feelings about the effects of "foreign" immigration. "I hope we have now done with making new Counties for some time," he wrote, "as they afford me no sort of satisfaction, being generally filled with such an exceeding barbarous kind of people, as makes it almost impossible to keep them in any sort of order." While the Germans were generally praised for their diligence, there was a growing concern about their political influence, leading many in both the Quaker Party and proprietary faction to try to draw county lines in a way that limited that influence. The Scots-Irish, the most numerous and perceived to be the most "disorderly," came in for the brunt of the abuse, reaching some sort of peak during the French and Indian Wars. When commenting on one backcountry skirmish, a Quaker member of the assembly from Chester County noted that the only casualties were "some Scotch-Irish killed, who could well be spared." These antipathies were not lost on the Scots-Irish, who were resigned to the fact that, as Paxton Presbyterian Church minister John Elder put it, "Representations from the back Inhabitants have but little weight with the Gentlemen in power, they looking on us, either as uncapable of forming just notions of things, or as biass'd by Selfish Views."[83]

One of the things that may have damped down ethnic and religious conflict was the tendency toward dispersion of settlement. Immigrants to Pennsylvania began to spread themselves out across the landscape almost as soon as William Penn established his "greene Country Towne," and there was almost nothing either in the institutional structure of the colony or in the inclinations of the settlers to halt that trend. Moreover, the citizens of the Pennsylvania backcountry were not only widely dispersed on individual farmsteads most commonly ranging from one hundred to three hundred acres, they were also impermanent to an extraordinarily high degree. Geographical mobility in Paxton itself in the mid-eighteenth century was phenomenal by almost any standard. In most years during the period from 1750 through the Revolution, the turnover in the township's population—measured both in terms of the entrance into the town of new settlers and the departure of old ones—was around 50 percent, with somewhat over 30 percent of the town's citizens disappearing from the tax rolls each year. During the thirty-two year period between 1750 and 1782 only 2 percent of the town's taxpayers were in continuous residence. These extraordinary rates of mobility, in conjunction with the absence of institutions—political or religious—that served to bring citizens together in common endeavor, made Paxton, in the words of George Franz, "a community of strangers."[84] It was in that context that the settlers of Paxton—diverse in religion and ethnic origins and largely alienated from the political institutions of the east—confronted the problems of Indian violence and of violence against Indians in their midst.

Perhaps the closest that the residents of the area had to a community institution was the trading post run by John Harris on the banks of the Susquehanna River near Paxton. And Harris was the closest thing that the Paxton residents had to a community leader. Harris's position as a merchant and trader inclined him to attempt to play a role as peacemaker in many of the conflicts between the Indians and white settlers of the area, and his trading post became the site for many of the negotiations between Indians and Europeans during the 1740s and 1750s. As a frontiersman with a record both of extraordinary bravery in battle against the Indians as well as of being a man who had demonstrated an ability as a negotiator among Indians, Harris was the one person in the area whose views might actually be listened to by officials in Philadelphia. By 1763, however, Harris had joined his neighbors in Paxton both in his dismay at the absence of a strong military response from the Pennsylvania government and in his implacable hostility to the Indians of the area, "friendly" or otherwise.[85]

In the absence of positive forces binding citizens of the region together, the events of the mid-1760s in and around Paxton unleashed a torrent of negative reference-group behavior. It would of course be Indians—friendly and otherwise—who would bear the brunt of discontent and frustration. The vituperation aimed at Indians by the defenders of the Paxton Boys was extraordinary by any standard of measure. In the pamphlet war that followed the Paxton massacre, defenders of the Paxton Boys repeatedly referred to the Indians of the region as "merciless savages," "Savage Indian Butchers," and "murderers," and poured forth a litany of the outrages they had committed upon white frontier settlements.[86] The pro-Paxton pamphlets are filled with gruesome descriptions of Indian "barbarism" which, in the intensity of the fear and anger they express, are difficult to capture in short compass. One of the passages from "The Apology of the Paxton Volunteers" gives some sense of the rage felt by the defenders of the Paxton Boys:

The Indians set Fire to Houses, Barns, Corn, Hay, in short to every thing that was combustible; so that the whole Country seemed to be in one general Blaze and involved in one common Ruin. Great Numbers of the back Settlers were murdered, scalped & butchered in the most shocking manner, & their dead Bodies inhumanly mangled; some having their Ribs divided from the Chine with the Tomahawk, others left expiring in the most esquisite [sic] Tortures, with Legs & Arms broken, their Skulls fractured, & the Brains scattered on the Ground. Many Children were either spitted alive & roasted or covered under the Ashes of a large Fire, before their helpless Parents Eyes. The Hearts of some taken out & eaten reeking hot, while they were yet beating between their Teeth and others, where Time & Opportunity would admit of it were skinned, boiled, and eaten. Hundreds were carried into the most miserable Captivity separated from all the Endearments of their Friends & the Privileges of the Christian Church and are daily tortured to Death in every Method of Cruelty which Indian Barbarity can suggest.[87]

The fear and hatred of the Indians by many backcountry settlers was visceral; the rage that the settlers felt toward the members of the eastern oligarchy and, in particular, toward the Quaker members of that oligarchy who had ignored their plight was, if less instinctively generated, long nurtured and deeply ingrained. And the most obvious focus for those feelings was the Quaker-dominated assembly, whose principal members—Quaker and non-Quaker alike—were located far from the scene of Indian warfare and who were therefore wholly unconcerned about voting the appropriations necessary to make war on the Indians. The author of "The Apology of the Paxton Volunteers," after chronicling the horrors visited on frontier residents by the Indians, asked rhetorically whether "a Government might do something to help a bleeding frontier . . . & who could suspect that the

Men in Power refused to relieve the Sufferings of their fellow Subjects?"
But, applying to the government for relief, "the far greater part of our Assembly were Quakers, some of whom made light of our Sufferings & plead Conscience, so that they could neither take Arms in Defense of themselves or their Country." The Paxton apologists believed that if the Quakers had been truly "conscientious in this matter, & found that it was inconsistent with their Principles to govern in a Time of War, why did they not resign their Seats to those who had no Scruples of this Kind?"[88]

The constant theme of the attacks on the Quakers was the hypocrisy with which they denied frontier residents adequate representation in the assembly and then, using their disproportionate power in that body, insisted on imposing their deviant views on the rest of the population. The Quaker belief that "divine Inspiration" prohibited them from having "any Hand in shedding Blood" was, quite simply, unnatural, and, therefore, why should any holding those beliefs "be intrusted as a Representative for People who look on themselves to be obliged by the Laws of God, the Laws of Nature, and the Laws of their King and Country to take up Arms to defend themselves, and punish those who deprive them of Life or Property?" War against savage peoples, the Paxton apologists insisted, was not only a necessity, but divinely sanctioned. In spite of that truth, however, the Quakers continued to show "more real Affection for Enemy Savages than for their fellow Subjects."[89]

While Quaker theology provided one focus for the frontier settlers' anger, there was also a component that emphasized ethnic difference. In "The Cloven-Foot discovered," one aspiring frontier poet declaimed:

> Go on good Christians, never spare
> To give your Indians Clothes to wear;
> Send'em good Beef, and Pork, and Bread
> Guns, Power, Flints, and store of Lead,
> To Shoot your Neighbours through the Head;
> Devoutly then, make Affirmation,
> You're Friends to George and British Nation;
> Encourage ev'ry friendly Savage,
> To murder, burn destroy and ravage;
> Fathers and Mothers here maintain,
> Whose Sons add Numbers to the slain,
> Of Scotch and Irish let them kill
> As many Thousands as they will
> That you may lord it o'er the Land
> And have the whole and sole command.[90]

In language nearly identical to that used by Charles Woodmason in defending the Regulators in the Carolina backcountry, "Philopatrius" noted the consistent refusal of the assembly to pay any attention to the petitions and remonstrances emanating from the backcountry, and he reminded his readers that "as the wise SOLOMON suggests, 'Oppression will make a Wise Man mad.' And have not all Nations and Generations found it so, that when People have been driven to Desperation by Oppression, they have broken thro' all Obstacles to right themselves, if at all in their Power?"[91]

Benjamin Franklin, though a master at straddling both sides of a dispute, had clearly placed himself in the line of fire on this issue, so he, too, came under attack from the defenders of the Paxtonites. A "Gentle-man in one of the Frontier Counties" was unimpressed with

the mighty Noise and Hubbub . . . made about killing a few Indians in Lancaster County; and even Philosophers and Legislators have been employed to raise the Holloo upon those that killed them; and to ransack Tomes and Systems, Writers ancient and modern, for Proofs of their Guilt and Condemnation! And what have they proved at last? Why that the WHITE SAVAGES of Paxton and Donnegal have violated the Laws of Hospitality! I can sincerely assure the ingenious and worthy Author of the NARRATIVE, that a Shock of Electricity would have had a much more sensible Effect upon these People than all the Arguments and Quotations he has produced.[92]

The responses from Quakers and non-Quakers alike to pro-Paxton pamphlets almost certainly inflamed the sense of cultural isolation felt by many on the Pennsylvania frontier. Certainly many of those writing pamphlets denouncing the Paxton killings were motivated, like Franklin in his "Narrative of the Late Massacres," by a desire to defend the essential humanity of peaceful Indians in the colony. But in the course of their defense of the Indians, some moved into other areas as well. Isaac Hunt, a recent graduate of the College of Philadelphia and the author of "A Looking Glass for Presbyterians," defended the Quakers for "wisely and judiciously" governing the colony and then lashed out at the ignorance and ingratitude of those "Adventurers from *Ireland*" who sent "their poor Relations to populate this Province; whose delightful Plains far surpass the barren Mountains of *Carentaugher, Slemish, Slevgallion.*"[93] While acknowledging some of the potential difficulties created by the Quaker stricture against serving in government during time of war, Hunt was of the opinion that if "their Seats [had] been fill'd with Presbyterians, we should inevitably have been in a much worse condition; for it is very evident, from undeniable Facts, that they are by no Means proper Men to hold the Reins of Government, either in War of Peace." Then followed a litany of Presbyterian unruliness in England, Scotland, and Ireland, including murders of "men, Women and Children in . . . much the same Manner their Offspring murder'd the *Indians at Lancaster.*" From all these instances, Hunt concluded, "Presbyterians have been always Enemies to *Kingly Government*, and consequently not fit to be entrusted with any Share of the *Civil Power*, when a king reigns." Noting that "the Presbyterians want more Members from the back Counties to represent them, and have added this to the Catalogue of their Grievances,"

Hunt countered that even within the present scheme of apportionment of representatives, the voters of Lancaster had "seldom sent a Presbyterian to represent them (one qualified being very rarely to be found)."[94]

Whether provoked by a Quaker-dominated legislature inattentive to their needs, by a philosopher-statesman likening them to "cruel Turks," or by an intemperate pamphleteer painting all Scots-Irish and Presbyterians with the same broad brush, the exasperation of the frontier residents toward their governors (and philosophers) in the eastern part of the colony went beyond differing conceptions of the Indian threat or unhappiness with the current formula for representation in the assembly. Although the frontier residents frequently invoked in their pamphlets a shared tradition of "English liberty" that, they insisted, made them just as loyal in their attachment to Crown and colony as their adversaries, there was in those same invocations a sense that they were a people apart, living a life in a land more dangerous, more disordered, more desperate, than their privileged and pampered neighbors to the east. They deeply resented the fact that the "Names of RIOTERS, REBELS, MURDERERS, WHITE SAVAGES & c have been liberally and indiscriminately bestowed upon them," and saw this as one more sign not only of the malevolence of Quaker political leaders, for whom they had special contempt, but also as another sign that the eastern and western residents were, quite literally, speaking a different language.[95]

This sense of separation and alienation from the provincial center was in fact one of the few points of cohesion for those individuals who were called Paxton Boys. Lacking any obvious physical community center and located a hard day's ride from the administrative and legal institutions of the county, the town of Paxton was not really a town, but only a string of mills, ferries, and taverns situated along the several crossroads of the township. The ethnic and religious makeup of the township almost certainly did not contribute to a cohesive community identity. Scots-Irish settlers initially composed the great bulk of Paxton's residents, but by the time of the march on Philadelphia there were at least as many Germans in the town as Scots-Irish, as well as a modest number of English. Even within those ethnic groups there was no single point of congregation in which the settlers might gather for religious observance. A German Reformed Church was not built in the township itself until the 1770s, and the Paxton Presbyterian Church was off in a remote corner of the township, away from most of the residents, with the consequence being that Scots-Irish Presbyterians in the eastern part of the township worshiped in neighboring Hanover and southern residents traveled to Derry. With the coming of the Great Awakening to the Pennsylvania backcountry, the inhabitants were further divided as New Light Churches sprang up to challenge Old Light ways.[96]

George Franz has called Paxton an "ad hoc" community—"transitory, individualistic, informal and fractionalized," one that "did not develop a continuum of concern or action among its inhabitants." It is therefore no surprise that there is little to be recovered of a discernible public political culture in this community. James Lemon, in his optimistic view of eighteenth-century Pennsylvania as a "Best Poor Man's Country," views the mobility, acquisitiveness, and individual striving that characterized life in Paxton as the essence of "liberal individualism," but even so ardent an admirer of democratic individualism as Frederick Jackson Turner recognized the dangers inherent in an individualism taken "beyond its proper bounds."[97] The individualism that thrived in Paxton, often born of alienation and manifested in violence against others, was hardly the stuff of a pluralistic, consensual democracy.

The only source of cohesion in Paxton was, in fact, the common animus that the town's citizens felt toward Indians and toward those in the east of the colony who failed to join with Paxton's white citizens in making war on those Indians. While the flurry of pamphlets and petitions following the Paxton uprising brought the town and a few of its residents into the public spotlight, it did not create within that troubled region a core of leaders capable of providing Paxton with either cohesion within or meaningful influence beyond. Political leadership at the local level within Lancaster County continued to be dominated by men living in or around the town of Lancaster, the county seat, far from Paxton. Although there may have been a lively local political culture, with occasional contests for public office in the area surrounding the town of Lancaster, none of that extended as far as Paxton. Indeed, during the critical period from 1748 to 1756 the Lancaster delegation to the assembly was either three-quarters or entirely Quaker in its religious orientation and consistently voted with the Quaker majority in the assembly either to weaken or defeat altogether defense bills aimed at providing relief from Indian hostilities. The situation did not improve markedly thereafter; the Lancaster delegation to the assembly continued to vote with the eastern majority right up to the end of the Revolution.[98]

Indeed, the reaction of many in the east to the Paxtonites was either instinctively hostile or self-consciously partisan. Benjamin Franklin was not alone in labeling them "barbarous men" and "WHITE SAVAGES;" much of the commentary following the uprising suggested that life on America's far frontier was an inherently uncivilizing and disintegrating process. That much of the violence and disorder of the uprising was associated with men of Scots-Irish background (an exaggeration as it turned out) only reinforced the impression among many easterners that those living on the Pennsylvania frontier were an alien race.[99]

These visceral fears—whether of Indians or of Scots-Irish frontiersmen—were also fuel for partisan advantage, whether among members of the proprietary faction who used the Paxton uprising as yet another example of misrule by the Quaker-dominated assembly or by the Assembly Party as proof of a plot by proprietary faction leaders, in league with disorderly

Scots-Irish Presbyterians, to destabilize the provincial government. In the atmosphere of overheated rhetoric that marked the aftermath of the Paxton uprising, it is sometimes difficult to know where visceral, virulent ethnocentrism ends and carefully calculated political partisanship begins, but whatever the precise mixture, few in the east exhibited any real desire to understand or serve the culture of the Paxton backcountry residents.[100]

The Meaning of Paxton

The legacy of the Paxton uprising is mixed. In the short run the beleaguered citizens of Paxton and their neighbors in the backcountry gained very little. Of the nine grievances listed in their remonstrance, only one was acted on, and a dubious one at that. In July of 1764 the General Assembly passed a law offering a bounty for Indian scalps. And for those, like Benjamin Franklin, revolted by the savagery displayed on those two days in December and eager for the perpetrators to be brought to justice, there would be very little satisfaction either. In spite of the boasting of many of the participants in the massacre of the Indians, no witnesses were willing to come forward to testify as to the identity of those present on those two bloody days, and no one was ever brought to trial. Whatever the outrage that may have existed in Philadelphia, the operation of the law on the frontier proved to be a thing apart.[101]

The immediate political consequence of the Paxton uprising on the politics of the east would be to give the members of the proprietary faction an opening to undercut their rivals in the assembly; in spite of the ultimately conciliatory role that Franklin played in the affair, proprietary leaders attempted to use his writing and the Quaker Party's past inaction on matters of defense as a means of winning western representatives in the assembly to their side. For their part Franklin and other members of the inner circle of the Assembly Party determined that the time had come to remove proprietary influence over the colony altogether, and in the spring of 1764 they began to lay plans for the revocation of the proprietary charter and the conversion of Pennsylvania to a royal colony. In March 1764 the assembly passed a set of resolves calling for a canvass of public opinion as to whether to request that the king "take the people of the Province under his immediate Protection." In May, Franklin presented to the assembly petitions containing 3,500 signatures asking for the transfer of power from the proprietors to the king, and with only three dissenting votes out of thirty, the assembly formally endorsed the recommendation.[102]

The timing of the call for conversion to royal government, occurring as it did at precisely the moment when British imperial policies were turning more and more Americans against royal government, could not have been worse, and, as we will see in chapter 9, Franklin and the Assembly Party would discover that they had greatly misjudged public opinion. The tem-

per of the public in Pennsylvania on a wide range of issues—the proprietors, royal authority, relations between east and west, and defense against
not only Indians, but now the British army—would become inflamed as
never before.

The issues of both proprietary and royal authority would be settled, although not necessarily to the assembly's liking, with the advent of independence. The resolution of the issues dividing east and west and of those
bringing Europeans and Indians into conflict on the frontier would take
much longer. It would take more than a new set of political institutions to
accomplish those feats of cultural integration. The combination of ethnic,
class, and political differences between east and west continued to keep in
place alternative and often militantly antagonistic identities among western
settlers, identities that made the threat of separatist movements in Pennsylvania nearly constant during the 1780s and 1790s. Indeed, the Pennsylvania backcountry would continue to mirror the sort of tribal behavior
exhibited in the Carolina backcountry: hostility among contending groups
(particularly between Indians and Scots-Irish settlers) in an environment of
material scarcity (if rough equality of condition) continued to threaten to
bubble to the surface and erupt into conflict. In Pennsylvania's "Western
Country," as in the Carolina backcountry, some of the payoff of these conditions would be dealt out during the War of Independence as British soldiers, western residents, and the various Indian tribes of the region
jockeyed for advantage. A Pennsylvania militia officer summed up the result and reported, "Our country is on the eve of breaking up. There is
nothing to be seen but disolation, fire, and smoak."[103]

Pennsylvania's revolutionary constitution would remove the westerners'
grievances about underrepresentation in the legislature, although as the
Whiskey Rebellion of 1794 would demonstrate, it would not remove altogether the western distrust of taxes imposed from afar. In Pennsylvania, as
in much of the north and southwest, the most important force working to
secure the loyalty of the backcountry resided less in the extension of political representation than in the eventual willingness of the Continental government to use force on the Indian adversaries. In that sense, tragically, the
revolutionary settlement of 1776 and the constitutional settlement of 1787
were less important to the history of political integration in the western
backcountry than was the decisive victory of Anthony Wayne over the Iroquois at Fallen Timbers in 1794.[104]

Chapter 9

Toward Democratic Pluralism
The Politics of the Cities of the Northeast

Back in Philadelphia in 1764 after a five-year stay in London as a colonial agent, Benjamin Franklin had good reason to rest content with a life well lived. By 1748, at age forty-two, he had accumulated enough wealth from his highly successful careers as a printer and author to retire to the life of scientist and civic activist. Over the course of the next sixteen years he earned for himself honorary degrees from Harvard, Yale, William and Mary, St. Andrews, and Oxford; election to the Royal Society; and an international reputation as a scientist for his experiments with electrity. His inventions—from the lightning rod to the Franklin fireplace to the flexible catheter—would extend his reputation as a man of uncommon genius. Franklin's record as a civic leader was no less luminous. He initiated all manner of projects for the improvement of his home city—the establishment of a municipal police force, the paving and lighting of city streets, the founding of the city's first hospital, and the establishment of a circulating library. And his accomplishments as a cultural and educational leader—as founder of both the American Philosophical Society and the Academy for the Education of Youth (later to become the University of Pennsylvania)—extended his fame still further. Finally, as we have seen, during the period from 1751 to 1764 he would emerge as a leader of the Quaker-dominated "Assembly Party" in the Pennsylvania legislature.[1] During all of those years, there is no indication that he ever had to worry about appealing aggressively to the voters in order to ensure his own election to office. Though his origins were humble, Franklin was clearly a man deserving the respect of his fellow citizens.[2]

By 1764 the long-standing battle between the proprietors and the Assembly Party was heating up once again. Such battles were by no means uncommon, nor was it unusual that leaders of the two sides would occasionally try to mobilize popular sentiment in their favor. For the most part, however, such political mobilizations had been top-down affairs, usually precipitated by attempts by the proprietary faction to broaden its political base in order to gain advantage over its legislative rival. In the elections of 1764, however, the voters of Philadelphia faced a broader range of substantive issues than they had ever faced in the past. Popular confidence in the assembly, which in the view of many had continued to drag its feet on the issue of defense, was sinking. Moreover, Franklin's decision to try to put the proprietors out of business once and for all by persuading the Crown to convert Pennsylvania into a royal colony, would have a far more destabilizing effect than he ever could have realized. To a significant degree the assembly elections of 1764 turned into a referendum not only on Franklin's political leadership but also on the soundness of the plan to convert the colony to royal government. Allied with the capable, but conservative, Joseph Galloway, Franklin took the lead both in writing pamphlets and organizing mass meetings in Philadelphia promoting the scheme for the transfer of power to the king. The leaders of the proprietary faction, normally unwilling to look beyond the circle of a few wealthy and well-born Anglicans for leadership, took the bold step in 1764 of including on their eight-person assembly slate two Germans and a Scots-Irishman. In all, the two sides produced no fewer than forty-four pamphlets and broadsides, many of them in German. Many of the pamphlets stuck to the issue of royal versus proprietary government. Franklin and his allies argued that in a proprietary form of government, conflict was inevitable, since the proprietors, occupying the executive branch, would always be guided by their concern for their private interests, rather than the public good. While acknowledging the validity of some of the concerns about royal government, Franklin and the Assembly Party pointed to the parliamentary tradition as one that had steadily defended, not usurped, the rights of Englishmen. John Dickinson, arguing the other side, noted the dangers of surrendering charters and rights without being certain that the privileges previously granted under those charters could be "perfectly secured" by a royal charter.[3]

Although there was plenty of sober, reasoned argument for the thoughtful voter to contemplate, much of the pamphlet, broadside, and newspaper coverage of the election of 1764 was of a more vituperative cast. Franklin's opponents attacked him as a person of "ingrate Disposition and Badness of Heart" who "By assuming the merit/of other mens *discoveries* . . . obtain'd the name of /A PHILOSOPHER." One publicist took aim at Franklin's sexual habits, berating him as a "letcher" who "needs nothing to excite him,/But is too ready to engage,/When yonder Arms invite him." He was also called a schemer, a squanderer of public funds, a man so disloyal that he had "cruelly suffer[ed]]" the mother of his illegitimate son, William, "TO STARVE," and a corrupt politician familiar with "every Zig Zag Machination," interested in the move for royal government only as a means of becoming the first royal governor.[4]

The 1764 campaign also engaged religious interests in a manner that allowed for a more far-reaching appeal to the electorate than had been possible earlier. Ministers and lay leaders of the contending religious groups of the city—Anglicans, Presbyterians, and German Reformed as well as Quak-

Figure 14. Benjamin Franklin. Ambitious aspiring entrepreneur and philosopher statesman. Courtesy of the Pennsylvania Academy of Fine Arts, Philadelphia.

ers—enlisted on one side or the other during this election, and Franklin discovered to his chagrin that not only would he have to deal with a mobilization of members of the German Reformed Church against him but also of Presbyterians (or, in the words of one Franklin supporter, "Piss-Brute-arians—a bigoted, cruel and revengeful sect").[5]

Election day brought an unprecedented popular upsurge. According to one observer, "never before in the history of Pennsylvania . . . have so many people assembled for an election." In Philadelphia a line of voters jammed the stairway of the courthouse from nine in the morning on October 1 until three in the afternoon the following day, with balloting continuing all through the night. In the end, aided by a substantial block of votes from Presbyterians and members of the German Reformed Church, the proprietary faction captured five of the eight assembly seats from Philadelphia County, with Franklin and Joseph Galloway among the casualties. One commentator noted, "Mr. Franklin died like a philosopher. But Mr. Galloway agonized in Death, like a Mortal Deist, who has no Hopes of a Future Existence." Franklin did his best to take defeat in stride. He acknowledged that popular feeling had played a significant role in the election; the major cause of his defeat, he believed, was the influx of German voters who had voted for his opponents on the basis of a misrepresentation of his position, taken twelve years earlier, respecting the immigration of Germans to Pennsylvania. By his analysis the proprietors "carried (would you think it!) above 1000 Dutch from me, by printing part of my Paper . . . on Peopling new Countries where I speak of the Palatine Boors herding together, which they explain'd that I call'd them a Herd of Hogs." "This," Franklin wrote, "is quite a laughing Matter."[6] But laughing matter or not, German annoyance at comments he had made twelve years earlier was not at the core of his problem; rather, the Germans, in their many pamphlets and broadsides, made it clear that they were deeply concerned about the prospect of a transfer to royal government, for they believed that their rights as an ethnic minority were well protected under the present charter and could not be similarly guaranteed under a new royal government.

Franklin discovered in 1764, as many others among America's traditional ruling class would in subsequent years, that his claim to political authority could no longer rest on personal authority alone. Rather, the outcome of the Philadelphia election of 1764 was shaped by a combination of forces—religious and ethnic identity, partisan maneuvering by two self-consciously organized political interest groups, and new sets of substantive political issues occasioned by imperial decision making in London—that would render the politics of deference obsolete.

The Eighteenth-Century American City

For better or worse modern America was born in the cities of the Northeast during the eighteenth century. It would be in New York, Philadelphia, and, to a lesser extent, Boston that pluralism would emerge in an increasingly variegated structure of economic endeavor, in the gradations of wealth and status that would result from that variegated economic structure, and in the ethnic and religious makeup of the population. And it would be from the political mobilization of those different identities and interests that a modern American conception of politics would be born.

As we have seen, there were two somewhat contradictory forces that helped propel the energies of most of the members of America's ruling class. The first, the desire to emulate the style and prerogatives of England's ruling elite, was confounded in nearly every colony by two factors. While some colonies may have come closer than others to emulating aspects of English society, the social structures of every colony in America were too unsettled and too open-ended to allow any one of those entities to replicate the English original. And however much American provincial leaders may have looked to England for a cultural model of correct political behavior, the political scene in England itself was too fluid, too contested, to provide a clear guide to behavior. The other and more dynamic force propelling America's provincial leaders was the contest for power with royal agents and agencies of government. Though the dynamic of that contest differed from place to place, the outcome was everywhere the same: the rise to power of provincial agents and agencies of government. The rationale behind this assertion of provincial political power was consistent everywhere as well: whether stridently, as in New York, or with genteel insistence, as in Virginia, the members of the provincial ruling class in America all claimed to be speaking and acting in behalf of the people whom they governed.

These representations had varying degrees of plausibility depending upon the setting. The inland members of the Massachusetts General Court, elected in their town meetings and living close by their neighbors in circumstances not dramatically different from those neighbors, had perhaps the best claim to be speaking and acting in behalf of their community. Though Virginia's burgesses stood far above the great mass of their constituents in terms of wealth and family prestige, they were able at least to persuade themselves that the interests of a largely English society overwhelmingly given over to staple agriculture were on the whole homogeneous.[7] And in the Mohawk and Hudson valleys of New York, the superior economic power of a William Johnson or a Henry Beekman was, at least for a while, sufficient to keep complaints about the unrepresentative character of provincial government to a minimum. But neither the natural convergence of interests prevailing in parts of Massachusetts and Virginia nor the conditions of unchallenged economic dominance that prevailed in the Hudson Valley could be obtained in the more fluid and complicated environments of America's northeastern cities. Political life in those cities—with electoral laws that were broadly inclusive, diverse population groups increasingly attuned to the practical necessity of working aggressively to promote their interests and identities, and a traditional ruling elite accustomed to defending their prerogatives by facile but substantively empty invocations of "popular rights"—was by the mid-eighteenth century ripe for insurgence.

In some important respects the nature of political discourse in New York City, Philadelphia, and Boston was shaped by institutional structures and political imperatives that were peculiar to the colonies to which they were joined. All three cities were the capitals of government in their colonies, and the character of political debate and contest in each city would be influenced by issues particular to its colony. In each of the three colonies there would be specific political issues—in Massachusetts the land bank, in New York military policy, in Pennsylvania multiple issues peculiar to early Quaker dominance—that would affect the political cultures of the three principal cities in distinctive ways. But Boston, New York, and Philadelphia—though by European standards still backward provincial towns—were becoming America's first "urban" centers, and the politics of each of those towns were being shaped by forces—both purely local and international—that pointed the way to a very different, American future.

In 1690 neither Boston, New York, nor Philadelphia could claim to be anything more than a small-sized town. Both the colony and the city of New York had grown relatively slowly since their founding by the Dutch in 1624; in 1690 New York City's 4,500 inhabitants constituted perhaps a third of the colony's total population. Boston, the longest-settled of the English colonial cities, had reached a population of about 6,000 in 1690, out of a total population for the colony of about 50,000. Philadelphia, only recently settled, in 1690 was a village of not more than 2,000 souls, and like Boston, was nearly wholly English in its composition.[8]

The next half century would bring dramatic changes to all three cities. Boston's population increased to 17,000, Philadelphia's and New York's to about 9,000. Whereas Boston remained primarily English, both New York and Philadelphia were beginning a process of transition by which they would become America's first multiethnic communities. The immigration of German Palatines, which began in New York in 1710 and then moved rather decisively toward Philadelphia in 1715, and of huge numbers of Scots-Irish would change both the structure and the cultural character of those two cities. The continued immigration of non-English peoples to New York and Philadelphia would propel the demographic growth of those two cities in the last half of the eighteenth century; not only would the immigration of Germans and Scots-Irish continue but the importation of

African slaves, who had constituted an insubstantial portion of the urban population earlier, would accelerate greatly in the years before the Revolution. By 1765 the population of Boston had actually dropped a few thousand from its 1740 level, but New York and Philadelphia, swelled by European immigration and by black slaves (who numbered about 2,500 in the former and perhaps 2,000 in the latter) had reached 17,000 and 18,000, respectively. By 1775 Boston's population had rebounded somewhat—to perhaps 17,000—and New York's and Philadelphia's continued their rapid ascent, to 23,000 and 25,000, respectively.[9]

While on the eve of the Revolution some Philadelphians boasted that their city was the largest in Great Britain's North American empire, the gap between their town of 25,000 and the city of London, with a population nearing a million, was a chasm that differentiated a real cosmopolitan center from a provincial town. For most of the eighteenth century, in spite of increasing population, the northeastern cities were face-to-face societies in which people lived in close proximity to one another, cities in which men like wealthy Philadelphian James Allen could boast that they "knew every person white & black, men, women & children by name."[10]

The peoples of the northeastern cities, increasingly numerous, diverse in ethnic and religious background, and differentiated by job skills and material attainments, would be brought closer together—and sometimes more closely into conflict—by the emergence of a popular press whose very prosperity depended on reaching out to citizens of all backgrounds. Not only did the number and circulation of newspapers in each of those cities rise during the eighteenth century, but the frequency with which individuals used the press to broadcast a political message through the device of the pamphlet increased markedly. Almost unheard of in America before 1700, by the 1730s it was not uncommon for local political issues to generate a dozen or more pamphlets in a given year. When the excise bill was being debated in Massachusetts in 1754, no fewer than seventeen pamphlets appeared in the streets of Boston in opposition to it; during the years 1752–56, when New Yorkers were debating whether King's College should have an Anglican affiliation, several dozen pamphleteers entered the fray in support and in opposition. And, as we have seen in the previous chapter, in the wake of the Paxton massacre in Pennsylvania, twenty-eight pamphleteers debated the various sides of that tragedy.[11]

As the seats of government of their colonies, the cities of the Northeast were centers of political activity, but the sources of political activism in those cities ran deeper than their status as capitals of government. It was in those cities that the notion of society as an organic whole began to be seen more clearly as the fiction that it was. The clash of interests, the differing agendas of merchants and lawyers, of mechanics and tradespeople, of seamen and day laborers was far more obvious in those cities than in the countryside. Perhaps most important, it was the individuals at the top of the variegated economy and social hierarchy of those cities who were the first to see that it was their interests that were most directly affected by the actions of provincial governors and legislators and who, consequently, took the responsibilities of leadership most seriously. Only in New York did the population of the principal city exceed 10 percent of the total population of the colony; in Boston and Philadelphia the proportion was significantly under 10 percent, but the influence wielded by representatives from those cities in the politics of their respective colonies far exceeded their numbers. During the years 1740–55, 28 percent of the leadership of the Massachusetts General Court came from Boston, with Bostonians occupying the position of Speaker of the lower house three out of every four years during that period. Most, but not all, of those influential Bostonians were merchants—men like Thomas Hutchinson, James Allen, and Thomas Hubbard—and many were lawyers. In Pennsylvania nearly the whole of the assembly leadership was resident either in Philadelphia or in adjacent counties and, as we have seen, overwhelmingly Quaker, at least up until 1756. In part because of the need to defend provincial interests against proprietary prerogatives, and in part because of their awareness that the society they governed was an increasingly diverse one, those political leaders recognized that aggressive involvement in politics was necessary if they were to protect their interests. New York City's political leaders had to share power more fully with rural oligarchs living in the Hudson River Valley, but they, no less than their counterparts in Boston and Philadelphia, recognized that it was in their interest to make certain that they be influential in shaping policy in their colony. Accordingly, throughout much of the eighteenth century, New York City contributed disproportionately to the colony's political leadership in the colony. As in Philadelphia, the range of interests—mercantile, legal, familial, ethnic, and religious—was varied, but all of those contesting for power and influence shared the understanding that politics mattered.[12]

The populations of Boston, New York, and Philadelphia were not only more numerous and more varied than in other parts of America but were also, to perhaps a greater extent than anywhere in the world, armed with the franchise. In Boston the percentage of eligible voters among free white males in the population was probably 80–90 percent; in New York, owing to more liberal suffrage requirements in the city than in the countryside, it may have been as high as 80 percent, compared with lows of 50 percent in some parts of the countryside; and in Philadelphia it probably approached 75 percent.[13]

Those large, varied populations, armed with the franchise, provided a tempting target for any insurgent group wishing to challenge the power of another group. As we have already seen, however, political organization and mobilization in the cities in the first half of the eighteenth century were mostly top-down affairs. While the degree of activity in organizing the electorate was often intense, that activity was nearly always initiated by one elite group seeking to gain advantage over another. As they struggled to wrest power from royal officials or proprietors, provincial elites in Boston, New York, and Philadelphia found it convenient to organize the townspeople to give substance to their claims that they were working for popular rights, but in most cases these political mobilizations were narrowly based, with individual families or groups of regional interests grappling for momentary advantage over their rivals. In their inception these efforts at organization—the nomination of candidates, the printing of pamphlets and broadsides, the circulation of petitions, and the orchestration of noisy public campaigns—were not intended to democratize political life in those cities. Though one can catch glimpses in these early political mobilizations of broader divisions of interest and ideology among the population at large—among social classes or different ethnic and religious groups—those divisions generally remained repressed. Beginning in the mid-1760s, however, as provincial and local conflicts were complicated and occasionally inflamed by the appearance of new conflicts generated by policymakers in London, the potential for a more meaningful awakening and mobilization of "opinion" increased.

Boston: "The Cancer of Sedition"

The American Revolution against British imperial authority began in the northeastern cities. And the revolution in American political behavior would find its beginnings in those same cities, for many of the same reasons that fueled the revolution against imperial rule. It was in those cities that the divergent interests both of Crown and colony and of different groups within the colonies became most visibly apparent.

As any royal official in London would have been ready to attest, it was in Boston that the "cancer of sedition" was most visibly rooted, and it would be in Boston as well that the autonomous power of ordinary people, properly organized, would be put most dramatically on display. The story of revolutionary mobilization in Boston—of Sam Adams and the Sons of Liberty and of Ebenezer Mackintosh and the South End Mob—has been told many times, with different historians drawing different morals from the tale. Mackintosh, in particular, has been described in disparate ways. To the Tory Peter Oliver he was a dupe of the Otises and Adamses, "always ready for the Drudgeries of his Employers." To Pauline Maier he was "an influential mob leader and potential rabble-rouser." And in Gary Nash's hands he becomes an astute leader of an army of unemployed and working poor enraged not only at the arrogance and pomposity of royal officials but also at a social structure that had deprived them of the opportunity to enjoy the blessings of either Lockean liberty or property. A close analysis of the immediate events of August to November of 1765 confirms a picture of Mackintosh and the South End Mob as autonomous actors playing critical roles in the drama taking place in the streets of Boston, although a longer view of the situation in Boston in the aftermath of the Stamp Act riots suggests as well some of the limits of such popular mobilizations.[14]

Anyone living in Boston in the 1760s no doubt would have had at least passing knowledge of both the name and person of Ebenezer Mackintosh. Twenty-eight years old in 1765 and a shoemaker, he had served his country as a private in the Ticonderoga campaign of 1758, and in 1760 he had been appointed a fireman in Engine Company Number 9, a position of some honor and public visibility for the son of a man who had been warned out of Boston in the 1750s as a vagrant. More important, he had by 1765 emerged as the leader of the South End Mob, a collection of tradespeople, artisans, laborers, and mariners who regularly matched brawn and masculine ego with a similarly composed gang from the north side of town. The citizens of puritan Boston and, in particular, the humbler citizens of that town had a special fondness for Pope's Day, the annual commemoration of the November 1605 thwarting of an alleged Catholic conspiracy to take over the English government. The relation of the South End Mob to "respectable" society was always somewhat problematic; while many, rich and poor alike, gathered to watch and even to applaud their antipopish and antiauthoritarian jousting on Pope's Day, there was always something unsettling, if not menacing, in their activities. In the November 1764 celebration it had been Mackintosh who had been at the head of the South End Mob as it pummeled rivals from the North End, a victory that earned for him the sobriquet of "Captain" Mackintosh of the South End.[15]

However formidable Ebenezer Mackintosh may have appeared as one passed him on the street, few could have been prepared for the nearly instant prominence he was to achieve beginning at about dawn on August 14, 1765. As Bostonians went to work on that morning they discovered an effigy of Andrew Oliver, a prominent member of the royal elite recently given the responsibility of implementing the Stamp Act, hanging from an elm tree in Boston's South End. Thomas Hutchinson, chief justice and lieutenant governor of the colony, was outraged by this insult to royal authority and to his brother-in-law, and he ordered Sheriff Stephen Greenleaf to cut the effigy down. When Greenleaf went to do so later that morning, he confronted a menacing crowd; convinced that discretion was the better part of valor, he left the scene with the effigy still swinging from what would soon be dubbed the "Liberty Tree." Hutchinson's embarrassment and outrage increased as crowds continued to gather; they ended the day by holding an elaborate mock funeral.[16] By this time Mackintosh had emerged, in Thomas Hutchinson's words, as the "principal leader of the mob," and at the end of the funeral he led the crowd, which included "40 to 50 tradesmen" and even perhaps a few "gentlemen," to the South End wharves, where a new customs house—presumably where the hated stamps were to be distributed—had recently been constructed.[17] The crowd demolished the building, "Pull[ing] it down to the Ground in five minutes," saving the timbers, which they "stamped" and carried across town to Fort Hill. Along the way they stopped at Andrew Oliver's house. Oliver was not home at the time, but Hutchinson, intent on doing his duty to uphold both royal authority and public order, tried to persuade the mob to disband. His presence only exacerbated the situation, and after the confrontation with Hutchinson the crowd began to destroy Oliver's stable, coach, and chaise. Later in the evening, after another confrontation with Hutchinson in which the lieutenant governor was pelted by a flurry of stones, the mob went to work on Oliver's house in earnest, ravaging the interior furnishings and making off with the contents of the wine cellar. The fury of the mob, directed pointedly at the property of the man thought most immediately responsible for the enforcement of a law that threatened the interests of all in the city, had the desired effect: Andrew Oliver promptly resigned his commission as stamp distributor.[18]

At this point the actions of the South End Mob, however unorthodox they may have been as expressions of political opinion, seem to have earned the approbation of nearly all in the city.[19] Twelve days later, in its attack on the home of Thomas Hutchinson, the mob moved in more controversial fashion. Hutchinson and his family were at the dining table when the mob struck. After sending the family scurrying from the house, with Hutchinson scantily clad in a "thin camlet surtout," the mob systematically destroyed the lieutenant governor's house, furniture, gardens, and personal possessions and papers.[20] The members of the mob appeared nearly obsessive in their determination to obliterate every feature of the house. Governor Bernard reported that "they worked three hours on the cupola before they could get it down," and noted that only the heavy brick construction of the walls prevented the total destruction of the building. The next day, according to Bernard, "the streets were found scattered with money, plate, gold rings, etc. which had been dropped in carrying off." As one contemporary observed, "Gentlemen of the army, who have seen towns sacked by the enemy, declare they never before saw an instance of such fury." Governor Bernard's testimony reinforces this sense of outrage; the mob, he wrote, worked "with a rage scarce to be exemplified by the most savage people." In the aftermath of the devastation some ten thousand people came to view the results of the night's work. Moreover, the royal government seemed powerless in the face of this aroused citizenry. Hutchinson himself reported that the friends of law and order were "intimidated and utterly dispirited," and Bernard, in defending his government's ineffectual response to the South End Mob's work, wrote that "the mob was so general and so supported that all civil Power ceased in an Instant, and I had not the least authority to oppose or quiet the Mob."[21]

At this point, however, the relationship between the mob and "the better sort" became more problematic. The day after the violence the Boston town meeting condemned the assault on Hutchinson's home, calling on town magistrates to "suppress the like disorders for the future." The *Boston Gazette* reported that "every Face was gloomy" in the aftermath of the event, and, while it defended the use of extralegal violence "in some extraordinary cases," it stated emphatically that "pulling down Houses and robbing Persons of their Substance" was "utterly inconsistent with the first Principles of Government."[22] Reverend Andrew Eliot, pastor of the New North Congregational Church in Boston, was even more explicit in making a distinction between defensible and indefensible extralegal violence. Discussing the events of August 14 and August 26, he noted that the actions of August 14 were "under the direction of some persons of character," but the activities of August 26, he believed, were "under a very different direction. It was a scene of riot, drunkenness, profaneness, and robbery."[23]

Hutchinson himself was convinced that "the people in general express the utmost detestation of this unparalleled outrage." But whatever concerns many felt about finding appropriate limits to extralegal opposition to what all agreed was an unjust parliamentary act, no one was willing to risk the consequences of an effort to punish Ebenezer Mackintosh, the man most visibly in charge of the mob's actions. Although Sheriff Greenleaf, who was the head of the fire company in which Mackintosh served, went through the motions of arresting his fellow fireman, he never made any attempt either to imprison him or to bring him to justice. Indeed, so great was Mackintosh's following that royal officials came to understand that if action were to be taken against him, it was likely that no government building would be safe from the mob's onslaught. Governor Bernard, reporting on the events of the rioting, admitted that the situation had gotten wholly beyond his control. He asserted that he had no more than ten men under his control and that he was, in effect, governor in name only.[24]

In the weeks between the ransacking of Hutchinson's house and the commemoration of the November 1765 Pope's Day, Mackintosh's influence grew by leaps and bounds. He had engineered a truce between his South End Mob and the rival North Enders, and plans for the two groups to unite in purposeful political protest rather than drunken brawling on the upcoming Pope's Day in November were moving forward. By that time the *Boston Gazette* was referring to Mackintosh as the "Commander of the South [End]", and even Governor Bernard spoke of "Captain" Mackintosh. The unfolding of events on November 5, 1765, marked both a triumph and a significant transformation for Ebenezer Mackintosh. "Commander Mackintosh" was clearly in charge. Decked out in a blue-and-gold uniform, wearing a gold-laced hat, and using a speaking trumpet through which to give orders to his troops, Mackintosh stood at the head of a force two thousand strong as it marched in formation past the statehouse. Such was Mackintosh's sense of command that "If a Whisper was heard among his Followers, the holding up of his Finger hushed it in a Moment; & when he had fully displayed his Authority, he marched his Men to their first Rendevouz, & order'd them to retire peaceably to their several Homes; & was punctually obeyed."[25] Ebenezer Mackintosh and the two-thousand-man "army" that he commanded were no longer marginal street brawlers, but the very embodiment of a virtuous, if outraged, citizenry.

Mackintosh would emerge into the spotlight one more time during the Stamp Act resistance. With the exception of the events of August 14 and 26, resistance to the tax had been solemn, orderly, and united, but members of the provincial elite in Massachusetts had still not mustered the courage to defy it outright. Both sides were playing a waiting game, with royal officials using as an excuse the fact that the official commission appointing Andrew Oliver stamp distributor had not yet reached Boston shores. Once it became clear that it had arrived, the Sons of Liberty published a letter in the *Boston Gazette* demanding that Oliver make his resignation official by appearing at the Liberty Tree to renounce his commission. Oliver was more than willing to resign his commission, but he wished to do so in a way that would allow him to avoid public humiliation. But he would not be granted his wish. On December 17, in a driving rainstorm, Ebenezer Mackintosh personally escorted Oliver to the Liberty Tree where, with several thousand people gathered, including "several selectmen and many other persons of condition," he was made to resign his commission. Thomas Hutchinson, whose suffering through the entire ordeal of the Stamp Act resistance would forever change his attitude toward his Boston neighbors, commented bitterly, "This indignity to the third crown officer in rank in the province passed without notice from any authority." In "regular times," he conjectured, the officials who allowed the humiliation to occur would have been dismissed from their positions, but these clearly were not regular times.[26] John Adams, who detested Oliver and Hutchinson, nevertheless shared some of Hutchinson's feelings about the episode. He reported in his diary that he had received the news of the actions of "the Sons of Liberty, on Tuesday last, in prevailing on Mr. Oliver to renounce his office of Distributor of Stamps, by a Declaration under his Hand and under his Oath, . . . under the very Tree of Liberty, nay, under the very Limb, where he had been hanged in effigy, Aug. 14th 1765. Their absolute Requisition of an Oath, and under that Tree, were circumstances extremely humiliating and mortifying."[27]

Defenders of royal authority, who in Boston were pitifully few, tried to raise the specter of class warfare in their descriptions of Mackintosh and his followers. Governor Bernard warned that the mobilization of the mob was becoming "a War of Plunder, of general leveling and taking away the Distinction of rich and poor," and he warned that if "persons of property and consideration" did not unite in support of government the inevitable result would be that the "anarchy and confusion which will ensue, [and] . . . will

Figures 15 and 16. Andrew and Peter Oliver. Like their close political associate
Thomas Hutchinson, Andrew and Peter Oliver became the most visible, and
detested, symbols of royal authority in pre-revolutionary Massachusetts. Andrew
Oliver (*above*). Painted by John Singleton Copley, Courtesy the National Portrait
Gallery, Smithsonian Institution. Peter Oliver (*right*). Artist unknown. Courtesy,
Winterthur Museum.

soon oblige and justify an insurrection of the poor against the rich, those that want the necessities of life against those that have them." And for their part the leaders of the newly formed Sons of Liberty tried to depict royal officials as privileged fat cats whose habits of "Luxury and extravagance are . . . destructive of those virtues which are necessary for the preservation of Liberty and the happiness of the people."[28]

However much the language of class may have been used in the contest of wills between royal officials and provincial resisters, what is striking is the extent to which class tensions were submerged in the overall show of unity among leaders of the resistance at all levels of Boston society. Although the role of Mackintosh and the South End Mob in preventing implementation of the Stamp Act was the most visible and colorful event of the Boston resistance, it was only one part of a triad of opposition, led at the top by James Otis, Speaker of the Massachusetts lower house, and mediated in the middle by men like Sam Adams and his compatriots in the Loyal Nine and, subsequently, the Sons of Liberty. To be sure, in the aftermath of the August 26 sacking of Thomas Hutchinson's house, there was a fissure in that tripartite alliance, with at least some members of the provincial elite expressing fears that mob violence was getting out of hand, but on the whole what is most striking about the scene in Boston in the wake of the Stamp Act controversy is the extent to which ordinary citizens like Mackintosh engaged themselves in purposeful political activity with the full support of the traditional political leaders of the city.

Less clear is the nature of the bonds of interest and ideology that knit the constituent parts of the resistance together or the character of the working relationships among the leaders of those constituent parts. While we can reject with some confidence Tory Peter Oliver's description of Ebenezer Macintosh as merely a tool of the provincial upper classes, we should perhaps be equally cautious about embracing the view that Mackintosh and his men represented an independent expression of proletarian rage at entrenched power and privilege. Crucial to an understanding of the dynamic of these relationships is the role of Sam Adams, the Loyal Nine, and the Sons of Liberty, for in important respects the insurgency of the sorts of upper middling citizens who were active in those two organizations was a more enduring consequence of the revolutionary struggle than the temporary fame of Ebenezer Mackintosh. In Boston the organization known as the Sons of Liberty, which numbered over 350 by 1769, grew out of a social club calling itself the Loyal Nine. John Adams, when he visited the group "at their own Apartment in Hanover Square, near the Liberty Tree" (actually, the second floor counting room of Chase's and Speakman's distillery), in January 1766, had by that time begun to call them the Sons of Liberty, and, as we have seen, the group itself was by December 1765 issuing calls to resistance in that name. Although historians differ over the exact composition of the original Loyal Nine, there is general agreement that the core of the group consisted of middling merchants and tradespeople. When Adams paid his visit, he met "John Avery, Distiller or Merchant, . . . John Smith the Brazier, [Thomas] Chase the Distiller, Joseph Field, Master of a Vessel, Henry Bass [merchant] George Trotter Jeweller," and Benjamin Edes, a printer. Although Samuel Adams may not originally have been a member of the Loyal Nine, he was certainly closely associated with them, and by the time they were calling themselves the Sons of Liberty, he had already taken a highly visible role in their activities.[29]

After many years of apparent aimlessness Sam Adams was rapidly ascending in power and influence. His father, Samuel Adams Sr., was a prosperous brewer and merchant, a "godly man" who served for many years as a deacon in the South End Congregational Church and, during the 1730s and 1740s, was a highly visible member of the "popular party" within the Massachusetts General Court. When the younger Samuel Adams was admitted to Harvard in 1736, at age fourteen, he was ranked fifth in his class, indicative of a social position higher than that accorded to his younger cousin, John, who ranked sixteenth in his class in 1752. Sam Adams stayed on at Harvard for three years after his graduation in 1740, earning a master's degree by writing on the question of "whether it be lawful to resist the Supreme Magistrate, if the Commonwealth cannot be otherwise preserved." After a couple of false starts as a merchant he went to work in his father's brewing business, even though it was clear to all that his heart was in politics, not beer making. From 1748, at the death of his father, until the early 1760s Adams struggled to find his calling. Although he had an abiding interest in politics, he had a hard time getting his political career on track. Elected one of the clerks of the Boston market in 1746, he found it difficult to move up the ladder. He went another seven years before gaining election to another office, and that office—town scavenger—hardly signified a meteoric rise. He was elected a town tax collector in 1756, an office at which he was notably unsuccessful; during that same period, Adams had so neglected his patrimony that his father's brewing business was virtually defunct and the small amount of capital that had come to him as part of his inheritance had disappeared. Adams was, as his biographer John C. Miller has noted, "incorrigibly indifferent to money making," and instead of tending to the business of making his fortune, he continued to be a fixture in Boston taverns and coffeehouses, talking politics and waiting for his chance.[30]

The passage of the Stamp Act—and the economic and political threat it brought with it—would be the catalyst for Sam Adams's emergence. During the summer of 1765, the Boston town meeting turned to him to draft the instructions respecting the Stamp Act to the town's representatives to the general court, and in September, with the death of Oxenbridge Thatcher, Adams got the chance he had been waiting for; with the strong support of his longtime power base, the Caucus Club, he was chosen to serve in the general court.

Sam Adams's subsequent career as legislator, revolutionary publicist, organizer, and, ultimately, governor of the independent Commonwealth of Massachusetts has been well told by his biographers. While his rise to power was facilitated by the imperial struggle in which he would play such a decisive role, it is also clear that his emergence as a political leader in his province, however belated, was achieved through largely traditional

Figure 17. Samuel Adams. Although born to wealth and high social status, Sam Adams would prove to be the ideal bridge between traditional Massachusetts provincial politicians and the ordinary residents of Boston. Museum of Fine Arts, Boston.

means—serving his time in local politics, winning the support of the Boston Caucus at a critical point in his election campaign, and, once arriving in the Massachusetts assembly, depending on the patronage of the senior member of the Massachusetts provincial elite, James Otis Jr., for the committee assignments and other political opportunities that would move him to the front rank of his fellow legislators.

Whatever the traditional aspects of Adams's career—a politically prominent father, a Harvard education, key support from important organizations and individuals—it was nevertheless his relationship with the ordinary citizens of Boston, and in particular with the mobs that made life so miserable for the agents and armies of the Crown, that would distinguish his service to the revolutionary cause. His ability to serve as mediator of the interests and ideologies of the traditional ruling class of Massachusetts and those of ordinary citizens secured his influence while infuriating his adversaries. Peter Oliver observed that if "one wished to draw the Picture of the Devil, [one] would get Sam Adams to sit" for the portrait; he was convinced that Adams "understood human Nature, in low life, so well, that he could turn the Minds of the great Vulgar as well as the small into any Course that he might chuse; perhaps he was a singular Instance in this Kind; & he never failed of employing his Abilities to the vilest Purposes."[31]

But which way were the currents of influence running? Were members of the provincial elite, through Sam Adams, manipulating and managing the minds and actions of the mob, as Peter Oliver and nearly all other royal officials charged, or was it Adams and his fellow provincial leaders who were having to adjust their aspirations and plans of opposition to those of the mob? While it is well documented that Sam Adams was in close touch with nearly every important street action that occurred in Boston between 1765 and 1775 and was often at the scene of the action himself, there is only the scantiest evidence testifying to the content of his relationship with either the mobs or their leaders. We have, dated August 12, 1765, just two days before the attack on Andrew Oliver's house, a scrap of information indicating that on that day Sam Adams, tax collector, took out a writ warranting the sheriff to collect a £10 12s debt from Mackintosh for back taxes; the penalty for failure to pay the debt—imprisonment. Mackintosh, we know, neither paid the debt nor paid the price for nonpayment. Shortly thereafter a deputy sheriff returned the warrant with the notation, "By order of the Creditor I Returne this Execution no part Satisfied."[32] Was this the leverage that Sam Adams and the Loyal Nine needed over Mackintosh? It may have helped, but it hardly seems sufficient to explain the enthusiastic participation of Mackintosh and his mob on August 14 and August 26. Following the devastation of August 26, Sam Adams was one of the many who bemoaned loudly the destruction and violence that had been visited on Hutchinson's house. It was, he said, a "high handed Enormity" committed by "vagabound Strangers"; he insisted that it should not in any way be connected to the justifiable protest over the Stamp Act and joined in the town's "detestation" of the lawlessness. But Thomas Hutchinson was certainly not convinced, and he complained that those who had been most visible in the Boston town meeting the next day lamenting the destruction that was wreacked on his house were among the foremost "villains" the night before.[33] In fact, Adams may have had something to do with keeping Mackintosh out of prison following the sacking of Hutchinson's house, but it seems clear that the principal factor insulating Mackintosh from the arm of the law was that none of the forces of "law and order" in Boston were strong enough to withstand the wrath of his supporters should he be imprisoned. Sam Adams may have been among those pointing this out to Sheriff Greenleaf and Governor Bernard, but the truth was evident to anyone.

Perhaps the most important bit of mediation on Adams's part came just before the critical 1765 Pope's Day march in which Mackintosh and both the North and South End mobs were so conspicuously peaceful and politicized. Adams probably was a key figure in arranging a "Union Feast" in which the leaders of the North and South End mobs were brought together sometime before the November 5 march. At that banquet Whig leaders like Sam Adams and other members of the Loyal Nine feasted with the members of the two mobs, "with Heart and Hand in flowing Bowls and bumping Glasses," until all were persuaded that the common good of Boston would be best served by a united front on November 5.[34]

But there the evidence ends. While friend and foe alike would credit Sam Adams with a key role in most of the mob-related activity in Boston subsequent to the Stamp Act, Ebenezer Mackintosh and, indeed, the North and South End mobs would largely disappear from public view as self-consciously organized instruments of political resistance. Mackintosh would later claim that he was a participant in the Boston Tea Party, but there is no solid evidence to establish that he was. And sometime between the Tea Party and the passage of the Coercive Acts he left town, apparently spurred to do so by reports that a sloop of war was on its way "with orders to bring to England, in irons, Messrs. Hancock, Row, Adams, and Mackintosh; the latter has been very active among the lower order of people and the other among the higher."[35] He took with him his two children, Elizabeth and Pascal Paoli (the child's name itself telling evidence of Mackintosh's heightened political consciousness), to Haverhill, New Hampshire, where he took up once again his trade as a shoemaker. He served in two relatively brief campaigns during the Revolution, first as a private and then as a scout, and then apparently lived out his life peacefully in Haverhill, dying in 1816 at the age of seventy-nine.[36]

The effect of Boston's revolutionary street politics on electoral politics was not immediately self-evident. There exists a nearly complete record of voter turnout in elections for the general court in Boston for the period 1696–1774. During that entire time, turnout fluctuated depending on the intensity of competition among rival elites. The low point in voter interest occurred during the decade of the 1720s, when Elisha Cooke Jr. and his followers established their dominance of provincial politics. Voter interest peaked only sporadically during the prerevolutionary years, rising above 30 percent a few times in the late 1740s and to 44.7 percent and 48.9 percent, respectively, in 1760 and 1763. The jump in interest in those two years was due, no doubt, to the heating up of the purely personal and local rivalry between James Otis and Thomas Hutchinson and not to the larger imperial questions that would later occupy the colony's attention. Voter turnout in the election in which Sam Adams finally gained entrance to the assembly in 1765 was 29 percent—about average for that decade. Turnout ranged from a low of 18 percent to a high of 33 percent during the whole of the period 1764–74, with very little apparent correlation with the events of revolutionary mobilization against Great Britain.[37]

TABLE 3. BOSTON VOTER PARTICIPATION, 1696–1774

Year	Number	Percent	Year	Number	Percent	Year	Number	Percent
1696	134	10.2	1730	530	21.9	1752	327	14.2
1798	340	25.0	1731	474	19.1	1753	445	20.0
				450	18.1			
1699	323	23.3	1732	655	25.8	1754	603	27.1
1703	459	31.1	1733	600	23.0	1755	492	22.1
	244	16.5						
1704	206	13.7	1734	604	22.6	1756	533	23.9
1709	204	12.6	1735	517	19.0	1757	528	23.7
1711	173	10.4	1736	266	9.8	1758	369	16.6
1715	262	14.9	1737	240	8.8	1759	469	21.0
1716	376	21.2	1738	481	18.9	1760	997	44.7
1717	283	15.7	1739	635	26.2	1761	334	15.0
1718	242	13.2	1740	418	18.3	1762	629	28.2
1719	454	24.6	1741	495	22.2	1763	1,089	48.9
				280	12.6			
1721	247	13.0	1742	525	23.6	1764	449	20.1
	322	16.9						
1722	205	10.7	1743	451	20.2	1765	641	29.1
1723	275	13.9	1744	532	23.9	1766	746	33.8
1724	209	10.2	1745	342	15.3	1767	618	28.0
1725	332	15.7	1746	443	19.9	1768	440	19.9
1726	203	9.4	1747	451	20.2	1769	508	23.0
1727	204	9.1	1748	723	32.4	1770	513	23.3
	214	9.6						
1728	248	10.8	1749	684	30.7	1771	410	18.6
1729	192	8.1	1750	541	24.3	1772	723	32.8
			1751	463	20.8	1773	419	19.0
						1774	534	24.2

Source: Robert Dinkin, *Voting in Provincial America*, p. 174.

Voter turnout is, of course, only one indicator of citizen involvement in the affairs of the polis. As the activities of Ebenezer Mackintosh and the South End Mob clearly suggested, formal elections were not the only vehicle through which an aroused citizenry could express its sentiments. As the Revolution neared, the emergence of new institutions as well as the redefinition of some older ones would serve to increase citizen participation in public affairs and, in the process, to alter the relationship between the many and the few. As historian Richard D. Brown has demonstrated, the Boston Committee of Correspondence, organized by Sam Adams and the Boston Sons of Liberty in 1772, would emerge as an active agent both in fanning the fires of revolt within the city and in igniting new fires of resistance in the countryside. The committee's use of circulars, pamphlets, mass meetings, and, probably, extralegal means such as those on display at the Boston Tea Party empowered ordinary citizens as never before and served to undermine still further traditional ways of transacting public business. By the early months of 1775, with the revolutionary movement in Boston and in the colony as a whole fully mobilized, the Boston Committee of Correspondence would fade into the background, giving way to the newly called Provincial Congress and the Boston town meeting, but the local activism generated by the committee would continue to flourish in those bodies as well.[38]

Revolutionary Politics in New York City

Of all the eighteenth-century American urban economies, Boston's was probably the most severely stressed by the political and military upheavals of the age, and conditions of economic hardship that hit prominent merchants like John Hancock as well as laborers like Ebenezer Mackintosh, made the resistance to the Stamp Act in that city particularly vociferous, widespread, and united. Resistance to that act in Philadelphia and New York was neither so concerted nor so united as in Boston, but those very facts would present opportunities as well as impediments to insurgents bent on using popular discontent with Great Britain as a springboard to greater political influence within their localities.

The distinctive political culture that had developed in the city and the colony at large over the course of the eighteenth century was more important than economic differences in shaping New York's reaction to the Stamp Act. Whereas the communitarian traditions of New England influenced the resistance in Boston, New York's reaction was conditioned by a culture in which the frank aggressive pursuit of self-interest was the norm, not the exception. As we have seen, New York City had a well-developed tradition of top-down political organization, one used with particular success by James and Oliver DeLancey during the 1740s and 1750s, when they were most successful in using the instruments of newspapers, caucuses, and the language of popular rights to gain advantage over their political rivals. It was in this context that rival political elites would confront the changes in British imperial policy after 1763. Those contending elites would not only have to examine the effect of those new policies on their conceptions of provincial liberty but would also be forced to make some calculated guesses about how their stands on those policies would "play" with the voters on whose suffrages they depended. And, for the very first time, the wealthy and well-born men who had traditionally composed the leadership of politics in the city and the colony would face at least a modest insurgency from individuals of a different social station.

The death of James DeLancey in 1760, the consequence of which was a weakening of that family's hold on New York politics, opened the way for an increase in the political factionalism that had sporadically marked politics in both the colony and the city. Indeed, in the assembly elections in 1761, after more than a decade of one-sided elections and voter disinterest, voter turnout in New York City, in an unusually large field of six candidates, increased to 56 percent. Although he did not choose to stand for the legislature in that year, the man who emerged as the chief beneficiary of the vacuum of power left in the wake of James DeLancey's death was William Livingston, a New York City lawyer and member of the family that had been the longtime rivals of the DeLanceys.[39] Livingston, along with his legal partners, William Smith Jr. and John Morin Scott, put together a coalition that would facilitate their prominence, if not dominance, in the politics of the colony. The three lawyers had proven themselves sincere and articulate defenders of popular rights against the claims of the Crown—in particular against the claims of Lieutenant Governor Cadwallader Colden, the longtime spokesman for royal interests in New York. When news of the Stamp Act reached New York, they led the opposition. While they were no doubt sincere in their commitment to the principles that underlay all American opposition to unjust taxation, it is also clear that the three saw in the rising popular resentment to the Stamp Act yet another opportunity to undermine further the power of their longtime adversary.[40]

In fact, events in Boston had already eliminated some of the principal sources of conflict in New York, for with the example of poor Andrew Oliver before them the likely candidates for stamp distributor in the city had immediately refused their commissions before being subjected to popular pressure to do so. But there were still rumors that Lieutenant Governor Colden intended to implement the act, rumors given greater substance by the claim of a British army officer, Major Thomas James, that he was sent to New York "to cram down the Stamp act upon them."[41] Sometime in the fall of 1765 a group of tradesmen, merchants, and ship captains, in many respects similar in economic standing and middling political influence to the Loyal Nine in Boston, began to form as "Sons of Liberty" in order to organize opposition to the Stamp Act in New York City. Unlike Boston, where

the mobs working in concert with the Loyal Nine had a discernible organizational structure and discipline, the mobs that the Sons of Liberty in
New York sought to control were more inchoate. When the mob struck on
November 1, 1765, the targets were Lieutenant Governor Colden and the
detested Major James. The example of Boston was everywhere evident—
solemn marches of townspeople who viewed hanging effigies of the lieutenant governor, followed by attacks on the residences of Colden and
James and four days later on Fort George, the place at which the hated
stamps were being stored. The destruction of private property in New York
City was if anything more unrestrained than in Boston, and the public reaction to that destruction was much more divided. Although the triumvirate of Livingston, Smith, and Scott had initially allied themselves with the
group calling themselves Sons of Liberty, they pulled back from that support in the wake of the destruction in early November. William Smith
warned of a "State of Anarchy" that might lead to a "general Civil War," and
when members of the Sons of Liberty asked the three lawyers to go ahead
with their business without the hated stamps, the three reiterated their determination to oppose the act by "Petitions, . . . representations, claims, ad-
dresses or remonstrances" but refused to engage in outright defiance of
the law.[42]

One of the members of the New York City elite who sought to take advantage of the timidity of Livingston and his cohorts was the son of the
former lieutenant governor, James DeLancey, Captain James DeLancey.
The younger James DeLancey had tried to gain election to the New York
Assembly in 1761 on a ticket fashioned by the triumvirate and had finished
dead last, beaten by two independents who entered the race at the last
minute. In late 1765, seeing Livingston's, Smith's, and Scott's lack of
courage, DeLancey publicly allied himself with the most radical members
of the Sons of Liberty, accusing the members of the triumvirate of timidity
in the cause of liberty.

Divisions within the New York City elite were mirrored in the leadership
of the Sons of Liberty. The radical leadership of the revolution in New York
was from the beginning more fragmented than that in Boston. During the
jockeying for position between the triumvirate and James DeLancey, one
portion of the Sons of Liberty, led by ship captain and merchant Alexander
McDougall, continued to support the moderate course of action being
championed by the three lawyers, while another portion, led by another
ship captain and merchant, Isaac Sears, advocated more radical activity.
Sears had been among those encouraging the mob to continue agitating
even after the ransacking of Colden's and James's houses on November 1,
and he continued to urge radical action in the weeks to come. At a town
meeting, itself an innovation in New York, where most political decisions
were made behind closed doors, Livingston and the moderate wing of the
Sons of Liberty won at least a temporary victory by getting those assembled

to agree to a set of instructions to New York's delegates to the legislature commanding them to vote for an embargo of British goods rather than outright defiance of the law as a means to secure repeal. Both Isaac Sears and James DeLancey criticized the timidity of the town meeting, and the following week, they won a victory of their own of sorts. In the first week of December the British customs officers responsible for ensuring that no trade through the port of New York occur without complying with the Stamp Tax decided to open the port and allow ships to pass through without the stamped paper. Justifying their actions to their superiors, they wrote, "This step we thought more adviseable as we understood the Mob (which are daily increasing and gathering strength, from the arrival of Seamen, and none going out, and who are the people that are most dangerous on these occasions, as their whole dependance for a subsistence is upon trade) were soon to have a meeting."[43]

Though the end result of the Stamp Act protest in New York City was identical to that in Boston—resistance and, ultimately, successful defiance of the law—the exact relationship between leaders of the Sons of Liberty and the mob was more problematic. Not only were the members of the Sons of Liberty themselves divided over what path of resistance was most efficacious, but the composition of the mob was more varied and more transitory. Both Isaac Sears and Alexander McDougall worked to control the actions of the mob, but at no point—neither in the riots of November 1 nor in the threatened action against the customs officials in early December—could it be said that anyone was fully in control.

The electoral consequences of these popular mobilizations would first be felt in 1768 at the first assembly elections held since the resistance to British imperial policy emerged. In that election James DeLancey and two candidates of like mind, Jacob Walton and James Jauncey, turned their guns on one of their opponents in particular, John Morin Scott. Aided by the aggressive intervention of Isaac Sears and those members of the Sons of Liberty who shared Sears's more radical views on the Stamp Act resistance, they emphasized two issues in their campaign. The first was a generalized sentiment toward the common profession of the triumvirate: "No Lawyer in the Assembly" was their cry, for lawyers, they charged, "fatten and grow rich upon the ruin of the people."[44] This anti-lawyer sentiment was not merely a code for opposition to Livingston, Smith, and Scott; rather, in the hands of DeLancey, Jauncey, and Walton, lawyers as a group were identified with conservative and landed interests against the interests of ordinary citizens. The second issue was Scott's unwillingness to oppose the Stamp Act. He was unfairly accused of refusing to support the Virginia Resolves (in fact, he opposed only those that urged defiance of the Stamp Act, a position taken as well by a majority of Virginia burgesses) and, in general, of not being willing to "employ . . . even . . . [a] Pen in Defiance" of the law.[45]

Fifty-three percent of the city's eligible voters participated in the 1768 election, and when the count was taken, Scott had suffered a humiliating defeat. The top vote getters for New York City's four assembly seats were Philip Livingston, a well-liked New Yorker who had avoided the partisan debates of the campaign and had been successful in winning election by more traditional means, with 1,320 votes, and Captain James DeLancey. Walton and Jauncey won the other two seats, with totals of 1,175 and 1,052 votes, respectively. Morris was a poor fifth, with 870 votes.[46] Certainly New York City had witnessed election campaigns at least as vituperative as this, and voter turnout, though high, was not unprecedented in the often faction-ridden politics of that city. What was unusual, though, was both the extent to which real issues—that of the candidates' attitudes toward British policy in particular—were focal points of the campaign and the extent to which men like Isaac Sears played visible, and independent, roles in lining up votes for candidates to their liking. New York City politics, even in 1768, continued to show many of the marks of the oligarchic, interested-oriented political culture of the colony as a whole, but the changing character of New York's political and economic relationship to the British Empire was all the while adding new elements to the game.

The Revolution in Pennsylvania Politics

This chapter opened with a brief glimpse of the way in which the conjunction of longtime political rivalries between assembly and proprietary factions, growing ethnic and religious consciousness, and the new issues arising from Great Britain's changing imperial policy caused even a demigod like Benjamin Franklin to lose his command of the suffrages of his fellow Philadelphians. Shortly after his defeat at the polls Franklin was narrowly elected by the assembly to a position as assistant agent for the colony to England, an election he secured in spite of John Dickinson's depiction of him as a person "extremely disagreeable to a very great number of the most serious and reputable inhabitants."[47] He served in London from December 1764 until May of 1775 and thus was not directly involved in the politics of his colony and city as the British sought to implement the Stamp Act there. In fact, though, Franklin's presence would continue to be felt in the politics of his home city. His supporters and fellow members of the Assembly Party, who had consistently used the language of popular rights in their battles with the proprietors, mounted a successful counter-attack in the October 1765 elections to avenge their defeat the year before. But interestingly, it was the supporters of the proprietors and not Franklin and those in his circle who were most vocal in their opposition to the Stamp Act.

The tepid reaction to the Stamp Act in Philadelphia can best be understood within the context both of general prosperity among merchants and artisans in the city and of Franklin's continuing influence among the artisan population of his hometown. Franklin lobbied hard in London against the Stamp Act, but he came to see that its passage was inevitable. Moreover, he was still pursuing the idea of converting Pennsylvania into a royal colony and thus was anxious to avoid conflict with the Crown. He rationalized the softening of his opposition to the act in a letter to Charles Thomson, a Presbyterian merchant who would eventually become one of the leaders of the radical resistance movement in Philadelphia, soon after Parliament had passed the bill: "We might as well have hinder'd the Suns setting," Franklin wrote, adding, "Let us make as good a Night of it as we can."[48] One of the ways in which Franklin hoped to make the best of a bad thing was by securing the appointment of John Hughes, a leader of the Assembly Party and a trusted associate, as stamp distributor. Franklin was successful in his bid to gain the post of stamp distributor for his friend, but as Hughes watched the fate of other distributors in New York and Boston, he must have found it difficult to feel much gratitude toward his patron in London. In some respects Hughes found himself in the same situation as his counterparts in Boston and New York; on September 16 and again during the first week in October he faced mobs that threatened the same kind of damage to his property as that suffered by Oliver and Colden. But in Philadelphia the antistamp mobs were countered by equally large groups of artisans and mechanics—in particular, ships carpenters, the White Oaks and Hearts of Oak—who, though no friends of the Stamp Act, were loyal to Franklin and willing to mass themselves to prevent mob violence.[49]

Hughes temporized, refusing to resign his post officially but making it clear that he would not try to enforce the act unless he had clearer instructions from the king or until the act had been put into execution in other colonies.[50] It was in this context that voters went to the polls to cast their ballots in the assembly elections of October 1765. Although some members of the proprietary faction sought to use the softness of Franklin, Hughes, and the Assembly Party on the subject of colonial rights to their advantage, the uneasy alliance between Presbyterians and Anglicans, Germans and Scots-Irish made it difficult to do so effectively. For their part, men like Joseph Galloway and Thomas Wharton of the Assembly Party had learned their lesson from the 1764 election. In spite of their tepid opposition to the Stamp Act, members of the Assembly Party in Philadelphia played down their earlier interest in converting the colony to royal government and instead emphasized the litany of complaints that had made the proprietors so unpopular in the first place—their continued evasion of a fair share of taxation, their attempts to manipulate the land office, and their attempts to control the judiciary. And they were able to recruit second-generation German merchant Michael Hillegas to help them woo German voters back into the fold. In the 1765 election unprecedented numbers of voters turned out, returning Galloway to the assembly as a representative from Philadelphia County and removing from the legislature five of the ten representatives who had voted against sending Franklin to London as the colony's agent.[51]

However high the political consciousness of ordinary Philadelphians may have been, they did not focus their concerns on issues of imperial authority and conduct in the way their fellow citizens in Boston and New York had. As the Sons of Liberty in Philadelphia confessed, "Our Body in this City is not declared Numerous, as unfortunate Dissentions in Provincial Politicks keep us rather a divided People." According to Alan Tully, imperial issues relating both to royalization and taxation would quickly recede from public view, and members of the Quaker Party would be able once again to use their advantage on purely local issues to reestablish their claim to being the truly "popular" party.[52] But it was a peculiar form of popular rule, as voter turnout at assembly elections, after reaching 46.1 percent in Philadelphia County and 61.8 percent in the city of Philadelphia in 1765, fell to 31.4 percent and 45.8 percent, respectively, in 1766. By 1771 the turnout in Philadelphia County had dropped all the way to 12.4 percent, and, even at the height of the Imperial Crisis in 1774–75 would rise to only 25–35 percent.[53]

The decline in voter interest in the assembly elections would obviously work to the advantage of Quaker Party members as they sought to control the assembly, but however much satisfaction they may have felt over their continuing dominance in the assembly, something far more profound was happening outside the legislative chamber that would render their claims to power and legitimacy far from secure. Even more than in Boston and New York, the most meaningful site of popular insurgence in Philadelphia was occurring not in assembly elections but in the streets. The citizens of Philadelphia were slower to react to British policies than their counterparts in Boston and New York, but as relations with the Crown continued to deteriorate, and as the Pennsylvania Assembly continued to remain passive in the face of the escalating conflict, it would be the citizenry out-of-doors, and not the assembly, that would lead the colony into Revolution.

The vehicles by which Pennsylvanians moved toward independence from Great Britain and by which they asserted a genuinely popular vision for their own government were the local militias and the several committees—of Observation, Officers, Privates, and Safety—organized outside of, and sometimes in direct opposition to, the formal structures of government. In the wake of the battles of Lexington and Concord the Pennsylvania Assembly had moved to put the colony in a state of defense, but as the military conflict escalated and avenues toward reconciliation seemed to be closing, a loose coalition of conservatives—whose most visible member was Joseph Galloway—and moderates—the most prominent of whom was John Dickinson—in the assembly continued to resist the call for independence. Historians have differed over the extent to which the emergence of the militia and the radical committees represented a fundamental rejection of elite rule in Pennsylvania, but all who have studied the coming of the Revolution in that colony Pennsylvania agree that during the years 1775–76 there was an unprecedented insurgence of artisans, craftsmen, mechanics, and shopkeepers into these extralegal organizations.[54] From the beginning of 1776 onward, the militia and the radical committees became less and less tolerant of foot-dragging by the assembly. On May 16, 1776, a caucus of committee members, with radical lawyer Thomas McKean in the lead, called for a provincial conference, enjoining the assembly from proceeding with its business until the proposed conference had articulated the public will. McKean and his fellow caucus members wasted no time; they distributed handbills throughout Philadelphia announcing an open meeting of all citizens on May 20, and on that day four thousand citizens braved the rain and, by acclamation, approved a set of resolutions proclaiming that the assembly was not "competent to the exigencies of [Pennsylvania's] affairs" and that it was therefore necessary that a convention "chosen by the people" form a new government. The resolutions also criticized the assembly for its dilatory response to independence, a response that had "a dangerous tendency to withdraw this province from that *happy union* with the other colonies."[55]

From that point on, the flow of power from the assembly to the people in the streets accelerated. The Philadelphia committee immediately sent out a circular letter with the details of the May 20 meeting to all of the counties in the colony, and by the end of May militia battalions and county committees in Lancaster, Northampton, York, and Chester counties had joined Philadelphia and Bucks counties in denying the authority of the assembly and calling for independence. The assembly, which began its spring session two days after the fateful May 20 open-air meeting, tried both to maintain its authority and to forestall a precipitous break with Great Britain. The proceedings of the officially constituted assembly between May 22 and its final demise on June 14 were marked by a combination of confusion, futility, and despair. During that period, proindependence radicals, though only a small minority within the assembly, would use their numbers to frustrate the gathering of a quorum for the legislature's proceedings. Moderates like John Dickinson, who continued to cling to the hope of reconciliation, and conservatives, who adamantly opposed independence, jockeyed for position, with the consequence being a legislative body that on many days could not muster enough members to do its business, and on those days that it did achieve a quorum, could not agree on a course of action that was satisfactory to anyone.

On June 8 the assembly did succeed in approving a new set of instructions to Pennsylvania's delegates to the Continental Congress authorizing, but not commanding, them to vote in favor of "measures as, upon a View of all Circumstances, shall be judged necessary for promoting the Liberty,

Safety, and Interests of America." That timid step toward independence—a word notably absent from the instructions—was a case of too little too late. By the next week proindependence radicals, now joined by some conservatives who felt an equal measure of despair on the other side of the question, were again boycotting the assembly sessions. On June 14 the assembly failed once again to reach a quorum. On that same day militia committees both of officers and privates informed the assembly that they considered that body no longer a legitimate decision maker with respect to military affairs. And with that rebuke to its authority, the Provincial Assembly of the colony of Pennsylvania adjourned, never again to muster a quorum.[56]

Although a part of the reason for the assembly's demise lay with the dissension it suffered from within, an even greater part rested with the active mobilization of Philadelphia's militia battalions against its authority. And it was the militia battalions, often working through their Committees of Privates, that mobilized support both within and beyond Philadelphia for the Provincial Conference. That body met in Philadelphia's Carpenter's Hall between June 18 and 25, and that assemblage would issue a call for a constituent convention to draft a new constitution for the province; and, taking the step that the assembly was unwilling to take, the Provincial Conference made explicit its "willingness to concur in a vote of the Congress, declaring the united colonies free and independent states."[57]

Of the 108 delegates to the Provincial Conference, only 3 had ever before served in the assembly, and 2 of those had only been elected to that body six weeks earlier. The delegates were, overwhelmingly, men of modest means, with shipwrights, shopkeepers, carpenters, bakers, and tanners outnumbering merchants and lawyers.[58] In laying out the procedures for electing delegates to the proposed Constitutional Convention, they made clear their intention to change dramatically the structure and elitist ethic that had characterized Pennsylvania politics in the past. Repudiating the colonial assembly's policies toward the apportionment of representation, the Provincial Conference gave each of Pennsylvania's counties as well as the city of Philadelphia eight representatives to the Constitutional Convention. The conference also significantly expanded the franchise for the elections of delegates to the convention, declaring all taxpaying, militia-members age twenty-one or over eligible to vote, a definition of the franchise that may have extended the suffrage to 90 percent of the adult male population. The use of the militia as the agency for determining the franchise was of course also consistent with the strong support that the militia units had given to independence, as was another provision that enabled election inspectors to require that prospective voters take an oath swearing to their loyalty to the cause of independence, a move that not only made it impossible for British Loyalists to vote but also enabled some election inspectors to exclude strict Quakers who had objections to oath-taking.[59]

The men who gathered at the statehouse in Philadelphia on July 15, 1776, to draft a new constitution for their newly declared independent state were an entirely different bunch from those who had ruled the colony for nearly a century. At its largest, the assembly had contained just thirty-six members; the delegates to the Constitutional Convention numbered ninety-six. More important, the delegates to the convention were by their geographic residence, social and economic background, and previous political experience as different from their colonial predecessors as one could imagine.[60] Thomas Smith, a representative from Bedford County, one of the few previous assembly members attending the convention and one who plainly disapproved of the plebian cast of the gathering, dejectedly observed that the prevailing principle of the convention "seems to be this: that any man, even the most illiterate, is as capable of any office as a person who has had the benefit of education; that education perverts the understanding, eradicates common honesty, and has been productive of all the evils that have happened in the world. . . . We are resolved to clear every part of the old rubbish out of the way and begin on a clean foundation."[61]

Although Benjamin Franklin was chosen president of the convention, he played only a passive role in the proceedings, leaving the task of leadership to a relatively unknown group of radicals, including James Cannon, Timothy Matlack, David Rittenhouse, and Dr. Thomas Young. Cannon, a mathematics professor at the College of Philadelphia and perhaps the prime organizer behind the Committee of Privates, was most likely the principal author of the constitution, with many of the ideas that he had earlier articulated in a June 16 pamphlet from the Committee of Privates finding their way into Pennsylvania's new frame of government. In that June 16 pamphlet Cannon had asserted that not only should the new government be founded on the authority of the people but that, once constituted, the people should have a direct hand in overseeing its operations. He insisted that "A Government made for the Common Good should be framed by Men who can have no Interest beside the common Interest of Mankind" and doubted the ability of "great and over-Grown rich Men" to be trusted with the reins of government. For Cannon, "Honesty, common sense, and a plain Understanding" were far more important than a fancy education or a lofty social status in the task of promoting the common good.[62]

The document that emerged from the Pennsylvania convention on September 28, 1776, was the most radically democratic frame of government that the world had ever seen. That constitution followed the lead of the Provincial Conference in enlarging the franchise, providing that "every [tax-paying] freemen of the full age of twenty-one shall enjoy the right of an elector"; it addressed in forthright fashion issues relating to the equitable apportionment of representation, giving six assembly representatives to each county and the city of Philadelphia for the years 1777 and 1778 and, more important, decreeing that "as representation in proportion to the number of taxable inhabitants is the only principle which can at all times secure liberty, and make the voice of a majority of the people the law of the land," called for a complete census of taxable inhabitants to be regularly conducted, with representation after 1776 to be based on those results.[63]

The framers of the Pennsylvania Constitution were intent on going far beyond reapportioning representation and equalizing access to the franchise. Following the lead of radicals like Cannon, Bryan, and Matlack and, no doubt, hearing at least echoes of Tom Paine, they eliminated altogether an upper house of assembly and drastically reduced executive power by creating a twelve member council with a rotating president in place of a unitary executive. More important, they articulated a much more explicit and direct relationship between elected officials in an annually elected, unicameral legislature than had ever before existed; the new constitution called for the operation of a suspending clause by which implementation of all laws passed in one session of the legislature would be "printed for the consideration of the people" and then held in abeyance until the next session of the legislature in order that representatives might return to their homes and collect the views of their constituents on the previous year's decisions.[64] Demophilus described the rationale behind the suspending clause: "You have the perusal, and consequent approbation of every law before it binds you; so that you must consent to be slaves before you can be made such."[65]

This explicit recognition of the potency and immediacy of the constituent power, in conjunction with changes eliminating the upper house and weakening the executive branch, would render the politics of postrevolutionary Pennsylvania volatile and often vituperative. What is perhaps surprising, though, is not that Pennsylvania politics took this explicitly democratic turn, but that it took so long for that development to occur. Penn's colony, and particularly the city of Philadelphia, had from the beginning been shaped by the founder's Whiggish and libertarian beliefs. Of course, those were seventeenth-century Whiggish and libertarian beliefs, and, as we saw in chapter 8, those who came to control politics in the Provincial Assembly were able quite easily to use the language of popular rights to justify oligarchical rule. But the rapidly growing economic, ethnic, and religious diversity of both the colony and its capital city were undermining their ability to keep that oligarchy in place. Moreover, the combination of the political and cultural alienation of western settlers, fueled by their increasingly virulent hatred of Indian peoples, made the mixture an even more explosive one. The Quaker Party oligarchs worked valiantly to keep a traditional system of politics in place, acting as if the colony continued to be composed entirely of middle-class English Quakers rather than a polyglot of differing interests and identities. They managed to maintain that fiction nearly to the very end, but in the months before and immediately after independence, it all gave way. The Pennsylvania Constitution pointed the way toward a democratic future, even if the path toward that future was not straight. As the Revolution in Pennsylvania played itself out and as Quakers and other pacifists found themselves disenfranchised by loyalty oaths, it would become clear that the concept of majoritarian democracy did not provide a guarantee either for liberty or for justice for all who resided in the commonwealth. But however imperfect the handiwork of the framers of the Pennsylvania Constitution of 1776, they had taken an important step in the right direction.

Chapter 10

The Unfinished Revolution in American Political Culture

Assessing the impact and meaning of the American Revolution in an essay sent to Hezekiah Niles some forty-two years after independence, John Adams posed and then answered a pair of questions:

> But what do we mean by the American Revolution? Do we mean the American War? The Revolution was effected before the War commenced. The Revolution was in the minds and hearts of the people; a change in their religious sentiments. Of their duties and obligations. . . . *This radical change in the principles, opinions, sentiments, and affections of the people was the real American Revolution.*[1]

Adams's assessment has been frequently cited by historians as evidence that much of what we think of as revolutionary about the American Revolution was in fact well advanced before the advent of independence. And, indeed, there is a good deal of evidence supporting that notion in the preceding chapters of this book. We have seen that even in eighteenth-century England there was no single agreed-upon formula for the proper conduct of politics and, moreover, that whatever passed for a traditional view of politics in colonial America was being constantly altered by a wide range of social and political forces in the institutionally and culturally diverse landscapes of Britain's colonies. We have also seen that in many respects the social and political structures of the American backcountry and of the cities of the American Northeast were on the eve of the Revolution as different from one another as those of London and rural provinces in France or Spain. And even in the more settled regions of rural America, local variations in economic organization or institutional traditions created strikingly different social and political arrangements.

In the North American mainland's two oldest colonies, Virginia and Massachusetts, those who dominated public life continued to use the language of classical republicanism, with its emphasis on personal virtue and the need to subordinate individual interest to the public good, both to justify their own claims to power and to describe their relationships with their fellow citizens. Political leaders in Virginia's Tidewater and Northern Neck, where the homogeneity of interests among white Englishmen living and working in a slave-based tobacco economy reduced opportunities for conflict among white residents, were perhaps more successful than any others in persuading their neighbors that they were the natural aristocrats most capable of promoting the public good. But even among those who seemed most naturally to embody the character of disinterested public servants—a George Washington or a John Robinson—such mastery required conscious effort. And among those who, like Landon Carter, yearned for the respect of their neighbors but lacked the personae and habit of command of a Washington, even strenuous effort at demonstrating superior wisdom and virtue might be met with rejection and humiliation at the hands of the multitude.

The social ethic of Massachusetts on the eve of the Revolution had changed markedly since John Winthrop proclaimed the divinely ordained existence of a social hierarchy in which "some . . . must be highe and eminent in power and dignitie; others meane and in subieccion," but members of the ruling elite of Massachusetts were similarly inclined to invoke classical republican values to justify their positions as power holders. As in Virginia, those values were challenged and undermined at every turn—as the ethnic and religious homogeneity of Massachusetts society gradually dissipated, as the nucleated New England village stretched out over space, and as the rhetoric of "popular rights," used so often against royal officials to justify provincial interests, was used by insurgents within the province to undermine the power of the traditional ruling elites. But in Massachusetts as in Virginia, at least for a time, the traditional rhetoric of republicanism and the actual operation of the polity were not wholly disconnected from each other.

Those who controlled the politics of the colonies of New York and South Carolina were every bit as self-consciously committed to upholding traditional English values in their domains as were their counterparts in Virginia and Massachusetts, but that commitment seemed to resemble more closely the oligarchic reality of eighteenth-century English political behavior than it did the idealized refrains of English commonwealth political philosophers. Whether in the inequitable division of wealth and political power between landlords and tenants in the Hudson River Valley or in the extraordinary privilege of South Carolina low-country oligarchs, the social and political orders of New York and South Carolina seemed unlikely places in which democratic ideas or practices might flourish. And, indeed, if those two societies had continued to exist in isolation from their neighbors, and if they had somehow been able to ignore the conflicts and intellectual logic of the American revolutionary movement, perhaps they would have remained—at least for a while—odd, hybrid outposts of English oligarchy within the American wilderness.

Certainly the societies that seemed farthest from their European origins were those of the eighteenth-century American backcountry and frontier. If the well-settled portions of the North American mainland colonies arrived at the moment of the Revolution with the outlines of a coherent American ethic of politics only hazily in view, the societies of the American backcountry, particularly in the western parts of North and South Carolina and Pennsylvania, presented even more basic challenges. As we catch glimpses of public life in those societies, we see contradictory elements of the modern and the tribal—aggressive, even exuberant, egalitarianism and volatile, virulent suspicion and distrust of "the other," whether that "other" was represented by eastern oligarchs or red-skinned Native Americans. The Regulator disturbances of North and South Carolina and the Paxton riots of Pennsylvania, all occurring nearly at the moment that America's traditional political elites were awakening to the challenges posed by changes in British imperial policy, were relatively easily contained. But the full integration of those regions into the larger American polity could not occur until the underlying sources of conflict between periphery and center were resolved.

Yet somehow, out of the formlessness and disorder of the frontier, out of the contest of interests, ethnicities, and ideologies of America's cities, and out of the diversity of political behavior across the rest of rural America, egalitarian and democratic forms of social and political behavior would become everywhere so prevalent by the early nineteenth century that they came to define the very meaning of what it was to be an American. Whatever the differences in attitude and style within the various political communities of colonial America, those political cultures nevertheless displayed some common tendencies and were moving, however unknowingly, toward greater convergence. The one thing that all free residents of the British colonies in America had in common before the Revolution was that they were all subjects of the king, a state that virtually all of the American political leaders discussed in this volume found wholly congenial. Indeed, this identity as subjects was probably more widespread in the American colonies than it was among the peoples of England. English common law had tended to convey a more restrictive definition of subjectship—creating a division between subjects and aliens—whereas the imperatives of attracting a wide variety of settlers to America led to more generous naturalization policies that enabled Germans, Swedes, or French Huguenots to claim the same rights as other British subjects in America.[2] That common experience of subjectship was, in fact, one of the few and essential concepts that bound all of America's free residents together.

There were other forces at work that in the long run would serve to undermine Americans' identity as subjects and to forge alternative sources of definition for a common identity. Although America was neither a land of unlimited economic opportunity nor an egalitarian paradise, it did display a variety of conditions—a higher proportion of residents owning land; remarkably high rates of economic growth; a relatively more fluid social, economic, and political hierarchy, an absence of a hereditary aristocracy; as well as the frailty of many of the imperial institutions of government—that impressed most European visitors to the colonies as distinctly different from the conditions prevailing in England. One of the consequences of this was that, however much American settlers may have shared a common allegience and obligation of obedience to the king, the condition of subjectship for the most part rested rather lightly on them. Yet another consequence was that it was often difficult for those among the provincial elite who claimed political power to maintain "that Decency and Respect, and Veneration . . . for Persons in Authority" so much desired not only by royal officials but also by American provincial leaders such as John Adams.[3] Whether one regarded it as a lack of "Decency and Respect" or as the legitimate exercise by freeholders of their political rights, there were in all of the polities of colonial America occasional assertions of the popular will—sometimes in spirited electoral contests but at others in the form of extralegal protest and violence. Whatever the differences in the political cultures of these American polities, they were moving in the same direction—toward a mode of political discourse and action that gave freer rein and greater legitimacy to those libertarian and popular impulses that would eventually be articulated in the Declaration of Independence.

However much the "minds and hearts" of colonial Americans may have inclined them to be sympathetic to the ideas and outcomes generated by the American Revolution, John Adams himself was aware that a real revolution both in thought and deed—involving radical upheaval and sustained violence—was necessary to effect the changes to which he had referred in his essay in the *Niles Weekly Register*. Writing to his wife, Abigail, on July 3, one day after the Continental Congress had passed its resolution endorsing independence, Adams—mistakenly, as it turned out—predicted that "the second day of July 1776 . . . will be celebrated by succeeding generations, as the great anniversary Festival." Although slightly off the mark with respect to the precise dating of America's "anniversary Festival," Adams did comprehend the magnitude of the change that the Americans were seeking to effect. "I am surprised," he wrote, "at the Suddeness as well as the Greatness of this Revolution." The most significant of the changes was also one that gave him greatest pause. "The People will have unbounded Power. And the People are extremely addicted to Corruption and Venality, as well as the Great—I am not without Apprehension from this Quarter. But I must submit all my Hopes and Fears to an overruling Providence, in which, unfashionable as it may be, I firmly believe."[4] A month later, writing to Abigail's brother-in-law, Richard Cranch, Adams continued in the same vein:

Is not the change we have seen astonishing? Would any Man, two years ago, have believed it possible to accomplish such an Alteration in the Prejudices, Passions, Sentiments of these thirteen little States to make every one of them completely republican, and to make them own it. Idolatry to Monarchs, and servility to Aristocratical Pride was never so totally eradicated from so many Minds in so short a time.[5]

In what seemed like a heartbeat the common identity of all free residents in America as fellow subjects of the king was obliterated. David Ramsay, the product of a culture of political leadership in South Carolina that was more self-consciously reverential of all things English than any in America, described the nature of the conceptual change "from subjects to citizens" as "immense." As Ramsay analyzed it:

Subject is derived from the Latin words, *sub* and *jacio* and means one who is *under* the power of another; but a citizen is an *unit* of a mass of free people, who, collectively, possess sovereignty. Subjects look-up to a master, but citizens are so far equal, that none have hereditary rights superior to others. Each citizen of a free state contains, within himself, by nature and the constitution, as much of the common sovereignty as another. In the eye of reason and philosophy, the political condition of citizens is more exalted than that of noblemen. Dukes and earls are the creatures of kings, and may be made by them at pleasure; but citizens possess in their own right original sovereignty.[6]

The functional difference between a near universal conception of subjectship and that of citizenship was brought into stark relief as Americans found themselves at war with Great Britain. In the immediate aftermath of the Declaration of Independence (and, in some cases, even before that moment), the residents of the American colonies faced the necessity of choosing between being British subjects or citizens of their now independent states. In fact, those newly independent state governments tended to define the requisites of citizenship differently, and in that sense, ironically, the concept of subjectship may have provided Americans more of a common basis for their political identity than the newly emerging, but still hazily defined, concept of citizenship.

Whatever the differences in definition, however, that act of casting aside an identity as British subjects and choosing the status of American citizen was the starting point for the tranformation in American political culture that would flow from the ideas, events, and aftermath of the American Revolution. Most historians agree on the general character—if not the precise social dynamic, timing, or completeness—of those ideological transformations.[7] Inextricably connected to the move from subjectship to citizenship was the transfer of political sovereignty from a hereditary monarch to collectivities of citizens. And in seizing that sovereign power, those collectivities of citizens, gathered together in the polities of their individual states, came to realize that written constitutions that were explicit both in the powers they delegated to the government and the fundamental rights that all citizens were to enjoy would provide a more secure means of achieving the public good than the conglomeration of laws, precedents, and customs on which the powers of government in the British Empire had previously rested.

However unselfconsciously, the American colonists had been moving toward some basic convergence in values and aspirations, and, further, the logic they used to justify their independence accelerated that process of convergence. But whatever the underlying forces working toward a common definition of America's political destiny, the differing forms and styles of politics existing from colony to colony before the Revolution would serve either to accelerate or to temper the immediate effects of the Revolution on those colonial entities. For that reason the extent to which revolutionary leaders of the newly independent states recognized the connection between their theoretical assertions about the sovereignty of the people and the need for explicitly written constitutions founded on the consent of the people varied across time and space. Most states simply converted their sitting legislatures or extralegal provincial congresses into Constitutional Conventions and proceeded to draft new frames of government, although five of those states—New Hampshire, Delaware, Maryland, North Carolina, and Georgia—did order new elections for representatives to those bodies before they met. In the first round of constitution making, only Pennsylvania convened something that looked like a special constituent convention, and the reasoning behind that action may have had less to do with a recognition that the act of legislating and constitution making were separate and distinct things than to the fact that the sitting Pennsylvania legislature had discredited itself by its refusal to endorse independence. Rhode Island and Connecticut did not even engage in a formal act of constitution making, instead simply accepting their old colonial charters as the basis for their independent governments. Only Massachusetts and New Hampshire submitted the product of their conventions' deliberations to the people for approval, and that only happened in 1780 in Massachusetts after a previous draft of a constitution drafted by an extralegal session of the Provincial Assembly had been rejected by the voters and in 1781 in New Hampshire under roughly similar circumstances.[8]

In the aftermath of independence, many, but not all states, revised their laws to make it easier for free white adult males to vote. Many states either eliminated or liberalized property qualifications for voting in the first round of constitution making and, by 1825, after many had completed a second round of constitutional revision, every one of the original thirteen states but Rhode Island and Virginia had moved to embrace the idea of universal free white male suffrage.[9] The authority, size, and composition of most postrevolutionary state legislatures would also show the effects of this democratization of attitudes toward office holding and governance. Every state with the exceptions of Connecticut and Rhode Island moved to strengthen the powers of the state legislature at the expense of their governors and upper houses, with Pennsylvania going so far as to eliminate both the upper house and the office of a unitary chief executive. Although these actions may have been primarily driven by a negative reaction to the excesses of royal officeholders in the years leading up to the Revolution, the practical effect was a more positive one—to more explicitly empower popular agencies of government.[10]

There were two means by which these popular impulses were explicitly embraced: the size of many state legislatures increased, thus extending opportunities for office holding, and the monopoly on legislative power by a distinctive economic and political elite was significantly weakened. In New Hampshire, for example, the lower house of assembly numbered 34 representatives in 1765, but by 1786 it numbered 88. As we have seen, New York's legislature, which numbered twenty-seven on the eve of the Revolution, was tiny given the size and population of the colony; although New York's constitution makers did not take dramatic steps to extend popular government in the drafting of their new frame of government, they did nearly double the number of representatives in the assembly after the Revolution. And South Carolina, whose prerevolutionary legislature may have been the least "representative" representative body in America in terms both of size and the extent of the disconnect between representatives and constituents, increased the size of its legislature from fifty-one representatives in 1775 to 184 after the Revolution.[11]

As the size of the legislatures increased, the characteristics of those serving as representatives, though certainly not mirroring those of the population at large, began to approximate them more closely. In New Hampshire, for example, the prerevolutionary legislature had been composed nearly exclusively of gentlemen from around the coastal town of Portsmouth; by contrast half of the members of the postrevolutionary legislature were yeoman farmers and only about 10 percent of the members could be considered genuinely wealthy. Similarly, in Maryland, Virginia, and South Carolina, the percentage of legislators who could be classed as wealthy declined from 52 percent before the Revolution to 28 percent after, with a corresponding increase in the percentage of men of moderate wealth—from 12 percent before independence to 30 percent after the Revolution.[12] Although public service in high office in most parts of America was still primarily the preserve of the wealthy and wellborn, that was less strikingly the case after the Revolution than before.

The process by which America's newly independent citizens came to embrace egalitarianism as a central value on which all of their social interactions would be founded was highly imperfect and halting, even more than that by which American political institutions came to function democratically. One does not have to look far to see the limits of the Americans' egalitarian vision: the continuation of the institution of chattel slavery in the independent southern states; legal impediments to full citizenship for women, free blacks, and unpropertied white males; and a confused and conflicted definition of the place of American Indian cultures within an emerging American nation-state are among the most obvious examples of the vagueness and incompleteness of the promise of equality contained in the Declaration of Independence. But progress toward an egalitarian future was not trivial. All of the newly independent states north of the Mason-Dixon Line initiated a process by which the institution of African slavery was to be eliminated within their borders. Although the timetable for abolition varied from state to state, the explicit recognition by those states that the values of equality and liberty were compromised by the holding of slaves was monumentally important.[13]

While the condition of bondage within the institution of chattel slavery defined the extreme version of dependence within colonial American society, there were other forms of dependency that were similarly weakened by the forces unleashed by the Revolution. Indentured servitude remained a fundamental part of the social and economic orders of most northern and southern states before the Revolution, and though the practice did not disappear overnight, it came to be seen increasingly as anachronistic. In the words of one New York group agitating for an end to indentured servitude, the practice was "contrary to . . . the idea of liberty this country has so happily established," and the combination of organized opposition to indentured labor and changing economic realities steadily diminished the number of American residents working in that status until the practice gradually disappeared altogether.[14]

Another sign both of the extent to which egalitarian ideas were well advanced before the Revolution and of the way in which the Revolution gave further impetus to the advancement of those ideas can be seen in the systematic attack on laws of primogeniture and entail. Those ancient laws restricting the descent of inherited property to the elder son were born of the desire to keep intact the wealth of the "Patrician order," to use Jefferson's derisive phrase. The strict operation of those laws had already been seriously undermined in the more open-ended social and economic order of eighteenth-century America, but the laws remained on the books, a reminder to men like Jefferson that there still existed within America a desire to maintain an "aristocracy of wealth," an impulse that ran directly counter to the goal of making "an opening for the aristocracy of virtue and talent, which nature has wisely provided for the direction of the interests of society, and . . . [has] deemed essential to a well-ordered republic."[15] Between 1776 and the mid-1780s every state in America abolished primogeniture and entail on the grounds that elimination of the practices would "tend to promote that equality of property which is of the spirit and principle of a genuine republic."[16]

The same impulses that caused all of the independent states to abolish primogeniture and entail also caused most states to move in other ways against patrilineal notions of kinship. Most of the new inheritance laws adopted in the immediate aftermath of the Revolution gave to daughters as well as sons the right to inherit property, as well as giving greater autonomy to widows in the inheritance of their husbands' property. These impulses to grant to women more expansive rights of citizenship were clearly limited, for it would be many decades before women possessed all of the property ownership rights of men, and many more decades before they could claim full equality as voters, but the egalitarian impulses unleashed by the Revolution did at least signal a beginning to the undermining of patriarchy in America.[17]

In the preceding chapters we have seen at least glimpses of the ways in which the ideology and social dynamic of the Revolution played out in the political communities that have been the subject of this book. Although past practices were certainly not fully determinative of the way the events of the Revolution would develop in these communities, the continuities between colonial traditions and revolutionary outcomes are nevertheless striking. In Virginia, in spite of the apparent effortlessness with which a small planter-gentry group claimed and exercised political authority, the clash of values and religious styles of Anglicans and Evangelicals would be brought into sharp focus during the crisis with Great Britain. One of the truly radical outcomes of the American Revolution—the formulation of the idea that "our civil rights have no dependence on our religions opinions, any more than our opinions on physics or geometry" and the consequent separation of church and state—was affected in part because men like Thomas Jefferson and James Madison took up their pens and applied the same libertarian logic they had used to justify separation from England to the subject of American religious liberty.[18] But their thoughts on that subject would have remained just words on a page had not the Evangelicals—and the Baptists in the Virginia backcountry in particular—mobilized themselves politically during the Revolution to force a legislature overwhelmingly dominated by Episcopalians to agree to that separation of church and state.

That political mobilization would have a lasting impact on the culture of religion in Virginia, and within just a few decades the landscape of Virginia would be markedly changed, with Episcopal churches in decline nearly everywhere within the state and a multiplicity of churches representing a vast array of Protestant denominations springing up across the countryside. But once the decision to secularize the state had been made and the most important area of contention between the evangelical and gentry cultures eliminated, the need for continuing political mobilization became less obvious. To a remarkable extent, the structure and style of Virginia's internal political culture was not altered by the Revolution. As late as 1949 the political scientist V. O. Key, describing the continuing dominance of governance in the state by members of a few prominent families and the persistence of uncontested elections, would conclude that Virginia was a "political museum piece," in which an "oligarchy" consistently "subverted democratic institutions and deprived most Virginians of a voice in their government."[19]

As we have seen, the revolution in Massachusetts did not end well for a few of those political leaders who chose allegiance to the king rather than secession. Thomas Hutchinson suffered humiliation and exile; Israel Williams, humiliation and imprisonment. But most of the members of Massachusetts's ruling elite, in part because they were so ardent in support of independence, found themselves comfortably in power once independence was declared and therefore in a good position to control and moderate the effects of the Revolution in their independent commonwealth. The result was a very slow movement toward either a democratic or a pluralistic conception of their polity. It would take another forty years before Massachusetts did away with its elaborately layered sets of property qualifications for voting and for service in high public office, and the connection between "good order" and "piety, religion and morality," with the Congregational Church retaining special status within that connection, would remain in place until 1833. The ideal of an organic social hierarchy, held in place by virtuous, disinterested public servants and undergirded by a collective commitment to piety and morality, would die hard in Massachusetts.

New York's provincial ruling elite was no less committed to its notion of an organic social hierarchy than that of Massachusetts, and, for the most part and for at least a few years after the Revolution, the principal leaders of the state managed to resist significant change in their traditional ways. The men who met to chart New York's political course after independence were, with a few notable exceptions, the same men who had dominated the politics of the colony, and few among them were inclined to propose significant changes of course for their independent polity. Many of New York's political leaders were prepared simply to have their extralegal Congress go ahead and draft a constitution, but, "doubts hav[ing] arisen whether this Congress are invested with sufficient power and authority to deliberate and determine on such an important subject," the Congress, in the upcoming elections for representatives, asked the voters to express their opinion about whether it should have the authority to draft a new constitution. If "the majority of the Counties, by their representatives in the Provincial Congress, shall be of opinion that such new Government ought to be instituted and established," the Congress would then feel itself empowered to draft a new constitution.[20]

Among the representatives who played the most active role in drafting that new constitution were some of the most prominent and familiar faces of prerevolutionary New York politics—Robert Livingston, Gouverneur Morris, John Jay, William Duer, John Morin Scott, and James Duane. There were a few relatively new faces in the group, such as Charles DeWitt, a shopkeeper from Ulster County, but for the most part the men who controlled the process of drafting the new constitution were committed to the status quo. The New York Constitution retained property qualifications in all aspects of political life, instituting a gradation of qualifications for holding office depending on the power and dignity of the office, and even requiring a higher level of property ownership for those voting for members of the postrevolutionary upper house and governor, a move that may have excluded about seven out of ten male citizens from voting in those elections. Although most states appended to their constitutions separate declarations of rights explicitly spelling out those fundamental liberties that were beyond the government's reach, New York included in the body of its constitution language protecting at least some of those rights—including freedom of religion. The constitution did not, however, end the privileged position of the Episcopal Church as the established, tax-supported church of the state.[21]

Although the outward form of the New York Constitution was distinctly conservative, the Revolution had other, more enduring effects that would work to transform the political culture of the state in decades to come. The choices of allegiance and identity necessitated by independence generated greater internal crisis among traditional elites in New York than in Virginia or Massachusetts, and when the Revolutionary War had ended, a significant transfer of both economic and political power had taken place. Although most of the members of New York's political ruling class decided, many of them reluctantly and belatedly, to cast their lot with the patriot cause, there was a sizeable class of large landowners in the colony—men such as Oliver DeLancey, Peter Van Schaack, Frederick Philipse, and William Johnson's heir, Sir John Johnson—who remained loyal to the king and who between 1776 and 1779 would face, in addition to the threat of mob violence and imprisonment, the confiscation of their property by the state. There was considerable controversy over what should be done with the confiscated property, but by 1780, and in spite of opposition from prominent New Yorkers such as Robert Livingston and Abraham Ten Broeck, who were nervous about the consequences of any attack on property, the New York Assembly began to enact legislation putting the confiscated lands up for sale, with the result being the most substantial redistribution of property to occur anywhere in America during the Revolution.[22]

Much of the impetus for the confiscation and sale of Loyalist estates came from a new class of politicians emerging in New York in the years following the Revolution. Although defenders of the traditional order like John Jay and members of the Livingston and TenBroek families had been successful in steering a cautious course in the drafting of the New York Constitution, the fractiousness among elites that characterized New York politics before the Revolution, in combination with the displacement of those Loyalists who had occupied places within those elite groups, would bring about fundamental changes in the style of New York politics after the Revolution. The leader of that new class of insurgent politicians was George Clinton, son of an Irish immigrant, who, through military service and timely marriage to a member of a politically powerful family in Ulster County, would rapidly ascend in the politics of the independent state. His election to the governorship in 1777—an election that caused John Jay to huff, "Clinton's family and connections do not entitle him to so distinguished a pre-eminence"—marked a real turning point in the style and substance of New York politics. And, like it or not, old-style politicians like Jay and members of the Livingston family would have to play Clinton's more populistic game if they hoped to unseat him and the men around him.

All of this electoral competition took place within a constitutional structure that remained relatively restrictive, but by 1820 to 1821, when the state held a second constitutional convention, it was clear that the tone and tenor of New York politics had irreversibly changed. By that time a new breed of politician, perhaps best represented by the humbly born Martin Van Buren, had seized the initiative in New York politics, leading a movement for constitutional revision that not only swept away all property qualifications for voting but also set forth the novel proposition that party loyalty rather than wealth or family distinction should be the basis on which voters should cast their ballots. Peter Jay, son of John Jay, and Chancellor James Kent pleaded with the delegates to retain some respect for traditional values based on family dignity, wealth, or individual achievement lest Federalists like themselves might "feel themselves aliens in their native land," but their opponents simply marveled that the old guard could not recognize that "the course of things in this country is for the extension and not the restriction of popular rights." In the view of the new political leadership class of New York, "the great fundamental principle that all men were equal in their rights was settled, forever settled, in this country."[23]

In some important senses South Carolina's Revolution never happened. We have seen in chapter 5 how three of the colony's most powerful leaders—William Bull, Henry Laurens, and Christopher Gadsden—responded to the crisis with England. William Bull would fall off the tightrope he had so skillfully walked and in the end would be forced to flee to England, salvaging as much as he could of the value of his South Carolina holdings once the war had ended. Laurens and Gadsden—the former a bit reluctantly and the latter enthusiastically—cast their lot with the patriot cause, and both would emerge from the Revolution with their power and property intact. When it came time for men like Laurens and Gadsden to create a new government for their state, the deep strain of traditionalism that had marked the political culture of the colony persisted with a vengeance.

In postrevolutionary South Carolina, even more than in New York, the constitutional changes accompanying independence were slight. The extralegal Provincial Assembly of South Carolina actually drafted two constitutions during the maelstrom of events surrounding independence. The first was drafted in February of 1776 and quite explicitly divorced the crafting of a frame of government for the state from the question of independence, for many of South Carolina's leaders continued to hold out the hope that a reconciliation with England might be reached. The committee that drafted the initial constitution consisted of eleven of the most prominent men in the colony—John Rutledge, Charles Cotesworth Pinckney, Henry Laurens, and Christopher Gadsden among them—and the product of their labors wholly reflected their conservatism. In a bow to the continuation of principles of mixed government, the lower house of assembly was empowered with the election of both the upper house and the president. The same property qualifications for both voting and office holding that prevailed under the colonial government were retained in the new one. Although the discontented and disadvantaged western districts were given additional representation in the lower house, the balance of power remained with the eastern parishes.[24]

A combination of dissatisfaction with the casual way in which the first constitution was drafted and put into effect and the fact of the adoption by the Continental Congress of a formal Declaration of Independence caused enough unease about the legitimacy of the new constitution that the South Carolina Assembly did it all over again in 1777. The new version was slightly more attentive to the popular will. Property qualifications for voting were lowered to a fifty-acre freehold or a town lot, and the voters were given the right to elect members to both the lower and upper houses. The governor continued to be elected by the legislature, and property qualifications for serving in the senate or as governor were actually raised to £2,000 and £10,000, respectively. Apportionment of representation in the legislature remained the same as in the earlier constitution. Finally, the extralegal assembly moved to disestablish the Anglican Church and to grant a full measure of religious liberty to all Protestant religious sects, although the "Christian Protestant Religion" remained the established religion of the state. As further evidence of the Provincial Congress's murky understanding of the distinction between the authority of an extralegal legislative body and that of a constituent convention, the members of the congress submitted the revised constitution to John Rutledge, serving as president of the state under the 1776 constitution, as simply another legislative act for his approval. Rutledge actually vetoed it on the grounds that the existing constitution was adequate and that reconciliation with England was still possible. He then resigned after vetoing the draft; he was subsequently replaced by Rawlins Lowndes, who, though nearly as conservative as Rutledge, added his approval to the constitution.[25]

The smoldering discontent in the western districts that had burst briefly into flame during the Regulator disturbances of 1768 to 1769 was hardly extinguished by the minimal reforms institutionalized by the constitution of 1778. As we have seen in chapter 6, the choice between identifying themselves as subjects of the king or citizens of an independent state ruled by eastern gentrymen was by no means an obvious one for many residents in the western regions of South Carolina, with that decision often turning more on the strength of negative and hostile feelings than on any positive sense of loyalty or affection. Some of the tension between east and west would be gradually defused in subsequent decades, as successive reapportionments of representation in the legislature gradually gave a fairer representation to western regions, but low-country planters and merchants would still retain disproportionate influence in the government.

Governance in South Carolina would have a distinctly elitist flavor right up to the Civil War. Although the 1778 constitution was amended in 1808 to provide something close to universal suffrage for free white males (under the condition that they had lived in the state for six months), other features of the constitution remained remarkably resistant to the democratizing forces that were sweeping other southern states during the decades of the 1820s and 1830s. For all of the first half of the nineteenth century the distribution of representatives in the South Carolina Assembly was based on a combination of population and the amount of taxes paid in each district, an indication of the attachment of South Carolina's leaders to traditional notions of property as the basis for the polis. Attempts to do away with distinctions based on wealth or to bring about popular election of the governor were consistently thwarted, usually on the grounds that the people of the state would be better served by concentrating their attentions on protecting South Carolina's interests from threat of encroachment from the federal government than they would by agitating purely local issues. Indeed, the only constitutional amendment adopted in the state between 1830 and 1850 was one that required all citizens to swear that "I will be faithful, and true allegiance bear to the state of the South Carolina, as long as I may continue a citizen thereof," a clear indication that South Carolina's political leaders retained as their primary identification their citizenship of their state and not their nation.[26]

As we have seen at the conclusion of chapter 9, Pennsylvania's revolution of 1776 was as complete a revolution as the world had ever seen. The men who drafted the state's revolutionary constitution were an altogether different bunch from those who had ruled the colony just a few months before, and the principles on which they based their new frame of government were explicitly democratic. The venerable Harvard historian Samuel Eliot Morison, no doubt swayed by his attachment to the orderly process of political change in his native commonwealth, termed the Pennsylvania Constitution of 1776 "the nearest thing to a dictatorship of the proletariat that we have had in North America; a real 'popular front' government."[27] Morison was no doubt influenced in his characterization by the campaign of retaliation against some of the more conservative Quakers in Penn's former colony, but his assessment both overstates the extent of illiberality embodied in the Pennsylvania revolutionary frame of government and fails to appreciate the genuinely egalitarian and libertarian character of that document. In addition to its aggressive embodiment of democratic principles in the structure of government and its articulation of a direct and immediate relationship between representatives and constituents, the constitution, in a lengthy preamble and an even lengthier declaration of rights, spelled out in stirring terms the principles so eloquently articulated by Tom Paine and Thomas Jefferson, that governments are "instituted and supported for the securing and protection of the community," and that their primary purpose is to "enable the individuals who compose it to enjoy their natural rights."[28]

The politics of postrevolutionary Pennsylvania would be unusually tumultuous, a consequence in part both of the relative inexperience of the state's new leadership class and the factionalism inherent in its unicameral legislature, which was, in effect, the sum and substance of government. Some of the sources of tumult would be reduced by a constitutional revision in 1790 that restored a bicameral legislature and a relatively independent chief executive, but that new constitution would continue to embrace the explicitly democratic principles on which the original constitution was based. Pennsylvania, perhaps alone among the American colonies, had during its revolution moved to an explicitly democratic conception of politics.

There is considerable irony, but also considerable logic, in the pace and substance of revolutionary political change exhibited during the transition to statehood of the colonial polities surveyed in this volume. In general those colonies whose political leaders were able, either by conviction or calculation, to keep themselves in the forefront of the move for independence and, as a consequence, to appear to be in full sympathy with the sentiments of the people whom they represented and ruled, displayed both stability and a continuing attachment to traditional republican notions of government as they constituted their new polities. Virginia and Massachusetts, whose provincial political leadership retained relatively secure control over events at every stage in the Revolution, were able to go through the revolutionary transition with remarkable ease and little disruption, and the governments they fashioned, with appropriate protections against excessive concentrations of power but also clear inhibitions on the direct expression of the popular voice, were models of traditional republican values. The political leaders of New York and South Carolina, though apparently less attentive to classical republican concerns about concentrations of power when it came to their own political behaviors, were no less committed than their counterparts in Virginia and Massachusetts to a conception of politics that gave a special place in the polity to men of "property and standing." Often less responsive to either the feelings or the interests of their more humble constituents, they nevertheless managed—some more reluctantly than others—to embrace the Revolution and to emerge from the event with their power intact. But, at least in New York, their days of un-challenged dominance were numbered.

That it was the independent state of Pennsylvania that would point the way most clearly to a democratic American future was a result both of its relatively progressive and Whiggish origins and of the unwillingness of the eighteenth-century Assembly Party leadership to move beyond those mildly populist beginnings to embrace a political culture that was more genuinely respectful of the popular voice. The American nation itself would eventu-ally come to embrace the sets of political values that had been articulated and institutionalized by the Pennsylvania insurgents during the revolution-ary crisis. But, as was the case with the evolution toward more popular, democratic forms of politics in the American colonies before the Revolu-tion, the continuation of that evolution in state and nation after the Revo-lution varied across time and space, and remained incomplete even up to the Civil War.

When the American nation was brought into being in 1787, it was, in the arresting phrase of historian John Murrin, a "roof without walls." Whereas Britain and allegiance to a sovereign monarch had been the primary focal points of American identity before the Revolution and opposition to Britain the primary unifying rallying point for Americans during that strug-gle, in the aftermath of the Revolution American identity remained, in Murrin's words, "unexpected, impromptu, artificial, and . . . extremely fragile." In his view it would be the "contrivance" of the United States Con-stitution that would "serve as a substitute for any deeper kind of national identity."[29] And, indeed, the diligence with which America's most talented political leaders—from Jefferson and Madison to John Marshall to John C. Calhoun, Daniel Webster and Henry Clay—devoted themselves to elabo-rating on the intricacies of the American constitutional system suggests the extent to which the constitutional definition of our nationhood was the re-sult of a conscious effort by those statesmen—actually, state builders—to forge a common conception of citizenship among a people whose diversity of belief and background made such a job so daunting.

The fashioning of a common American identity has, however, not rested solely, or even primarily, on constitutionalism. The essential elements of a common sense of citizenship among Americans were contained not in the federal Constitution, but in the Declaration of Independence, in those eternal, and eternally elusive, phrases of the preamble holding out the promise of a society founded on principles of democracy and equality. While neither the pathway nor even the vista toward that democratic and egalitarian future was very clear to most Americans on the verge of the American Revolution, there were at least a few who were able, on the eve of America's experiment in independence, to imagine what shape Amer-ica's future might take. The person with the clearest vision of that Ameri-can future would not even arrive in America until the fall of 1774, and, perhaps because he had arrived so late, he was better able to see both those things that Americans possessed in common and how very different the American colonies had become from their English parent. "It hath lately been asserted," Tom Paine wrote in *Common Sense*, "that the colonies have no relation to each other, but through the parent country, i.e. that Pennsylvania and the Jerseys, and so on for the rest, are sister colonies by the way of England." This was, in Paine's view, patent nonsense. Even if one admitted to some portion of parental connection to England, how ridiculous it was to assert that "because a child has thrived upon milk, that it is never to have meat; or that the first twenty years of our lives is to become a precedent for the next twenty." More important, the parental bond between an English sovereign and his American subjects was a trivial form of connection compared to those things that Americans held in common. "This new world hath been the asylum for the persecuted lovers of civil and religious liberty from every part of Europe," Paine argued, and it was that common love of liberty that would be the enduring tie that would bind Americans together. "We have every opportunity," Paine argued, to

form the noblest, purest constitution on the face of the earth. We have it in our power to begin the world over again. A situation, similar to the present, hath not happened since the days of Noah until now. The birth-day of a new world is at hand, and a race of men perhaps as numerous as all Europe contains, are to receive their position of freedom from the events of a few months. The Reflexion is awful—and in this point of view, How trifling, how ridiculous, do the little, paltry, cavellings, of a few weak or interested men appear, when weighed against the business of a world.[30]

Paine was both a polemicist and an optimist. The British system of government was not nearly as terrible as Paine made it out to be, and the men entrusted with forming those noble and pure state constitutions in the aftermath of independence were for the most part souls far more timid than Paine, unprepared to seize the moment of independence to "begin the world over again." The interconnected stories of the process by which America's political cultures were democratized and by which Americans embraced egalitarianism as a central value on which their nation was to be founded was indeed, as Paine and his oft-vocal critic, John Adams, recognized, one that began well before the American Revolution commenced. Equally assuredly, and contrary to Paine's optimistic prediction, it was hardly complete by the time the Revolution ended. Indeed, the story continues today, perpetually unfinished.

Appendix 1

Connecticut	Income of 40 shillings per year from rent of freehold (1689) Personal property valued at £40 (1702) Age: 21 Persons of "peaceable and honest conversation"
Delaware	Freehold of 50 acres: 12 acres cleared (1734) Personal property valued at £40 (1734) Age: 21 Natural-born subject of Great Britain or a naturalized citizen of England or Delaware and have resided for 2 years
Georgia	Freehold of 50 acres (1754) Age: 21 Minimum 6 month residence in Georgia Suffrage restricted to "white adult males"
Maryland	Freehold of 50 acres (1670) Personal property valued at £40 (1670) Suffrage for Catholic voters restricted (1718)
Massachusetts	Income of 40 shillings per year from rent of freehold (1691) Personal property valued at £40 Age: 24 for non-freeman and non-churchmembers; 21 otherwise Suffrage of non-church members restricted to those "non vicious in life"
New Hampshire	Freehold valued at £50 (1728) Age: 21 Natural-born subject of Great Britain or naturalized citizen of England or New Hampshire Suffrage restricted to those "not vicious in life"

New Jersey Freehold of 100 acres (1705)
Personal property valued at £50 and own a freehold of any amount (1705)
Age: no specification
Resident of the county, city or town where vote is cast

New York Freehold of 100 acres (1705)
Age: 22
Owner of land for at least 3 months prior to election
Suffrage barred to Catholics and Jews

North Carolina Freehold of 50 acres (1735)
Age: no specification
Natural-born subject of Great Britain or a naturalized citizen of England or North Carolina and resident of North Carolina for 6 months
Suffrage barred to negroes, mulattoes and Indians

Pennsylvania Freehold of 50 acres: 12 acres cleared (1705)
Personal estate valued at £50 (1705)
Age: 21
Natural-born subject of Great Britain or a naturalized citizen of England or Pennsylvania and resident of Pennsylvania for 2 years

Rhode Island Freehold valued at £40 (1760)
Income of 40 shillings per year from freehold (1723–1730, 1760)
Age: no specification
Suffrage barred to Catholics

South Carolina Freehold of 100 acres unsettled or a settled plantation (1759)
Real estate valued at £60 (1745) or payment of 10 shillings per year in taxes (1759)
Age: 21
Resident of South Carolina for 1 year
Suffrage restricted to white protestants

Virginia Freehold of 100 acres unsettled (1736)
25 acres settled with a house or possession of a house or lot in a legally established town (1762)
Age: 21
Suffrage barred to negroes, mulattoes and Indians

Appendix 2

Days in Session of Colonial Assemblies, 1752–1756

	1752	1753	1754	1755	1756
Massachusetts	75	66	118	117	70
New York	12	38	40	61	75
Pennsylvania	40	65	124	139	175
South Carolina	98	54	74	103	119
Virginia	44	41	37	39	43

Craig W. Horle, *Lawmaking and Legislators in Pennsylvania: A Biographical Dictionary.* (Philadelphia, 1991).

New York (Colony) Council. *Journal of the Legislative Council of the Colony of New York.* Began the 9th day of April, 1691; and ended the [end of April 1775]. Vol. (New York, 1861).

Massachusetts (Colony). General Court. House of Representatives. *Journal of the House of Representatives of Massachusetts.* Vol. (Boston, 1919).

H.R., McFluaire, ed., *Journals of the House of Burgesses of Virginia: 1752–1755, 1756–1758.*

H.R., McFluaire, ed., *Journals of the House of Burgesses of Virginia: 1758–1761.*

South Carolina. General Assembly. Commons House. *The Journal of the Commons House of Assembly,* vols. 11–14. Ed. J.H. Esterby. (Columbia, 1951).

Appendix 3

AVERAGE NUMBER OF LAWS ENACTED BY COLONIAL ASSEMBLIES ACROSS SELECTED
FIVE-YEAR PERIODS

	1730–1735	1740–1745	1760–1765
Connecticut	15.0	10.8	8.0
Maryland	22.6	18.2	24.8
Massachusetts	17.1	23.1	31.5
New Jersey	6.2	5.0	18.5
New York	13.3	25.5	27.0
North Carolina		11.5	26.2
Pennsylvania	4.3	5.0	12.1
Rhode Island	11.3	23.0	10.4
South Carolina	13.8	16.0	12.0
Virginia	31.3	31.6	37.8

Adapted from Alison G. Olson, "Eighteenth-Century Colonial Legislatures and Their
Constituents," *JAH,* 79 (1992): 563.

Appendix 4

Average Number of Petitions Received Annually by Colonial Assemblies

	1715–1720	1750–1755	1760–1765
Connecticut	39.0	90.3	130.3
Maryland	17.8	16.3	28.0
Massachusetts	95.2	212.0	257.0
New Jersey	13.6	18.5	43.1
New York	13.8	13.2	12.2
Pennsylvania	18.0	26.6	25.5
Rhode Island	2.2	58.1	100.3
South Carolina	10.8	17.6	9.6
Virginia	28.5	60.0	88.8

From Alison G. Olson, "Eighteenth-Century Colonial Legislatures and Their Constituents," *JAH,* 79 (1992): 557.

Appendix 5

NUMBER OF ASSEMBLY ELECTIONS PER DECADE

	1696–1705	1706–1715	1716–1725	1725–1735	1736–1745	1746–1755	1756–1765	1766–1775
Connecticut	20	18	20	20	20	20	20	20
Delaware				6	10	10	10	10
Georgia						4	5	
Maryland	3	4	4	3	4	4	4	3
Massachusetts	10	10	12	12	11	10	10	10
New Hampshire	6	3	4	8	6	3	3	4
New Jersey	14	2	2	5	4	1	2	
New York	5	6	1	3	4	3	2	2
North Carolina		4	3	7	6	4	5	6
Pennsylvania	2	10	10	10	10	10	10	10
Rhode Island	10	17	19	12	10	10	11	10
South Carolina	5	7	5	8	4	7	6	6
Virginia	6	2	3	1	2	2	3	5

From Jack P. Greene, "Legislative Turnover in British America, 1696 to 1775: A Quantitative Analysis," *WMQ*, 3d ser., 38 (1981): 446–48.

Average Turnover Rate of Legislators in North American Colonial Mainland Assemblies by Decade

	1716–1725		1726–1735		1736–1745		1746–1755		1756–1765		1766–1775	
	Number of Elections	Mean %	Number of Elections	Mean %	Number of Elections	Mean %	Number of Elections	Mean %	Number of Elections	Mean %	Number of Elections	Mean %
Connecticut	20	49.0	20	46.5	20	43.2	20	46.3	20	48.2	20	41.9
Delaware			6	29.8	10	15.0	10	20.7	10	25.6	10	20.4
Georgia									4	49.7	5	47.4
Maryland	4	52.7	3	39.3	4	28.5	4	33.7	4	37.5	3	47.3
Massachusetts	12	52.3	12	42.7	11	43.4	10	44.3	10	37.0	10	33.6
New Hampshire	4	32.9	8	30.1	6	39.0	3	35.3	3	40.7	4	30.2
New Jersey	2	81.0	2	54.5	5	38.6	4	36.2	1	29.0	2	50.0
New York	1	38.0	3	26.7	4	32.5	3	22.3	2	44.5	2	35.0
North Carolina	3	63.7	7	36.0	6	39.5	4	40.5	5	44.8	6	40.0
Pennsylvania	10	48.0	10	30.4	10	16.9	10	19.6	10	22.3	10	17.6
Rhode Island	19	59.1	12	54.2	10	60.1	10	56.8	11	55.4	11	49.8
South Carolina	5	61.0	8	46.1	4	69.7	7	62.4	6	43.5	6	34.7
Virginia	3	39.0	1	55.0	2	64.5	2	44.5	3	41.3	5	29.4

Adapted from Jack P. Greene, "Legislative Turnover in British America, 1696 to 1775: A Quantitative Analysis," *WMQ*, 3d ser., 38 (1981): 446–48.

Notes

Introduction

1. David Hume, "Of the First Principles of Government," *Essays and Treatises on Several Subjects,* 1758 edition, quoted in Edmund S. Morgan, *Inventing the People: The Rise of Popular Sovereignty in England and America* (New York, 1988), p. 13.

2. The works of those historians who have been most influential in shaping the republican paradigm will be cited extensively in the pages that follow. For overviews of that work see Isaac Kramnick, *Republicanism and Bourgeois Radicalism: Political Ideology in Late Eighteenth Century England and America* (Ithaca, N.Y., 1990); Joyce Appleby, *Liberalism and Republicanism in the Historical Imagination* (Cambridge, Mass., 1992); see also Richard R. Beeman, "Deference, Republicanism, and the Emergence of Popular Politics in Eighteenth Century America," *William and Mary Quarterly* (hereafter *WMQ*), 3d ser., 49 (1992): 401–30; and Robert Shalhope, "Republicanism," in Jack P. Green and J. R. Pole, eds., *A Companion to the American Revolution* (Oxford England, 2000), 668–73. Another useful glimpse into the overwhelming importance of Bernard Bailyn in shaping conceptions of politics and ideology in eighteenth-century America can be gained from perusing James A. Henretta, Michael Kammen, and Stanley N. Katz, *The Transformation of Early American History: Society, Authority, and Ideology* (New York, 1991), a book of essays written by Bailyn's former students in his honor.

3. See, for example, David Waldstreicher, *In the Midst of Perpetual Fetes: The Making of American Nationalism, 1776–1820* (Chapel Hill, N.C., 1997); Saul Cornell, *The Other Founders: Anti-federalism and the Dissenting Tradition in America, 1788–1828* (Chapel Hill, N.C., 1999); Sean Wilentz, *Chants Democratic: New York City and the Rise of the American Working Class* (New York, 1984); and Edward Countryman, *The American Revolution* (New York, 1985).

4. Two useful guides to the range of definitions given to politics and political behavior are Iain McLeon, *The Concise Oxford Dictionary of Politics* (Oxford, 1990), p. 309, and Frank Bealy, *The Blackwell Dictionary of Political Science* (Oxford, 1999), p. 261.

5. There has been a recent outpouring of work using public celebrations and civic rituals as a means of understanding social relations among groups within America. Among the most impressive of these are Waldstreicher, *In the Midst of Perpetual Fetes*; Simon Neumann, *Parades and the Politics of the Street: Festive Culture in the Early American Republic* (Philadelphia, 1997); David Conroy, *In Public Houses: Drink and the Revolution of Authority in Colonial Massachusetts* (Chapel Hill, N.C., 1995); and Peter Thompson, *Rum Punch and Revolution: Tavern-Going and Public Life in Eigh-*

teenth Century Philadelphia (Philadelphia, 1999), esp. pp. 111–44. Waldstreicher and Neumann are most effective in gleaning from public rituals something of the character of the relationship between leaders and ordinary citizens, but their work focuses on urban areas within postrevolutionary America and on a political context that was national rather than provincial and local. Thompson's and Conroy's studies of Philadelphia and Massachusetts tavern life focus more directly on prerevolutionary behaviors; of the two, Thompson is more successful in establishing the importance of taverns as important sites of public, political discourse.

6. The two words most often used to denote those regions of North America more recently settled by Europeans—frontier and backcountry—carry with them some very heavy historical and ideological baggage. From the time of Frederick Jackson Turner forward, the concept of the frontier has often been associated with a Eurocentric view of settlement in which democracy and individualism were inevitable results. And, as Daniel Richter has observed, what may have seemed like backcountry to European settlers was in fact a long-occupied front country to Indian inhabitants. Whatever their drawbacks, however, the words were part of the eighteenth-century vocabulary, often used interchangeably. In the chapters that follow, I will use backcountry when discussing those more recently settled regions of the colonies that were *not* engaged in consistent conflict with Native Americans and will use the word frontier when discussing those regions where the contest between Europeans and Indians was a more active feature of daily life. The original, Turnerian statement of the "frontier thesis" was presented in "The Significance of the Frontier in American History," delivered as the Presidential Address at the annual meeting of the American Historical Association in 1893, but subsequently published in Turner, *The Frontier in American History* (New York, 1920), pp. 1–38. Richter's formulation is in *Facing East from Indian Country: A Native History of Early America* (Cambridge, Mass., 2001), pp. 1–10.

7. I have also decided against including a discussion of the evolving political cultures of the British West Indian colonies. Although the economic connections between England's West Indian colonies and those on the mainland of North America were important, the political cultures of the mainland colonies and the islands of the West Indies were, in my opinion, different not only in degree but also in kind. For an excellent effort at incorporating the West Indian colonies within the larger context of England's Atlantic empire see Andrew J. O'Shaughnessy, *An Empire Divided: The American Revolution and the British Caribbean* (Philadelphia, 2000).

Chapter 1. The Traditional Order of Politics in England and America

1. J. H. Plumb, *The Origins of Political Stability: England, 1675–1725* (Boston, 1967), p. 29. In particular, Plumb emphasized the turbulence of seventeenth-century English politics in order to argue for the relative stability produced by a Whig oligarchy in the eighteenth century. Linda Colley, *In Defense of Oligarchy: The Tory Party, 1714–1760* (Cambridge, 1982), has argued that the Whig oligarchy was neither as dominant nor the Tory party as enfeebled as Plumb has claimed and, moreover, that the underlying sources of political stability in eighteenth-century England were economic and social rather than strictly political. Other important works on eighteenth-century England are: John Brewer, *Party Ideology and Popular Politics at the Accession of George III* (New York, 1976); J. C. D. Clark, *English Society, 1688–1832: Ideology, Social Structure, and Political Practice During the Ancien Regime* (Cambridge, 1985), *Revolution and Rebellion: State and Society in England in the Seventeenth and Eighteenth Centuries* (Cambridge, 1986), and *The Language of Liberty, 1660–1852: Political*

Discourse and Social Dynamics in the Anglo-American World (Cambridge, 1994); Linda Colley, *Britons: Forging the Nation, 1707–1837*, (New Haven, Conn., 1992); H. T. Dickinson, *Liberty and Property: Political Ideology in Eighteenth Century Britain* (New York, 1977), and *The Politics of the People in Eighteenth Century Britain* (London, 1995); Paul Langford, *A Polite and Commercial People: England, 1727–1783* (Oxford, 1989); and Kathleen Wilson, *The Sense of the People: Politics, Culture and Imperialism in England, 1715–1785* (Cambridge, 1995).

2. Plumb, *Political Stability*, p. 2.

3. *Ibid.* While Colley, *In Defense of Oligarchy*, passim, argues persuasively that Robert Walpole and the circle of men around him were neither so powerful nor so effectively dominant as Plumb made them out to be, it certainly was the case that *parliamentary politics* during the period 1714–1760 were decidedly oligarchical.

4. The author who has written most perceptively about the "object of government" in early modern England is J. G. A. Pocock. See especially his *Virtue, Commerce, and History: Essays in Political Thought and History, Chiefly in the Eighteenth Century* (London, 1985); and *The Machiavellian Moment: Florentine Political Thought and the Atlantic Republican Tradition* (Princeton, N.J., 1975). Working within the same historiographical tradition, Eliga H. Gould, *The Persistence of Empire: British Political Culture in the Age of the American Revolution* (Chapel Hill, N.C., 2000), surveys the ways in which traditional attitudes toward liberty within England weathered the crisis of the American Revolution. An excellent brief summary of English traditions of liberty and citizenship is Richard D. Brown, *The Strength of a People: The Idea of an Informed Citizenry in America, 1650–1870* (Chapel Hill, N.C., 1996), pp. 1–25. For the American echoes of this long tradition see Gordon Wood, *The Creation of the American Republic, 1776–1787* (Chapel Hill, N.C., 1969), esp. pp. 53–70, *The Radicalism of the American Revolution* (New York, 1991), pp. 11–94. See also Jack P. Greene, "The Concept of Virtue in Late Colonial America," in Greene, *Imperatives, Behaviors and Identities: Essays in Early American Cultural History* (Charlottesville, Va., 1993), pp. 208–35.

5. Following Aristotle and Livy, Harrington argued that the only governments that could serve that common interest were those based on the rule of "laws and not of men." James Harrington, *The Commonwealth of Oceana* (1656), in Pocock, ed., *The Political Works of James Harrington* (Cambridge, 1977), p. 161. My understanding of Harrington, like that of so many historians, is founded upon the work of Pocock. See, for example, *Machiavellian Moment*, esp. pp. 383–400. "Machiavelli, Harrington and English Political Ideologies in the Eighteenth Century," *WMQ,* 22 (1965): 549–83; and "The Classical Theory of Deference," *American Historical Review,* 81 (1976).

6. William Blackstone, *Commentaries,* ed. John Taylor Coleridge, 16th ed. 4 vols. (London, 1825), 1, pp. 49–50, 154–55; John Adams to Mercy Warren, quoted in Forrest McDonald, *Novus Ordo Seclorum* (Lawrence, Kans., 1985), p. 72; Tom Paine, *The Rights of Man*, pt. 2, in Bruce Kuklick, *Paine: Political Writings* (Cambridge, 1989), pp. 167–68.

7. See especially the writings of Gordon Wood, *Creation of the American Republic,* pp. 3–45; and *Radicalism of the American Revolution*, pp. 11–94. See also Bernard Bailyn, *Ideological Origins of the American Revolution* (Cambridge, Mass. 1967), pp. 55–93, and *Origins of American Politics* (New York, 1967), pp. 3–58.

8. Tom Paine, *Common Sense,* ed. Isaac Kramnick (New York, 1986), pp. 65–66.

9. This point is made and elaborated most effectively by Edmund S. Morgan in *Inventing the People,* esp. pp. 55–121.

10. For extended discussions of these themes see Bailyn, *Ideological Origins,* pp. 55–93; and Wood, *Creation,* pp. 18–28. See also H. Trevor Colbourn, *The Lamp of Ex-*

perience: Whig History and the Intellectual Origins of the American Revolution (Chapel Hill, N.C., 1965).

11. John Adams to Mercy Otis Warren, July 20, 1807, *Massachusetts Historical Society Collections* 5th ser., 4, p. 353; John Adams to J. H. Tiffany, April 30, 1819, in Charles F. Adams, ed., *The Works of John Adams* (Boston, 1850–56), 10, pp. 377–78. The literature on republicanism—classical and modern—is vast. In addition to the previously cited works of Bernard Bailyn and Gordon Wood, see Joyce Appleby, *Capitalism and a New Social Order: The Republican Vision of the 1790s* (New York, 1984); J. G. A. Pocock, *Machiaveillian Moment,* esp. pp. 462–552. For historiographic overviews of the subject see two articles by Robert Shalhope, "Toward a Republican Synthesis: The Emergence of an Understanding of Republicanism in Early American Historiography," *WMQ,* 3d ser., 29 (1972): 49–80, and "Republicanism and Early American Historiography," *WMQ,* 39 (1982): 334–56; and Daniel Rogers, "Republicanism: The Career of a Concept," *Journal of American History* (hereafter as JAH) 79 (1992): 11–38.

12. Wood, *Radicalism,* p. 99.

13. David Hume, "The Rise and Progress of the Arts and Sciences," in Eugene F. Miller, ed. *Essays: Moral, Political and Literary* (Indianapolis, 195), p. 125. Baron de Montesquieu, Spirit of the Laws, trans. by Thomas Neumann (New York, 1949) pt. 1, bk. 5, ch. 19, p. 68, and bk. 5, ch. 9., as quoted in Wood, *Radicalism,* pp. 97–98.

14. Benjamin Rush to Ebenezer Hazard, 22 October 1768 in L. H. Butterfield, ed. Letters of Benjamin Rush (Princeton, 1951), I, 68, quoted in Wood, *Radicalism,* p. 15.

15. Edmund Burke, *Reflections,* Works of Edmund Burke (London, 1887), III, 308–10; [Samuel Adams], Committee of Correspondence of Boston, March, 31, 1773, Harry A. Cushing, ed., *The Writings of Samuel Adams* (New York, 1904–08), Papers, 3, p. 15.

16. For an elaboration of this point, see Morgan, *Inventing the People,* pp. 107–14; and Gould, *The Persistence of Empire,* pp. 14–30. See also Wood, *Creation,* pp. 10–18, and *Radicalism,* pp. 98–99.

17. Dr. William Douglass, *Summary, Historical and Political . . . of the British Settlements in North America* (1749–51), quoted in Bailyn, *Origins of American Politics,* p. 59.

18. Although the English king in the eighteenth century continued to have a theoretical claim to veto parliamentary legislation, in fact, none of the English sovereigns had dared to veto a bill since Queen Anne had done so in 1707. One of the clear lessons flowing from the Parliamentary Revolution of 1688 was that any sovereign who sought to impose his will over that of Parliament did so at his or her peril. See Morgan, *Inventing the People,* p. 140, and, for a more detailed analysis, Geoffrey Holmes, *British Politics in the Age of Anne* (London, 1967), pp. 82–115.

19. Leonard Labaree, *Royal Government in America: A Study of the British Colonial System before 1783* (New Haven, Conn. 1930); Ronald Butt, *The Power of Parliament* (New York, 1907), pp. 49 ff.; and George M. Trevelyan, *The English Revolution, 1688–89* (London, 1938), pp. 180–92.

20. For country party politicians in England, however, the parliamentary ascendancy seemed to have a bogus quality, for in their view the "robinarchy" of Robert Walpole and successive Whig political leaders seemed nearly as dangerous as the despotism of the Stuart kings. For an excellent discussion of the "robinarchy" see Bailyn, *Origins,* pp. 45–51.

21. Jack P. Greene, *The Quest for Power: The Lower Houses of Assembly in the Southern Royal Colonies, 1689–1776* (Chapel Hill, N.C., 1963), p. 9; Bailyn, *Origins of American Politics,* p. 96. There is an immense body of historical writing on the evolving institutional relationship between the royal and provincial governments. The starting

point is Labaree, *Royal Government in America*, already cited, but see also Charles M. Andrews, *The Colonial Period of American History* 4 vols., (New Haven, Conn. 1938); Arthur Berriedale Keith, *Constitutional History of the First British Empire* (Oxford, 1930); Lawrence Henry Gipson, *The British Empire Before the American Revolution*, 15 vols., (New York, 1936–67). The essays by John Murrin on "Anglicization" are particularly suggestive; see, in particular, Murrin, "Political Development," in Jack P. Greene and J. R. Pole, eds., *Colonial British North America: Essays in the New History of the Early Modern Era* (Baltimore, 1984), pp. 408–56; and Murrin, "The Great Inversion, or Court versus Country: A Comparison of the Revolution Settlements in England (1688–1721) and America (1776–1816)," in J. G. A. Pocock, *Three British Revolutions: 1641, 1688, 1776* (Princeton, N.J., 1980), pp. 368–453.

22. John Winthrop, "A Modell of Christian Charity, *Winthrop Papers*, 5 vols., (Boston, 1927–47), 2, p. 282. John Adams to James Warren, April 2, 1776, in Worthington C. Ford, ed., The Warren-Adams Letters. . . .", *Massachusetts Historical Society Collections*, 72–73 (1917–25), 1, p. 234; and George Sandys to Mr. Farriss, March, 1622–23 in Susan M. Kingsbury, ed., *Records of the Virginia Company of London*, 4 vols. (Washington D.C., 1906–35), 4, pp. 110–11. The relationship between social and political authority in early America is brilliantly analyzed by Bernard Bailyn, "Politics and Social Structure in Virginia," in James Morton Smith, ed., *Seventeenth Century America* (Chapel Hill, N.C., 1959), pp. 90–115.

23. For a concise and illuminating discussion of the logic and logical contradictions inherent in notions of divine right, see Edmund S. Morgan, *Inventing the People*, pp. 17–37.

24. Morgan, *Inventing the People*, pp. 66–97; although there were echoes of Leveller thought in that of the seventeenth-century commonwealthmen and that of radical Whigs in the eighteenth century, there were important differences among those groups as well. For the best explication of those differences, see Caroline Robbins, *The Eighteenth Century Commonwealthmen: Studies in the Transmission, Development, and Circumstance of English Liberal Thought from the Restoration of Charles II until the War with the Thirteen Colonies* (Cambridge, MA, 1959) pp. 3–19. Considering the subsequent importance of many of the ideas articulated by the Levellers, the scholarly literature on them and their movement is relatively slight. But see G. B. Macpherson, *The Political Theory of Possessive Individualism* (New York, 1964), pp. 107–59; G. E. Aylmer, ed., *The Levellers in the English Revolution* (New York, 1975), pp. 9–55; and, for a detailed, but somewhat disorganized account, the posthumously published, H. N. Brailsford, *The Levellers and the English Revolution* (Stanford, CA, 1961).

25. Wood, *Radicalism*, p. 104; see also Wood, *Creation*, pp. 65–70. For the English conception of virtue see Pocock, *Machiavellian Moment*, pp. 462–505; and *Virtue, Commerce, and History: Essays on Political Thought and History, Chiefly in the Eighteenth Century* (Cambridge, 1985), esp. pp. 37–50.

26. Harrington, *The Commonwealth of Oceana*, in Pocock, ed., *Political Works*, pp. 155–359; and Pocock, *Machiavellian Moment*, pp. 383–96.

27. Ibid. See also J. G. A. Pocock, "The Classical Theory of Deference," *American Historical Review* (hereafter AHR) 81 (1976): 516–23; and Richard R. Beeman, "Deference, Republicanism, and the Emergence of Popular Politics in Eighteenth Century America," *WMQ*, 49 (1992): 401–7.

28. John Cotton to Lord Say, as quoted in Morgan, *Inventing the People*, p. 45.

29. As Bernard Bailyn notes, democracy was "a word that denoted the lowest order of society as well as the form of government in which the commons ruled [and] was generally associated with the threat of civil disorder and the early assumption of power by a dictator. *Ideological Origins*, p. 282.

30. Harrington, Oceana, in *Political Works*, p. 261.

31. Pocock, "Classical Theory of Deference," pp. 516–17.

32. Ibid.

33. The first historian to use the concept of deference to describe social and political relations in England was Walter Bagehot, who in his study of *The English Constitution* (London, 1867), pp. 236–39, was much impressed by the genius of a political system in which the great "mass of the people yield obedience to a select few." For a more extensive discussion of the use of the concept in both English and American historiography, see Beeman, "Deference, Republicanism and Popular Politics," pp. 401–12; and David Spring, "Walter Bagehot and Deference," *AHR*, 21 (1976): 524–31.

34. Plumb, *Origins of Political Stability*, p. 188.

35. Dickinson, *Liberty and Property*, p. 165.

36. Dickinson, *Politics of the People*, pp. 31–32. For varying estimates of the voting population in eighteenth-century England, see J. H. Plumb, "The Growth of the Electorate in England from 1600–1715," *Past and Present* 45 (1969): 90–116; and Derek Hirst, *The Representative of the People: Voters and Voting in England Under the Early Stuarts* (Cambridge, 1975), p. 105.

37. Colley, *In Defense of Oligarchy*, pp. 19, 118. For more extended discussions of electoral practices in England, see ibid., passim; Sir Lewis Namier, *The Structure of Politics at the Accession of George III*, 2d ed. (London, 1970); and Geoffrey Holmes, *The Electorate and the National Will in the First Age of Party* (London, 1976).

38. Colley, *In Defense of Oligarchy*, pp. 118–19; and Dickinson, *Liberty and Property*, pp. 13–31.

39. Dickinson, *Liberty and Property*, pp. 184–92; and Colley, *In Defense of Oligarchy*, pp. 142–45.

40. Nicholas Rogers, *Whigs and Cities: Popular Politics in the Age of Walpole and Pitt* (Oxford, 1989); and Wilson, *Sense of the People*, pp. 315–440. These historians have made significant contributions to our understanding of the increasing political activism of middle-class and working-class Englishmen and have, in their investigations of nontraditional sites of political activity—e.g., taverns and coffeehouses—broadened our conception of "politics." Their contributions with respect to the increasing political radicalism of the lower orders of English society build on the work of an earlier group of English social historians, among them E. P. Thompson, *The Making of the English Working Class* (London, 1963); *Whigs and Hunters: The Origins of the Black Act* (New York, 1975); "Patrician Society, Plebian Culture," *Journal of Social History* 7 (1974): 382–405; and *Customs in Common: Studies in Traditional Popular Culture* (New York, 1991); and George Rude, *Wilkes and Liberty* (Oxford, England 1962).

Nearly all of the evidence that we have on "popular" political practices in England comes from large urban centers or, in the case of the work of Kathleen Wilson, sizeable provincial towns. London, with 700,000 residents, may have accounted for about 10 percent of England's total population in 1775, and provincial towns with populations over 5,000 may have constituted another 5 percent. In America in 1775 Boston, New York, Philadelphia, and perhaps Charleston were the only population centers that were comparable in size even to provincial towns like Norwich and Newcastle-on-Tyne, and the combined population of those towns, even on the eve of the Revolution—about 76,000—was less than 3 percent of the total American population of around 2.2 million. Lester J. Cappon, ed., *Atlas of Early American History: The Revolutionary Era, 1760–1790* (Princeton, 1976), pp. 97–100.

41. See Beeman, "Deference, Republicanism, and Popular Politics," pp. 401–11 for a discussion of the historiography of deference in the context of colonial American politics.

42. Alan Everitt, *Change in the Provinces: The Seventeenth Century* (Leicester, 1969), pp. 5–14.

43. Peter Laslett, *The World We Have Lost: England Before the Industrial Age,* 2d ed. (London, 1971), pp. 55–83.

44. Long ago Edmund S. Morgan wrote that "we probably know more about the Puritans than we ever would want to," and since that time the literature on the establishment and evolution of New England society has grown exponentially. The localistic, even insular, character of the New England communities—together with some of the stresses and strains undermining that character—are ably discussed, for example, in Kenneth Lockridge, *A New England Town: The First Hundred Years: Dedham, Massachusetts, 1636–1736* (New York, 1979); David Grayson Allen, *In English Ways* (Chapel Hill, N.C., 1981), passim; and Michael Zuckerman, *Peaceable Kingdoms: New England Towns in the Eighteenth Century* (New York, 1970).

45. Jack P. Greene, *Pursuits of Happiness: The Social Development of Early Modern British Colonies and the Formation of American Culture* (Chapel Hill, N.C., 1988), passim.

46. For the unsuccessful attempts of Virginia royal governors to shape the Virginia economy to suit English mercantilist needs, see John C. Rainbolt, *From Prescription to Persuasion: Manipulation of Seventeenth Century Virginia Economy* (Port Washington, N.Y. 1974), passim.

47. Richard J. Hooker, ed., *The Carolina Backcountry on the Eve of the Revolution: The Journal and Other Writings of Charles Woodmason, Anglican Itinerant* (Chapel Hill, N.C. 1953), p. 52.

48. Baron de Montesquieu, *Spirit of the Laws* (London, 1823), 1, p. 161.

Chapter 2. Eighteenth-Century Virginia: In Pursuit of the Deferential Ideal

1. Jack P. Greene, "Virtus et Libertas: Political Culture, Social Change, and the Origins of the American Revolution in Virginia, 1763–1776," in Jeffrey J. Crow and Larry E. Tise, eds., *The Southern Experience in the American Revolution* (Chapel Hill, N.C., 1978), pp. 55–108, uses the Virginia seal as his point of departure for an illuminating discussion of the role of virtue in defining the character of Virginia's ruling class, and my discussion here relies heavily on his. The illustration of the Virginia seal reprinted here was slightly revised in 1779, substituting for *Deus nobis. . . .* the single word *Perseverando,* an impulse no doubt propelled by the dark days of the Revolution before Yorktown. The earliest account of the Virginia seal is by Edmund Randolph, in his *History of Virginia,* Arthur Shaffer, ed. (Charlottesville, Va., 1970), p. 76. See also W. Edwin Hemphill, "The Symbolism of Our Seal," *Virginia Cavalcade,* 2 (1952): 27–33.

2. Charles Syndor, *Gentlemen Freeholders: Political Practices in Washington's Virginia* (Chapel Hill, N.C., 1952), though he did not actually use the word deference, was perhaps the first historian on eighteenth-century Virginia to incorporate the concept.

3. For almost a half century nearly every historian of early American politics has made conspicuous use of *The Candidates,* often for radically different purposes. Sydnor, in *Gentlemen Freeholders,* esp. pp. 39–47, 149–50, used the play to illustrate the simultaneous operation of democratic and aristocratic forces on Virginia politics. J. R. Pole, in "Historians and the Problem of Early American Democracy," *AHR,* 67 (1962): 626–46, and *Political Representation in England and the Origins of the American Republic* (Berkeley, Calif., 1966), pp. 159–69, was the first to explicitly link the behavior described in the play to a deferential system; he described the play as "as

keen a commentary on its subject as could be found in any treatise," and used it to demonstrate the persistence of the deferential ideal not only in Virginia but in American politics more generally. Robert E. and B. Katherine Brown, *Virginia, 1705–1786: Democracy or Aristocracy?* (East Lansing, Mich., 1964), pp. 212, 236–37, view the play, anachronistically, as a description of democratic politics at work. Most recently, John Gilman Kolp, *Gentlemen and Freeholders: Electoral Politics in Colonial Virginia* (Baltimore, 1998), pp. 13–15, 35, 166, 189, has interpreted *The Candidates* in a way that emphasizes the considerable diversity of belief and behavior that existed within Virginia's political culture. See also Edmund S. Morgan, *Inventing the People*, p. 185, and *American Slavery, American Freedom: The Ordeal of Colonial Virginia* (New York, 1975), pp. 363–64. The full text of *The Candidates* is in Jay B. Hubbell and Douglass Adair, "Robert Munford's *The Candidates*," *WMQ*, 3d ser., 5 (1948): 227–57.

4. Ibid., pp. 256–57.

5. It seems likely that the only person Munford thought worthy of true gentry status was himself. For some of the gap between the real and the ideal in Munford's work see Richard R. Beeman, "Robert Munford and the Political Culture of Frontier Virginia," *Journal of American Studies* 12 (1978): 169–83.

6. John Pendleton Kennedy and H. R. McIlwaine, eds., *Journals of the House of Burgesses of Virginia* (hereafter *JHB.*), 13 vols. (Richmond, Va., 1905–15) 1727–40: 9, 29. The best brief treatments of Robinson's life are David John Mays, *Edmund Pendleton*, 2 vols. (Richmond, Va. 1952): 1, pp. 63–65, 174–78; and Thomas Perkins Abernathy's sketch in Dumas Malone, et al. eds, *Dictionary of American Biography*, 20 vol.s (New York, 1935), 16, p. 46.

7. Jackson Turner Main, "The Virginia 100," *WMQ*, 3d ser., 11 (1954): 354–84.

8. Mays, *Pendleton* 1, pp. 64–65; and Abernathy, "John Robinson," *Dictionary of American Biography*, 16, p. 46.

9. Francis Faquier to the Board of Trade, April 10, 1759, quoted in Jack P. Greene, "The Attempt to Separate the Offices of Speaker and Treasurer in Virginia, 1758–1766," *Virginia Magazine of History and Biography* (hereafter *VMHB*) 71 (1963): 12. For a contrasting view of Robinson, see Joseph A. Ernst, "The Robinson Scandal Redivivus: Money, Debts, and Politics in Revolutionary Virginia," *VMHB* 77 (1969): 146–73.

10. Randolph, *History of Virginia*, pp. 173–4.

11. Jack P. Greene, ed., *The Diary of Landon Carter*, 2 vols. (Charlottesville, Va., 1965), 1, pp. 82, 85.

12. *Virginia Gazette*, May 16, 1766.

13. Douglas Southall Freeman, *George Washington: A Biography*, 7 vols. (New York, 1948–57), 2, p. 147.

14. For the full documentation on the election of 1758, see *The Papers of George Washington: Colonial Series*, 6 vols. to date (Charlottesville, Va., 1983), 5, pp. 332–43.

15. The merchant accounts for Washington's liquor expenditures are printed in *Washington Papers: Colonial Series*, 5, pp. 331–33.

16. Washington to Wood, July 28, 1758, ibid., p. 349.

17. Captain Robert Stewart to Washington, February 13, 1761, in Stanislaus M. Hamilton, *Letters to George Washington and Accompanying Papers*, 5 vols. (Boston and New York, 1898–1902), 2, p. 202; and *GW to Captain Van Swearingen, May 15, 1761*, in John C. Fitzpatrick, ed., *The Writings of George Washington*, from the *Original Manuscript Sources, 1745–1799*, 39 vols. (Washington, D.C., 1931–44); 2, pp. 358–59.

18. William Byrd II to Charles, Earl of Orrery, July 5, 1726, in "Virginia Council Journals, 1726–1753," *VMHB* 32 (1924): 27.

19. The tensions and contradictions inherent in a patriarchal world that de-

pended on the coerced labor of unfree Africans are both obvious and exceptionally difficult to identify precisely. Among the historians who have explored that subject are Kathleen M. Brown, *Good Wives, Nasty Wenches, and Anxious Patriarchs: Gender, Race, and Power in Colonial Virginia* (Chapel Hill, N.C., 1996), esp. pp. 251–53, 318–66; Timothy H. Breen, *Tobacco Culture: The Mentality of the Great Tidewater Planters on the Eve of Revolution* (Princeton, N.J., 1985); Rhys Isaac, *The Transformation of Virginia, 1740–1790* (Chapel Hill, N.C., 1982), esp. pp. 330–446; Alan Kulikoff, *Tobacco and Slaves: The Development of Southern Culture in the Chesapeake, 1680–1800* (Chapel Hill, N.C., 1986); Morgan, *American Slavery, American Freedom,* esp. pp. 295–388; Philip Morgan, *Slave Counterpoint: Black Culture in the Eighteenth Century Chesapeake and Low Country* (Chapel Hill, N.C., 1988), esp. pp. 257–99; Gerald W. Mullen, *Flight and Rebellion: Slave Resistance in Eighteenth Century Virginia* (New York, 1972); and Mechal Sobel, *The World They Made Together: Black and White Values in Eighteenth Century Virginia* (Princeton, N.J., 1987).

20. Greene, *Landon Carter Diary,* 1, pp. 3–61 has an excellent overview of Landon Carter's life and lineage. For other members of the Carter family see Louis B. Wright, *The First Gentlemen of Virginia: Intellectual Qualities of the Early Colonial Ruling Class* (San Marino, Calif., 1940), pp. 248–85; and Richard B. Morton, *Robert Carter of Nomini Hall: A Virginia Tobacco Planter of the Eighteenth Century* (Williamsburg, Va., 1941).

21. Greene, *Carter Diary,* 1, pp. 3–6. The precise number of Carter's slaves when he began his career is not known, but the inventory of his estate taken at his death in 1779 listed over 400 slaves. Lucille Griffith, *The Virginia House of Burgesses, 1750–1774,* rev. ed. (University, Ala. 1970), p. 83.

22. Greene, *Carter Diary,* 1, pp. 25, 27; 2, p. 668.

23. *JHB* (1742–47) 34–35; accounts of the election are in Robert E. and B. Katherine Brown, *Virginia, 1705–1786: Democracy or Aristocracy?* (East Lansing, Mich., 1964), pp. 157–58.

24. Brown, *Virginia, 1705–1786,* pp. 157–58. Ibid.

25. Greene, *Carter Diary,* 1, pp. 27, 286–92.

26. Greene, *Carter Diary,* 1, pp. 116–17.

27. Quoted in Greene, *Carter Diary,* 1, p. 39. Of course, in comparing the sloth and dissipation of the Virginia ruling elite with a virtuous and decorous parliamentary elite, Carter was constructing a highly idealized and inaccurate picture of the conduct of members of Parliament.

28. Ibid., 1, pp. 77–78, 86, 87, 89.

29. Griffith, *House of Burgesses,* p. 72.

30. Ibid., pp. 85–87.

31. Greene, ed., *Carter Diary,* 2, pp. 1008–9.

32. Brown, *Virginia,* pp. 197–203; Griffith, *House of Burgesses,* p. 87.

33. Sydnor, *Gentlemen Freeholders,* pp. 74–85; Greene, *Quest for Power,* pp. 467–74.

34. George Webb, *The Office and Authority of a Justice of the Peace* (Williamsburg, 1736), pp. 200–02, quoted in Jack P. Greene, "Society, Ideology, and Politics: An Analysis of the Political Culture of Mid-Eighteenth Century Virginia," in Greene, ed., *Negotiated Authorities: Essays on Colonial Political and Constitutional History* (Charlottesville, Va., 1994), p. 269.

35. Kolp, *Gentlemen and Freeholders,* pp. 119–120.

36. Sydnor, *Gentleman Freeholders,* pp. 76–83, 100–101, 111–12; Albert O. Porter, *County Government in Virginia: A Legislative History* (New York, 1947), pp. 9–226.

37. A. G. Roeber, *Faithful Magistrates and Republican Lawyers: Creators of Virginia Legal Culture, 1680–1810* (Chapel Hill, N.C., 1981), esp. pp. 73–159. For the importance of the petitioning process, which tied localities to provincial leaders in

Williamsburg, see Raymond C. Bailey, *Popular Influence on Public Policy: Petitioning in Eighteenth Century Virginia* (Westport, Conn., 1979).

38. As we will see, there is controversy among historians about the extent of the franchise in nearly every colony throughout colonial America. The initial source of that controversy has been statements by Progressive historians such as Charles Beard and Carl Becker that suffrage was severely restricted, even among free white males, throughout all of America (see, for example, Charles A. Beard and Mary Beard, *The Rise of American Civilization*, 2 vols. (New York, 1927), 1, p. 110; and Carl Becker, *Beginnings of the American People* (Boston, 1915), pp. 165–66. Charles Sydnor, in *Gentlemen Freeholders*, pp. 34–38, estimated that more than half of Virginia's free white males were disenfranchised by a combination of property and religious requirements. Robert Brown, who made it his life's work to prove that the Progressive historians had greatly understated the democratic character of American political life, argues that over 85 percent of the colony's free white males were able to vote in provincial elections (Brown, *Virginia*, pp. 136–47). Most recently, John Kolp, *Gentlemen and Freeholders*, pp. 38–49, has done an extensive analysis of voting qualifications and property ownership in selected Virginia counties and has concluded that about two-thirds of Virginia's free adult males attained freeholder status by the mid-eighteenth century.

39. Kolp, *Gentlemen and Freeholders*, pp. 62, arrives at this calculation based on an analysis of 491 elections during that period.

40. Ibid., pp. 49–58; Kolp, "The Dynamics of Electoral Competition in Pre-Revolutionary Virginia," *WMQ*, 3d ser., 49 (October 1992): 666–68.

41. Ibid., p. 657.

42. Jack P. Greene, "Legislative Turnover in British America, 1696–1775: A Quantitative Analysis," *WMQ*, 3d ser., 38 (July 1981): 461.

43. *Cato's Letters; or, Essays on Liberty, Civil and Religious . . .* , 3d ed. (London, 1733), 1, pp. 182–83.

44. Alison Olson, "Eighteenth Century Colonial Legislatures and their Constituents," *Journal of American History* (hereafter *JAH*) 79 (1992): 543–67. Professor Olson suggests that this increase in petitions to the legislature was a reflection of a decline in the ability of local governments to satisfy constituent needs. In fact, though, given the close connection between local officials and the burgesses who represented each locality, it seems more likely that the increase in petitioning was a reflection of a much more active government at all levels. For the general pattern of petitioning across the colonies, see Appendix 4, p. 297.

45. Kolp, *Gentlemen and Freeholders*, p. 42.

46. Bailey, *Petitioning in Eighteenth Century Virginia*, pp. 43–45.

47. Raymond Bailey has analyzed the signatories on a sampling of prerevolutionary petitions and finds that to a remarkable extent they represented a cross section of the whole population of a given locality. Ibid., pp. 41–46, 68–89, 137–50.

48. Ibid., pp. 159–65.

49. Olson, "Eighteenth Century Colonial Legislatures," p. 563 calculates the laws enacted for a dozen colonies from 1730–35, 1740–45 and 1760–65. For New York they are, respectively, 13.3, 25.5, and 27.0. For Pennsylvania, 4.3, 5, and 12.1. For Virginia, 31.3, 31.6, and 37.8. For the legislative activity of other colonies, see Appendix 2, p. 295.

50. Bailey, *Petitioning in Eighteenth Century Virginia*, pp. 90–113.

51. Greene, *Quest for Power*, passim.; and Greene, "Political Mimesis: A Consideration of the Historical and Cultural Roots of Legislative Behavior in the British Colonies in the Eighteenth Century," *AHR* 75 (1969–70): 337–67.

52. *JHB*, 1742–49: 406–7.

53. Quoted in Morgan, *American Slavery, American Freedom*, p. 258.

54. Francis Faquier to the Board of Trade, April 10, 1759, quoted in Greene, "Attempt to Separate Offices of Speaker and Treasurer," *VMHB*, 71 (1963); 12. For Jefferson's relationship with the royal governor see Dumas Malone, *Jefferson the Virginian* (Boston, 1948), pp. 73–74.

55. Rhys Isaac, "Evangelical Revolt: The Nature of the Baptists' Challenge to the Traditional Order in Virginia, 1765 to 1775," *WMQ*, 3d ser., 31 (1974): 362. For a fuller discussion which places the Baptist insurgence in the larger context of Virginia's social and economic development, see Isaac, *The Transformation of Virginia*, esp. pp. 148–54, 161–77.

56. Because the most visible manifestation of the "evangelical revolt" was seen in the Virginia backcountry—among Baptists of the Southside and southwest and among Presbyterians in parts of the Piedmont and the Shenendoah Valley—most of the discussion of the intersection of politics and religion will be found in chapter 6. See, for example, Richard R. Beeman, *The Evolution of the Southern Backcountry: A Case Study of Lunenburg County, Virginia, 1746–1832* (Philadelphia, 1984), pp. 97–119.

57. Quoted in Isaac, "Evangelical Revolt," p. 347.

58. There is no single adequate overview of religious life in eighteenth-century Virginia, and the history of dissenting religious groups other than the Baptists, about which much has been written, remains very sketchy. In addition to the work of Rhys Isaac, previously cited, Wesley M. Gewehr, *The Great Awakening in Virginia, 1740–1790* (Durham, N.C., 1930), gives a general account of the rise of Protestant dissenting religion. Mark A. Beliles, "The Christian Communities, Religious Revivals, and Political Culture of the Central Virginia Piedmont, 1737–1813," in Garrett Ward Sheldon and Daniel L. Dreisbach, eds., *Religion and Political Culture in Jefferson's Virginia* (Lanham, Md., 2000), pp. 3–41, is a brief overview for one region of Virginia. For the Anglicans see Joan Gundersen, *The Anglican Ministry in Virginia, 1723–1776* (New York, 1989). For the German Lutherans see A. G. Roeber, *Palatines, Liberty, and Property: German Lutherans in Colonial British America* (Baltimore, 1993), pp. 101–108, 140–52.

59. Malone, *Jefferson the Virginian*, pp. 50–60; and J. E. Morpurgo, *Their Majesties' Royall Colledge: William and Mary in the Seventeenth and Eighteenth Centuries* (Williamsburg, 1976), pp. 123–26. For the state of education in Virginia more generally see Lawrence Cremin, *American Education: The Colonial Experience, 1607–1763* (New York, 1970), pp. 527–34.

60. Linda Kerber, *Women of the Early Republic: Intellect and Idealogy in Revolutionary America* (Chapel Hill, N.C., 1980); Marybeth Norton, *Liberty's Daughters: The Revolutionary Experience of American Women, 1750–1800* (Boston, 1980); and Cynthia Kierner, *Beyond the Household: Women's Place in the Early South, 1700–1835* (Ithaca, N.Y. 1998).

61. This evidence and the discussion that follows are drawn from the illuminating essay, by John. G. Kolp, and Terri L. Snyder, "Gender, Property, and Voting Rights," in Christopher L. Tomlins and Bruce H. Mann, *The Many Legalities of Early America* (Chapel Hill, N.C., 2001), pp. 272–92.

62. Kierner, *Beyond the Household*, p. 20.

63. Brown and Brown, *Virginia*, pp. 138–39.

64. "Munford's *The Candidates*, p. 240. Kolp and Snyder, "Gender," pp. 280–82.

65. Kolp and Snyder, "Gender," pp. 272–73, 288, 292.

66. Cynthia Kierner, "Genteel Balls and Republican Parades: Gender and Early Southern Rituals, 1677–1826," *VMHB* 104 (1996): 185–210.

67. Cynthia Kierner, *Southern Women in Revolution, 1776–1800: Personal and Politi-*

cal Narratives (Columbia, S.C., 1998), pp. xx–xxii. Kierner notes a dramatic increase in petitioning in general once the Revolution gets under way, but she notes, in particular, the paucity of petitions from females before the Revolution. Only 11 of the 239 petitions heard by North Carolina's provincial assembly and 21 of the 690 sent to the South Carolina House of Commons between 1750 and 1775 were from women.

68. The historians who have argued most persuasively about these underlying states of tension are Brown, *Good Wives*, esp. pp. 319–66; Woody Holton, *Forced Founders: Indians, Debtors, Slaves and the Making of the American Revolution in Virginia* (Chapel Hill, N.C., 2000); and Michael McDonnell, "Popular Mobilization and Political Culture in Revolutionary Virginia: The Failure of the Minutemen and the Revolution from Below," *JAH*, 85 (1998): 946–81.

69. Patrick Henry to Robert Pleasants, in Robert Vaux, *Memories of the Life of Anthony Benezet* (Philadelphia, 1817), pp. 55–57.

70. The contradictions inherent in a society that espoused so emphatically doctrines of liberty and at the same time depended on chattel slavery have been thoroughly explored by historians. Perhaps the best introduction to that problem is Morgan, *American Slavery, American Freedom*, esp. pp. 295–388, but see note 19 for additional works that explore this vexing subject.

71. Perhaps the best account of the Robinson affair is in Mays, Pendleton, 1, pp. 174–208. See also Greene, "Attempt to Separate Office of Speaker and Treasurer," and, for a more critical treatment of the same subject, Joseph Ernst, "The Robinson Scandal Redivivus: Money, Debt and Politics in Revolutionary Virginia" *VMHB*, 67 (1969): 146–73.

Chapter 3. The Character of the Good Ruler in Eighteenth-Century Massachusetts

1. By far the most insightful portrait of Hutchinson is Bernard Bailyn, *The Ordeal of Thomas Hutchinson* (Cambridge, 1974). For Hutchinson's early life and background see Bailyn, pp. 9–34. See also the excellent extended biographical sketch in Clifford K. Shipton, *Sibley's Harvard Graduates*, 8 (Boston, 1951), pp. 149–217.

2. Shipton, 8, p. 150. For a discussion of the ethic behind the Harvard system of class ranks see Robert Zemsky, *Merchants, Farmers, and River Gods: An Essay on Eighteenth Century American Politics* (Boston, 1971), pp. 35–38.

3. Zemsky, *Merchants, Farmers, and River Gods*, p. 38.

4. Thomas Hutchinson to Israel Williams, August 8, 1759; Francis Bernard to Thomas Hutchinson, November 17, 1769, both quoted in Bailyn, *Hutchinson*, pp. 17–18.

5. Thomas Pownall to the Earl of Halifax, September 4, 1757, quoted in Bailyn, *Hutchinson*, p. 13.

6. Richard Bushman, *King and People in Provincial Massachusetts* (Chapel Hill, N.C., 1985), pp. 3–7, 122–32; Wood, *Creation*, pp. 53–65. John Adams to Mercy Otis Warren, quoted in Forrest McDonald, *Novus Ordo Seclorum*, p. 72.

7. St. George Tucker to William Wirt, September 25, 1815, quoted in Greene, *Negotiated Authorities*, p. 281.

8. Bushman, *King and People*, p. 13.

9. Ibid., pp. 11–12. For the early evolution of relations between Crown and province in Massachusetts see George Lee Haskins, *Law and Authority in Early Massachusetts: A Study in Tradition and Design* (New York, 1960).

10. Bushman, *King and People*, esp. pp. 88–134.

11. Address of the House to the King, November 22, 1728, quoted in ibid., p. 124.

12. Ibid., p. 89.

13. Alexis d'Tocqueville, *Democracy in America* (New York, 1945), 1, p. 65.

14. The phrase is from Kenneth Lockridge's study of local government in Dedham, *A New England Town: The First Hundred Years: Dedham, Massachusetts, 1636–1736* (New York, 1970), p. 38.

15. Michael Zuckerman, *Peaceable Kingdoms: New England Towns in the Eighteenth Century* (New York, 1970). Zuckerman uses the term "ruling fathers" in *Peaceable Kingdoms* p. 116.

16. Like Puritanism itself, New England political life has attracted a disproportionate amount of attention from historians, some bent on establishing the region's reputation as a cradle of democracy and others intent on proving just the opposite. James Truslow Adams, *The Founding of New England* (Boston, 1921), and Thomas Jefferson Wertenbaker, *The Puritan Oligarchy* (New York, 1947), are perhaps the most influential of those historians arguing that New England was the seedbed of an antidemocratic oligarchy that little resembled modern America. The most vociferous assault on that notion was mounted by Robert E. Brown, *Middle Class Democracy and the Revolution in Massachusetts, 1691–1780* (Ithaca, N.Y., 1955). More nuanced, though often conflicting, accounts have been offered by Lockridge, *A New England Town*; John Murrin, "Review Essay," *History and Theory: Studies in the Philosophy of History* 11 (1972), pp. 226–75; and John Dinkin, "Provincial Massachusetts: A Deferential or a Democratic Society?" (Ph.D. diss., Columbia University, 1971).

17. Ratable estate was defined as the assessed value, as opposed to the market value, of a person's estate. Although there continues to be controversy over the extent of the suffrage in Massachusetts, even severe critics of Robert and B. Katherine Brown agree that they have done more to explain the intricacies of the franchise in that colony than any other historians. See both Robert Brown, *Middle Class Democracy*, pp. 21–37, 79–99; and B. Katherine Brown, "Freemanship in Puritan Massachusetts," *AHR* 59 (1954): 865–83; "Puritan Democracy: A Case Study," *Mississippi Valley Historical Review* 50 (1963–64): 377–96; and "Puritan Democracy in Dedham, Massachusetts: Another Case Study," *WMQ* 24 (1967): 378–96. More recent work, while lowering the Brown's estimates on the extent of the suffrage, does not dramatically change those estimates. See, for example, Zemsky, *Merchants, Farmers, and River Gods*, pp. 230–52; and Zuckerman, *Peaceable Kingdoms*, pp. 164–65, 187–90, 190–200.

18. Zuckerman, *Peaceable Kingdoms*, pp. 206–8, 274–76; Dinkin, "Provincial Massachusetts," pp. 47–53; and Lockridge, *A New England Town*, pp. 43–46, 119–26, present contradictory evidence on length of service among selectmen in the eighteenth century. Zuckerman, who samples selectmen service in fifteen towns in Massachusetts, concludes that tenure of service among selectmen was relatively short—usually under five years—and that those short terms were in part the consequence of decidedly undeferential attitudes on the part of the voters. Dinkin, who argues for the persistence of deferential attitudes in Massachusetts, presents evidence indicating that the length of service among selectmen was increasing as the eighteenth century progressed, often averaging ten years or more. Lockridge's study of Dedham, by contrast, indicates that average terms of service among selectmen in that town were declining from the seventeenth to the eighteenth century.

While it is difficult to compare or reconcile these pieces of conflicting evidence, many of them collected across different periods of time and for different towns, it does appear that neither Zuckerman's picture of an aggressively independent electorate nor Dinkin's of a submissive and deferential one is wholly on the mark.

19. Zuckerman, *Peaceable Kingdoms*, pp. 201–2: Lockridge, *New England Town*, pp. 122–23.

20. John Adams, *Defense of the Constitutions of the United States*, 3 vols. (Philadelphia, 1797), 1, pp. 110–11.

21. John Murrin, "Review Essay," *History and Theory* 11, p. 268.

22. Ibid., pp. 254–55.

23. Robert Dinkin, *Voting in Provincial America: A Study of Elections in the Thirteen Colonies, 1689–1776* (Westport, Conn. 1977), pp. 168–73; Brown, *Middle Class Democracy*, pp. 65–66; John Waters, *The Otis Family in Provincial and Revolutionary Massachusetts* (Chapel Hill, N.C., 1968), pp. 83–84.

24. David Conroy, *In Public Houses: Drink and the Revolution of Authority in Colonial Massacusetts* (Chapel Hill, N.C., 1995), pp. 190, 196–7. The complaints from Adams appear in *Diary and Autobiography* 1, pp. 96, 128–29, 211, 224.

25. Conroy, *In Public Houses*, pp. 196–249, infers the connection between tavern keeping and political power, but I am more impressed by the absence of evidence making that connection at least in those Massachusetts towns other than Boston. The case for the radicalizing influence of taverns is much stronger when one looks at America's seaport cities, especially as the conflict with Great Britain intensified. Another noteworthy attempt to uncover the roots of popular politics in New England is Christopher Grasso, *A Speaking Aristocracy: Transforming Public Discourse in Eighteenth Century Connecticut*, (Chapel Hill, N.C., 1999). Drawing on notions of "public discourse," Grasso's evidence on the democratization of political discourse is more impressive for the period of the early republic than it is for the prerevolutionary period.

26. Dinkin, *Voting in Provincial America*, p. 8.

27. Waters, *Otis Family*, pp. 79–86. In his sampling of representation in eleven Massachusetts counties during the years 1742–1758, Waters discovered that incumbents were reelected in about 60 percent of the cases, former members of the House in another 10 percent, leaving 40 percent of the seats to newcomers.

28. Ibid., pp. 86–87. Zemsky, *Merchants, Farmers, and River Gods*, pp. 17–18.

29. Zemsky, *Merchants, Farmers, and River Gods*, pp. 28–38.

30. Ibid.

31. Virtually all historians of colonial Massachusetts agree on the localist ethic that prevailed in the colony. Michael Zuckerman, *Peaceable Kingdoms*, pp. 261–64 has made the most emphatic case for the prevalence of that localism.

32. Nearly all colonial legislatures received petitions from individuals pertaining to their own personal circumstances as well as petitions on matters of public policy from groups.

33. Olson, "Eighteenth Century Colonial Legislatures," pp. 543–67.

34. Dinkin, "Provincial Massachusetts," p. 133.

35. Ibid., pp. 128–50.

36. Quoted in Zemsky, *Merchants, Farmers, and River Gods*, p. 280; see also Morgan, *Inventing the People*, pp. 216–18.

37. Bushman, *King and People*, pp. 260–61.

38. John Brook, *The Heart of the Commonwealth: Society and Political Culture in Worcester County, Massachusetts, 1713–1861* (Cambridge, Mass., 1989), pp. 97–128, has argued that, at least in the southeastern portion of Worcester County, there did exist a prerevolutionary political culture in which representatives based their authority not on property and personal virtue, but on service to constituent interests.

39. Morgan, *Inventing America*, pp. 216–18; Zemsky, *Merchants, Farmers, and River Gods*, pp. 276–81.

40. All quotes are from Hutchinson, *Dairy*, 1, pp. 49–50, in Dinkin, "Provincial Massachusetts," pp. 139–40. See also Brown, *Middle Class Democracy*, pp. 53–54; Bushman, *King and People*, p. 148.

41. The best sources on Williams's social background and political activities are Shipton, ed., *Harvard Graduates*, 8, pp. 303–33; Kevin Michael Sweeney, "River Gods and Related Minor Deities: The Williams Family and the Connecticut River Valley, 1637–1790," (Ph.D. diss., Yale University, 1986); Ronald Snell, "Ambitious of Honor and Places: The Magistracy of Hampshire County, Massachusetts, 1692–1760," in Bruce C. Daniels, ed., *Power and Status: Officeholding in Colonial America* (Middletown, Conn., 1986), pp. 17–35; and Gregory Nobles, *Divisions Throughout the Whole: Politics and Society in Hampshire County, Massachusetts, 1740–1775* (New York, 1983), pp. 30–35.

42. Snell, "Ambitious of Honor and Places." See also Zemsky, *Merchants, Farmers, and River Gods*, pp. 32–33; and Nobles, *Division Throughout the Whole*, pp. 19–50.

43. Robert J. Taylor, *Western Massachusetts in the Revolution* (Providence, R.I., 1954), p. 25.

44. Sweeney, "River Gods," pp. 496–515, 538–69; and Nobles, *Divisions Throughout the Whole*, pp. 169–70.

45. Nobles, *Divisions Throughout the Whole*, pp. 176–78. Nobles's analysis of the political culture of Hampshire County emphasizes the extent to which the apparent "deference" on the part of ordinary citizens was in fact founded on the exertion and manipulation of economic and family power by members of the leading families. The decisiveness of the collapse of Williams's power provides compelling evidence for that point of view.

46. Ibid.; Taylor, *Western Massachusetts*, pp. 64–67.

47. Waters, *Otis Family*, pp. 3–28.

48. Ibid., pp. 29–39.

49. Ibid., pp. 40–60.

50. Ibid., pp. 62–63; Shipton, *Harvard Graduates*, 5, pp. 339–40.

51. Waters, *Otis Family*, pp. 64–77. John Adams's assessment is in Lyman Butterfield, ed., *Diary and Autobiography of John Adams*, June 8, 1762 (Cambridge, Mass., 1961), 1, p. 227.

52. Ibid., pp. 75–104.

53. James Otis Sr. memorandum, ca. August 1757, quoted in ibid., p. 105.

54. Ibid., pp. 105–8.

55. Ibid., pp. 111–19; Peter Oliver, *Origins and Progress of the American Rebellion*, Douglass Adair and John A. Schutz, eds. (San Marino, Calif., 1961), pp. 28, 35.

56. For accounts of the activities of James Otis Sr. and Jr. in the Revolution see Waters, *Otis Family*, pp. 132–203; Ellen Brennan, "James Otis: Recreant and Patriot," *New England Quarterly*, 12 (1939): 691–715; and Edmund S. and Helen M. Morgan, *The Stamp Act Crisis: Prologue to Revolution* (Chapel Hill, N.C.), pp. 140–43.

57. Greene, *Pursuits of Happiness*, p. 25.

58. Zemsky, *Merchants, Farmers, and River Gods*, pp. 35–38.

59. Morgan, *Inventing the People*, pp. 258–59; Elisha Douglass, *Rebels and Democrats: The Struggle for Equal Political Rights and Majority Rule During the Revolution* (Chapel Hill, N.C., 1955), pp. 137–213; Marc Kruman, *Between Authority and Liberty: State Constitution Making in Revolutionary America* (Chapel Hill, N.C., 1997), pp. 15–16, 30–33, 69–70, 92–94, 106–7, 125–26, 148, 158; and Ronald Formisano, *The Transformation of Political Culture: Massachusetts Parties, 1790–1840* (New York, 1983), pp. 29–30.

Chapter 4. Uneasy Oligarchs: The Manor Lords of Upstate New York

1. Johnson's colorful life has attracted the attention of several biographers, the most recent of whom is James Thomas Flexner, *Lord of the Mohawks: A Biography of*

Sir William Johnson (Boston, 1979). See also Arthur Pound, *Johnson of the Mohawks* (New York, 1950); and Flora Seymour, *Lords of the Valley: Sir William Johnson and His Mohawk Brothers* (New York, 1930). Unfortunately, an up-to-date, scholarly biography of this extraordinary Anglo-American does not exist.

2. John C. Guzzardo, "Democracy Along the Mohawk: An Election Return, 1773," *New York History* 51 (1976): 35. My own account of Johnson's extraordinary influence in New York politics closely follows that of Guzzardo.

3. Pound, *Johnson*, p. 138.

4. Flexner, *Lord of the Mohawks*, pp. 307–9.

5. Sir William Johnson to H. Glen, December 28, 1772, quoted in Guzzardo, "Democracy Along the Mohawk," pp. 51–52. The account of the election itself is also from Guzzardo, pp. 33–52.

6. Ibid., p. 49.

7. Hutchinson most often resolved these internal conflicts by choosing to serve the interests of the Crown, but he most always justified that decision—to himself as well as to others—by claiming that he had the best interests of the people at heart. See, for example, Bailyn, *Hutchinson*, esp. pp. 39–45, 63–64, 79–80.

8. Carl Becker, *The History of Political Parties in the Province of New York, 1760–1775*, (Madison, Wiss., 1909), p. 8.

9. Historical interpretations of the landholding system and social structure of the Hudson River valley have, since the time of Carl Becker, been dominated by historians writing in the Progressive and neo-Progressive traditions. In addition to Becker, see Edward Countryman, *A People in Revolution: The American Revolution and Political Society in New York, 1760–1790* (Baltimore, 1981); and Irving Mark, *Agrarian Conflict in Colonial New York* (New York, 1940). For a more benign view of the operation of the manor system see Sung Bok Kim, *Landlord and Tenant in Colonial New York: Manorial Society, 1664–1775* (Chapel Hill, N.C., 1978).

10. The quotation is from Alan Tully, *Forming American Politics: Ideals, Interests, and Institutions in Colonial New York and Pennsylvania* (Baltimore, 1994), p. 333. Tully, pp. 331–34, has argued that though there was some sentiment in the eighteenth century to make more of the local offices elective, for the most part, local oligarchs like Johnson were able to resist that demand.

11. Peter Warren to George Clinton, August 22, 1742, quoted in Nicholas Varga, *New York Government and Politics during the Mid-Eighteenth Century* (New York, 1960), p. 21; Tully, *Forming American Politics*, pp. 314–15.

12. Becker, *Political Parties*, p. 15.

13. The most influential interpretation of the factious character of New York society and politics is Patricia Bonomi, *A Factious People: Politics and Society in Colonial New York* (New York, 1971). Benjamin N. Newcomb, *Political Partisanship in the American Middle Colonies, 1700–1776* (Baton Rouge, La., 1995), argues that the partisan politics of colonial New York were part of a pattern common to all of the middle colonies and that the political factionalism of the early eighteenth century gave way by the 1730s to a more stable form of protoparty organization. See also Tully, *Forming American Politics*, especially pp. 126–45, 165–82, 213–52, 400–407; Mary Lou Lustig, *Privilege and Prerogative: New York's Provincial Elite, 1710–1776* (Madison, Wis., Teaneck, N.J., 1995), passim; and Milton Klein, *The Politics of Diversity: Essays on the History of Colonial New York* (Port Washington, N.Y.), 1974. For the ethnic and religious foundation of some of New York's political conflict see Randall Balmer, *A Perfect Babel of Confusion: Dutch Religion and English Culture in the Middle Colonies* (New York, 1989).

14. The one fascinating exception to the generalization that the history of frontier New York was largely separate from that of the European settlements in the

colony was William Johnson himself. As we have seen, from his feudal castle in the Mohawk Valley, Johnson moved reasonably comfortably between the two cultures. In general, though, the history of the political culture of the New York frontier is better conceived in the context of the larger history of the mid-Atlantic frontier. The literature on the Iroquois is considerable but on the Algonquians much less so. The best starting point on the Iroquois is Daniel Richter, *The Ordeal of the Longhouse: The Peoples of the Iroquois League in the Era of European Colonization* (Chapel Hill, N.C., 1992) and on the Algonquians, Bruce Trigger, *The Huron: Farmers of the North* (New York, 1969). There is a vast literature on European-Indian relations in the mid Atlantic. See, for example, Douglas E. Leach, *The Northern Colonial Frontier, 1607–1763* (New York, 1966); Thomas E. Norton, *The Fur Trade in Colonial New York* (Madison, Wis., 1974); Howard Peckham, *The Colonial Wars* (Chicago, 1964); and, for a polemical view, Francis Jennings, *The Invasion of America: Indians, Colonization, and the Cant of Conquest* (Chapel Hill, N.C., 1975). More recently Fred Anderson, *Crucible of War: The Seven Years' War and The Fate of Empire in British North America, 1754–1766* (New York, 2000), has in masterful fashion integrated the political and military histories of the New York frontier. For an outstanding recent account of the conflicts between Europeans and Indians on the frontier see Daniel Richter, *Facing East from Indian Country: A Native History of Early America* (Cambridge, Mass., 2001).

15. Dinkin, *Voting in Provincial America*, pp. 8, 9, 56. Dinkin notes at least one case in New York, in a June 1737 election in Queens County, in which two widows voted. It seems likely, as we have already seen in Virginia, that propertied widows probably wielded more political power than any other group of females.

16. Ibid. For discussions of the extent of the franchise in New York see Carl Becker, "Nominations in Colonial New York," *AHR*, 6 (1900–01): 260–75; Milton Klein, "Democracy and Politics in Colonial New York," *New York History*, 40 (1959): 221–246; Nicholas Varga, "Election Procedure and Practices in Colonial New York," *New York History*, 41 (1960): 249–77; Roger Champagne, "Family Politics Versus Constitutional Principles: The New York Assembly Elections of 1768 and 1769," *WMQ* 20 (1963): 57–79; and Bonomi, *A Factious People*, pp. 3–19, 32–36. For the extent of the franchise in England see Derek Hirst, *Voters and Voting in England*, pp. 29–43, passim; J. H. Plumb, "The Growth of the Electorate in England from 1600 to 1715," *Past and Present*, 45 (1969): 90–116; G. Holmes, *The Electorate and the National Will in the First Age of Party* (Lancaster, 1976); John Phillips, "The Structure of Electoral Politics in Unreformed England," *Journal of British Studies* 19 (1979): 76–100; and J. C. D. Clark, *English Society, 1688–1832*, pp. 15–26.

17. Becker, "Nominations in Colonial New York," 265; Becker, *Political Parties*, p. 15; Dinkin, *Voting in Provincial America*, pp. 54, 135–36.

18. Milton Klein, "Democracy and Politics," pp. 231–32 notes that those people who perhaps should have been most vocal in opposition to viva voce voting—the tenants on the manors—did not seem to care about the issue; conversely, many of those who were the strongest supporters of a move to written ballots before 1777 were the most prominent members of New York's political and economic oligarchy, including members of the Livingston family.

19. Bonomi, *A Factious People*, pp. 10, 294–311; see also Table 1, p. 54. Greene, "Legislative Turnover," p. 461.

20. Patricia Bonomi, *A Factious People*, pp. 296–311.

21. Greene, "Legislative Turnover," pp. 446–48. For turnover rates across the North American mainland colonies, see Appendix 6, p. 299.

22. Tully, *Forming American Politics*, pp. 320–30; Dinkin, *Voting in Provincial America*, p. 68.

23. Bonomi, *A Factious People*, pp. 296–311.

24. The most important studies of eighteenth-century New York politics, in addition to Becker's *Political Parties*, are Bonomi, *A Factious People*; Tully, *Forming American Politics*; Michael Kammen, *Colonial New York: A History* (New York, 1975); Edward Countryman, *A People in Revolution*; Lawrence Leder, *Robert Livingston, 1654–1728, and the Politics of Colonial New York* (Chapel Hill, N.C., 1961); Stanley Katz, *Newcastle's New York: Anglo-American Politics, 1732–1753* (Cambridge, Mass., 1968).

25. Tully, *Forming American Politics*, pp. 241–49.

26. Countryman, *People in Revolution*, pp. 77–78.

27. Becker, *Political Parties*, p. 22.

28. Dinkin, *Voting in Provincial America*, p. 152.

29. Dinkin, *Voting in Provincial America*, pp. 151–56. Tully, *Forming American Politics*, p. 328, asserts that "the number of uncontested elections in New York . . . seems likely to have been considerably less than the 65 percent Virginia experienced between 1728 and 1775." In fact, the available evidence on elections in New York does not permit one to draw any meaningful comparison between New York and Virginia on that score, but nearly everything we know about the character of the relationship between voters and representatives in upstate New York seems to contradict Tully's contention.

30. Becker, "Nominations in Colonial New York," pp. 260–75. Abraham Ten Broeck to James Duane, February 22, 1768, quoted in Dinkin, *Voting in Provincial America*, p. 74.

31. Quoted in Dinkin, *Voting in Provincial America*, p. 57.

32. Jacob Ten Eyck and Volkert Douw to Sir William Johnson, February 3, 1761; John Duncan to Johnson, November 19, 1763, in John Sullivan, et al., eds. *The Papers of William Johnson*, (14 vols. (Albany, 1921–1966), 3, p. 324, 13, p. 302.

33. Richard Cartwright to Sir William Johnson, January 8, 1768 in Sullivan, et al., eds., *Johnson Papers*, 12, p. 408. See also Becker, "Nominations in Colonial New York," pp. 266–68.

34. William Johnson to Hugh Wallace, quoted in Becker, "Nominations in Colonial New York," p. 268.

35. Full accounts of the election between Morris and Forster can be found in Tully, *Forming American Politics*, p. 344; Bonomi, *A Factious People*, pp. 114–16. The literature on the Zenger trial is vast. For an analysis that joins that trial to the political turmoil of the 1730s, see Katz, *Newcastle's New York*, pp. 76–77.

36. *New York Weekly Journal*, November 5, 1733, quoted in Tully, *Forming American Politics*, p. 344; and Bonomi, *A Factious People*, pp. 114–15.

37. Dinkin, *Voting in Provincial America*, p. 103.

38. Ibid., p. 104.

39. Ibid.

40. New York General Assembly, *Journal of the Votes and Proceedings of the General Assemblies of the Colony of New York*, 2 vols., (New York, 1764–66), I. p. 711.

41. Bonomi, *A Factious People*, p. 133; Dinkin, *Voting in Provincial America*, pp. 151–52.

42. James Alexander, *A Brief Narrative of the Case and Trial of John Peter Zenger, Printer of the New York Weekly Journal*, Stanley Katz, ed. (Cambridge, Mass., 1963), pp. 134–38.

43. Tully, *Forming American Politics*, p. 82.

44. The tenant unrest in upstate New York during the 1750s and 1760s has provided Progressive and neo-Progressive historians with what they believe to be the most dramatic evidence of class conflict prevailing in colonial America. See, for example, Mark, *Agrarian Conflict*, pp. 131–63; and Countryman, *A People in Revolution*

pp. 40–42; For a view that emphasizes intercolonial, rather than class, conflict see Kim, *Landlord and Tenant*, passim.

45. Mrs. Anne Grant, *Memoirs of an American Lady*, 2 vols. (New York, 1901), 2, pp. 136–39, 147–56.

46. Kim, *Landlord and Tenant*, pp. 346–415; Tully, *Forming American Politics*, pp. 382–84.

47. Ibid.

48. Livingston to Jacob Windell, then to William Alexander, quoted in Bonomi, *A Factious People*, p. 214.

49. Ibid., pp. 217–18.

50. Ibid., p. 219; Countryman, *A People in Revolution*, p. 40.

51. Ibid.

52. Bonomi, *A Factious People*, pp. 223–24; Mark, *Agrarian Conflict*, pp. 153–54.

53. My discussion of Livingston's values relies on Cynthia Kierner, *Traders and Gentlefolk: The Livingstons of New York, 1675–1790* (Ithaca, N.Y., 1992), especially pp. 119–25. More generally, Kierner argues that New Yorkers, like the members of the Livingston family, in spite of their reputation for factiousness, shared with political leaders in colonies such as Massachusetts and Virginia a strong desire to present themselves to their fellow citizens as virtuous leaders guided by principles of gentility and public-spiritedness. Kierner makes a strong case for the desire of New York's oligarchs to gain the esteem of their fellow citizens, but the evidence for their ability to embody that desire in their own behavior is much less persuasive.

54. For the highly localized character of political life in New York see Tully, *Forming American Politics*, pp. 330–31.

55. Ibid., p. 336.

56. Ibid., pp. 340–41.

57. Ibid., p. 343.

58. New York Assembly Journal, 2, 1756, pp. 487–89, quoted in Leonard Levy, "Did the Zenger Case Really Matter," *WMQ* 3d ser., 17, (1960): 41.

59. The assembly continued to be aggressive in defense of its prerogatives even as the Revolution approached. In 1770 it prosecuted one of the leaders of New York City's Sons of Liberty, Alexander McDougall, for seditious libel; McDougall would spend three months in prison before the public outcry against his incarceration caused charges against him to be dropped. Ibid., pp. 41, 46–49.

60. Olson, "Eighteenth-Century Colonial Legislatures and Their Constituents," *JAH*, 79 (1992): 556.

61. Colden to the Earl of Hillsburough, New York, April 25, 1768, cited in Bonomi, *A Factious People*, p. 245.

62. Staughton Lynd, *Antifederalism in Dutchess County, New York* (Chicago, 1962), pp. 52–53.

Chapter 5. Complacent Oligarchs: The Merchant Planters of South Carolina

1. My account of the changing fortunes of the Bull family is indebted to Kinloch Bull Jr., *The Oligarchs in Colonial and Revolutionary Charleston: Lieutenant Governor William Bull II and His Family* (Columbia, S.C., 1991).

2. Ibid., p. 11, notes that Westminster at the time was seen as the "House of Lords," and Eton the "House of Commons" of the English public-school establishment, and thus William Bull II's entrance into Westminster was highly unusual, especially by colonial standards.

3. Ibid., p. 232.

4. Ibid., pp. 17, 18.

5. Philip Hamer, ed., *The Papers of Henry Laurens*, 16 vols. (Columbia, SC, 1968), 1, pp. xiv–xxii.

6. Walter Edgar and N. Louis Bailey, *Biographical Directory of the South Carolina House of Representatives*, vol. 2, *The Commons House of Assembly, 1692–1775* (Columbia, SC, 1977), pp. 391–94. See also David D. Wallace, *The Life of Henry Laurens*, (New York, 1967) p. 109.

7. My account of Gadsden is based on E. Stanly Godbold Jr. and Robert H. Woody, *Christopher Gadsden and the American Revolution* (Knoxville, Tenn., 1982), p. 12.

8. Richard Waterhouse, *A New World Gentry: The Making of a Merchant and Planter Class in South Carolina, 1670–1770* (New York, 1989), p. 189; Eugene Sirmans, *Colonial South Carolina* (Chapel Hill, N.C., 1966), p. 239; and Robert Weir, "The Harmony We Were Famous For: An Interpretation of Pre-Revolutionary South Carolina Politics, *WMQ*, 3d ser. vol. 26 (1969): 473–501, and *Colonial South Carolina: A History* (Columbia, S.C., 1997).

9. John Drayton, *A View of South Carolina* (Charleston, S.C., 1802), p. 217.

10. "Journal of Josiah Quincy," *Proceedings of the Massachusetts Historical Society* (Boston, 1915–1916), 49, p. 454; and Johann David Schoepf, *Travels in the Confederation*, 2 vols., (Philadelphia, 1911), 2, p. 205.

11. Weir, *South Carolina*, p. 251; Waterhouse, *New World Gentry*, p. 87.

12. Weir, *South Carolina*, pp. 246–48.

13. Carl Bridenbaugh, *Myths and Realities: Societies of the Colonial South* (New York, 1963), pp. 76–79, 86–89; and Waterhouse, *New World Gentry*, pp. 92–96.

14. Johann Bolzius, "Johann Martin Bolzius Answers a Questionnaire on Carolina and Georgia, 1751," *WMQ*, 3d ser., vol. 14 (1957): 243; and Schoepf, *Travels*, 2, p. 168.

15. Schoepf, *Travels*, 2, p. 172; and Weir, *South Carolina*, pp. 206–7. Health conditions in Charleston were probably just as bad as they were in the low country surrounding the capital; it wasn't until population started to move out of the low country that mortality rates improved.

16. The standard work on slavery in colonial South Carolina remains Peter Wood, *Black Majority: Negroes in South Carolina from 1676 to the Stono Rebellion* (New York, 1974); see also Weir, *South Carolina*, pp. 173–93.

17. Bull, *Oligarchs*, p. 16; and Schoepf, *Travels*, p. 220.

18. Wallace, *Henry Laurens*, p. 89.

19. Sirmans, *Colonial South Carolina*, p. 254.

20. Ibid., pp. 142–44.

21. Ibid., p. 143.

22. Waterhouse, *New World Gentry*, p. 127.

23. Sirmans, *Colonial South Carolina*, pp. 166, 250–52; Waterhouse, *New World Gentry*, pp. 126–28; Weir, *South Carolina*, pp. 106–8; and Richard J. Hooker, ed., *The Carolina Backcountry on the Eve of the Revolution: The Journal of Charles Woodmason, Anglican Itinerant* (Chapel Hill, N.C., 1953), p. 262.

24. Quoted in Waterhouse, *New World Gentry*, p. 159.

25. Sirmans, *Colonial South Carolina*, pp. 257–61, 263, 274, 280.

26. Waterhouse, *New World Gentry*, p. 157.

27. Ibid., pp. 157–58.

28. Sirmans, *Colonial South Carolina*, p. 237.

29. Waterhouse, *New World Gentry*, pp. 163, 168, 170, 175, 181–82, 188; Sirmans, *Colonial South Carolina*, pp. 247, 312.

30. Those individuals who were not planters, merchants, lawyers, or doctors constituted only 4.2 percent of the total number serving in the Commons House during the period 1692–1775. W. B. Edgar, et al., eds., *Biographical Directory of the South Carolina House of Representatives*, vol. 2, *The Commons House of Assembly, 1692–1775* (Columbia, S.C., 1974), p. 5.

31. Greene, "Legislative Turnover," p. 461, and see also Table I, p. 54.

32. Dinkin, *Voting in Provincial America*, p. 179.

33. Richard Walsh, *The Writings of Christopher Gadsden* (Columbia, S.C., 1966), p. 18; and Jack P. Greene, *Quest for Power*, pp. 192–96. Greene has analyzed this election and argued that it did mark an important chapter in the ascendancy of the lower house over royal governors, but even if that was the case, there is little evidence that the people at large were much involved in the conflict.

34. Greene, "Legislative Turnover," pp. 442–63; and Waterhouse, *New World Gentry*, pp. 160–61.

35. Waterhouse, *New World Gentry*, pp. 176–77, 180.

36. Ibid., p. 161.

37. "Quincy Journal," *Proceedings*, 49, p. 451–52.

38. See Appendix 2.

39. Olson, "Colonial Legislatures," *JAH*, 79 (1992): 557.

40. Weir, "Harmony We Were Famous For," p. 496.

41. Rebecca Starr, *A School for Politics: Commercial Lobbying and Political Culture in Early South Carolina* (Baltimore, 1998), pp. 17–23. For her description of the prevailing cultural ethic of the Virginia elite, Starr relies on the interpretation of Timothy Breen, *Tobacco Culture: The Mentality of the Great Tidewater Planters on the Eve of the Revolution* (Princeton, N.J., 1985).

42. Starr, *School for Politics*, pp. 24–43.

43. Gadsden, "To the Public," July 17, 1784, in Walsh, *The Writings of Christopher Gadsden*, p. 207.

44. Woodmason, *Carolina Backcountry*, pp. 272, 278.

45. "Quincy Journal," *Proceedings*, 49, pp. 456–57.

46. Bull, *Oligarchs*, pp. 118–19.

47. This account is drawn from Bull, *Oligarchs*, pp. 258–317.

48. Laurens to Joseph Brown, October 1765, in *The Papers of Henry Laurens*, 5, pp. 23–24.

49. Laurens to Brown, October 22, 1765, in ibid; pp. 26–27.

50. Laurens to Brown, October 28, 1765, in ibid., pp. 29–31.

51. John Alden, *The South in the Revolution* (Baton Rouge, La., 1957), pp. 94–95.

52. Gadsden to William Samuel Johnson and Charles Garth, December 2, 1765, in Walsh, *The Writings of Christopher Gadsden*, pp. 66–67.

53. Pauline Maier, *The Old Revolutionaries: Political Lives in the Age of Samuel Adams* (New York, 1980), especially pp. 173–74, 270–74.

54. *The Papers of Henry Laurens*, 16, p. 181.

55. Alan Nevins, *The American States During and After the Revolution* (New York, 1924), pp. 402–3.

56. Gadsden, "To the Public," *Gazette of the State of South Carolina*, July 17, 1784, in Walsh, *The Writings of Christopher Gadsden*, pp. 225–27.

57. Ibid., pp. 227–28.

58. "Quincy Journal," *Proceedings*, 49, p. 451.

59. Ibid., p. 454.

60. Gadsden to William Samuel Johnson, April 16, 1766, in Walsh, *The Writings of Christopher Gadsden*, p. 72.

Chapter 6. The Unsettling Political Cultures of the Backcountry: The Southern Backcountry

1. Turner, *Frontier in American History*, pp. 1–38. The more recent formulation by Greene is in his essay, "Independence, Improvement, and Authority: Toward a Framework for Understanding the Histories of the Southern Backcountry during the Era of the American Revolution," in Ronald Hoffman, Thad Tate, and Peter J. Albert, eds., *The Southern Backcountry During the American Revolution* (Charlottesville, Va., 1985), pp. 3–36. For discussions of the frontier from the perspective of the wider Atlantic world see the essays in Bernard Bailyn and Philip Morgan, *Strangers Within the Realm: Cultural Margins of the First British Empire* (Chapel Hill, N.C., 1991). For an overview of the colonial American frontier experience that focuses on the European encounter with American Indian cultures see Gregory Nobles, *American Frontiers: Cultural Encounters and Colonial Conquest* (New York, 1997).

2. The historians who have applied Turner's notion of the frontier to the American colonial experience most literally, arguing that frontier conditions contributed to a thoroughly egalitarian economic and social order, are Robert and B. Katherine Brown; see especially Robert Brown, *Middle Class Democracy and the Revolution in Massachusetts,* and Robert and B. Katherine Brown, *Virginia, 1705–1786.*

3. Greene, "Independence, Improvement, and Authority," p. 12.

4. Turner, "Significance," p. 32.

5. This section draws in large measure on Richard R. Beeman, "The Political Response to Social Conflict in the Southern Backcountry: A Comparative view of Virginia and the Carolinas during the American Revolution," in Hoffman, et al., *Uncivil War,* pp. 213–39.

6. Michael L. Nicholls, "Origins of the Virginia Southside, 1705–1753" (Ph.D. diss., College of William and Mary, 1972), pp. 28–55; Freeman H. Hart, *The Valley of Virginia in the Revolution, 1763–1789* (Chapel Hill, N.C., 1942), p. 7; A. Roger Ekirch, *Poor Carolina: Politics and Society in Colonial North Carolina, 1729–1776* (Chapel Hill, N.C., 1981), p. 6; and Weir, *Colonial South Carolina,* p. 209.

7. For arguments emphasizing inequality and social conflict in the southern backcountry see Marvin M. Michael Kay, "The North Carolina Regulation, 1766–1776: A Class Conflict," in Alfred F. Young, ed., *The American Revolution: Explorations in the History of American Radicalism* (DeKalb, Ill., 1976), pp. 84–103; and Kay and Lorin Lee Cary, "Class Mobility and Conflict in North Carolina on the Eve of the Revolution," in Jeffrey J. Crow and Larry E. Tise, eds., *The Southern Experience in the American Revolution* (Chapel Hill, N.C., 1978), pp. 109–51.

8. Beeman, "Political Response," pp. 219–20.

9. Ibid., pp. 221–23; Weir, *Colonial South Carolina,* pp. 210–11.

10. Louis B. Wright, ed., *The Prose Works of William Byrd of Westover: Narratives of a Colonial Virginian* (Cambridge, Mass., 1966), p. 204. The phrase "Best Poor Man's Country," which we most often associate with New York and Pennsylvania, was also used to describe Virginia and North Carolina. S. Johnson Jr. to Robert Cathcart, November 28, 1745, quoted in Ekirch, *Poor Carolina,* p. 26.

11. Beeman, "Political Response," pp. 222–23.

12. Ibid., pp. 223–24.

13. Ibid.

14. For ethnic diversity within the Virginia backcountry see Warren Hofstra, "Ethnicity and Community Formation on the Shenandoah Valley Frontier, 1730–1800," and Richard K. MacMaster, "Religion, Migration, and Pluralism: A Shenandoah Valley Community, 1740–1790," in Michael J. Puglisi, ed., *Diversity and Accommodation: Essays on the Cultural Composition of the Virginia Frontier* (Knoxville, Ky., 1997), pp. 59–81, 82–98.

15. William Byrd, "A Journey to the Land of Eden, Anno 1733," in Wright, ed., *The Prose Works of William Byrd*, pp. 381–412.

16. Hooker, ed., *The Carolina Backcountry on the Eve of the Revolution: Journal of Charles Woodmason*, pp. 52, 60.

17. For a discussion of Woodmason's exceptional life see ibid., pp. xi–xxxix.

18. Rhys Isaac, "Evangelical Revolt: the Nature of the Baptists' Challenge to the Traditional Order in Virginia, 1765–1775," *WMQ*, 3d ser., vol. 31 (1974): 345–68.

19. Ibid.

20. Glen to Lords of Trade, Ninety-Six, October 23, 1753, quoted in Hooker, ed., *Journal of Charles Woodmason*, p. xxv.

21. Ibid., p. 56.

22. For a provocative discussion of the savage and disintegrating forces at work on the "periphery" see Bernard Bailyn, *The Peopling of British North America* (New York, 1986), pp. 114–18.

23. These and other contested elections in Virginia are discussed in Beeman, "Robert Munford and the Political Culture of Frontier Virginia," *Journal of American Studies* 12 (1978): 169–83.

24. Ekirch, *Poor Carolina*, pp. 177–78.

25. Ibid., pp. 94–96; Sirmans, *Colonial South Carolina*, pp. 241–42, 244–48.

26. "Regulators Ad. No. 10, May 21, 1768," in William S. Powell, James Huhta, and Thomas Farnham, *The Regulators of North Carolina: A Documentary History, 1759–1776* (Raleigh, N.C., 1971), p. 113. See also "Regulators Ad. No. 3, October 10, 1766."

27. John Lord Carteret was one of the original Lords Proprietors of the Carolina colony and the only one who chose to remain a proprietor and retain his claim to land in the region. His claim to a proprietary grant of land remained contested between 1729 and 1744, at which time his increasing power back in England—he had just been named Secretary of State for the Northern Department—enabled him to obtain a grant from the Privy Council. His new grant, the Granville District (Carteret had gained the title of Earl Granville that same year upon the death of his mother), contained more than 26,000 square miles along the northern border of Virginia southward. Ekirch, *Poor Carolina*, pp. 128–129.

28. Robert Ramsey, "James Carter: Founder of Salisbury," *North Carolina Historical Review*, 39 (1962): 131–39; William L. Saunders, Walter Clark, and Stephen B. Weeks, ed., *The Colonial and State Records of North Carolina*, 3 vols. (Raleigh, N.C., 1886–1914), 5, pp. 846, 1092.

29. Ekirch, *Poor Carolina*, pp. 169–72.

30. "Theodurus Swain Drage to Benjamin Franklin, March 2, 1771," in William B. Wilcox, ed., *The Papers of Benjamin Franklin* (New Haven, 1974), 28, p. 47.

31. James Whittenburg, "God's Chosen in the Backcountry" (unpublished paper presented at Southern Historical Association annual meeting, 1979), p. 5.

32. Alan D. Watson, "The Origin of the Regulation in North Carolina," *Mississippi Quarterly* 47 (1994): 568–69, in his assessment of the historiography on the North Carolina Regulator Movement, has noted that "the Regulator Movement has been described variously as a mob action, a reaction to British tyranny, a sectional confrontation, a class struggle against aristocratic dominance, a manifestation of status anxiety on the part of Western farmers, and an attempt to purge the colonial government of its pervasive corruption." And, in fact, the movement did contain elements of all of those things.

The oldest, and in many respects still the standard, analysis of the North Carolina Regulation is John Spencer Bassett, "The Regulators of North Carolina," *American Historical Association Annual Report for 1894* (1895), pp. 141–212. Other useful works are: Ekirch, *Poor Carolina*, esp. pp. 161–220 and "A New Government of Liberty: Hermon Husband's Vision of Backcountry North Carolina," *WMQ*, 3d ser., 34 (1977): 632–46; and James Whittenburg, "Planters, Merchants, and Lawyers: Social Change and the Origins of the North Carolina Regulation," *WMQ*, 3d ser., 34 (1977): 215–38. Marvin L. Michael Kay, "The North Carolina Regulation, 1766–1776: A Class Conflict," in Alfred F. Young, *The American Revolution: Explorations in the History of American Radicalism* (DeKalb, Ill., 1976), pp. 71–123; and Kay and Lorin Lee Cary, "Class, Mobility, and Conflict in North Carolina on the Eve of the Revolution," in Crow and Tise, eds., *The Southern Experience in the American Revolution*, pp. 109–51, have argued, not entirely persuasively, for an exclusively class-based explanation of the Regulators' behavior. Andrew C. Denson, "Diversity, Religion, and the North Carolina Regulation," *North Carolina Historical Review* 74 (1995): 30–53, has added yet another dimension, noting the ways in which religion and politics converged for many Regulators.

33. Richard Maxwell Brown, *The South Carolina Regulators* (Cambridge, Mass., 1963), pp. 38–39, 90. For the South Carolina Regulator Movement see also Rachel Klein, "Ordering the Backcountry: The South Carolina Regulation," *WMQ*, 3d ser., 38 (1981): 661–80; and George Lloyd Johnson Jr., *The Frontier in the Colonial South: South Carolina Backcountry, 1763–1800* (Westport, Conn., 1997), pp. 113–37.

34. Brown, *South Carolina Regulators*, passim. See also Weir, *Colonial South Carolina*, pp. 275–80.

35. Ekirch, *Poor Carolina*, p. 178.

36. Brown, *South Carolina Regulators*, pp. 113–34; and Rachel Klein, *Unification of a Slave State: The Rise of the Planter Class in the South Carolina Backcountry* (Chapel Hill, N.C., 1990), p. 51.

37. This account is taken from Hooker, *Carolina Backcountry*, pp. xxvii–xxix.

38. Charles Woodmason, "The Remonstrance," November 7, 1767, in ibid., p. 225.

39. Woodmason would be a significant exception, for he would move on, first to Maryland and finally to Bristol, England, in search of a "proper" parish. Alas, his quest would be filled with disappointment and frustration. See Hooker, *Carolina Backcountry*, pp. xxxi–xxxii.

40. For example, John Pryor, who was elected a representative for Orange County in 1769 along with Husband, owned 3,500 acres and twenty-one slaves by 1772. Ekirch, *Poor Carolina*, p. 190.

41. The clearest statement of this connection is Whittenburg, "God's Chosen in the Backcountry," but see also Ekirch, *Poor Carolina*, pp. 274, 284.

42. Hermon Husband, "An Impartial Relation of the First Rise and Cause of the Recent Differences, in Publick Affairs, In the Province of North Carolina . . . ," 1770, in William K. Boyd, ed., *Eighteenth-Century Tracts Concerning North Carolina* (Raleigh, N.C., 1927) pp. 303, 322–23.

43. Ibid., pp. 285, 303; Husband, "A Fan for Fanning and a Touch-Stone for Tyron . . . ," 1771, in Boyd, ed., *Eighteenth-Century Tracts*, p. 343.

44. "Regulator Advertisements No. 1", August 1766, in Powell, et al., eds., *The Regulators*, p. 35.

45. Dinkin, *Voting in Provincial America*, pp. 178–79.

46. Ekirch, *Poor Carolina*, pp. 194–96.

47. Quoted in ibid., p. 164.

48. Ibid., p. 165.

49. Quoted in Ronald Hoffman, "The 'Disaffected' in the Revolutionary South," in Young, *The American Revolution*, pp. 294–95. Hoffman's essay, pp. 273–318, is the

best brief analysis of the consequence of provincial government irresponsibility on revolutionary loyalties in the backcountry.

50. This account of Marrable's political career is drawn from Beeman, "Deference and Republicanism," *WMQ*, 3d ser. 49 (July 1992): 401–30.

51. Beeman, *Evolution of Southern Backcountry*, pp. 93–94. Read's authority in the House of Burgesses is supported by Greene, *Quest for Power*, p. 473, who places Read in the second rank of burgesses in terms of the importance and number of committee assignments he received.

52. See for example, *Journal of House of Burgesses, 1761–65*, pp. 106, 107, 111–12.

53. Kolp, *Gentlemen and Freeholders*, pp. 165–90. Albert Tillson, *Gentry and Common Folk: Political Culture on a Virginia Frontier, 1740–1789* (Lexington, Ky., 1991), pp. 20–44, has found that the political elite in Virginia's upper Shenandoah Valley were able to assimilate the values and habits of the eastern political elite somewhat more easily than their counterparts in Virginia's Southside.

54. One notable exception was a communication from Lunenburg County's Henry Blagrave to Rind's *Virginia Gazette* on June 4, 1769, in which Blagrave reported that he had "made a strict inquiry amongst my constituents concerning the taxes the Parliament of Great Britain insist on." Their attitude, as reported by Blagrave, differed little from the constitutional orthodoxy of provincial leaders in the east, namely, that "the people do not think they ought to be taxed there [in Parliament], as they may have authority from their most gracious Sovereign to hold Assemblies here, for that purpose."

55. The one notable source of internal discord was the campaign of persecution aimed by backcountry residents at Scottish merchants, who were despised not only because of their failure to rally around the patriot cause, but also because of their growing dominance over all aspects of the tobacco trade. Beeman, "Political Response," pp. 235–36.

56. Ibid., pp. 237–38; and Rhys Isaac and Richard R. Beeman, "Cultural Conflict and Social Change in the Revolutionary South: Lunenburg County, Virginia," *Journal of Southern History* 46 (1980): 538–50.

Chapter 7. The Unsettling Political Cultures of the Backcountry: The Northern Frontier

1. The best general treatments of the New England frontier are Charles E. Clark, *The Eastern Frontier: The Settlement of Northern New England, 1610–1763* (New York, 1970); Douglas Edward Leach: *The Northern Colonial Frontier, 1607–1763* (New York, 1966); and Lois Kimball Mathews, *The Expansion of New England* (Boston, 1909).

2. Clark, *Eastern Frontier*, pp. 55–56, 335–40.

3. John Adams, *Diary*, quoted in ibid., p. 340.

4. Gordon Kershaw, *Gentlemen of Large Property and Judicious Men: The Kennebec Proprietors, 1749–1775* (Portland, Maine, 1975), pp. xi, passim. For a much more hostile view of the proprietors as the root of all evil and inequality in Maine's social order see Alan Taylor, *Liberty Men and Great Proprietors: The Revolutionary Settlement on the Maine Frontier, 1760–1820* (Chapel Hill, N.C., 1990).

5. "Report of Committee on Claims, Massachusetts General Court, May 27, 1715," from James B. Baxter, *Documentary History of the State of Maine*, 24 vols. (1869–1916), 24, p. 239. See also Leach, *Northern Colonial Frontier*, p. 176.

6. Clark, *Eastern Frontier*, pp. 228–35.

7. William Bently, *The Diary of William Bently*, 4 vols. (Gloucester, Maine, 1962), 1,

p. 64, and Baron La RocheFoucauld-Liancourt, Travels, 1, p. 443, both quoted in Taylor, *Liberty Men.* p. 73.

8. Adele E. Plachta, "The Privileged and the Poor: A History of the District of Maine, 1771–1793" (Ph.D. diss., University of Maine, 1975), pp. 93–99.

9. Taylor, *Liberty Men*, p. 3.

10. Roy H. Akagi, *The Town Proprietors of the New England Colonies* (Philadelphia, 1924), esp. pp. 73–80, 85–96.

11. Clark, *Eastern Frontier*, p. 198.

12. This discussion owes heavily to ibid., pp. 199–223.

13. Plachta, "Privileged and the Poor," p. 142.

14. Edward Cass, "A Town Comes of Age: Pownalborough, Maine, 1720–1785" (Ph.D. diss., University of Maine), pp. 71, 130.

15. Plachta, "Privileged and the Poor," pp. 116–22, notes that in some years as high as 76 percent of the judges in Maine were wealthy, while as few as 7 percent could be classed as not wealthy. Unfortunately, she does not provide a precise definition of those terms.

16. Neal Allen, *Province and Court Records of Maine*, 5 vols. (Portland, Maine 1958–60), 5, p. liv.

17. Plachta, "Privileged and the Poor," p. 158, bases this conclusion on an analysis of roll call votes between 1782 and 1786.

18. "Impatialis Secondus," *Falmouth Gazette*, July 9, 1783, quoted in Plachta, "Privileged and the Poor," p. 165.

19. Ibid., pp. 140–58.

20. Samuel Nasson to George Thatcher, 26 February 1788, *Historical Magazine* 6: 341, quoted in ibid., p. 154.

21. Allen, *Province and Court Records* 4, pp. xiii–xvi; 5, pp. xxi–xxv.

22. The information on Thomas Chute is taken from a handwritten index compiled by George M. Bodge in the *Thomas Chute Ledger Book, 1725–1779*, Maine Historical Society; Samuel T. Pole, *Windham in the Past* (Windham, Maine, 1916), pp. 20–21, 33–34, 67–16, 77, 104–8, 225; *Collections of the Maine Historical Society*, 2d ser. vol. 7 (1896): pp. 416–19; and Clark, *Eastern Frontier*, pp. 191–95, 233–35, 244–48, 260–63.

23. Dole, *Windham*, pp. 33–34, 109, 215; and Clark, *Eastern Frontier*, pp. 244–45.

24. Indeed, the prospect of establishing a family dynasty went up in smoke when Thomas Chute's son, Curtis, was killed by lightning in 1767, at which time Thomas Chute was seventy-seven years old. *Collections*, 2d ser. 7, p. 419.

25. James Leamon, *Revolution Downeast: The War for American Independence in Maine* (Amherst, Maine, 1993), pp. 14–18, 46, 66, 77–78, 190–91; William Willis, ed., *Journals of the Rev. Thomas Smith and the Rev. Samuel Deane* (Portland, Maine, 1849), p. 363; and Clark, *Eastern Frontier*, pp. 157–60.

26. This account and the quotation are taken from Clifford K. Shipton, *Sibley's Harvard Graduates* (8 (Boston, 1951), pp. 572–81.

27. *Collections of the Maine Historical Society* 2d ser., vol 13, pp. 236, 239; and Willis, *Journals*, p. 363.

28. William Willis, *History of Portland from 1632–1864* (Portland, Maine, 1865), p. 807.

29. Leamon, *Revolution Downeast*, pp. 62–80; and Shipton, *Harvard Graduates*, 8, pp. 572–81.

30. This account of the Pepperrells draws mainly on the excellent study by Byron Fairchild, *Messrs. William Pepperrell, Merchants at Piscataqua* (Ithaca, N.Y., 1954), pp. 18–20.

31. Ibid. pp. 31–125.

32. Ibid.

33. Ibid., pp. 124–41, 160–77.

34. Ibid., p. 166.

35. Clarke, *Eastern Frontier*, p. 289. The fighting force consisted of about 500 men from New Hampshire, 3,250 from the Massachusetts Bay Colony—about a third of which were from Maine—and another 550 from Connecticut.

36. Ibid., pp. 288–92; Fairchild, *Pepperrell*, pp. 171–77.

37. Silas Lee to George Thatcher, February 28, 1788, quoted in Ronald Banks, *Maine Becomes a State: The Movement to Separate Maine from Massachusetts, 1785–1820* (Middletown, Conn., 1970), pp. 10–11.

38. Petitions from Kittery and, no doubt, other Maine towns to the general court, usually conveyed by the town selectmen, suggest that the principal point of conflict with the general court was the towns' belief that they were carrying an undue share of the burden—financial and otherwise—for defense. This was, as we have seen, a predictable subject of complaint from almost any backcountry region in America, but Pepperrell's effective advocacy was almost certainly a force for moderating that unhappiness. Fairchild, *Pepperrell*, pp. 166–71.

39. Leamon, *Revolution Downeast*, pp. xiv–xv.

40. Henry Sewall to Henry Sewall Sr., June 18, 1783; *Jonathon Sayard Diaries*, vol. 26, January 1, 1785, both quoted in Leamon, *Revolution Downeast*, p. 188.

41. Ronald Banks, *Maine Becomes a State*, and Alan Taylor, *Liberty Men and Great Proprietors*, argue for a much greater sense of alienation between Maine residents and political leaders in postrevolutionary Massachusetts, Taylor citing incidents of agrarian unrest, and Banks seeing a greater level of "constitutional" dispute. While both economic injustice and constitutional conflict certainly were in evidence in postrevolutionary Maine, those sources of conflict, when compared with similar sets of conditions in other parts of the eighteenth-century backcountry, seem remarkably muted.

Chapter 8. The Paradox of Popular and Oligarchic Behavior in Colonial Pennsylvania

1. William Penn, *Frame of Government of Pennsylvania*, May 1682, in Richard S. and Mary Maples Dunn, eds., *The Papers of William Penn*, 5 vols. (Philadelphia, 1981–87), 2: p. 225, thereinafter referred to as *PWP*. The standard account of William Penn and the Quaker founding of Pennsylvania is Gary Nash, *Quakers and Politics: Pennsylvania, 1681–1726* (Princeton, 1968). See also Melvin Endy Jr., *William Penn and Early Quakerism* (Princeton, 1973); Barry Levy, *Quakers and the American Family: British Settlement in the Delaware Valley* (New York, 1998); Joseph Illick, *Colonial Pennsylvania: A History* (New York, 1976); and Frederick B. Tolles, *Meeting House and Counting House: The Quaker Merchants of Colonial Philadelphia, 1682–1763* (Chapel Hill, N.C., 1968).

2. William Penn to the Kings of the Indians, October 18, 1681, in *PWP*, 2: p. 128; Nash, *Quakers and Politics*, pp. 90–91; and James Lemon, *The Best Poor Man's Country* (Baltimore, 1972), pp. 54–57.

3. William Penn, *England's Present Interest Discovered* (1675), quoted in J. R. Pole, *Political Representation* (New York, 1966), p. 79. For an elaboration on Penn's views and on other matters concerning the relationship between representatives and constituents in pre-revolutionary America see ibid. esp. pp. 76–93. For a less sanguine view of the democratic potential of Penn's political ideas see Gary Nash, "The Framing of the Government of Pennsylvania: Ideas in Conflict with Reality," *WMQ*, 3d ser., 23 (1966): 183–209.

4. Penn to Robert Turner, December 1, 1696, *PWP*, 3, p. 472; and Penn to Thomas Lloyd and Others, August 15, 1685, *PWP*, 3, p. 50.

5. Tolles, *Meeting House and Counting House*, pp. 19–20; and Nash, *Quakers and Politics*, esp. pp. 41–47, 67–83.

6. Lemon, *Best Poor Man's Country*, pp. 12–19; Tully, *Forming American Politics*, p. 285. Cappon, *Atlas of Early American History*, pp. 24, 98–99; and *Historical Statistics of the United States: Colonial Times to 1970*, 2 vols. (Washington, D.C., 1975) 2, p. 1168.

7. Lemon, *Best Poor Man's Country*, pp. 55–57.

8. Ibid., pp. 42–45.

9. Much of the discussion that follows is informed by Tully, *Forming American Politics*, esp. pp. 417–21.

10. Ibid., p. 420.

11. Ibid., pp. 408–10 has articulated this notion most persuasively. There are numerous accounts of the contest between the assembly and proprietary parties in colonial Pennsylvania. Perhaps the best starting point is Tully, *William Penn's Legacy: Politics and Social Structure in Provincial Pennsylvania, 1726–1755* (Baltimore, 1977), but see James Hutson, *Pennsylvania Politics, 1740–1770: The Movement for Royal Government and Its Consequences* (Princeton, 1972); William Hanna, *Benjamin Franklin and Pennsylvania Politics* (Stanford, Calif., 1964); and Theodore Thayer, *Pennsylvania Politics and the Growth of Democracy, 1740–1776* (Harrisburg, 1953).

12. Chilton Williamson, *American Suffrage From Property to Democracy, 1760–1860*, (Princeton, 1960) pp. 12–14, 27–28, 33–34. See also Sister Joan de Lourdes Leonard, "Elections in Colonial Pennsylvania," *WMQ*, 3d ser., 11 (1954): 385–401.

13. Ibid. Tully, *Forming American Politics*, p. 470, estimates that the percentage of those eligible to vote in Pennsylvania ranged from 50 percent to 80 percent depending on the locality.

14. Craig Horle, et al., *Lawmakers and Legislators in Pennsylvania: A Biographical Dictionary*, 2 vols. (Philadelphia, 1991–97), 2, pp. 20–21, has a full description of the many changes made in the election laws respecting election inspectors. The very fact that the legislature was constantly tinkering with the laws regulating the conduct of elections suggests at least the theoretical importance of the popular voice in the making of public policy in Pennsylvania.

15. Tully, *Forming American Politics*, pp. 346–47.

16. Ibid., 330–35; see also Claire Keller, "Pennsylvania Government, 1701–1740: A Study of the Operation of Government" (Ph.D. dissertation, University of Washington, 1967).

17. Quoted in Tully, *William Penn's Legacy*, p. 110.

18. Ibid., p. 114.

19. Quoted in Thayer, *Pennsylvania Politics*, 41–42. See also Horle, *Lawmaking and Legislators* 2, pp. 1125–27.

20. Horle, *Lawmaking and Legislators* 2, pp. 132–34.

21. Ibid., p. 128; and Greene, "Legislative Turnover," pp. 446–47.

22. The ratio in New York, which like Pennsylvania, had a small assembly, was 1:1,065, the second highest in America. Greene, "Legislative Turnover," p. 460.

23. Charles H. Lincoln, *The Revolutionary Movement in Pennsylvania: 1760–1776* (Philadelphia, 1901), p. 47. The taxable population theoretically represented all of the eligible voters of the colony, although in reality the number of people capable of casting a vote was probably larger. Peter Rhoads Silver, "Indian-Hating and the Rise of Whiteness in Provincial Pennsylvania" (Ph.D. diss., Yale University, 2000), pp. 366–69, using records of loan-office activity as an index of property ownership within each county, argues that the western counties were not underrepresented if one uses value of property, as opposed to population, as the basis for representa-

tion. While there was ample tradition in England supporting the notion that representation should be based on property as well as population, it is unlikely that western residents saw things that way.

24. Tully, *William Penn's Legacy*, p. 95.

25. Tully, *Forming American Politics*, p. 339. The most comprehensive discussion of the reluctance of the Quaker Party leaders to use their power to govern the colony actively is Robert S. Hohwald, "The Structure of Pennsylvania Politics, 1739–1766" (Ph.D. diss., Princeton University, 1979), passim.

26. Horle, *Lawmaking and Legislators* 2, pp. 18–19, 81–114; Olson, "Colonial Legislatures," p. 563; and Hohwald, "Structure of Pennsylvania Politics," pp. 22, 95. The number of days that the legislature was in session during this period ranged from a low of 15 in 1732 to a high of 139 in 1755. See Appendices 2 and 3.

27. About 40 percent of the laws enacted by the legislature during the period between 1710 and 1756 were in response to petitions from individuals or groups asking for the legislation, with most of the remainder being initiated by the legislators themselves, sometimes with a little prompting from the governor. Horle, *Lawmaking and Legislators* 2, pp. 18–19.

28. Olson, "Colonial Legislatures," p. 557. See also Appendix 4, p. 247.

29. Tully, *Forming American Society*, pp. 336–37.

30. Horle, *Lawmaking and Legislators* 2, pp. 18–19.

31. Tully, *Forming American Society*, pp. 335–37.

32. Ibid.

33. Tully, *William Penn's Legacy*, p. 84; and Horle, *Lawmakers and Legislators* 2, pp. 23–26.

34. Tully, *William Penn's Legacy*, pp. 83–87.

35. William Smith, *A Brief History of the Province of Pennsylvania* (London, 1755), p. 28. Smith would prove to be a disruptive figure not only in Pennsylvania politics but also in his role as provost of the College of Philadelphia, where he would develop a particular antipathy for Benjamin Franklin, ousting him from the college's board of trustees. For a brief, but excellent, summary of Smith's combative role in Pennsylvania politics see Tully, *Forming American Politics*, pp. 150–59.

36. Tully, *William Penn's Legacy*, pp. 81–83.

37. Ibid., p. 83.

38. Horle, *Lawmaking and Legislators* 2, pp. 24–26.

39. Dinkin, *Voting in Provincial America*, p. 183, notes that on some occasions a larger number of votes were cast in the elections for sheriff than in those for the assembly seats.

40. Tully, *William Penn's Legacy*, p. 115; Shippen's reluctance is quoted in Dinkin, *Voting in Provincial America*, p. 102.

41. Horle, *Lawmaking and Legislators* 2, p. 375; Leonard, "Elections in Colonial Pennsylvania," p. 386; and Tully, *William Penn's Legacy*, pp. 90–91.

42. Horle, *Lawmaking and Legislators* 2, p. 72.

43. The attack was made in a private letter to the board of trade, but the colony's agent in London, Richard Portridge, obtained a copy, and it and parts of it were subsequently published. Tully, *William Penn's Legacy*, p. 29.

44. Horle, *Lawmaking and Legislators* 2, p. 228.

45. Ibid., 2, pp. 27, 228.

46. Ibid.; Tully, *William Penn's Legacy*, pp. 90–91.

47. Horle, *Lawmaking and Legislators* 2, p. 27.

48. Tully, *Forming American Politics*, pp. 350–52.

49. Cohen, "Election of 1742," pp. 308–10; Dinkin, *Voting in Provincial America*, p. 159.

50. This account is taken principally from Cohen, "Election of 1742", pp. 310–11.

51. William T. Parsons, "The Bloody Election of 1742," *Pennsylvania History*, 36 (1969): 297.

52. Ibid., p. 298.

53. Dinkin, *Voting in Provincial America*, pp. 130–31, 157; Parsons "Bloody Election," p. 300; and Cohen, "Election of 1742," pp. 314–19.

54. Dinkin, *Voting in Provincial America*, p. 203.

55. Ibid., p. 158.

56. Quoted in Tully, *Forming American Politics*, p. 371. Tully, ibid., pp. 370–74 takes an appropriately skeptical attitude about the operation of deference in Pennsylvania's political culture and emphasizes the ways in which the egalitarianism of Quaker theology—with its discouragement of "words or signs of respect tainted by artificiality or insincerity"—worked to undercut traditional notions of deference. His view stands somewhat in contradiction to his earlier assertion, in *William Penn's Legacy*, p. 79, that "deference was relatively high and access to provincial office was restricted to appropriate members of the colonies' elite."

57. Quoted in Tully, *Forming American Politics*, p. 372.

58. Quoted in Edward Beatty, *William Penn as Social Philosopher* (New York, 1939), pp. 102, 268.

59. The consistent conflict between Quakers and proprietors on the issues of defense and of the taxing of proprietary lands can be followed in Tolles, *Meetinghouse and Counting House*, pp. 9–32; Hanna, *Franklin and Pennsylvania Politics*; Thayer, *Pennsylvania Politics*, pp. 42–46, 57–59, 71–74, 83–85; and Horle, *Lawmaking and Legislators* 2, pp. 57–78.

60. Hohwald, "Structure of Pennsylvania Politics," pp. 92–140, provides a detailed discussion of the way in which the Quaker Party tendency toward "passive sovereignty" led to a near total failure of governance in the matter of defense.

61. Horle, *Lawmaking and Legislators* 2, p. 73.

62. Ibid., p. 74; and Tolles, *Meeting House and Counting House*, p. 23.

63. Ibid., 24. A thousand men quickly joined Franklin's voluntary "Association," but, as it turned out, their services were not immediately needed.

64. William Smith, *Brief View*, pp. 52, 70, quoted in Hutson, *Pennsylvania Politics*, p. 25.

65. Ibid., pp. 23–26.

66. Tolles, *Meeting House and Counting House*, pp. 24–28.

67. Ibid; Tully, *Forming American Politics*, p. 158; and Eric Hinderaker, *Elusive Empires: Constructing Colonialism in the Ohio Valley, 1673–1800* (Cambridge, 1997), pp. 140–44.

68. Tolles, *Meeting House and Counting House*, pp. 24–28; and Horle, *Lawmaking and Legislators* 2, pp. 76–78.

69. Benjamin Franklin to Peter Collinson, August 27, 1755, *Franklin Papers* 6, pp. 170–71; and Tully, *Forming American Politics*, p. 152.

70. Ibid., pp. 156–59; see also Hanna, *Franklin and Pennsylvania Politics*, pp. 102–14 and Thayer, *Pennsylvania Politics*, pp. 55–65.

71. Edward Shippen to Joseph Shippen, July 21, 1763, quoted in John Dunbar, ed., *The Paxton Papers* (The Hague, 1957), p. 17.

72. Edward Shippen to Joseph Shippen, July 30, 1763, in ibid., p. 18.

73. Brooke Hindle, "The March of the Paxton Boys, *WMQ*, 3d ser., 3 (1946): 466–67; and Benjamin Franklin, "A Narrative of the Late Massacres in Lancaster County . . . ," in Labaree, ed., *Franklin Papers* 11, pp. 48–52.

74. J. S. Mombert, *An Authentic History of Lancaster County in the State of Pennyslvania* (Lancaster, Pa., 1869), p. 185, quoted in Dunbar, *Paxton Papers*, p. 29.

75. Labaree, *Franklin Papers* 11, pp. 42–47, 53, 56–65.

76. Dunbar, "A Declaration and Remonstrance of the Distressed and Bleeding Frontier Inhabitants," *Paxton Papers*, p. 103.

77. Hindle. "Paxton Boys," pp. 474–79.

78. The "Declaration and Remonstrance" is reprinted in Dunbar, *Paxton Papers*, pp. 101–10.

79. My account of the political and social organization of Paxton relies heavily on George Franz, "Paxton: A Study of Community Structure and Mobility" (Ph.D. diss., Rutgers University, 1974).

80. Horle, *Lawmaking and Legislators* 2, pp. 25–29.

81. The body of historical literature on the expansion of settlement in southeastern Pennsylvania in the eighteenth century is large. Among the most helpful are Solon J. Buck and Elizabeth Buck, *The Planting of Civilization in Western Pennsylvania* (Pittsburgh, 1939); Wayland Dunaway, *The Scots Irish of Colonial Pennsylvania* (Chapel Hill, N.C., 1944); E. R. L. Gould, *Local Government in Pennsylvania*, Johns Hopkins University Studies in Historical and Political Science, vol. 3 (Baltimore, 1883); Jerome Wood, *Conestoga Crossroads: Lancaster, 1730–1790* (Harrisonburg, PA, 1979); Jerome Wood, "The Town Proprietors of Colonial Pennsylvania, 1730–1790; and *Pennsylvania Magazine of History and Biography* 106 (1972): 346–68.

82. Quoted in Franz, "Paxton," p. 145.

83. Quoted in ibid., pp. 49, 51.

84. Ibid., pp. 200–255.

85. Ibid; James Merrell, *Into the Woods: Negotiations on the Pennsylvania Frontier* (New York, 1999), pp. 169, 231, 232, 233, 235, 237, 285, 286. There is at least a hint of some collective political organization in Paxton in response to the danger on the frontier. Harris, in a 1756 letter to the colony's secretary, Richard Peters, asking for a stronger militia law "that will oblige us all to Doe our Duty," reported that the Paxton residents had held a "town meeting," most likely at his store, in which they unanimously agreed to supply a twenty-man force to guard the town, "Day and Night." John Harris to R. Peters, November 5, 1756, in *Pennsylvania Archives*, ser. 1, 3: 33–34.

86. Silver, "Indian-Hating and the Rise of Whiteness in Provincial Pennsylvania," pp. 311–401, uses the Paxton incident as the culminating event in what he sees as the gradually building phenomenon of Indian-hating within prerevolutionary Pennsylvania. He correctly connects, I think, some of the colony's first popular political mobilizations to the rise of Indian-hating.

87. "The Apology of the Paxton Volunteers addressed to the candid and impartial world," in Dunbar, *Paxton Papers*, pp. 185–86. For other descriptions in a similar vein see "A Declaration and Remonstrance," pp. 101–10; "The Quaker Unmask'd," pp. 208–15; and "The Conduct of the Paxton-Men Impartially Represented," pp. 269–98, all in Dunbar, *Paxton Papers*. The pamphlet "The Conduct of the Paxton Men," although seemingly of a piece with most of the other pro-Paxton pamphlets written at the time, is of particular interest since it was most likely written by the Reverend Thomas Barton, an Anglican minister who had attempted to Christianize Indians of the regions both before and after the Paxton uprising. Barton had also previously gone on record opposing mob actions against Indians and, indeed, was not considered particularly friendly to the Scots-Irish Presbyterians of Lancaster County. James Myers, "The Reverend Thomas Barton's Authorship of *The Conduct of the Paxton Men, Impartially Represented (1764)*," *Pennsylvania History* 61 (1994): 155–84, argues that Barton's pamphlet, and perhaps other pro-Paxton writings, were an orchestrated part of the proprietors' campaign to oust the Quakers from political power. Silver, "Indian-Hating," pp. 336–63, has carved out the most exten-

sive and provocative analysis of the pro- and anti-Paxton pamphlets. He skillfully traces the way in which the pamphlets on both sides "illustrated an overarching, paranoid interpretation of events, an interpretation that brought Quaker Party writers to see a Presbyterian, and proprietary ones an Indian, in every closet." As illuminating as Silver's analysis is, in my view, it understates the substantive content of the westerner's political grievances against the Quaker oligarchy.

88. "Apology," in Dunbar, *Paxton Papers*, pp. 187–88.

89. "Quaker Unmask'd," in ibid., p. 211.

90. "The Cloven Foot discovered," in Dunbar, *Paxton Papers*, p. 85.

91. "The Quaker Unmasked, or Plain Truth Humbly Addressed to the Consideration of all the Freeman of Pennsylvania," 1764, in Dunbar, *Paxton Papers*, p. 209.

92. "A Gentleman of the Frontier Counties," 1764, in ibid., p. 282.

93. "A Looking Glass for Presbyterians," in ibid., p. 245. Carntogher and Sleve Gallion Mountains are in Londonberry County, the Slemish Mountains in Antrim County, in Northern Ireland.

94. Ibid., pp. 245–49; and "A Looking Glass for Presbyterians,", p. 304.

95. "Conduct of the Paxton Men," in ibid., p. 274. James E. Crowley, "The Paxton Disturbance and Ideas of Order in Pennsylvania Politics," *Pennsylvania History* 37 (1970), pp. 317–39, has argued that the fundamental division between the Paxtonians and political leaders in the east rested on fundamentally different conceptions of the very purposes of government, with the Paxtonians holding to a "simple view of social relations"—that gave to ordinary citizens the right to take authority into their own hands on occasion—and the assembly leaders possessing a more sophisticated sense of a society's need for a delicate balance between order and liberty. While this interpretive framework helps us understand some of the nature of the cultural conflict between east and west in Pennsylvania, it does, by its abstractness, obscure some of the visceral, emotional power of that conflict. For a more recent analysis of the Paxton pamphlets, one that analyzes the Paxton pamphlet war as an example of the revolution in print culture occurring at the time, see Alison Olson, "The Pamphlet War Over the Paxton Boys," *Pennsylvania Magazine of History and Biography* (hereafter *PMHB*) 123, (1999): 31–55.

96. Franz, "Paxton," pp. 274–76.

97. Ibid., pp. 405–6; and Lemon, *Best Poor Man's Country*, pp. 218–28.

98. Horle, *Lawmaking and Legislators* 2, pp. 1126–27; and Thayer, *Pennsylvania Politics*, pp. 120–21, 170–83. There is a substantial body of work on local politics in Lancaster County, including Wayne Bockelman, "Local Politics in Pre-Revolutionary Lancaster County," *PMHB* 97 (1973): 45–74; Russell Nelson, "Backcountry Pennsylvania: The Ideals of William Penn in Practice" (Ph.D. diss., University of Wisconsin, 1968); and Jerome Wood, *Conestoga Crossroads*, pp. 23–46. While all of these authors are able to demonstrate that there was active participation in local politics in the town of Lancaster, the absence of evidence on Paxton confirms the sense of that region's estrangement from all of the province's political centers.

99. The tone of the denunciations of the Paxtonites issued by eastern pamphleteers is fully congruent with Bernard Bailyn's characterization of much of the frontier experience as operating on the "margin" of British North American culture. Bernard Bailyn, *The Peopling of British North America: An Introduction* (New York, 1986), passim.

100. Tully, *Forming American Politics*, pp. 83–96.

101. Hindle, "Paxton Boys," pp. 481–86.

102. For discussion of the move toward regal government see Hutson, *Pennsylvania Politics*, pp. 122–77; Hanna, *Benjamin Franklin*, pp. 154–68; and Thayer, *Pennsylvania Politics*, pp. 89–110.

103. Quoted in Anthony F. C. Wallace, *The Death and Rebirth of the Seneca* (New York, 1972), p. 141.

104. For a depiction of unrest and cultural isolation on the Pennsylvania frontier after the Revolution, see Thomas Slaughter, *The Whiskey Rebellion: Frontier Epilogue to the American Revolution* (New York, 1986).

Chapter 9. Toward Democratic Pluralism: The Politics of the Cities of the Northeast

1. There are numerous accounts of the contest between the Assembly and proprietary "parties" in colonial Pennsylvania. Among them are James Hutson, *Pennsylvania Politics*; William Hanna, *Benjamin Franklin and Pennsylvania Politics*; Theodore Thayer, *Pennsylvania Politics and the Growth of Democracy*; Alan Tully, *William Penn's Legacy*; and Tully, *Forming American Politics*.

2. In many respects the best full biography of Franklin is still Carl Van Doren, *Benjamin Franklin* (New York, 1938). Two recent biographies are: Edmund S. Morgan, *Benjamin Franklin* (New Haven, 2002); and Walter Isaacson, *Benjamin Franklin: An American Life* (New York, 2003). Additional works include David Freeman Hawke, *Franklin* (New York, 1976); Ronald W. Clark, *Benjamin Franklin: A Biography* (New York, 1983); Esmond Wright, *Benjamin Franklin and American Independence* (London, 1966); Wright, *Franklin of Philadelphia* (Cambridge, Mass., 1986); and Ralph Ketcham, *Benjamin Franklin* (New York, 1965).

3. For extended discussions of the election of 1764 in Pennsylvania see Gary B. Nash, *The Urban Crucible: Social Change, Political Consciousness and the Origins of the American Revolution* (Cambridge, Mass., 1979), pp. 282–91; Nash, "The Transformation of Urban Politics, 1700–1764," *JAH*, 60 (1973): 605–32; Hanna, *Franklin and Pennsylvania Politics*, pp. 54–68; James Hutson, "The Campaign to Make Pennsylvania a Royal Province, 1764–1770," *PMHB*, 94 (1970): 427–63; and Philip Gleason, "A Scurrilous Colonial Election and Franklin's Reputation," *WMQ*, 18 (1961): 68–84.

4. Nash, "Transformation of Urban Politics," pp. 616–17, 627–8, and Gleason, "A Scurrilous Election," pp. 68–84. See also *Franklin Papers* 11, pp. 369–90.

5. Isaac Hunt, "A Letter from a Gentleman in Transilvania," p. 4, quoted in Nash, *Urban Crucible*, p. 287.

6. Theodore Tappert and John W. Doberstein, eds. and trans., *The Journals of Henry Melchior Muhlenberg in Three Volumes* (Philadelphia, 1945) 2, p. 123; Mr. Petit to Mr. [Joseph] Reed, November 3, 1764, in William B. Reed, ed., *Life and Correspondence of Joseph Reed* (Philadelphia, 1847), pp. 36–37; *Franklin Papers* 11, pp. 397. It is important to emphasize that the victory of the proprietary candidates in the Philadelphia area was still not sufficient to swing the balance of political power within the colony in favor of the proprietors.

7. This, at least, was the ideology created by the planters of the colonial South. To embrace that ideology required of course not only overlooking differences of ethnicity, religion, and social class among whites but also, and more fundamentally, denial of the fact that nearly the whole of the bottom half of southern society was composed of unfree Africans who shared very little of the English values of the ruling class.

8. The discussion in this and subsequent paragraphs on the demographic growth of Boston, New York, and Philadelphia is taken primarily from Nash, *Urban Crucible*, pp. 54–55.

9. Ibid., pp. 54–55, 107–8, 194–95, 313–15.

10. Lester Cappon, *Atlas of Early American History*, pp. 97–98; and "Diary of James

Allen, Esq., of Philadelphia," *PMHB* 9 (1885): 185. In their pioneering work *Rebels and Gentlemen: Philadelphia in the Age of Franklin* (New York, 1942), p. 4, Carl and Jessica Bridenbaugh mistakenly claimed that Philadelphia was the second largest city in the entire British empire, a mistake subsequently repeated by many other historians.

11. Nash, *Urban Crucible*, pp. 85–86, 199–204, 280–81; Tully, *Forming American Politics*, pp. 134–43; and Dunbar, *Paxton Papers*, passim.

12. Robert Wells, *The Population of the British Colonies in America Before 1776: A Survey of Census Data* (Princeton, 1975), pp. 79, 112, 143; Zemsky, *Merchants, Farmers and River Gods*, pp. 28–38; Lincoln, *Revolutionary Movement*, pp. 43–50; and Tully, *Forming American Politics*, pp. 5–8.

13. Williamson, *American Suffrage*, pp. 12–14, 27–28, 33–34.

14. Peter Oliver, *Origins and Progress of the American Rebellion* (Stanford, 1961), p. 55. Pauline Maier, *From Resistance to Revolution: Colonial Radicals and the Development of American Opposition to Britain, 1765–1776* (New York, 1972), p. 69; and Nash, *Urban Crucible*, pp. 293–300. The most detailed discussion of Mackintosh's activities during the Stamp Act Crisis remains George P. Anderson, "Ebenezer Mackintosh, Stamp Act Rioter and Patriot," *Colonial Society of Massachusetts Publications* 26, (1924–26), pp. 15–64.

15. Nash, *Urban Crucible*, pp. 293–300; and Anderson, "Mackintosh," pp. 15–64.

16. Nash, *Urban Crucible*, p. 293.

17. Thomas Hutchinson, *The History of the Colony and Province of Massachusetts Bay*, ed. Lawrence Shaw Mayo, 3 vols. (Cambridge, Mass., 1930), 3, p. 120.

18. Francis Bernard to Lord Halifax, August 15, 1765, in Edmund S. Morgan, *Prologue to Revolution: Sources and Documents on the Stamp Act Crisis* (Chapel Hill, N.C., 1959), pp. 106–7.

19. One exception was John Adams, who referred to the events of August 14 as a "very atrocious Violation of the Peace and of dangerous tendency and consequence." *Adams Diary*, August 15, 1765, p. 260.

20. Robert St. George, in a chapter on "Attacking Houses," in his *Conversing by Signs: Poetics of Implication in Colonial New England Culture* (Chapel Hill, N.C., 1998), pp. 205–95, has done a provocative analysis of the symbolic meaning of the assaults on the houses of Oliver and Hutchinson. Gary Nash, *Urban Crucible*, p. 294, argues that the destruction of Oliver's coach and chaise can be viewed as an assault not merely on British, but also upper-class, authority.

21. Bernard Bailyn, *The Ordeal of Thomas Hutchinson* (Cambridge, Mass., 1974), pp. 36–39, has an excellent account of the reaction of royal officials to the sacking of Hutchinson's house.

22. *Boston Gazette*, September 2, 1765, quoted in Maier, *Resistance to Revolution*, p. 63.

23. Andrew Elliot to Thomas Hollis, August 27, 1767, in *Massachusetts Historical Society Collections*, 4th ser. (1858), 4, p. 407.

24. Hutchinson to Richard Jackson, August 30, 1765, in Morgan, *Prologue to Revolution*, p. 109; Edmund S. and Helen M. Morgan, *The Stamp Act Crisis: Prologue to Revolution* (Chapel Hill, N.C.), pp. 128–29.

25. Maier, *Resistance to Revolution*, p. 70; and Oliver, *Origins and Progress*, p. 54.

26. Hutchinson, *History of Massachusetts*, 3, p. 102.

27. Adams, *Diary*, p. 265.

28. Henry A. Cushing, ed., *The Writings of Samuel Adams*, 4 vols. (New York, 1904–08), 4, p. 67. Nash, *Urban Crucible*, pp. 297–98, interprets the language of both Bernard and the Sons of Liberty as proving the class-based character of the conflict in Boston over the Stamp Act. There is no question that, at the extremes, both sides

evoked the specter of class, but support for the Stamp Act rioters among nearly all classes of provincial citizens suggests that there was more to the conflict than class alone.

29. For a good discussion of the relationship between the Loyal Nine and the Sons of Liberty, see Maier, *Resistance to Revolution*, pp. 85–86, 307.

30. The standard, though misleadingly titled, biography of Sam Adams remains John C. Miller, *Samuel Adams: Pioneer in Propaganda* (Stanford, Calif., 1960). For an illuminating discussion of Sam Adams's place within the American republican tradition see Pauline Maier, "A New Englander as Revolutionary: Samuel Adams," in *The Old Revolutionaries: Political Lives in the Age of Samuel Adams* (New York, 1980), pp. 3–50.

31. Oliver, *Origins and Progress*, p. 39.

32. Both Gary Nash, *Urban Crucible*, p. 296, and Dirk Hoerder, *Crowd Action in Revolutionary Massachusetts, 1765–1780*, (New York, 1977), pp. 97–101, interpret the matter of Mackintosh's debt and possible imprisonment as indicative of a struggle for power and control between Adams and Mackintosh.

33. Sam Adams to John Smith, December 20, 1765, in Cushing, ed., *Adams Letters* 1, p. 60; and Miller, *Sam Adams*, p. 67.

34. Hoerder, *Crowd Action*, p. 203.

35. Anderson, "Mackintosh," p. 53.

36. Ibid., pp. 55–64.

37. Dinkin, *Voting in Provincial America*, p. 174. Nash, *Urban Crucible*, pp. 226–27, 246–65, has argued that assertions of the popular will in politics tended to occur during times of economic depression and had a strong, class-based flavor, but it is difficult to correlate the fluctuations in Boston voting with changing economic conditions. It is of course possible that other, extra-legal assertions of popular sentiment were connected to issues of economic hardship.

38. Richard D. Brown, *Revolutionary Politics in Massachusetts: The Boston Committees of Correspondence and the Towns, 1772–1774* (New York, 1976), esp. pp. 58–91, 164, 210–12.

39. Dinkin, *Voting in Provincial America*, p. 156.

40. For accounts of the events surrounding the protest against the Stamp Act in New York, see Pauline Maier, *Resistance to Revolution*, pp. 69–73, 78–112; Bonomi, *A Factious People*, pp. 233–34; Tully, *Forming America Politics*, pp. 167–75; and P. D. G. Thomas, *British Politics and the Stamp Act Crisis: The First Phase of the American Revolution, 1763–1767* (Oxford, 1975), pp. 150–51, 293–94, 305–7.

41. Quoted in Tully, *Forming American Politics*, p. 169.

42. Ibid., pp. 170, 171.

43. Ibid.; Bonomi, *A Factious People*, pp. 233–35; and Morgan and Morgan, *Stamp Act Crisis*, p. 162.

44. "No Lawyer in the Assembly," *Parker's New York Gazette* February 15, 1768, quoted in Tully, *Forming American Politics*, p. 173.

45. Ibid.

46. Bonomi, *A Factious People*, pp. 240–44; and Dinkin, *Voting in Provincial America*, p. 156.

47. Quoted in Hawke, *Franklin* pp. 224–25.

48. *Franklin Papers*, 11, pp. 207–8.

49. There is a small historiographical tempest over the reasons why laborers in Boston and New York were so militantly antiestablishment in their opposition to the Stamp Act, while laborers in Philadelphia were more closely connected to traditional political elites. The sharpest statements of the controversy are James Hutson, "An Investigation of the Inarticulate: Philadelphia's White Oaks," *WMQ*, 3d ser., 27

(1971): 3–25; and Jesse Lemisch, "Jack Tar in the Streets: Merchant Seamen in the Politics of Revolutionary America," *WMQ,* 3d ser., 25 (1968): 343–70.

50. Morgan and Morgan, *Stamp Act Crisis,* pp. 250–52.

51. Dinkin, *Voting in Provincial America,* pp. 157–61.

52. Sons of Liberty in Philadelphia to Brethren, February 15, 1766, John Lamb Papers, New York Historical Society, quoted in Tully, *Forming American Politics,* pp. 201–2.

53. Dinkin, *Voting in Provincial America,* p. 159.

54. The historiography on the coming of the Revolution in Pennsylvania is nearly as contentious as was the revolutionary movement itself. The starting point is Lincoln, *Revolutionary Movement in Pennsylvania,* previously cited. Lincoln's treatment of Pennsylvania was one of the earliest progressive arguments in favor of a radical, internal revolution, and although his argument is overstated, there is still much to admire in the book. Among more recent studies that view the Pennsylvania Revolution through similar progressive, or neoprogressive, lenses, are Nash, *Urban Crucible,* esp. pp. 374–82; Steven Rosswurm, *Arms, Country, and Class: The Philadelphia Militia and the "Lower Sort" during the American Revolution* (New Brunswick, N.J., 1987); and Eric Foner, *Tom Paine and Revolutionary America* (New York, 1976), esp. pp. 107–44. Charles Olton, *Artisans for Independence: Philadelphia Mechanics and the American Revolution* (Syracuse, N.Y., 1975), discusses the political awakening of the artisan classes in Philadelphia during and after the Revolution. Richard A. Ryerson, *The Revolution Is Now Begun: The Radical Committees of Philadelphia, 1765–1776* (Philadelphia, 1978), while it does not deny either the radical or working-class components of the movement for independence, nevertheless downplays its class-based character. Theodore Thayer, *Pennsylvania Politics and the Growth of Democracy, 1740–1776* (Harrisburg, Pa., 1953), is openly admiring of the radical achievement of the Pennsylvania revolutionaries. David Hawke, *In the Midst of Revolution: The Politics of Confrontation in Colonial America* (Philadelphia, 1961), is a somewhat grumpy account of Pennsylvania's radical revolution, with an emphasis on the ways in which the radicals used propaganda and demagoguery to obtain their goals.

For some of the individual personalities involved in the struggle see David Jacobsen, *John Dickinson and the Revolution in Pennsylvania, 1764–1776* (Berkeley, Calif., 1965); Bond Schlenther, *Charles Thomson: A Patriot's Pursuit* (Newark, Del., 1990); Benjamin H. Newcomb, *Franklin and Galloway: A Political Partnership* (New Haven, Conn., 1972); and Burton Konkle, *George Bryan and the Constitution of Pennsylvania, 1731–1791* (Philadelphia, 1922).

55. *Pennsylvania Gazette,* May 22, 1776, quoted in Ryerson, *Revolution Is Now Begun,* p. 214.

56. Ibid., pp. 219–26.

57. *Pennsylvania Archives,* 2d ser. (Harrisburg, Pa., 1874–80) 3, p. 658; and Ryerson, *Revolution Is Now Begun,* pp. 226–36.

58. Ryerson, *Revolution Is Now Begun,* p. 229. Historians have written extensively, from varying points of view, about the inexperience and modest social and economic standing of the delegates both to the Provincial Conference and the subsequent Constitutional Convention. The most negative appraisal is Hawke, *In The Midst of Revolution,* pp. 172, 181–92. J. Paul Selsam, *The Pennsylvania Constitution of 1776* (Philadelphia, 1936), pp. 148–51, also emphasizes the inexperience of the delegates but views them more sympathetically.

59. Ryerson, *Revolution Is Now Begun,* pp. 231–34; Hawke, *In the Midst of Revolution,* pp. 173–75; and Selsam, *Pennsylvania Constitution,* pp. 136–45.

60. See note 5 above. Robert Gough, "Can a Rich Man Favor Revolution? The

Case of Philadelphia in 1776," *Pennsylvania History* 48 (1981): 235–50, has done an analysis of attitudes among the wealthiest Philadelphians toward the events of 1776 and has concluded that, in spite of the fall from political power of the traditional ruling elite, the coming of the Revolution in Philadelphia was not primarily a class-based movement.

61. Thomas Smith to Arthur St. Clair, August 22, 1776, in William Henry Smith, *St. Clair Papers: The Life and Public Services of Arthur St. Clair*, 2 vols. (Cincinnati, 1882), 1, p. 374.

62. Quoted in Hawke, *In the Midst of Revolution*, pp. 176–77. Remarkably little is known about the prime movers of the 1776 Pennsylvania Constitution. There are brief biographical sketches of the delegates to the Constitutional Convention in *PMHB* 3: 96–101, 194–201, 319–30, 438–46; 4: 89–98, 225–38, 361–72. See also Hawke, *In the Midst of Revolution*, pp. 186–92; and Selsam, *Pennsylvania Constitution*, pp. 169–254.

63. The 1776 Pennsylvania Constitution can be found in Thayer, *Pennsylvania Politics*, pp. 211–27.

64. Ibid. The most recent analysis of the Pennsylvania Constitution, though it does not supplant the work of Hawke, Selsam, and Ryerson, is Marc W. Kruman, *Between Authority and Liberty* pp. 24–28, 73–74, 92–93.

65. Demophilus, "Genuine Principles," Philadelphia, Pa. *Packet*, November 26, 1776, quoted in Wood, *Creation of the American Republic*, pp. 231–32.

Chapter 10. The Unfinished Revolution in American Political Culture

1. John Adams to Hezekiah Niles, *Niles Weekly Register*, March 7, 1818.

2. James Kettner, *The Development of American Citizenship, 1608–1870* (Chapel, N.C., 1978), pp. 9, 65–105; see also Brown, *Strength of a People*, esp. pp. 26–48.

3. Adams to Warren, *Massachusetts Historical Society Collections* 1, p. 234.

4. Adams to Abigail Adams, July 3, 1776, *Adams Family Correspondence*, 2, p. 28.

5. Adams to Richard Cranch, August 2, 1776, ibid., p. 74.

6. David Ramsay, *A Dissertation on the Manner of Acquiring the Character and Privilege of a Citizen of the United States* (Charleston, S.C., 1789), p. 3.

7. Kettner, *American Citizenship*, p. 208.

8. For a general discussion of constitution-making after the Revolution see Wood, *Creation of the American Republic*, pp. 124–255, and Wood, *Radicalism*, pp. 80, 290. See also Kruman, *Bettween Authority and Liberty*, passim; and Elisha Douglass, *Rebels and Democrats: The Struggle for Equal Political Rights and Majority Rule During the American Revolutionv* (Chapel Hill, N.C., 1955).

9. Wood, *Radicalism*, p. 294.

10. Jackson T. Main, *The Sovereign States 1775–1783* (New York, 1973), pp. 186–209.

11. Main, "Government by the People: The American Revolution and the Democratization of the Legislatures," *WMQ*, 3d ser. 23 (1966): 391–407; and Fletcher M. Green, *Constitutional Development in the South Atlantic States, 1776–1860* (Chapel Hill, N.C., 1930), pp. 60–61.

12. Main, "Democratization of the Legislatures," pp. 398–405.

13. An excellent introduction to this subject is Ira Berlin, "The Revolution in Black Life," in Young, *The American Revolution* (DeKalb, Ill., 1976), pp. 351–82.

14. Wood, *Radicalism*, p. 184.

15. Thomas Jefferson, Autobiography, in Adrienne Koch and William Peden, *The

Life and Selected Writings of Thomas Jefferson (Modern Library Edition, New York, 1944), pp. 38–39.

16. Quoted in Stanley N. Katz, "Republicanism and the Law of Inheritance in the American Revolutionary Era," *Michigan Law Review*, 86 (1977): 1–29.

17. Mary Lynn Salmon, "Republican Sentiment, Economic Change, and the Property Rights of Women in American Law," in Ronald Hoffman and Peter J. Albert, *Women in the Age of the American Revolution* (Charlottesville, Va., 1989), pp. 448–52.

18. *Virginia Statute of Religious Liberty,* October, 1785, in Samuel Eliot Morison, *Sources and Documents Illustrating the American Revolution and the Formation of the Federal Constitution, 1764–1788* (Oxford, 1923), pp. 206–7.

19. V. O. Key, *Southern Politics in State and Nation* (New York, 1949), p. 19.

20. Kruman, *Between Authority and Liberty,* pp. 20–21.

21. Main, *Sovereign States,* pp. 172–76; and Nevins, *The American States,* pp. 158–64.

22. For a full discussion of the consequences of the Revolution in New York see Edward Countryman, *A People in Revolutionv,* esp. pp. 103–160.

23. Wood, *Radicalism,* pp. 268–70, 299–302; and Dixon Ryan Fox, *The Decline of Aristocracy in the State of New York, 1801–1840* (New York, 1919), esp. pp. 229–70.

24. Douglass, *Rebels and Democrats,* pp. 39–42.

25. Ibid., pp. 42–44.

26. Green, *Constitutional Development in the South Atlantic States,* pp. 201–2, 248–51.

27. Samuel Eliot Morison, *The Conservative American Revolution* (Washington, D.C., 1976), p. 12.

28. The Constitution of Pennsylvania, 28 September, 1776, in Morison, *Sources and Documents,* pp. 162–177.

29. John Murrin, "A Roof Without Walls: The Dilemma of Amerian National Identity," in Richard R. Beeman, et al., *Beyond Confederation: Origins of the Constitution and American National Identity* (Chapel Hill, N.C., 1987), pp. 333–48.

30. Paine, *Common Sense,* pp. 83, 84, 120.

Index

Acknowledgments

I began this book long ago—too long ago—while a fellow at the Institute for Advanced Study in Princeton in 1989–90. During that idyllic year I profited from the wisdom of innumerable colleagues at the Institute, but, in particular, benefited from the insight and friendship of John Elliot. While at the Institute I had the rare privilege, at a moment of momentous change around the world, of having several absorbing conversations with George Kennan on the complicated relationship between democracy and political stability in the history of Europe in the nineteenth and twentieth centuries, conversations which, as it has turned out, have profoundly affected my views on both of those subjects. During that initial year of my work on this project I presented a paper at the Shelby Cullom Davis Center at Princeton outlining my preliminary thoughts on the subject, and received helpful and constructive criticism from the participants at that seminar, most notably from the seminar's formidable director, the late Lawrence Stone.

Since that year at Princeton my progress on the book has proceeded in fits and starts, as too many of the intervening years have been spent as a dean at the University of Pennsylvania, but along the way I have been given aid, comfort, and constructive criticism from a variety of sources. I spent brief, but vitally important periods of time both at the Rockefeller Study Center at Bellagio and at the Huntington Library in Pasadena, and on both occasions I was able not both to focus entirely on my research and writing and to rekindle my excitement about the project in which I was engaged.

I have had several undergraduate research assistants who have not only helped with some of the basic research on the book, but who have also been valuable critics along the way. In particular, Jacob Cogan, Elizabeth Figueira, and Morgan Hughes made important contributions to my progress on the book and, hopefully, learned something about the historian's craft along the way. At a particularly crucial stage in my progress, when I had a semi-completed and very rough draft of a manuscript, my long-time Penn colleague, dear friend, and relentless critic Richard S. Dunn read the manuscript and provided both crucially important encouragement and sound advice for revision and further work. Richard's advice and counsel sustained me for several years as I tried to juggle the responsibilities of being a university administrator, teacher, and part-time scholar. At a much later stage in my work on the book, my long-time friend and colleague Rhys Isaac offered incisive criticism mixed with just the right amounts of encouragement. Professor Alison Olson, one of the external readers of the manuscript for the University of Pennsylvania Press, offered some exceptionally helpful advice on ways to improve the book, and I have tried to incorporate her suggestions into the final product. John Murrin, although he did not read any of the manuscript and bears absolutely no responsibility for any of the interpretation contained therein, has been a constant source of wisdom and good advice for me at every stage in this project. It is the case that John knows more about the subject of eighteenth-century American politics than any person alive, and I profited enormously from his knowledge.

Many of my history colleagues at Penn and all of the people who make up the wonderfully supportive community that comprises the McNeil Center for Early American Studies have helped along the way. Bruce Kuklick and Walter McDougall read a completed draft of the manuscript in its entirety and made helpful suggestions, and Dan Richter, Director of the McNeil Center and editor of the series in which this book appears, provided an exceptionally detailed and wholly helpful critique of the manuscript during the final stages of my writing. Similarly, Robert Lockhart, history editor at the University of Pennsylvania Press, has helped me move this project forward not only by encouraging me to produce a completed manuscript, but also by his many helpful suggestions along the way. Finally, my good friend and fanatically loyal secretary during my service as Dean of the College of Arts and Sciences, Doris McLeod, played a dual, and indispensable, role in bringing this book to completion. Not only did she type and enter corrections into innumerable drafts of each chapter in the manuscript, but she also, in her role as "Dragon Lady," was relentless in fending off the hordes of students, parents, and faculty who demanded to see me during those times that we had carved out on my calendar for "research." It was less my discipline that allowed me to complete this book than it was hers.